Bicycling® Magazine's

Complete Guide To

Upgrading Your Bike

Bicycling® Magazine's

Complete Guide To

Upgrading Your Bike

By Frank J. Berto

West Coast editor, *Bicycling®* Magazine

Rodale Press, Emmaus, Pennsylvania

To the memory of Archibald Sharp, B.Sc., a Victorian engineer, who wrote *Bicycles and Tricycles* in 1896. His splendid book punctured the folklore of the time and provided a sound engineering basis for bicycle design in that first great period of bicycle development. Like Good King Wenceslas's page, I hope that I'm treading in his footsteps.

Printed in the United States of America

Senior Editor: Ray Wolf
Editor: Larry McClung
Photographer: Donna Hornberger
Book Designer: Denise Mirabello
Illustrator: Sally Onopa
Copy Editor: Lisa Baker Andruscavage

Library of Congress Cataloging-in-Publication Data
Berto, Frank J.
Bicycling magazine's complete guide to upgrading your bike/by Frank J. Berto.
p. cm.
Includes index.
ISBN 0-87857-751-3 paperback
1. Bicycles–Design and construction. I. Bicycling. II. Title III. Title: Complete guide to upgrading your bike.
TL410.B46 1988
1629.2'272–dc19 87-28886
CIP

Distributed in the book trade by St. Martin's Press

4 6 8 10 9 7 5 3 paperback

Contents

Acknowledgments

I want to thank the following friends and bicycle experts:

- Paul Brown, of Cycle Dynamics in Novato, Ca., for his help on chapters 2 and 3 and his review of the entire book.
- Eric Hjertberg, of Wheelsmith in Palo Alto, Ca., for his help on the wheel chapter.
- Jobst Brandt, of Avocet, for his review of the wheel and tire chapters.
- Imre Barsy and Jim Merz, of Specialized, for their review of the tire chapter.
- Mathew Aaron, of Michelin, for his review of the tire chapter.
- Fred DeLong for his help on bicycle history, ISO standardization, and his review of the entire book.
- My son, Ben Berto, for his help on bicycle racing details and his review of the entire book.
- Don Cuerdon, of *Bicycling,* for his review of the entire book.
- Larry McClung, of Rodale Press Book Division, for editing with such a light hand.

Introduction

Bicycling is an exercise you can pursue during your entire lifetime and if you bicycle regularly, it will be a healthier, more satisfying lifetime. The bicycle is a marvelous tool that lets you walk with 12-foot strides. Bicycling improves your health and your disposition. Using your bike for short trips leaves you and your car in better shape and leaves some of the world's finite supply of petroleum for your grandchildren.

I wrote this book to share my enthusiasm and knowledge about the splendid sport of bicycling. This book tells you how to upgrade your bicycle to fit your needs. It will help you to get more enjoyment and use from your bicycle. You should buy this book rather than, say, a nice new saddle because this book tells you which saddle to buy and why it's the right saddle for you.

Upgrading Your Bicycle

Upgrading your bicycle is a two-step process. First, you make sure that your bicycle is worth upgrading. If it is, then you upgrade the wheels, tires, gear train, and other components. You don't want to upgrade a frame that is the wrong size, or the wrong kind, and you don't want to invest more in a bicycle than the bicycle is worth. When you decide that your bicycle is worth upgrading, spend your money on the important items and do it right the first time.

Chapter 1 tells you about bicycle quality, bicycle costs, and upgrading costs. Chapter 2 tells you about the different kinds of bicycles for the different kinds of riders and about sizing bicycle frames to suit your dimensions. The rest of the book tells you about the various parts of the bicycle, so that you can determine what needs to be upgraded and how you should upgrade.

What's Different about This Book?

The bookshops are full of books written by enthusiastic bicyclists whose main research consists of reading books written by other enthusiastic bicyclists. These cycling authors piece together the conventional wisdom on the subject, add their personal opinions or biases, and voilà, another new bicycle encyclopedia. As the song goes, "Son, this one is different." It's based on the 80 technical articles that I've written for *Bicycling* magazine since 1974, as well as countless hours spent in my home workshop conducting the tests that furnished the data for the numerous tables found in this book.

Over the years, I've answered more than a thousand readers' letters. One hundred fifty have appeared in *Bicycling*'s "Technical Questions and Answers" column. The common theme to most of these letters has been, "Frank, what should I do to upgrade this part or that part of my bicycle?" Some questions have been asked so often that I have refined the answer and have stored it in my computer's memory. This book answers those questions in an organized, up-to-date manner. It tells you how to take the bicycle you have now and upgrade it to fit your needs. With gearing, tires, wheels, and everything else optimized to suit you, you'll enjoy your bicycle more and ride it more.

This book is primarily about "10-speeds"—that is to say, skinny-tired, dropped-handlebar bicycles equipped with 10 to 21 speeds. Except for occasional references, I have ignored mountain bikes, 1-speeds, 3-speeds, track bikes, and tandems; if I had thoroughly discussed them, the book would have been too long.

This book isn't a rehash of my *Bicycling* articles. To be sure, the timeless prose that I wrote about gear selection five years ago hasn't changed much in the interval, so I have drawn on earlier research where it is relevant. But all of the component ratings found in this book are based on new tests of the latest models.

The ratings found in this book cover only the best-performing and most available models in each component category. By contrast, my *Bicycling* articles often cover a much larger number and variety of models. That's because the magazine tries to be as comprehensive as possible in its coverage. Since this book is not bound by such constraints, I have limited my focus to those products worthy of consideration for a serious bicycle upgrade.

I agonized for a while over units of measure. Should I use all metric, all Anglo-Saxon, or cite both units while placing one or the other in brackets? (I really wish that the United States would switch to the international metric standard, but I don't expect to see it happen in my lifetime.) I finally decided to do what the bicycle industry has done: that is, to use whatever comes naturally. So you'll find components weighed in grams and bicycles weighed in pounds, cranks measured in millimeters and seat tubes measured in inches. Because this isn't a textbook, I didn't include the alternate units in parentheses. If you want to make your own conversions, remember there are 2.54 centimeters to the inch and 454 grams to the pound.

Finally, even though it bears the *Bicycling* name, this book is a truly personal statement that reflects my own preferences and biases rather than those of the *Bicycling* staff as a whole. Printed material is sometimes edited to conform with the established "voice" or "style" of a publication. I have experienced that to some degree in writing for cycling magazines. However, rest assured that the voice you hear ringing throughout the pages of this book is truly that of Frank Berto. Enjoy!

CHAPTER 1

Bicycle Economics

As I stated in the Introduction, the primary focus of this book is on dropped-handlebar, derailleur bicycles that are equipped with 10 to 21 speeds—the type of bikes commonly referred to as "10-speeds." But, since not all 10-speed bikes are created equal, before we can seriously begin talking about "upgrading," we have to define what is worth upgrading and what isn't.

Broadly speaking, 10-speed bikes can be divided into four quality-price categories:

- *Gaspipe quality,* less than $150.
- *Standard quality,* $150 to $250.
- *Good quality,* $250 to $700.
- *Top quality,* $700 and up.

The price ranges are approximate and are based on 1987 dollar-to-yen conversion rates. The bicycle market has sailed through many crosscurrents in the last decade. At the low end, prices have stayed low because of competition, automation, and the shift of production to lower-wage countries like Taiwan. At the upper end, the decline in the value of the dollar since 1985 has pushed up the price of good-quality imported bicycles. The price of top-quality models has increased even more because they take so much hand labor to produce.

During the course of the last decade, the overall quality of bicycle frames and components has improved significantly, especially at the standard- and good-quality levels. Today's $200 standard-quality bicycle has better wheels, better components, and a stronger, lighter frame than a good-quality bicycle that cost $200 ten years ago.

Part of army training is an exercise called "naming the parts." You learn to name all of the different parts of your rifle, for example, and you shout them out on command. Figure 1-1 names all of the parts of the bicycle. If I use an unfamiliar term in my description of bicycle components, most likely you'll find it there.

Gaspipe-Quality Bicycles

Gaspipe is a derogatory term and it's meant to be. These are the lowest-priced and the lowest-quality 10-speeds available. The name is derived from the frame construction. Gaspipe frames are welded together from thick, seamed, low-carbon steel tubes—the same material used for water and gas pipes. Gaspipe bicycles are sold through department stores, discount houses, and automobile supply stores. Better-quality bicycles are sold through bicycle stores. Until 1984, almost all gaspipe bicycles sold in the USA were made by four companies: Murray, Huffy, Roadmaster, and Ross.

In 1985, Taiwan's excess bicycle production capacity led to severe price cutting. Taiwanese 10-speeds were leaving the factories for less than $20 apiece. Some of these inexpensive Taiwanese bicycles have lugged and brazed frames, but they're still gaspipe quality.

The American factories that churn out gaspipe bicycles by the millions (literally) are models of automation and efficiency, but they're finding it difficult to withstand the intense competition from Taiwan. Ross no longer makes gaspipe bicycles. Huffy, Murray, and Roadmaster are currently lobbying for a tariff on all imported bicycles and components.

Here are some reasons why you shouldn't buy either an American or a Taiwanese gaspipe bicycle:

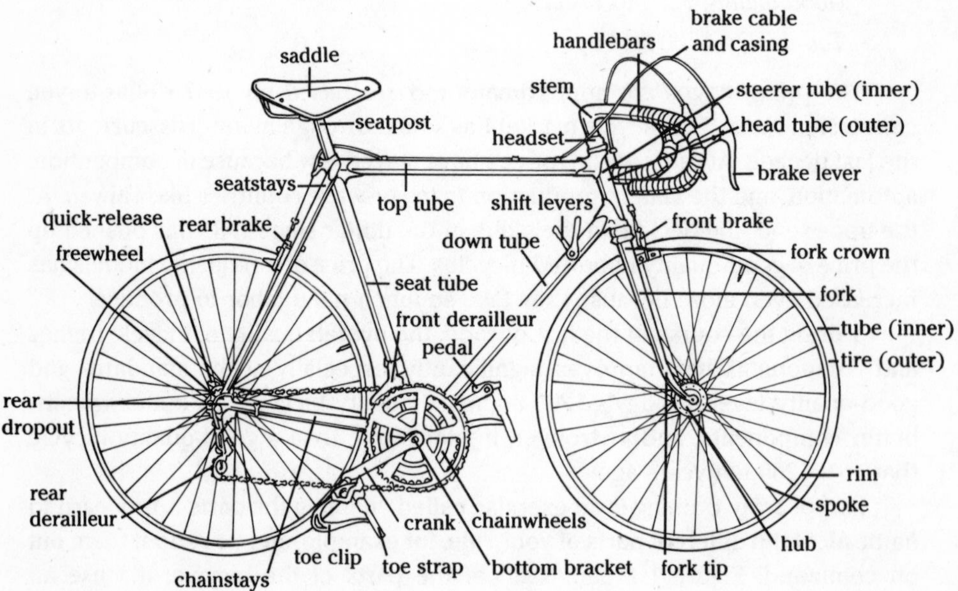

FIGURE 1-1 Naming the parts.

- The frames are heavy and they have an unresponsive inert feel.
- The bottom-of-the-line components are heavy, short-lived, and hard to adjust. They often use unique gaspipe-standard threads.
- The steel rims are heavy and stop poorly in the rain.
- Gaspipe bicycles are sold by stores that don't understand bicycles. They don't know how to fit you properly and they don't provide service.
- Gaspipe bicycles are a headache to maintain and many good bicycle shops won't work on them. If the shop charges fairly for labor, even a simple overhaul costs more than the bicycle is worth.

It's poor economics to try to upgrade a gaspipe bicycle. It's like fixing squeaks on an old car. Each time you upgrade something, another problem shows up. When you're all finished, you've done extra work, spent extra money, but you still have a heavy, poor-handling bicycle. It makes more sense to sell your gaspipe bicycle (though not to a friend) and use the money to buy a ten-year-old, inexpensive Japanese bicycle from a thrift shop. They're easy to work on because they use standard English-threaded parts. When you finish upgrading one of these bikes, you'll have something worth keeping.

The exception to the rule on upgrading gaspipe bicycles is replacing parts as they wear out. If you need to buy a new tire, new brake pads, or a new chain, you can afford to spend a few extra dollars to buy good-performing components of this type.

Standard-Quality Bicycles

Standard-quality bikes are the least expensive models sold by bicycle shops. Their frames are made from seamed, low-carbon steel tubing brazed together with lugs. More standard-quality bicycles are sold than all of the higher-priced models combined. Until about five years ago, bicycles in this quality range were made in America by Schwinn, Ross, and Trek or imported from Japan, France, England, or Taiwan. Now, Taiwan dominates the market and virtually every brand name has its Taiwanese low-end models.

Standard-quality bikes are often worth upgrading. However, you should limit what you spend because you won't get your money back on the resale. For example, it usually doesn't pay to install new wheels with aluminum (alloy) rims. Many current standard-quality bicycles come with alloy rims; such bikes are better candidates for an upgrade than those equipped with steel rims.

Time-out for terminology. Bicycle components come in many quality levels. The lowest-quality components are stamped out of steel. Higher-quality components are made of aluminum or aluminum alloy. Aluminum components are called "alloy" components in the bicycle literature. This use of the word is different from the metallurgist's definition. To a metallurgist, alloy means a high-quality steel alloyed with strengthening elements like chromium and molybdenum. Chrome-moly is an alloy steel used in bicycle frames.

Ten years ago, standard-quality bicycles sold for about $100. Generally, they had low-quality components and their gearing was often poorly selected. I used to dread doing the *Bicycling* road tests on such bikes. We call the current standard-quality bicycles "UJBs" (universal Japanese bicycles), even though they're mostly made in Taiwan. They have few design goofs and the Shimano, SunTour, Sugino, Sakae, and Dia-Compe low-end components with which they are equipped perform very well. Low-end components wear out more rapidly than higher-priced components because they have lower-quality bearings, but most of them perform quite adequately.

The mail-order catalogs used to show page after page of components to replace the duds that came with standard-quality bicycles. Today's bicycles are so much better equipped that the aftermarket for components is much smaller and the catalogs are full of clothing and accessories.

Old French standard-quality bicycles from Peugeot, Motobecane, or Gitane are worth upgrading because their frames are made of lightweight straight-gauge tubing. Upgraded, these bicycles will be light, nice handling, and slightly delicate.

There are millions of Schwinn Varsitys and Continentals around. Like the French bicycles, they're worth upgrading but for a different reason. Varsitys look like and weigh like gaspipe bicycles but they aren't. They're heavy, reliable bicycles for kids or for people who want a sturdy bicycle for short rides. You can afford to spend $30 to replace the original Huret Allvit derailleurs or to install more appropriate freewheel sprockets.

Good-Quality Bicycles

Good-quality bicycles are the hardest to define. They're better than the standard-quality low-end models and worse than the top-quality models. The $250 to $700 price range is very broad. Defining good-quality bicycles used to be easier. Good-quality bicycles had alloy rims and standard-quality bicycles had steel rims. Now, I walk through the bicycle shows looking at standard- and good-quality bikes, wondering how so much bicycle can sell for so little.

The Japanese makers still dominate this quality level, but the decrease in the value of the dollar has made American-made Cannondale, Raleigh, Schwinn, and Trek bicycles real competitors. Frames are greatly improved because machines can now automatically braze double-butted alloy steel tubing. This quality of tubing used to require hand brazing. The frame on today's $300 bicycle weighs a pound or two less than it did five years ago. The decals on a lot of good-quality bike frames say Reynolds 501, Mangaloy, VALite, or Cr-Mo, while many of the large Japanese bicycle manufacturers now have facilities to make their own butted tubing. Cannondale, Raleigh, and Trek offer aluminum-framed bicycles in this price range.

More terminology. *Butting* is a process for making tubing walls thicker at the ends where they're joined than in the mid-sections where they are less subject to stress. Butted tubes are stronger and lighter than straight-gauge tubes. *Double-butted* tubes are butted at both ends. *Triple-* and *quad-butted* tubes have their thickness expanded in stages. I suspect that anything more than double butting is just advertising pizzazz.

Good-quality bicycles use good-quality, all-alloy components, which often work a bit better and always last longer than low-end components. The component makers provide numerous lines of components to the bicycle makers. Each line is designed to fit into a particular marketing niche. For example, Shimano sells eight racing rear derailleurs: Skylark, Z501, 105/SIS, 600 EX, L522, 600 EX/SIS, Santé/SIS, and Dura-Ace/SIS. With the exception of the indexed shifting (SIS) models, they all shift very much the same. Moving up the price scale, you find less steel and more alloy as well as better bearings in the cage pivots and pulleys. The top-quality models will retain their good shifting ability for years.

Good-quality bicycles sometimes come with stems and cranksets matched in size to the frame. The bicycle maker can only go so far in offering size variations and you can often uprade the fit of your bicycle by fine-tuning the size of the stem, handlebars, and cranks.

Bicycle value peaks around $400. Spend less money and you get less bicycle. Spend more money and you get more prestige, but not a lot more performance. If you plan to buy a new, good-quality bicycle, take your time. Knowledgeable buyers can find a model to closely match their needs, but it isn't always easy. I had a sign on my wall at Chevron that read, "You get what you pay for if you know what you're doing—otherwise, you get what you deserve." There are 40 different bicycle makers struggling for survival and each maker has two or three good-quality models. *Bicycling* magazine's annual Buyer's Guide issue is loaded with information to help you make your selection.

Good-quality bicycles are definitely worth upgrading. The best possible value is often a secondhand, good-quality bicycle with upgraded components to exactly match your needs. When you get a good-quality bicycle that fits you properly, with appropriate gearing and wheels, you might as well propose and get married to it.

Top-Quality Bicycles

Top-quality bicycles are just what the name implies—the best that money can buy. Although there's only a slight difference in weight and performance between a good- and a top-quality bicycle, there can be an enormous amount of personal satisfaction. The top-quality market falls into three categories:

- *Top-of-the-line bicycles,* like the Schwinn Paramount and the Trek 2500, from the major bicycle makers.
- *Stock racing bicycles* from the major European frame builders like Colnago, Cooper, DeRosa, or Merckx. You can buy them as fully equipped bicycles or you can buy a frameset and have it equipped with components of your choice. Italian builders currently dominate this market.
- *Custom-built frames* made to your dimensions and needs and equipped with braze-ons and components of your choice. American frame builders dominate this market.

There are two general price levels for top-quality bikes. In the $700 to $1,000 range, the makers compromise a bit on components and braze-ons. SunTour Superbe Pro is a favorite component group for bikes at this price level. Above $1,000, you're paying for prestige, and traditionally that's been spelled C-A-M-P-A-G-N-O-L-O. Currently, Shimano's Dura-Ace is challenging Campagnolo's position at the top of the heap.

When purchasing a super bicycle, it's hard to decide between stock and custom-made models. It's a bit like buying a top-quality suit versus having a suit made to measure. It depends on your body's dimensions. If you fit an off-the-shelf racing bicycle, a fully equipped top-of-the-line model will be your best buy. The big makers get mass production benefits and a better price on components. The stock frameset will be next in value and the custom-built frame will be the most expensive.

Prestige is an ephemeral quality. Some people like one decal and others another. A custom-made bicycle is very satisfying because everything is made exactly to your specifications, including all the braze-ons. Custom-made bicycle frames are splendid bargains because there's so much competition among the frame builders. You pay a much higher premium to buy a custom-made rifle, for instance. However, I'd worry about buying a frame from a start-up builder; I'd rather he learn his trade on someone else's frame.

Starting in 1985, many major makers switched to aluminum and carbon-fiber frames for their top-of-the-line models. This fouls up the old value equations. Bicycles like my aluminum Trek 2000 offer a combination of weight, comfort, and stiffness that steel frames can't provide, regardless of price. I suspect that this means that the custom frame builders are going to be selling more custom-built frames and fewer stock frames.

It's fun to take an old racing frame and deck it out with modern wheels, components, and gearing to suit your needs. However, racing frames that use nonstandard threads pose special problems, which I will tell you about a bit later on.

Tubing Quality

The tubing decal on a frame probably tells you more about quality than any other single item. Top-quality bicycles will be made with double-butted tubing from one of the five prestige tubing makers: Reynolds, Vitus (Ateliers de la Rive), Columbus, Tange, and Ishiwata. Reynolds 531 tubing is a manganese-molybdenum alloy steel. The others are all AISI (American Iron and Steel Institute) 4130 chromium-molybdenum alloy steel.

The manufacturers make bicycle tubing in a range of qualities. The very best tubing is found only on the best bicycles. The names of the various prestige tubes are listed in table 1-1. Table 1-2 shows the descriptive terms found on tubing decals used by a representative group of bicycle makers.

On good-quality bicycles, it's more difficult to determine frame quality from the tubing decal. The tubing used at this price level is often a manganese alloy steel designed to withstand the higher temperatures involved in automated frame brazing. The bicycle maker may use double-butted name-brand tubing for only the three main tubes (top tube, down tube, and seat tube) and something less expensive for the forks and stays. Many of the Japanese makers now make their own butted tubing. Some makers use bulk chrome-moly tubing for the three main tubes. New companies like True-Temper are getting into the butted chrome-moly bicycle tubing business.

Table 1-1.

Tubing Makers' Quality Levels

Tubing Maker	Standard Quality	Good Quality	Top Quality
Columbus	—	Tenax	SLX, SL, SP, OR, GT
Ishiwata	—	Magny X & V	015, 017, 019, 021, 022, 024
Reynolds	—	501	531, 753
Tange	High-Ten	Mangaloy	Champion, Prestige
Vitus	—	Durifort	Super Vitus 980

Table 1-2.

Tubing Decal Descriptive Terms

Bicycle Maker	Standard Quality	Good Quality	Top Quality
Bridgestone	High Tensile	Cr-Mo	Cr-Mo
Fuji	High Tension	VALite	9658 Chrome-Moly
Miyata	Mangalite	Cr-Mo	Cr-Mo
Motobecane	2040	Motolite	Columbus
Nishiki	High Tensile	Cr-Mo	Tange
Panasonic	High Tensile	Tange CrMo	Columbus
Peugeot	Carbolite	Reynolds 501	Super Vitus, Columbus SLX
Schwinn	High Tensile	Columbus Tenax	Columbus SL
Trek	—	Reynolds 501	Reynolds 531

Even standard-quality bicycles have tubing decals. After all, decals help sell bicycles. The frames on these bicycles are made from low-carbon steel. (The numbers 1010 and 1020 are AISI designations for low-carbon steel.) This tubing has a seam because it is formed from strip stock that is rolled and welded. Nearly all of the better-quality tubes are seamless. They're formed from steel billets that are rolled and pierced.

Standardization and Nonstandardization

Before you start to upgrade your bicycle, check the bottom bracket. If the cups are 1.37 inches in diameter and have 24 tpi (threads per inch) and the bottom bracket is 68mm (2.68 inches) wide, you're in luck. Your bike uses English threads, the de facto industry standard.

If you have an English-threaded bike, your headset will be 27mm in diameter, while the steerer tube will be 1 inch in diameter and will have 24 tpi. The cranks will accept 20 tpi pedal threads that are 9⁄16 inch in diameter. You will be able to get standard parts from almost any supply source.

If your frame has a 70mm (2.76 inches) bottom bracket width, then it probably has French, Italian, or Swiss threads and I advise you to sell it to someone who hasn't read this book. Start anew with an English-threaded frame. Don't spend your time back-ordering bastard parts, waiting for them, and then finding that they don't fit. Buy standard parts. Then, two years from now, if you decide to transfer your fancy new parts to your next frame, they'll fit.

Italian-threaded frames deserve more respect than those with French or Swiss threads, because virtually all Italian racing frames imported into the USA have Italian threads. If you buy a new or used, top-quality, Italian racing bicycle, you'll get Italian threads. The importers and the pro bike shops that sell these frames also carry the Italian-threaded parts. They are available, though not nearly as available as English-threaded parts.

I admit I'm on a crusade here, but it's you, dear reader, trying to upgrade your bicycle, who is being hurt by nonstandardization. The lack of standardization in the bicycle industry is a horror story. It just proves that we're still basically a cottage industry. Each country has its own national standard. In addition to the fairly common French, Italian, and Swiss standards, there are German, Spanish, and Austrian standards. There are also some truly weird British threads produced by Raleigh and Chater Lea that plague the restorers of antique bikes.

In the early 1970s, the Japanese makers picked English threads for their exports to the USA, which is why English threads became today's de facto standard. When English threads accounted for 90 percent of the business, knowledgeable buyers insisted on English threads, and we had de facto standardization. The next step, true standardization, will be more difficult to achieve, because it requires industry or government standards that include dimensions and tolerances. The ISO (International Standards Organization) is slowly developing an international standard around English threads. Fred DeLong, *Bicycling*'s emeritus technical editor, has labored manfully on ISO standardization for many years.

Some bicycle dimensions, like seatpost diameters, simply can't be standardized. The seatpost has to fit inside the seat tube, and seat tube inside diameters vary according to the weight and kind of tubing. But in many cases, delays in standardization are caused by economics or national pride. Stick with the ISO-English thread standard and you'll be able to get replacement parts for your bike ten years from now.

The drive toward standardization involves more than thread sizes. Tire sizes, crankset bolt circle diameters, spindle lengths, dropout widths, and handlebar diameters are also slowly becoming standardized. Always buy the de facto standard component if you have a choice. It encourages a healthy trend for the user. More important, if your favorite company goes broke, you'll be able to buy replacement parts. (I'll talk more about this in the component chapters.)

Investing in Bicycles

Let's put the initial cost of a top-quality bicycle into perspective. Suppose you visit five Buick dealers and haggle to get the best possible deal. When you drive your $20,000 Buick Riviera out of the dealer's showroom, you're immediately $5,000 poorer. That's the typical depreciation for a "new" used Buick. Yet your neighbors admire your financial acumen and good taste.

Buy a $1,500 custom-built bicycle or two and you're considered a bicycle freak and a wastrel. Yet custom-made bicycles last for at least 20 years and they depreciate very slowly. A custom-made bicycle is truly unique, in the same league as a Ferrari or a Maserati; whereas, you'll see sister ships to your Riviera every day. Cars, boats, cameras, high-fidelity equipment, home computers, skis—they all depreciate while you look at them. By contrast, good bicycles retain their value indefinitely and pay rich dividends in physical and mental health.

Buy a top-quality bicycle because you want one, not because you need one. Use this book to specify a custom-made bicycle that exactly fits your needs. Spend some of your children's inheritance on a good bike and maybe they won't have to support you in a retirement home.

The Economics of Upgrading

Overall, bicycling is an inexpensive hobby, even for component freaks. So spend as much as you like on a favorite bicycle. That said, there are a few guidelines worth following when upgrading a bike.

Bear in mind that the OEM (original equipment maker) bicycle manufacturer pays about one-third as much for components as you do. This doesn't mean that you're getting ripped off. There are at least two extra people (importer and wholesaler) between you, the bicycle store, and the component factory. Each one has to run a business: which means paying rent, utilities, employees, liability insurance, and taxes; carrying inventory; and, hopefully, making a small profit. What it does mean is that your favorite *gruppo* may be cheaper with a new bicycle attached than when purchased separately. (You show your expertise by calling a complete line of components a "gruppo," which is the Italian word for "group.")

Therefore, keep this principle in mind: Don't spend so much on upgrading that you could sell your upgraded bicycle and buy a higher-quality bicycle with the same components attached. The exception to this rule arises when you decide to acquire your dream components in installments. Later, after your old frame is completely upgraded, you move the dream components onto a new dream frame and sell the old frame with the original components (which you thoughtfully saved).

Here are a couple of additional guidelines to observe. Don't spend more on upgrading than about half of the original cost of the bicycle. And don't invest a lot of money in a frame that doesn't fit you or doesn't suit your riding style. (There's more about this in chapter 2.)

As a rough rule of thumb, the following upgrades make economic sense.

Gaspipe bicycles will never be pleasant to pedal. You're buying cheap transportation. So minimize your investment. Install better tires, a better chain, better brake pads, and better, low-priced derailleurs as the originals wear out. Some gaspipe saddles are so uncomfortable that you may have to buy a new saddle to allow longer trips. Keep the saddle when you throw the gaspipe bicycle off the bridge.

Standard-quality bicycles are pleasant recreation and transportation vehicles. But you don't want to spend more than, say, $75 on the upgrade because it still makes more sense to sell and buy a new or secondhand good-quality bicycle. Bicycles with aluminum (alloy) rims are more desirable than those with steel rims. Therefore, you can spend more on them. As the originals wear out, buy better tires and a better chain. Buy a more comfortable saddle and better pedals with toe clips and straps. Optimize the gearing inexpensively by changing the inner chainwheel and the freewheel sprockets.

Good-quality bicycles have good-quality frames and wheels. You can reasonably spend $200 upgrading a bicycle that fits you properly. The important thing is to start with the right frame. Don't convert a racing frame to touring or the reverse. Each frame is too well adapted to one style of riding to serve well in the other style.

Optimize the gearing to exactly match your needs. This might involve a new freewheel, new chainwheels, and new derailleurs. If the bike is worth more than, say, $400, you can justify a new triple crankset to convert a 10-speed to a 15-speed. The wheels and the tires should match your needs. This might involve a second set of wheels. A new stem and handlebars and a new saddle can help the bike fit you perfectly.

Top-quality bicycles allow you to spend as much as you can afford. At this price level, you are building a dream machine to meet your exact specifications. You may be building a new bicycle from scratch or you may just be fine-tuning your present bicycle. Install top-quality components to match your style and improve your riding pleasure.

Who Does the Upgrading?

I like to work on my own bicycle. I carry a minimal tool kit and I'm prepared to make minor repairs on the road. Bicycles use "soft" technology. They aren't very complicated and it's easy and satisfying to work on them. In most cases, when you make an adjustment you can see what happens. Cycling is more pleasant when you know what the squeaks and rattles are telling you. Lawyers, doctors, ministers, and stockbrokers can all learn to fix their own bicycles. You can get a good set of basic maintenance tools for $25 and you can do a complete upgrade and overhaul with $100 worth of tools.

This is a what-to-do book, not a how-to-do book. *Bicycling Magazine's Complete Guide to Bicycle Maintenance and Repair* is a splendid companion volume to tell you how to install and fine-tune the new components. If the *Complete Guide* is a bit too complete for your pocketbook, *Richard's Bicycle Book,* by Richard Ballantine, is the best of the low-priced books.

I suggest that you do your own upgrading. Perhaps you'll need some help with the hardest parts, like the bottom bracket. This is where you need a good "pro" bike shop. A pro bike shop is operated by knowledgeable professionals. They hire professional bicycle mechanics and they cater to the serious cyclists in their area. They have the tools and the skills to do the more complicated modifications and repairs. They carry top-quality bicycles and, usually, a decent selection of tools and components. Talk to half a dozen serious local cyclists and you'll soon come up with a short list of pro bike shops.

One of the best ways to size up a bicycle shop is to ask for advice on upgrading your bicycle. If the store says it can't be done and tries to sell you a new bicycle, they're really saying that they aren't a pro bike shop. If your bicycle is truly an upgrade candidate, take your trade elsewhere.

If you're mechanically inadequate or if you just don't have the time, your pro bike shop can do your upgrading for you. Don't ask for half an hour of free advice and then buy your parts by mail order. Be prepared to pay a fair price for pro service. Thirty-five dollars an hour isn't too much. The shop has to pay the mechanics a decent wage and still make a reasonable profit or they won't be able to give you the kind of service that you want. Most shops have had to raise their rates to cover liability insurance. That's the ransom we pay to the trial lawyers.

If you live in Lodgepole, Montana, and the nearest decent bicycle shop is 300 miles away, you'll have to do your own work and buy your components from a mail-order source.

Component Makers

All things being equal (and they never are), your bicycle should use components from the same maker. This is more important in the drive train than elsewhere. If you buy your crankset, freewheel, derailleurs, and shift levers from the same maker, you'll avoid compatibility problems. Chains are an exception, and you can read all about them in chapter 9.

Campagnolo, Shimano, and SunTour are the three major makers of gruppos. A bicycle consists of a frame and a gruppo, plus tires, rims, spokes, and a saddle. A typical gruppo consists of pedals, brakes, derailleurs, shift levers, crankset, hubset, headset, and seatpost. It can also include the stem, freewheel, and chain. According to the ancient folklore, Campagnolo gruppos didn't include these components because Tullio Campagnolo didn't want to compete with his friends at Cinelli and Regina. All things change and Campagnolo now makes freewheels.

Most of the French and Italian component makers are smaller companies that don't make complete gruppos. Galli, Mavic, Nervar, Ofmega, and Zeus all sell nearly complete gruppos but their U.S. distribution is very limited. I won't use a lot of space describing these smaller companies. Rather, I'll concentrate on the components with the widest distribution.

When you upgrade your bicycle, you will probably be deciding between the "big three" component makers: Campagnolo, Shimano, and SunTour. You'll also be looking at Specialized and Avocet for tires, saddles, and other components. To help inform your decisions, let me tell you something about these five companies.

The big three gruppo companies are similar in many ways. All three are small, family-run companies that were started by dynamic patriarchs in the 1920s. Campagnolo has 700 employees, Shimano 1200, and SunTour 400. SunTour has the smallest sales. Campagnolo sells twice as much and Shimano four times as much as SunTour. Each company has a different attitude toward design and innovation.

Campagnolo

Founder Tullio Campagnolo was a bicycle racer who invented the quick-release hub in 1927. Since then, the company that bears his name has produced a series of race-proven components that are works of art in addition to being splendid examples of engineering. As a company, Campagnolo is slow to innovate. New ideas are tested by the Italian racing teams for a few years before they are marketed. They stick with a successful design for years. Campagnolo Nuovo Record cranksets, brakes, hubsets, headsets, pedals, and derailleurs are essentially unchanged from the 1970 models. In the 1960s, the key Campagnolo bolt circles and dimensions became de facto industry standards for racing components.

Dealers can afford to stock Campagnolo parts because they don't become obsolete every few years. Campagnolo also has a unique reputation for quality. The tolerances and the finish of Campagnolo's top-of-the-line components are second to none. Inside and outside the bicycle industry, "tout Campagnolo" describes perfection. They are expensive, but Campagnolo components hold their value well.

Campagnolo generally prices their top components at the top of the connoisseur market. In the mid-1980s, there was considerable price cutting. With the latest dollar to lire rates, most of the price cutting has ceased. If you find yourself priced out of the Record–Super Record market, take a look at Chorus, Nuovo Victory, and Nuovo Triomphe. They offer the same performance at a much lower price.

Campagnolo's parts naming and numbering system is Byzantine. I maintain that when Niccolo Machiavelli finished his book, *The Prince*, he was hired by Campagnolo to name new components. No one else could create such confusion.

There are seven Campagnolo gruppos. The newest gruppos are C-Record, Nuovo Triomphe, Nuovo Victory, and Chorus. The old Campagnolo gruppos are Super Record, Nuovo Record/Record, and Nuovo Gran Sport/Gran Sport. When Campagnolo introduced their new top-of-the-line gruppo in 1985, they had run out of superlatives (Super-Duper Record?). They decided to call the new line "Record" and they renamed all of the old components that still used the name Record. This caused so much confusion that everyone called the new line "C-Record." But Campagnolo is determined to call it Record, no matter what. They're also replacing their old, familiar, four-digit model numbers with new computer-generated model numbers.

Campagnolo's touring components have never shared the reputation of their top-of-the-line racing components. Today, Campagnolo is being hurt by their slow response to the superior performance of the latest Shimano Dura-Ace components.

Shimano

Shozaburo Shimano produced the company's first freewheel in 1921. Today, the Shimano company is run by his three sons. Shimano is the innovative leader of the component industry. Innovation has been the key to their acquiring the large market share they currently enjoy, especially for the low-priced lines. Shimano probably has more engineers working on component development than the rest of the industry combined.

Shimano is noted for short-lived technical "breakthroughs" that fade away after two or three years. Even Shimano's successful models are usually replaced after two or three years. Not surprisingly, many bike stores shy away from stocking Shimano components or spare parts. Who wants a store full of passé aerodynamic components? Shimano has responded to complaints about parts availability by setting up a complete inventory in Los Angeles with a hot line for dealers.

The new Dura-Ace gruppo, introduced in 1985, represents Shimano's best shot at displacing Campagnolo as the professional racers' favorite. With the development of this gruppo, Shimano demonstrated it has finally recognized the racers' inherent conservatism. Where they didn't have a major performance gain, they simply fine-tuned the basic Campagnolo designs. The Shimano Index System (SIS) for the rear derailleurs is a major improvement. SIS has now trickled down to Shimano's lower-priced lines and the component market will never be the same.

Shimano's naming system is complex, because they introduce new models almost every year. Shimano makes six main gruppos for the replacement market. Dura-Ace, 600 Ultegra, Santé, and 105 are for racers and sport tourists. Deore XT and Deore are for tourists and mountain bikers. (The 600 Ultegra replaced 600 EX in 1988.)

SunTour

The SunTour company was founded by Shikanosuke Maeda in 1922. Their key products in the 1970s were the slant parallelogram rear derailleur and the wide-range Perfect freewheel. I've always been partial to SunTour because it was their VGT derailleur that made wide-range gearing practical.

SunTour's design philosophy is similar to that of Campagnolo. SunTour concentrates more on offering value than on constant innovation, so their components change more slowly than Shimano components. Also, they do not manufacture their entire gruppo themselves. Sugino makes their cranksets, Sanshin makes their hubs, and Dia-Compe makes their brakes.

In 1987, SunTour replaced virtually every gearing component in their catalog to include AccuShift, their new indexed shifting system. The racing–sport touring gruppos offered by SunTour are Superbe Pro, Sprint 9000, Sprint, Cyclone 7000, and Cyclone. The touring–mountain bike gruppos are XC-9000 and XC-Sport. There are also two new Alpha lines for the OEM market. In these lines, Dia-Compe, Sugino, and Sanshin make the Alpha components in their own names. For 1988, X-9010 has replaced XC-9000. XCD-6000 is a new mountain bike gruppo.

SunTour's top-of-the-line Superbe Pro gruppo sells at a lower price level than Dura-Ace or Nuovo Record and it's not quite as highly finished. Both SunTour and Shimano have used mountain bikes as test beds to develop bulletproof touring components.

Over the last decade, the intense competition between SunTour and Shimano has dramatically improved the perfomance of bicycle components. The traditional European component companies have found it harder and harder to compete.

Specialized

In 1974, 24-year-old Mike Sinyard was on a bicycle tour of Italy, where he met Andrea Cinelli. After being introduced to Papa Cinelli, Sinyard convinced him that he should be the Cinelli company's U.S. distributor. He managed to borrow small sums from several Northern California pro bike shops to start importing Italian components. This was the beginning of Specialized Bicycle Imports, now known simply as Specialized.

The company has grown steadily over the years and currently has large warehouses on both coasts as well as a major distribution network. Specialized has had two major marketing breakthroughs. The first was their decision to import and distribute a broad line of high-performance, premium-priced, skinwall tires. The second was recognizing the potential of mountain biking and mass marketing the Stumpjumper.

Specialized is the largest U.S. manufacturer of bicycle water bottles. All of their other components are imported. They listen to the bike stores and they use their distribution network to supply hard-to-find components. Their imported components are designed to unique Specialized specifications.

Avocet

Avocet is the other major Northern California component distribution company. It was founded by Bud and Neal Hoffacker in 1976. Their first product was an anatomic saddle and they have a patent on saddles with thinned shells and bumps. After achieving success with the anatomic saddle, Avocet began importing and distributing Ofmega cranksets, hubsets, and pedals under the Avocet name.

In its early days Avocet was driven by the dream of producing "Made in the USA" bicycle components. They developed a line of super-quality hubsets, headsets, and bottom brackets. They also built a large saddle factory. Unfortunately, foreign competition made these ventures uneconomic and the saddle factory moved offshore. Only Avocet cyclometers are now made in the USA.

In 1985, Avocet developed FasGrip, a complete line of bald tires. Currently, Avocet's major emphasis is on saddles, cyclometers, tires, and shoes.

Retail Prices

As I write this, the dollar has fallen off a cliff versus the Japanese yen, the Italian lire, and the French franc. The prices of imported bicycle components are rising dramatically. Many bike dealers sell their old stock at the old marked prices and then find that their replacement wholesale cost is more than the old retail price. This is a good way to go bankrupt.

The prices found in the tables represent a range of current retail prices derived from a comparison of every source available to me. If your bike store sells components at the lower end of this range, it's making a minimal profit. If it sells at the higher price, it's paying its overhead and making a modest profit. If the current price inflation continues, even the higher prices found in these tables will soon be low.

CHAPTER 2

Racing, Sport Touring, or Loaded Touring?

Before beginning the upgrading process, you need to define your riding style so that you can determine what kind of bicycle suits you best. For example, it makes no sense to spend a lot of money on fancy racing components if you plan to use your bike mostly for loaded touring. You also should learn how to measure your body and your bicycle to determine if they're compatible. If your bicycle doesn't match your riding style, or if the frame is the wrong size, there's no use spending a lot of money upgrading. Sell your bike and buy one that suits you better.

Types of 10-Speeds

Some people divide the 10-speed market into just two categories: racing and touring. However, there's such a great difference between sport touring and loaded touring that lumping them together just causes confusion. Therefore, I prefer to divide 10-speeds into three categories: racing, sport touring, and loaded touring. Since the majority of cyclists are neither serious racers nor loaded tourists, but something in between, the sport touring category provides an important middle ground.

I'm going to define my three categories exactly so that we can communicate. I'll try to use neutral words so my prejudices don't show through. I own a Trek 2000 racer, a Schwinn Paramount racer, a custom-built Redcay sport tourer, and a custom-built Columbine loaded tourer. The fact that I own at least one bike in each category should make me impartial.

Racing Bicycles

A racing bicycle is designed to win races. Everything about the bike is slanted toward that goal. The frame dimensions stretch the rider out in a low, crouched position for minimum wind resistance. The frame angles provide quick handling for maneuverability in tight quarters and stiffness for maximum efficiency. The wheels and tires (invariably tubulars for serious racers) are designed for minimum weight and wind resistance. The gearing is designed for strong racers who can put out ¼ horsepower for a long period and still have something left for the final sprint. If you can't climb steep hills in a 50-inch gear, you won't stand a chance in a serious race. (My son Ben, the bike racer, read this last statement and noted "True, true.")

A long ride on a genuine criterium racing bicycle is uncomfortable for nonracers. Racing bicycles aren't designed for comfort; they're designed to win races. Racers don't talk about comfort. They talk about quickness and stiffness, which are almost the reverse of comfort. Racing bicycles are uncomfortable for three main reasons:

- The stiff, quick-handling forks and the steep head angle have little shock absorption, which beats up your hands and arms.
- The good-climbing short chainstays put the rear wheel nearly under the saddle, which beats up your backside.
- The light, narrow, high-pressure tires transmit road bumps with full fidelity.

Criterium Racers There are degrees of discomfort. Criterium racing bicycles are the least comfortable because they're designed for short races with lots of turning and sprinting. They have the stiffest frames, the steepest angles, the most rigid forks, and the shortest wheelbases in order to provide quick handling in a criterium pack. The bottom bracket is higher to allow pedaling around corners. Top-of-the-line Japanese racing bicycles are usually criterium racers.

Road Racers Road racing bicycles are made more comfortable than criterium racers because road races are much longer. They often cover more than 100 miles per day on consecutive days. In these longer events, the rider can't survive on an ultra-stiff criterium frame. Road racing frames are designed to soften the ride so that the rider will have something left for the closing sprint and the next day's stage. Top-quality Italian racing bicycles are usually road racers.

More than half of the racing bicycles sold are never raced in formal competition. They're bought by riders who appreciate lightness, stiffness, and efficiency and accept the accompanying discomfort. Triathlon bicycles are special cases. Triathletes have to be proficient in three sports, so they can't pile on training mileage like ordinary bicycle racers. Triathletes need a lightweight, high-performance racing bicycle, but they don't need quick handling because they don't race in a pack. They also want a fairly soft ride so they will have something left over at the end of the bicycle race to put into the running race.

Everything is done to reduce the weight of racing bicycles. The old truism is that one pound off the wheels is worth two pounds off the frame and ten pounds off the rider. Wheel weight is important because light wheels accelerate faster, which is critical in races where the pace is constantly changing.

Loaded Touring Bicycles

I've switched the order between loaded and sport touring to cover the extremes first and then the compromise. Loaded touring bicycles are designed to carry a heavy touring load reliably on a long cross-country tour with maximum rider comfort. The load is carried in *panniers* (a fancy French word for packsacks), which are fastened to racks mounted on the bike. The bicycle frame dimensions and angles are designed to provide stability on long descents with the touring load.

Everything on a loaded touring bicycle is designed for comfort and reliability because bicycle touring is supposed to be enjoyable. There aren't any record times for loaded touring. The rider is assumed to be a normal mortal capable of putting out about 1/10 horsepower for long periods of time. The gearing is designed so that the loaded bicycle can be pedaled (albeit slowly) up any hill that's encountered. The forks are designed to absorb front shocks and the long chainstays are designed to absorb rear shocks. Loaded touring wheels and tires are designed to avoid flats and to help absorb shocks from potholes and rough roads.

Loaded touring bicycles are very stable, especially if the weight is carried in low-mounted front panniers. They keep going in a straight line and they corner sedately and serenely. You don't tour in a *peleton* (another fancy French word for a bunch of bicycles in a line). Bicycle weight isn't so critical with 40 pounds or so in the panniers.

Sport Touring Bicycles

Most 10-speeds are sport tourers, neither racers nor loaded tourers, which is as it should be since most cyclists neither race nor go on loaded cross-country tours. Sport touring bicycles fall somewhere between the other two categories; they're called "sport tourers" both for want of a better name and because it's a useful marketing term. The bicycle makers design for a particular kind of rider at each price level. The makers know that standard-quality 10-speeds will never be raced and they design them for entry-level riders.

At the $400 to $500 price level, many makers supply two models: one for sporting and one for touring. Two recent trends have made the bicycles sportier. The growing number of triathletes has created a demand for high-performance almost-racing bicycles. At the same time, the market for comfortable touring bicyles is drying up because increasing numbers of riders are touring on mountain bikes. Some sport tourers are actually "platypi" with odd combinations of touring gears on racing frames.

Sport touring bicycles are designed to provide a more comfortable ride than road racing bicycles. Most sport tourers have modest clearance for fenders and they can be fitted with racks and used for loaded touring. Their gearing usually provides a compromise Low. The maker often signals the intended market for a particular bike by his tire selection. Touring bicycles have 27 × 1¼ or 27 × 1⅛ tires. Sporting bicycles have 700 × 23C or 700 × 25C tires.

Most of you have only one bicycle, which is a compromise to fit all of your different kinds of riding. If most of your riding is slow and leisurely (the kind the bicycle clubs call "flower watching"), then you want a comfortable sport tourer that is closer to a loaded tourer. If you like to really cover the distance on your recreational rides, then you want a light sport tourer that's closer to a road racer.

The big problem in selecting a sport touring bicycle isn't defining what you want, it's trying to determine if the bicycle that you're reading about or looking at meets your requirements. The differences are subtle and bicycle advertising offers little assistance. The catalogs don't tell you where the various models fit in the racing–touring spectrum. The more expensive sport tourers tend to have more racing character, but that's a very general observation.

Picking a Bicycle to Suit You

In an ideal world, 10-speed advertising would show a comfort rating (C) and a performance rating (P), like the sun protection factor (SPF) on sun tan lotions. The performance rating could just as readily be called an "efficiency" or a "stiffness" rating. A criterium racer would then be labelled C-0/P-10 and an unabashed loaded tourer would be marked C-10/P-0. To be sure, comfort and performance are not entirely reciprocals of each other. A properly designed aluminum frame, for example, increases the comfort rating at small cost to its performance rating. Also, on most any bike you can change both numbers by installing different wheels or tires.

Table 2-1 shows typical dimensions and component selection for a C-1/P-9 criterium racer, a C-4/P-6 sport tourer, and a C-9/P-1 loaded tourer, all for a 5-foot, 10-inch rider with average body dimensions. I developed this table by

TABLE 2-1.

Typical Racing, Sport Touring, and Loaded Touring Bicycles

Specifications	Racing	Sport Touring	Loaded Touring
Weight	21 lb.	25 lb.	28 lb.
Bottom bracket height	10.7 in.	10.6 in.	10.3 in.
Chainstay length	16 in.	16.5 in.	18.5 in.
Fork rake	1.4 in.	1.8 in.	2 in.
Frame size	22 in.	22.5 in.	23 in.
Head tube angle	74 deg.	73 deg.	72 deg.
Seat tube angle	74 deg.	73 deg.	73 deg.
Top tube length	22.5 in.	22 in.	21.5 in.
Wheelbase	39.5 in.	40.5 in.	42.5 in.
Crankset	53/42	50/40	48/43/24
Freewheel	13–21 (N-7)	13–28 (W-6)	13–34 (W-5)
High gear	110 in.	104 in.	100 in.
Low gear	55 in.	41 in.	19 in.
Rims	tubular	27 × 1	27 × 1¼
Spokes	32 × 15-16-15 gauge	36 × 15 gauge	36 × 14 gauge
Tires	250 gr., 700C tubulars	27 × 1⅛ clinchers	27 × 1⅜ clinchers

averaging the catalog specifications for typical bicycles from Cannondale, Nishiki, Panasonic, Peugeot, Specialized, and Trek. These nice companies show frame dimensions in their catalogs. There aren't many stock loaded touring bicycles, so I applied my own experience and preferences to the loaded touring category.

Note that the same rider uses a smaller frame for racing than for touring. The seatpost is set higher for racing, and the stem is usually about ½ inch longer to put the racer in a lower, more streamlined position. It's amazing that small changes in wheelbase, head angle, and fork rake make such a dramatic difference in the way the bike feels and handles out on the road. Figures 2-1 and 2-2 exaggerate the differences so you can see them.

Ask yourself two questions. First, where does your riding style fit within the comfort–performance spectrum? Second, where does your present bicycle fit within the same spectrum? Use the description of the different kinds of bicycles to answer the first question. As for the second, if you are a C-8 rider on a C-2 bicycle, you don't need to upgrade, you need a different bicycle.

FIGURE 2-1 Basic geometry of a racing bike.

FIGURE 2-2 Basic geometry of a loaded touring bike.

Picking the Right Bicycle Size

The previous section told you how to get the right *kind* of bicycle. This section will tell you how to get the right *size* bicycle. In order to do that, you need to understand the basic geometry of a bicycle frame and the way a frame is measured. This information is shown in figure 2-3. Look at the figure and note in particular these two dimensions: the seat tube length and the top tube length. These are the key dimensions to take into account when determining whether or not a bike is the right size for you. Note that the seat tube length determines the nominal size of the bicycle frame.

Bicycle Height or Size

The basic method used to determine what size bicycle frame is correct for you is to stand astride it and measure the distance between the top tube and your crotch. You should be able to stand flat-footed on the ground and still have some clearance.

How much is "some?" It depends on how you ride and who you ask for advice. I ride in a comfortable upright position, usually on the tops of the handlebars. My handlebars are about level with my saddle. I pick a frame that I can just straddle and I raise the handlebars to the mark on the stem. Thus, for me "some" means about ¼ inch. Racers ride in a lower, more efficient position with the handlebars of their bicycles set well below the saddle height. They use smaller frames because they are stiffer and lighter. A typical racing bicycle has 1½ inches of crotch clearance.

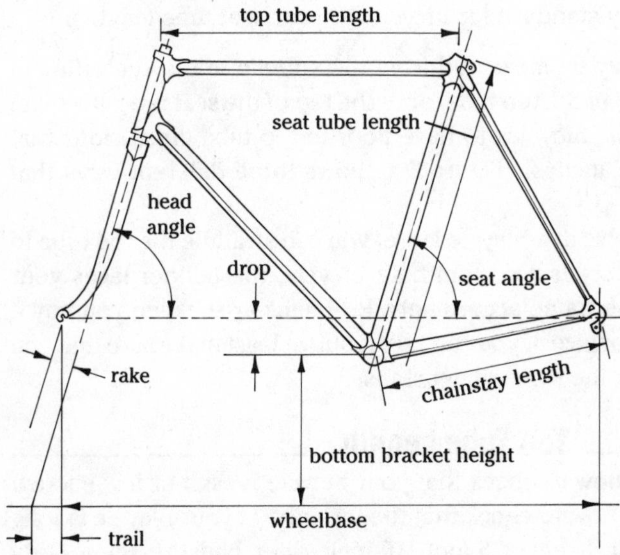

FIGURE 2-3

Key dimensions of a bicycle frame.

FIGURE 2-4

Different measurements of bicycle size.

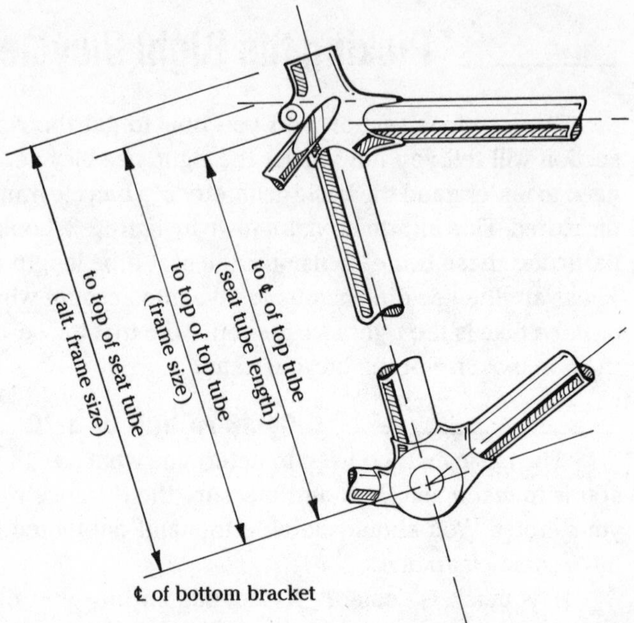

Most bicycle books tell you to multiply your inseam dimension by 0.70 or to subtract 9 or 10 inches from your inseam to get the right frame size. Both of these formulas have the following problems:

- The bottom bracket height can vary between 10¼ inches and 11 inches, moving the top tube up with it and changing your crotch clearance.
- There's no industry standard for bicycle size (or seat tube length).

A 23-inch bicycle may be measured from the spindle to the centerline of the top tube, or to the top of the top tube, or to the top of the seat tube. It's quite possible for two "23-inch" bicycles to have floor-to-top tube dimensions that differ by as much as 1½ inches. (Figure 2-4 shows three different ways that bicycle sizes are measured.)

When you buy a bicycle at a bicycle store, you can straddle the top tube to check the fit. When you order a custom-built bicycle, the builder takes your dimensions, and sizes the frame accordingly. Problems arise when you buy a bicycle without trying it for size. If you can't try it out, at least make sure that you and the seller are talking the same dimensions.

Top Tube Length

So far, I've told you how to check that your bicycle is high or low enough for you. Now, I'll tell you how to check that the top tube of your bicycle is long or short enough for you. If every 5-foot, 10-inch rider had the same body dimensions, it would be easy to design bicycle frames. But not all men have average dimensions. Neither do all women. Moreover, women's average dimensions are different from those of men.

The bicycle makers assume a set of average dimensions and they expect nonaverage riders to adjust for any misfit by moving the seat forward or back a bit and by using a longer or shorter stem. These methods provide no more than about an inch of adjustment. Interestingly, different makers make different assumptions about what is average because top tube lengths vary from maker to maker by about an inch.

Paul Brown's Sizing Method

Paul Brown runs the Cycle Dynamics bicycle shop in Novato, California. Over the past five years, Paul has sold more than a thousand custom-built bicycles. The sizing procedure given below is a simplification and condensation of the method Paul uses to measure his customers for custom-made frames.

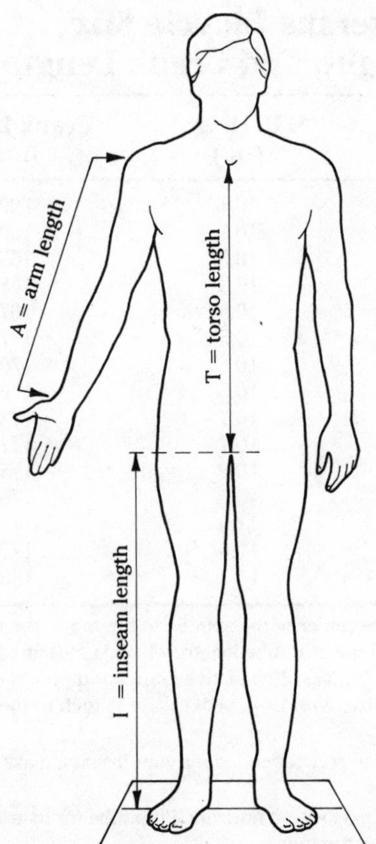

FIGURE 2-5

Body measurements for a perfect fit on a bike.

The method requires you to take three body dimensions: inseam length, torso length, and arm length. Figure 2-5 shows these three dimensions. Stand up against a wall with your bare feet close together. Insert a record album between your legs. Raise it until it touches your crotch and mark the wall at that point. The distance from the floor to this mark we will call "I" for inseam length.

Now find the top of your sternum (a.k.a. breastbone). That's the vertical bone under your Adam's apple that ties your ribs together at the front. Make another mark on the wall. The distance from the inseam mark to the sternum mark we will call "T" for torso length. Finally, have a friend measure your arm from the acromion process (that's the bone at the tip of your shoulder) to your wrist to get "A" or arm length.

Table 2-2 shows the bicycle size, bottom bracket height, and crank length

TABLE 2-2.

Inseam Length versus Bicycle Size, Bottom Bracket Height, and Crank Length

Inseam (in.)	Bicycle Size[1] (in.)	B.B. Height (in.)	Crank Length[2] (mm)
28	—[3]	10.1	160
29	20.0	10.1	160
30	20.7	10.3	165
31	21.3	10.3	165
32	22.0	10.5	167.5
33	22.6	10.5	167.5
34	23.3	10.6	170
35	23.8	10.6	170
36	24.3	10.7	172.5
37	24.7	10.7	172.5
38	25.1	10.8	175
39	25.4	10.8	175
40	25.8	11.0	177.5
41	26.2	11.0	177.5
42	26.7	11.1	180

1. The bicycle size shown is measured from the center of the spindle to the top of the top tube. Subtract ½ inch from the bicycle size to obtain the seat tube length, which is measured from the spindle to the centerline of the top tube. With Shimano Dyna-Drive cranks and pedals or Aero-Lite pedals, subtract ½ inch from the bicycle size. With Look pedals, add ½ inch to the bicycle size.

2. If you select a crank length other than the one recommended for your inseam, make the appropriate adjustment in the bicycle size.

3. It is not practical to make a conventional bicycle with a horizontal top tube for inseams below 29 inches. Use smaller front wheels or a sloping top tube.

TABLE 2-3.

Top Tube Length versus Combined Torso plus Arm Length

Torso plus Arm Length (in.)	Top Tube Length[1] (in.)	Stem Length[2] (mm)
40	19.5	90
41	19.9	90
42	20.3	90
43	20.6	90
44	21.0	90
45	21.3	90
46	21.6	100
47	21.9	100
48	22.2	100
49	22.5	100
50	22.8	100
51	23.1	100
52	23.4	100
53	23.7	100

1. The top tube length is measured horizontally from the centerline of the head tube to the centerline of the seat tube.
2. The stem length is measured from the center of the binder bolt to the center of the handlebars.

that matches your inseam (leg length). Table 2-3 shows the top tube length and stem length that matches your combined torso plus arm length.

The two tables give the key dimensions of a road racing bicycle. A loaded touring bicycle should be about an inch larger and have an inch shorter top tube. At least it should in my opinion. I admit that loaded touring bicycle dimensions are controversial. In any case, the dimensions of a sport touring bicycle should be somewhere in between, depending on your style of riding.

Here's an example of how the tables work. My measurements are I = 34 inches, T = 26 inches, and A = 24 inches. Paul's tables suggest that I should ride a racing bicycle with a 23.3-inch frame, a 22.8-inch top tube, and a 10.6-inch bottom bracket height. Table 2-4 shows how these optimum dimensions compare with the actual dimensions of four of my five bicycles.

Dealing with Nonaverage Dimensions

There's quite a variation in top tube lengths between bicycles of the same size from different makers. If you have dimensions that are different from average, this let's you pick a bicycle that fits you. If, like me, you have long legs and a short upper body, pick a frame with a shorter than average top tube. If you're like my touring friend, Paul Schafer, who has short legs and a long torso, pick a frame with a longer than average top tube. You can compensate for about an inch or so of top tube–upper body mismatch by installing a longer or a shorter stem.

Short people have special problems finding bicycles to fit them properly. The worst bicycles for short people come from the makers who use the same top tube length for all frame sizes. By shortening the seat tube and the head tube, they can use the same jigs and lugs for all frame sizes. The smallest frame size has an excessively long top tube and no possibility of a comfortable riding position. Even when the maker tries to proportion the top tube to the other tubes, the 19-inch frame will usually have an overlong top tube to prevent the toe clips from overlapping the front wheel.

Short people should also watch out for bicycles with extra-high bottom brackets (more than 10½ inches). This is another sneaky way that the makers use stock lugs. The right frame for short riders usually has a combination of sloping top tube, slightly higher bottom bracket, and smaller front wheel. Fuji, Shogun, and Univega now make properly proportioned stock bicycles for petite people. Among the custom builders, Bill Boston, Georgena Terry, and Paul Brown have made numerous small-framed bicycles.

Now that you've read the first two chapters and measured yourself and your bicycle, you should know if your bicycle is worth a major upgrade, a minor upgrade, or only a clean and polish job so that you can sell it.

TABLE 2-4.

Ideal versus Actual Dimensions of Frank Berto's Bicycles

Bicycle	Type	Bicycle Size (in.)	Top Tube Length (in.)	B.B. Height (in.)	Crank Length (mm)
Recommended	R	23.3	22.8	10.6	170
Columbine	LT	25.0	22.2	10.3	175
Redcay	ST	25.0	22.7	10.7	175
Trek 2000	R	23.4	22.5	10.6	175
Windsor Carrera	R	25.0	23.0	11.3	175

CHAPTER 3

Upgrading Your Gear Train

No matter how much money you put into your bike and how refined its componentry, if its gearing system is not well thought out or well suited to your riding style, the bike will not be a pleasure to ride. This chapter tells you how to get the right gears on your bicycle: the right number of chainwheels on the front, each with the right number of teeth, and the right number of freewheel sprockets on the rear, each with the right number of teeth. It tells you how to select the highest gear, the lowest gear, and the in-between gears to precisely match your needs. Later chapters will cover selection of the ironmongery—cranksets, freewheels, derailleurs, and the like—to accomplish the desired gearing results.

There's a lot of meat in this chapter. So take the time to read it and understand it. Once you have a good understanding of gearing and gear pattern design, you will be ready to benefit from the next five chapters, which tell you all about gear-train hardware. Taken as a whole, these six chapters will help you to upgrade the gears on your bicycle so that they exactly match your riding needs.

Long-term readers of *Bicycling* magazine know that bicycle gearing is my first love. I wrote my first gearing article in 1973. Since then I've written 20 gearing articles and another 20 articles about gear-train components. I'm a gear fanatic. I'm convinced that many beginners give up bicycling because they can't pedal up hills, whereas a change of gearing would make all the difference. It's actually quite pleasant to pedal a bicycle that's geared to suit your particular level of strength. And if you learn to use your 1⁄10-horsepower engine efficiently, eventually it will become a 1⁄4-horsepower engine.

Your present bicycle probably has the wrong gearing for your specific needs. There are two exceptions to that bold statement: (1) you may have lucked out when you bought your bicycle, or (2) you know enough about gearing that you have already revised the gearing that came with your bike.

The bicycle maker has a basic problem. He can only put one set of gears on each model of bicycle. He must select compromise gearing because his bicycles will be sold in both flat Florida and hilly Colorado and to both weak beginners and strong, serious cyclists. So he tries to choose a gearing system that will be appropriate for the "average" rider and the "average" terrain. Unfortunately, many makers do a poor job of devising compromise gearing and they end up with poorly spaced gears and duplicates. There's really no excuse for a maker to put "dumb" gearing on a bicycle because the right intermediate freewheel sprockets cost exactly the same as the wrong ones.

In theory, bicycle stores could customize the gearing of each bicycle they sell. In practice, bicycle stores sell low-profit items in a competitive marketplace. You have to do the customizing yourself, or at least tell your bicycle shop what you want done. This chapter will tell you how to determine your gearing needs and how to convert those needs into a practical gear train.

Thinking in Gear Inches

Before you can properly design a gear system for your bike, you have to understand the numbers used to describe gearing. If you're already familiar with *gear inches,* just skip to the end of this section. Otherwise, keep reading.

The gear inch numbers have a colorful history. During the first bicycle boom in the late 1800s, *ordinaries* (a.k.a. *high-wheelers* or *penny-farthings*) were specified by the diameter of the front wheel. A child might ride an ordinary with a 36-inch front wheel, whereas the average adult might ride a 45-inch model. Tall adults with long legs could just about reach the pedals on a 52-inch ordinary. Since the pedals were connected directly to the front wheel without gearing (or the ability to coast), the bigger "wheels" went farther for each pedal revolution. They were faster on the level but harder to pedal up hills. (A typical high-wheeler is shown in figure 3-1.)

Ordinaries were truly unsafe at any speed. (It's a good thing that bicycles were invented before trial lawyers took cases on contingency). You had to stop very carefully or you sailed over the handlebars. In the 1900s, the geared *safety* bicycle was invented to overcome the safety problems inherent with the older bikes. A 1900 safety looked very much like today's diamond-framed 10-speed.

The bicycle buyer was used to thinking in wheel diameters so the new safeties were advertised with a "gear number" that was the wheel diameter of an equivalent ordinary. This practice continues to this day. Thus, a bicycle with a 52-tooth chainwheel, a 13-tooth freewheel sprocket, and a 27-inch-diameter rear wheel has a gear of 108 inches ($52/13 \times 27$). It's equivalent to an ordinary with a nine-foot-diameter front wheel except that you can reach the pedals. Both bicycles go the same distance with one turn of the pedals.

FIGURE 3-1

A typical high-wheeler.

Because the literature uses gear inches, the numbers are meaningful to experienced readers. One hundred inches is a "tall" gear that enables you to go downhill at 25 mph. Eighty inches is a nice, level cruising gear. Forty inches is for climbing medium hills. Twenty inches is for climbing steep hills with a touring load, and so on.

In place of gear inches, the Europeans refer to "development"—the number of meters traveled in one turn of the pedals. This is a more logical system because it allows you to directly relate the number of your pedal revolutions to the distance you are traveling, but we're used to thinking in terms of gear inches.

While we're talking terminology, I should point out that I number bike gears like gears on an automobile. On a 10-speed, "first" is *Low,* the lowest gear, and "tenth" is *High,* the highest gear. You "downshift" to a lower gear for hill climbing and you "upshift" to a higher gear for level cruising.

Designing Your Own Gear Train

There are four essential steps to follow when designing a gearing system for your bike:

- Pick your ideal high gear.
- Pick your ideal low gear.
- Pick a shift pattern that you understand and will properly use.
- Select chainwheels and freewheel sprockets you need to produce the desired pattern and range of gears.

If you're doing an economy upgrade, you may not be able to pick the optimums. You may have to compromise the gear selection to match the capacity of your present components.

How High the High?

Selecting your highest gear is a reasonably straightforward process. The ergonomics of cycling narrows the options; even a very well-tuned bicycle engine can only put out about ¼ horsepower (HP) on a sustained basis.

Within a limited range, human horsepower capabilities can vary considerably. An out-of-shape beginner pedaling along at 14 mph only puts out about 1⁄10 HP. By contrast, Freddy Markham put out 1 HP for a whole minute when he went 65.5 mph for 200 meters in a human-powered vehicle (HPV) in 1986.

Although Markham put out ten times as much horsepower during his short ride as the beginner does while traveling 14 mph, he didn't go ten times as fast. In fact, if his HPV hadn't been completely streamlined, Freddy would have gone only about 35 mph. That's because most of the bicycle pedaling effort goes toward overcoming wind resistance.

Wind resistance absorbs 67 percent of your pedaling effort at 15 mph and 85 percent at 25 mph. Wind resistance increases with the cube of the speed, so it takes eight times as much horsepower to go twice as fast.

Finally, almost everyone pedals between 60 and 100 rpm. Pedal rpm is called "cadence." A cadence of 80 with a 100-inch gear equals 24 mph, which requires about ⅓ HP in a crouched position. Most bicycles have a 52-tooth large chainwheel and a 14-tooth small sprocket, a combination that produces a 100-inch High. That's about the highest gear that most cyclists have the strength to use at a reasonable cadence.

There are exceptions. Strong racers sometimes use 110- or even 115-inch gears for drafting the pack on the level or for sprinting downhill. Time trialists push very tall gears in their all-out races against the clock. Tourists with 40 pounds of luggage may be quite happy with a High of 85 or 90 inches.

Tall, long-legged riders with long (175mm or 180mm) cranks and a slower cadence might prefer a 110-inch high gear, especially for barreling down hills. Short-legged riders with short (160mm or 165mm) cranks often develop a faster cadence and they might prefer a 90-inch High.

The second highest gear affects the selection of High. With a nice 85- to 90-inch Ninth for level cruising, you can afford to carry an "overdrive" Tenth for pedaling downhill. If your Ninth is 75 to 80 inches, you'll probably be happier with a 90- to 95-inch Tenth.

If you think your High is too low, ask yourself if you are really ready for higher gears. Competitive racers who use 110-inch Highs spent years spinning in low 60-inch gears to develop their leg strength. Many macho cyclists buy extra-high gears, then find that the only thing that speeds up is knee deterioration.

To sum up, most cyclists are well served with the standard 100-inch High. If your own pedaling experience indicates that this is too high or too low, change it, but keep the changes within a narrow range.

The easy way to modify high gear is to change the small freewheel sprocket. The standard 52-tooth chainwheel × 14-tooth sprocket gives a High of 100 inches. A 13-tooth sprocket raises High to 108 inches. A 15-tooth sprocket lowers High to 93 inches. If those changes are too great, keep the 14-tooth sprocket and change the big chainwheel to 54 teeth for 104 inches or 50 teeth for 96 inches. But in deciding how to alter your gearing, keep in mind that chainwheels cost much more than freewheel sprockets.

Finally, I may be accused of falling into the "do as I say, not as I do" syndrome, since I have a 120-inch gear on my sport touring bicycle (48-tooth chainwheel × 11-tooth sprocket). I have that tall gear because I love to pedal down hills at 40 mph.

I've been working for the past five years to get my cadence up to 80. The Avocet Cyclometer has helped this program. It has shown me that when my cadence drops much below 80, I can go faster by shifting to a lower gear and speeding up my cadence. I assure you I'm very careful of my knees when using the 120-inch gear. As soon as the hill levels out and my speed drops below 30 mph, I shift out of the 11-tooth sprocket. I can afford to carry 2 extra downhill gears on the sport tourer because it's an 18-speed with 15 useful gears.

This is a nuts and bolts book, not a diet and exercise book, but I urge you to work on increasing your cadence. Bicycling avoids most of the physical pitfalls of other sports. So don't put gears on your bicycle that damage your knees.

How Low the Low?

If selecting High is straightforward, selecting Low is more personal, more controversial, and more expensive. Your lowest gear is used to climb the steepest hills. You're only in Low for a small fraction of your mileage. It's easy to convince yourself (or let yourself be convinced) that you should struggle on with your present gearing until you get stronger. That's bad reasoning if the hassle of hill climbing causes you to limit your cycling. The idea is to get stronger first and then raise your low gear.

There's a macho image associated with big chainwheels and little freewheel sprockets. The slightly derisory term "granny gear," used to describe very low gears, is part of the macho syndrome. I've been on a reverse ego trip for ten years. I flaunt the most anemic granny available (24-tooth chainwheel × 34-tooth freewheel). I don't use the 19-inch Low that often, but it's nice to have when I want it.

On a loaded tour, with 30 or 40 pounds of luggage, you need the lowest gear that you can get. If you average 15 mph on your fun training rides without any load, you're putting out something under ¼ HP. With 40 pounds of luggage, that horsepower will take you up a 6 percent hill at 4 mph. Sit down and figure it out for yourself. One horsepower raises 550 pounds 1 foot per second.

If your loaded touring bike has a 19-inch Low like mine, you can climb that 6 percent hill at a cadence of 70. If it has a 27-inch Low, your cadence will be about 50 because you are horsepower limited. You can't convert oatmeal to glycogen fast enough. At a cadence of 50, your bike will slow down each time you go through the dead centers. As you sway back and forth, your knees will tell you that you're pushing 1½ times as hard.

PHOTO 3-1 Gear train on Frank Berto's loaded touring bicycle.

As the hills get steeper, your speed and cadence become that much slower. At some point, you get off and walk. It's both faster and more efficient to pedal up hills. You know that. That's why you bought a bicycle. I suspect that there's a Low that's too low for loaded touring, but I haven't found it yet.

A Low of 19 inches certainly isn't the ergonomic limit, but it is the practical mechanical limit of today's equipment. On my bicycle tour of England, when I got off and walked up the one-in-five hills (that's a 20 percent grade, folks), the cyclometer said 2½ mph. I can easily balance a loaded touring bicycle at 2½ mph, but I can't push hard enough at 40 rpm in a 19-inch gear.

Fifteen years ago, cyclists avoided very low gears because of the lousy derailleurs that were available at the time. There was only one decent-shifting rear derailleur, the Campagnolo Record, and it didn't have the capacity to handle wide-range gearing. The Huret and Simplex wide-range rear derailleurs were fragile mechanical disasters. The old Campagnolo Gran Turismo was hell-for-stout, but it was arguably the worst-shifting rear derailleur ever made.

In 1970, wide-range touring gearing, even with 28-tooth freewheels, involved a significant sacrifice in shifting ease. You put up with narrow gearing in order to get good shifting.

Shimano and SunTour ended all that in the early 1970s with their GS and GT rear derailleurs. (Somebody ought to build a monument to the SunTour VGT.) To show that they were serious, the Japanese introduced 34-tooth freewheel sprockets. The Europeans still dispute the need for very low gears. You can't buy a 34-tooth sprocket for a European freewheel. But today, thanks to the Japanese, you can pick from dozens of good-shifting, wide-range rear derailleurs, freewheels, and cranksets.

The front derailleur situation was worse. Fifteen years ago, the common front derailleurs were the Campagnolo Gran Sport and the Simplex Prestige. They shifted poorly on doubles and worse on triples. In 1970, "alpine" gearing used 52/40 chainwheels and the front derailleurs were overwhelmed at that level. Good-shifting, wide-range front derailleurs are a recent development. Mountain bikes have provided the testing ground for most recent front derailleur improvements.

Today's wide-range front and rear derailleurs can comfortably handle low gears as low as you want to install, yet the old macho mythology persists. Ask yourself how you feel about your present bicycle. Are you straining and suffering going up hills or are you avoiding hilly rides? If so, then get a lower Low and smile as you slowly ride up your steepest hill.

Conversely, are you so strong that you never use your Low because you sprint up hills in second or third? Then rearrange your gearing around a higher Low and get easier shifting and closer steps between your level cruising gears.

PHOTO 3-2

SunTour VGT rear derailleur.

I pedal in hilly country and my cycling companions are not very competitive. With this admitted bias, I see ten over-geared bikes for every one that's geared too low. Based on many letters and conversations, I've developed table 3-1, which gives my arbitrary low-gear recommendations. In later chapters I'll tell you about the equipment decisions and compromises that are involved as you plumb the low-gear depths.

Logical Gearing Arrangements

At this point, you've tentatively selected your highest gear (High) and your lowest gear (Low). Now you have to convert the numbers into ironmongery. You must pick the big chainwheel–little sprocket combination that gives you High and the little chainwheel–big sprocket combination that gives you Low. In the process of picking these combinations, you will have selected two chainwheels and the smallest and largest freewheel sprockets.

Now things begin to get complicated. First, you have to decide on the number of "speeds" for your bike. Do you want one, two, or three chainwheels on your crankset; do you want five, six, or seven sprockets on your freewheel? These decisions will determine whether your bike becomes a 5-, 6-, 7-, 10-, 12-, 14-, 15-, 18-, or 21-speed.

TABLE 3-1.

Recommended Low Gears

Kind of Riding	Strong Young Riders (gear in.)	Wise Old Riders (gear in.)
Racing (level course)	60	55
Racing (hilly course)	50	45
Triathlon (level course)	60	55
Triathlon (hilly course)	45	40
Recreational riding (flat terrain)	45	40
Recreational riding (medium hills)	36	32
Recreational riding (steep hills)	32	27
Loaded touring (flat terrain)	32	24
Loaded touring (hilly terrain)	19	19

Time-out for terminology. A bicycle with three chainwheels and five sprockets is called a "15-speed," even if two of the speeds are unusable and three of the speeds are exact duplicates. Cranksets with three chainwheels are called "triples."

When you've selected High and Low and you've established the number of speeds, you're ready to pick the intermediate gears between High and Low. Bear in mind that when you choose the intermediate sprockets (and the middle chainwheel on a triple), you're also choosing the shifting pattern for your bicycle. Actually, it's easier to decide on the shifting pattern first and then choose the chainwheels and freewheel sprockets that fit the pattern.

So welcome to "Gearfreakland." I'll try to make your visit as pleasant and productive as possible. I will get right to the point by saying, I believe that there are just five logical and practical shift patterns to be considered. They're listed in table 3-2 on page 38. The table shows typical high and low gears and the chainwheel and freewheel combinations often used to create these basic gearing systems.

There are many other less practical and less convenient gearing patterns, and I'll talk briefly about them at the end of this chapter. But first, let's look at the five basic patterns one at a time.

Crossover

Crossover is the pattern for racers, triathletes, and anyone riding on level terrain. It's very straightforward. You have one set of gears on the big chainwheel for level roads and a second set of gears on the little chainwheel for hills. You make most of your shifts with the rear derailleur. Racers like this because rear shifts are faster and more reliable than front shifts. When you run out of lower gears on the big chainwheel, you shift to the little chainwheel. When you run out of higher gears on the little chainwheel, you shift back to the big chainwheel.

It isn't quite that simple, because you don't normally use the two cross-chain gears—the big chainwheel with the biggest freewheel sprocket or the little chainwheel with the smallest freewheel sprocket. You avoid these "forbidden" cross-chain gears so that the chain doesn't have to deflect at extreme angles. Of course they're not really forbidden. But if you use them, your chain will be noisy, less efficient, and it will wear faster. Racers don't use the cross-chain gears because they put so much tension on the chain that it can pull off the chainwheels. (Chain deflection is most severe on racing bicycles with short chainstays.) It's not a big deal to avoid the forbidden gears. You just switch to the other chainwheel one gear earlier.

Crossover gearing wastes gears. You give up the two cross-chain gears and there are often duplicates between the big and the little chainwheel gears. A typical 12-speed crossover system has seven or eight useful gears. Wasted gears aren't a problem for racers because in a typical race they normally use only five or six gears. Moreover, today's racers use six- or seven-sprocket freewheels to get more useful gears. They want a maximum number of one-tooth steps between adjacent sprockets because that gives them small, 7 percent changes.

TABLE 3-2.

Logical Shift Patterns

Pattern Name	High Gear	Low Gear	Chain-wheels	Freewheel Sprockets	Double Shifting	Shift Sequence
Crossover	110	50	52/42	13-14-15-17-19-21	no	easy
Half-step	100	45	52/47	14-17-21-26-32	yes	easy
Alpine	100	35	52/39	14-17-21-26-32	yes	hard
Half-step plus granny	100	20	52/47/24	14-17-21-26-32	yes	easy
Crossover plus granny	100	20	52/42/24	14-16-19-22-26-32	no	easy

Racers sometimes change sprockets before each race to customize the gearing to the course. On a level course, they use a "corncob" or "straight-block" freewheel (12-13-14-15-16-17-18) with one-tooth steps between sprockets. On a hilly stage, they use something like 13-14-15-16-18-20-23.

In the half-step and alpine patterns, there's a rigorous relationship between the gears on the two chainwheels. In a crossover system, there isn't a similar relationship so you can arrange the sprockets any way you please.

There's nothing magic about the 52/42 chainwheels either. When Campagnolo introduced the Record front derailleur in the late 1960s, it could reliably handle a 10-tooth chainwheel difference. Shortly afterward, Campagnolo revised the Record crankset so that it would take a 42-tooth minimum chainwheel. Shortly after that, most racers were using 52/42 chainwheels. Today, it's usually 53/42.

In the 1960s and 1970s, the smallest freewheel sprocket was a 13-tooth, and extra-strong racers had to use 54- or 56-tooth chainwheels to get extra-high gears. Today's racers can use 12-tooth sprockets and smaller inner and outer chainwheels. The latest generation of cranksets can handle 39-tooth chainwheels. Today's racers could use 50-tooth outer chainwheels instead of 53s or 54s, but most of them don't. In theory, racers could change chainwheels before each race, but they don't. They just install the smallest inner chainwheel that fits the crankset (39 or 42 teeth) and leave it alone.

The crossover shift sequence is very simple. As you approach a hill, you shift down with the rear derailleur until you get to the second largest rear sprocket. Then you "cross over" to the small chainwheel. That's the reason for the name.

Crossover works best as a narrow-range pattern for racers or for mere mortals in level country. It's less pleasant if there's more than two-tooth steps between the small sprockets or three-tooth steps between the larger sprockets, because large tooth steps result in 15 percent or larger steps between gears. Crossover is also a pattern best adapted to six- or seven-sprocket freewheels.

Though I have just described crossover as a narrow-range pattern, I think that a properly arranged wide-range crossover with seven or eight useful gears is more pleasant than alpine for many riders. Over the years I've often recommended wide-range crossovers to poor souls whose top-of-the-line "touring" bicycle came equipped with a racing crankset and a 42-tooth inner chainwheel. Combining the 42-tooth chainwheel with a 14-16-18-21-26-34 freewheel gives a 34-inch Low and an acceptable shifting pattern.

Half-Step

Half-step gearing is an old favorite of mine, but you rarely see it these days. Half-step was the standard racing pattern in the 1960s, with something like a

13–24 five-sprocket freewheel and a 52/49 crankset. Campagnolo Record derailleurs and six-sprocket freewheels ended half-step gearing and double shifting for racers.

With both half-step and alpine, the rules are rigid. The freewheel sprockets must be selected to give even percentage steps between gears. The "perfect" freewheel is 13-16-20-25-31, which provides uniform 24 percent steps between sprockets. The chainwheel step must be 12 percent, half of the freewheel step, hence the name.

Half-steps have three advantages: evenly spaced gears, an easy shift sequence, and easy front shifts. They also have three companion disadvantages: a Low that isn't very low, the need for wide-range freewheels and rear derailleurs, and the need to double shift to use the half-steps.

The half-step shift sequence is easy to remember. You get full steps with the right lever and half steps with the left. If the front derailleur is on the "wrong" chainwheel, you shift half a step in the "wrong" direction on the front and a full step in the "right" direction on the rear. That's called a "double shift."

The half-step pattern works very nicely to modify an alpine-geared bicycle for level country. If your alpine gearing is too low for you, replace the inner chainwheel with the appropriate half-step chainwheel.

In spite of all of my evangelizing, I have to admit that the most useful half-step application is the triple half-step plus granny pattern.

Alpine (A.K.A. One-and-a-Half-Step)

The majority of today's bicycles have *alpine* gearing or something that would have been alpine gearing if the designer understood gearing. Ten years ago, half of the bicycles sold had 10-speed alpine gearing with 52/40 chainwheels and a 14-17-20-24-28 freewheel. When SunTour introduced the narrow-spaced six-sprocket freewheel in 1978, there ceased to be a standard pattern.

Terminology time. A *narrow-spaced* freewheel has narrow spacers between the sprockets so that six sprockets can be crammed into the same width as five wide-spaced sprockets. A *narrow-range* freewheel has small tooth differences between the sprockets.

The macho experts put down alpine gearing because it's used on so many inexpensive bicycles. However, alpine has some major advantages, which is why it's so widely used. It's a compromise that takes maximum advantage of inexpensive, medium-capacity components. The 12-tooth chainwheel difference is about the largest front shift that can be handled by a novice with an inexpensive front derailleur. The 14–28 freewheel was about the limit of the old Huret Allvit and Simplex Prestige rear derailleurs.

A 10-speed alpine has ten useful gears with a big step on either end and half-steps between the eight intermediate gears. You normally use the forbidden little-little gear with an alpine.

The main disadvantage of alpine gearing is the bizarre shift sequence, which is hard to remember and hard to perform. The double shifting drill—left lever forward, right lever forward two steps; left lever back, right lever back one step—isn't easy, even with good-shifting derailleurs. Most beginners never figure out how to properly shift their alpines, and they end up with six rather poorly arranged gears.

The second disadvantage of alpine gearing is that the step between High and Ninth is too big. Once you've pedaled a 90-inch gear, you won't be happy with alpine's 83-inch Ninth. Especially worse off are cyclists with SunTour's old 14–34 five-sprocket freewheel. Its fourth sprocket has 18 teeth instead of 17, giving a 79-inch Ninth. This trivial change dooms the cyclist to a hopeless hunt for the missing 90-inch gear. SunTour's current Perfect and Pro-Compe freewheels use 14-17-21-26-34 sprockets and I like to think that my articles nagged SunTour into making the change. (Gear freaks get their jollies in strange ways.)

The rules for alpines are rigid, just like those for half-steps. The freewheel must have even percentage steps and the chainwheel step must be one-and-a-

PHOTO 3-3 Alpine gearing on Berto's Trek 2000 racing bicycle.

half freewheel steps, which is why alpine is often called "one-and-a-half-step" gearing. Many bicycle designers don't understand these rules and many alpines have less than the best sprocket arrangements.

Summing up, rats can be trained to navigate mazes and cyclists can train themselves to shift alpines. It takes the same kind of low animal cunning. If you can put up with the shifting sequence, alpines make sense for Lows between 30 and 40 inches, especially for 10-speeds.

The gearing on my Trek 2000 is closet alpine with 51/39 chainwheels and a 12-14-17-20-24-28 freewheel. That's the lowest Low I can get with the Dura-Ace EX crankset and the Dura-Ace/SIS rear derailleur. I double shift surreptitiously so my gear freak friends won't know.

Doubles versus Triples

There's a major difference between bicycles with two chainwheels *(doubles)* and bicycles with three chainwheels *(triples)*. Therefore, I want to make some observations about triple systems in general, before describing the two common gearing arrangements that make use of three chainwheels: the half-step plus granny and the crossover plus granny.

If you want a really low Low, you need three chainwheels. The purpose of adding a third chainwheel is not to create 14 narrow steps between gears rather than 9 wide steps. Instead, the third chainwheel lets you put all of your hill-climbing gears onto an inner, granny chainwheel so that you can use the outer two chainwheels to provide a pleasant pattern for riding on level terrain.

In short, triple cranksets offer the following advantages:

- Really low gears (below 25 inches).
- Lots of nicely spaced, level cruising gears and an easy shift sequence.
- Five or six usable gears on the middle chainwheel with less chain deflection, because the middle chainwheel really is in the middle.

However, triples also have a couple of disadvantages:

- Higher cost.
- Fussier shifting onto the middle chainwheel. (You have to look down and center the front derailleur whenever you shift onto the middle chainwheel.)

Here are some basic ground rules to observe when designing a triple chainwheel gearing system:

- Triples should have a Low lower than 27 inches. Don't put up with the problems and the expense of a triple unless you need a really low Low.

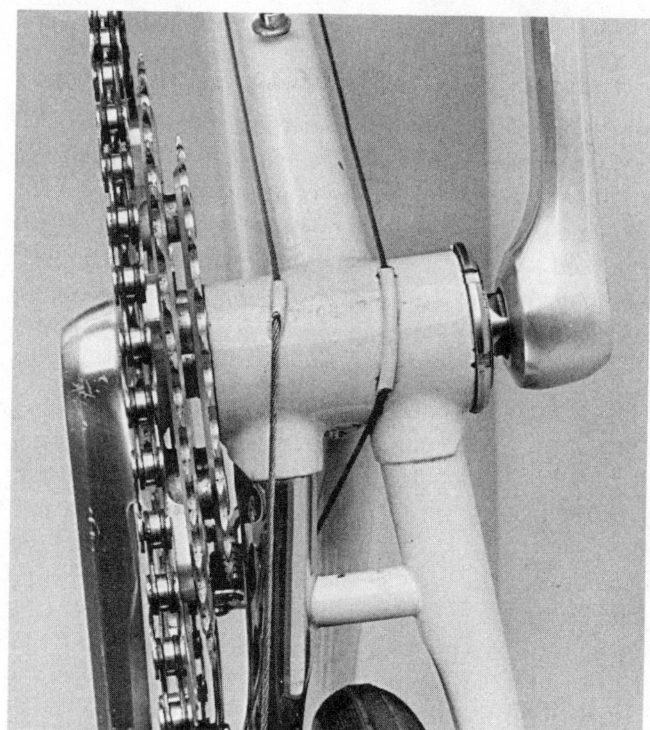

PHOTO 3-4

Closely mounted inner chainwheel on a triple crankset.

- The inner chainwheel should have 28 or fewer teeth. This is an extension of the first item. I don't think that cranksets that have 36-, 34-, or 32-tooth minimum sprockets are suitable for triples. You can get the same Low with a double.
- The inner chainwheel should be the smallest one that fits the crankset. If you don't want the lowest possible Low, use something less than the largest inner sprocket on your freewheel. The smaller inner chainwheel and smaller freewheel sprocket weigh less and make for easier rear shifts. If you decide later that you need a lower Low, you can change sprockets inexpensively.
- Triples shouldn't use narrow-spaced freewheels. Narrow-spaced freewheels and narrow chains shift adequately on racing freewheels with one- or two-tooth differences between sprockets. Narrow-spaced, wide-range, touring freewheels shift poorly, regardless of chain or rear derailleur. (I'll talk more about this in chapter 6 on freewheels.) On a triple, you're much better off with a wide-spaced five-sprocket freewheel than with a narrow-spaced six-sprocket freewheel.

- Triples should be mounted with the inner chainwheel as close as possible to the chainstay. You don't use the inner chainwheel with the small sprockets so don't provide a chainline for the unused gears. With the inner chainwheel just clearing the chainstay, the middle chainwheel will be in the middle, and you can use all five (or six) gears. The front shifts will be easier because the front derailleur doesn't have to reach out so far. I've set up more than 20 triples and most of them have used spindles designed for doubles rather than triples. Phil Wood and SunTour sealed-bearing bottom bracket sets allow you to adjust the chainline to set the inner chainwheel right next to the chainstay.
- Triples shouldn't be limited by the chain wrap-up capacity of the rear derailleur since you don't use the inner chainwheel with the small freewheel sprockets. With a proper chain length (two extra links in the big chainwheel–big sprocket gear), the chain will probably hang loose in the little chainwheel–little sprocket gears. So what? The bicycle makers can't exceed derailleur capacity because of trial lawyers and product liability, but you can. Forget about the wrap-up capacity of the rear derailleur and set up your triple with the Low that you really want.

Half-Step plus Granny

Now, let's talk about the difference between *half-step plus granny* triples and crossover plus granny triples. I prefer the half-step plus granny combination. A 15-speed has five gears on the middle chainwheel, each 24 percent apart. It has four more usable gears on the outer chainwheel, each 12 percent higher. I don't usually use the big chainwheel–big sprocket gear, but I have on occasion.

Front derailleur shifts are easier with a half-step plus granny, especially the upshift from the inner to the middle chainwheel. That sounds odd, doesn't it. (It's explained in chapter 8 on front derailleurs.) The main liability with this system is that the lowest gear on the middle chainwheel is around 35 or 40 inches, so you use the inner chainwheel more often.

Half-step plus granny triples are for dedicated gear freaks who appreciate 12 or 13 useful gears, each 12 percent apart, and who are willing to double shift to get them.

Crossover plus Granny

The *crossover plus granny* is the ideal pattern for mountain bikes. You have street gears on the outer chainwheel, off-road gears on the middle chainwheel, and mountain-climbing gears on the inner chainwheel. Almost all of the shifts are made with the rear derailleur, which is a major advantage in the hills. The smaller middle chainwheel gives a lower gear, so you don't have to use the inner chainwheel as often.

Many loaded tourists prefer the crossover plus granny shift pattern. The late Dr. Clifford Graves, the founder of the International Bicycle Touring Society, was a strong supporter. You're in the middle chainwheel most of the time. The steps between gears are larger, but a loaded bicycle slows down in a hurry so that's less of a disadvantage. The typical crossover plus granny has two tailwind or downhill gears on the outer chainwheel, six level gears on the middle chainwheel, and two steep-hill gears on the inner chainwheel.

The main drawback with this pattern is that it provides only ten useful gears with an 18-speed. Crossovers waste gears, and because of this, the pattern works better with a six-sprocket freewheel. If you have to use a narrow-spaced six-sprocket freewheel to get an 18-speed, you are probably better off with two fewer gears and a wide-spaced five-sprocket freewheel.

Crossover chainwheel combinations like 52/38/24 are a torture test for front derailleurs. The new mountain bike front derailleurs with deep inner cages can handle this kind of gearing, but the upshift from the 24 to the 38 is a bear. The smaller the difference between the middle and outer chainwheels, the better the shifts. I recommend a ten-tooth maximum difference.

PHOTO 3-5 Crossover plus granny gearing on Berto's Redcay sport tourer.

In this system, you arrange the freewheel sprockets to suit your needs. There are no rigid rules. I usually provide smaller differences between the small level-pedaling sprockets and larger differences between the large hill-climbing sprockets. When you shift down on a hill, you want a significantly lower gear.

Plotting Gear Patterns Graphically

Though I have just attempted to explain five popular gear patterns in words, I think that it's easier to explain gear arrangements with graphs. A graph of gearing consists of a series of dots, each dot representing the gear formed by one chainwheel-sprocket combination. The dots are arranged in horizontal rows, each row representing the gears formed on one chainwheel. In the graphs created for this chapter, the row that represents the outer chainwheel in each system is placed on top, the one for the middle chainwheel in the middle, and the one for the inner chainwheel on the bottom. Solid horizontal lines have been placed between rows for clarity.

The dots in these gearing graphs are laid out on logarithmic graph paper. You don't need to understand logarithms to appreciate logarithmic gear plots. They are valuable because they show the actual percentage relationship between gears and thus the way a change in gears will actually feel through the pedals. By looking at the dots, you can tell several other things about your gearing arrangement. For example, if one dot is on top of another, you have duplicate gears. This waste of gears is inevitable with gearing patterns like crossover. Conversely, if there's a wide gap on the graph between two dots, then there's a gap between those two gears, and when you're pedaling them, you'll shift back and forth looking for the "missing" gear. The dots also show you the relationship between the little chainwheel gears and the big chainwheel gears. You can see what happens when you shift from one chainwheel to the other.

To understand how to read logarithmic graphs, look ahead to figure 3-3. There you will see a variety of different gearing patterns graphed out. Look at the graph of the wide-range alpine. Suppose you're lugging along at 18 mph at a cadence of 60 in the 100-inch High (52-tooth chainwheel × 14-tooth sprocket). This feels a bit slow, and you're pushing too hard on the pedals. So you downshift one step on the rear derailleur to the 83-inch gear (52-tooth chainwheel × 17-tooth sprocket). This moves you to the left on the graph to the next dot. This is a 21 percent change (17/14). At the instant that you shift, your cadence speeds up 21 percent to 73 rpm, and the pressure on the pedals is reduced by 21 percent.

Suppose another time that you're pedaling up a hill at 6.5 mph and at a cadence of 60 in the 39-inch gear (40-tooth chainwheel × 28-tooth sprocket), and you downshift on the rear to your Low, the 34-tooth sprocket. That's also a 21 percent change (34/28). This also moves you to the left on the graph to the next dot. The two 21 percent changes feel the same to your legs and they plot the same on the logarithmic chart. That's why I use logarithmic graph paper.

Figure 3-2 shows a logarithmic gear plot with the gear inches labelled for different speeds and conditions. Figure 3-3 shows seven different gear patterns plotted on logarithmic paper.

How Many Speeds: 10, 12, 14, 15, 18?

When you modify the gearing on your bicycle, first decide on the High, the Low, and the gear pattern. Then the number of speeds will usually drop into place. Crossover patterns work best as 12- or 14-speeds because they need the extra gears to make up for the duplicates. Half-steps and alpines usually work best as 10-speeds. When six- and seven-sprocket freewheels became common, the gear freaks found that there weren't many really uniform equal-percentage six- or seven-sprocket freewheels (except those with 11-tooth small sprockets.)

The first derailleur bicycles had three-sprocket freewheels, probably to compete with 3-speed, Sturmey-Archer internally-geared hubs. As time passed, incredulous mechanical engineers watched in awe as four-, five-, six-, and then seven-sprocket freewheels were developed and chains were deflected at ever more painful angles. All mechanical engineers were taught in ME-100 that chain drives require perfectly aligned sprockets.

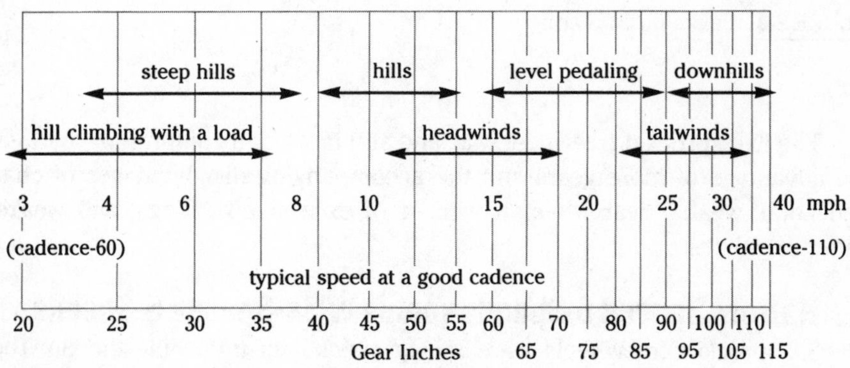

FIGURE 3-2 Gears for different speeds and conditions.

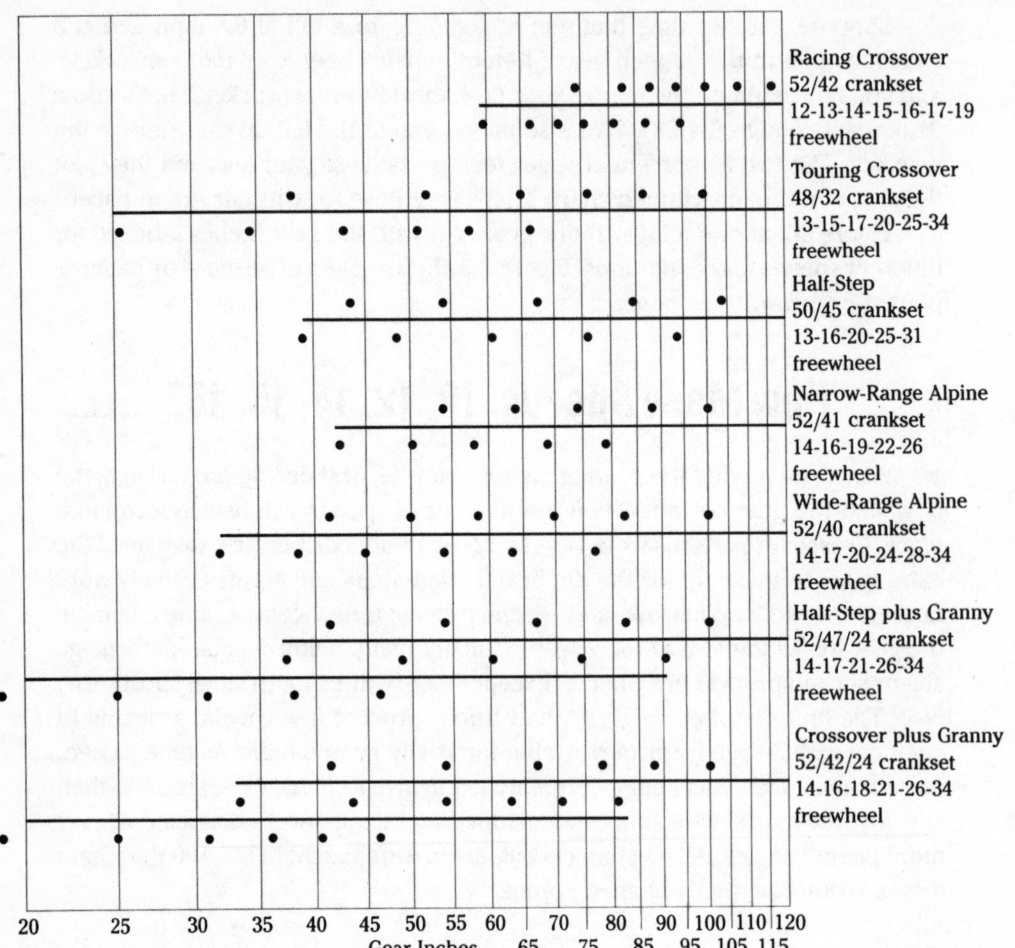

FIGURE 3-3 Seven basic gearing patterns.

The five-sprocket freewheel was, and still is, a good compromise between the advantage of more gears and the accompanying disadvantages of chain deflection, weaker rear wheels (because of excessive dishing), and weaker, wider rear axles.

Narrow-Spaced 6-Speeds versus Wide-Spaced 5-Speeds

Six-sprocket freewheels were racing specialties until Fuji and SunTour introduced the narrow-spaced Ultra-6 freewheel in 1978. It was a marketing success and a practical failure. From an advertising standpoint, a 12-speed bicycle was 20 percent better than a 10-speed, but narrow-spaced freewheels shift worse than wide-spaced freewheels.

On low-priced bicycles, the extra two gears were a minor improvement because the High and Low were usually the same as they were on the previous 10-speed. Narrow-spaced freewheels shift worse than wide-spaced freewheels on the rear and narrow chains shift worse than standard chains on the front. I kept waiting for a "miracle" narrow chain to solve the shifting problems, but it didn't come along and the narrow-spaced touring freewheel finally died in 1987. Rest in peace!

Nearly all of today's racers use narrow-spaced freewheels and narrow Sedisport chains. The shifting penalty is minor because there's only a one- or two-tooth difference between the sprockets on racing freewheels. Mountain bikes have gone in a different direction—toward wider rear axles so that they can use wide-spaced six-sprocket freewheels. That's where the racers were in 1978.

Unusual Gear Patterns

Now that we have looked at the most common and sensible gearing patterns, we will take a brief look at some unusual and less practical patterns.

Wide-Step

The basic idea behind the *wide-step* pattern is to combine a narrow-range freewheel with wide-range double chainwheels. In my very first gearing article in 1975, I talked about "three-steps," "four-steps," and "five-steps." Now I just call them "wide-steps" and I don't recommend them.

My disenchantment with wide-step patterns came when Sakae sent me a crankset with a complete set of chainwheels from 28 to 54 teeth. This allowed me to build and pedal some of the unusual gear trains that I had been writing about.

Wide-steps look pretty on graph paper but they are unpleasant to pedal, without exception. The problem is the double shifts. You shift on the front derailleur and then you have to shift four or five gears on the rear derailleur. By the time you find the right gear, your bicycle has slowed down so much that you have to shift back to where you started.

The beauty of a crossover pattern is the overlap between the high and the low ranges. This lets you stay on whatever chainwheel you're in until you run out of gears. Then you shift on the front. You don't have to make the front shift very often because there are duplicate or near duplicate gears on both ranges. A wide-step pattern has less overlap, so it requires more frequent front shifting.

Wide-Step Triple

The *wide-step triple* is an expansion of the basic wide-step pattern. The veteran racer finds that he can't muscle up the steep hills any more, but he has learned to love his corncob freewheel. So he adds a 28-tooth inner chainwheel to his racing crankset. The problem is that he loses the quick, easy front shifts onto the middle chainwheel. Now he has to look down every time he makes a front shift to center the derailleur and the Low of 40 inches or so isn't very low. You have the complication of a triple without the benefit.

Rhumba Gear

In the exotic pattern I call *rhumba,* the freewheel provides three closely spaced small sprockets, then a big gap, then the two large sprockets. The chainwheel difference is ingeniously selected so that when you shift from the big to the little chainwheel, the three little chainwheel gears just fill the gap. From High to Low, the shift sequence is as follows:

- Big chainwheel—one, two, three on the rear.
- Shift to the little chainwheel, shift down two gears on the rear—then four, five, six on the rear.
- Shift to the big chainwheel—seven, eight on the rear.
- Shift to the little chainwheel, shift down one gear on the rear—nine, ten.

One, two, three, one, two, three, one, two, one, two. Shall we dance?

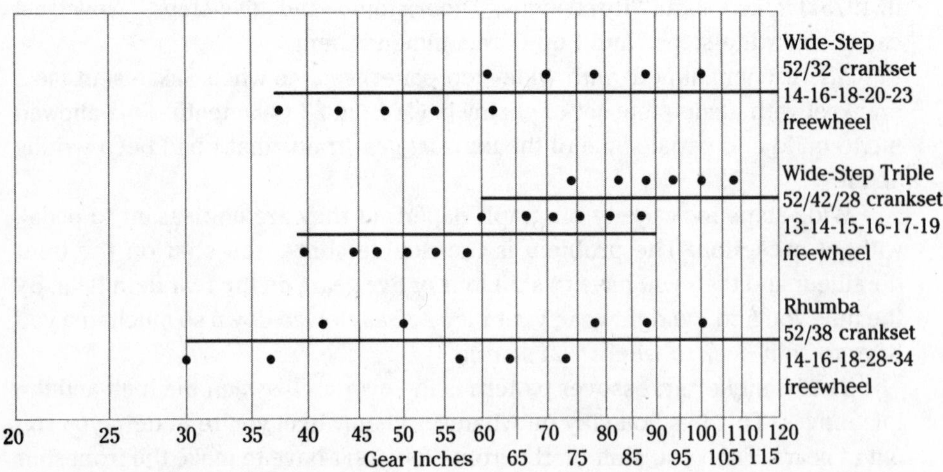

FIGURE 3-4 Unusual gear patterns.

The six-sprocket freewheel version with a three-three split is called "cha-cha" gearing. Both of these patterns are for people who just love to double shift and who have very mathematical memories.

Figure 3-4 plots these patterns. Just remember, they plot better than they pedal.

Frank's Favorite Gears

I have created table 3-3, which shows my 14 favorite gear patterns. They will take care of 90 percent of your needs.

TABLE 3-3.

Frank's Fourteen Favorite Gear Patterns

Pattern Name	High Gear	Low Gear	Chainwheels	Freewheel
Classic alpine	100	39	52/40	14-17-20-24-28
Frank's SIS alpine	115	38	51/39	12-14-17-20-24-28
Franks's super half-step plus granny	118	19	48/43/24	11-13-16-20-26-34
Gear freak's half-step	104	38	50/45	13-16-20-25-32
Loaded touring crossover	96	22	46/28	13-15-17-20-26-34
Loaded touring crossover plus granny	96	19	50/40/24	14-16-18-21-26-34
Loaded touring half-step plus granny	96	19	50/45/24	14-17-21-26-34
Medium-range crossover	104	39	50/40	13-14-16-19-23-28
Mountain bike crossover plus granny	93	22	48/38/28	14-16-18-21-26-34
Racing six-sprocket crossover	110	54	53/42	13-14-15-17-19-21
Racing seven-sprocket crossover	113	48	50/39	12-13-14-15-17-19-22
Sport touring half-step plus granny	104	27	50/45/28	13-16-19-23-28
Wide-range alpine	100	30	52/38	14-17-21-26-34
Wide-range crossover	104	30	50/36	13-15-17-20-24-32

CHAPTER 4

All about Shift Levers and Indexed Shifting

You can upgrade your bicycle's gear train by converting to indexed shifting. It will let you shift on the rear just by moving the shift lever to the next setting. It will also make it much easier for you to shift while you're pedaling uphill. Indexed shifting is a greater improvement over manual shifting than push button radio tuning is over manual tuning. If you're upgrading your gear train, consider one of the new indexed shifting packages. Test ride a friend's bicycle and it may convert you.

I have placed all of the significant background on indexed shifting in this chapter, rather than scattering it through the rear derailleur, freewheel, and chain chapters. In my discussion of shift levers, I cover both indexed and conventional friction types.

Indexed Shifting

In 1985, Shimano perfected a reliable indexed shifting package, which they called *Shimano Index System* or *SIS*. It was a genuine breakthrough in shifting performance. It took two years for the SIS to trickle down from Dura-Ace to Shimano's lower-priced lines, but by 1987, the U.S. market was sold on the benefits of indexed shifting. SunTour introduced the *AccuShift* package and Campagnolo introduced *Syncro* shift levers for the 1987 market, and Huret introduced their *Advanced Rider Index System (ARIS)* in 1988. A new bicycle simply won't sell in today's market if it doesn't have indexed shifting. Only the highest-priced racing bicycles and the least expensive gaspipe bicycles now come with friction shift levers.

It takes more than a new set of shift levers to convert a bicycle to indexed shifting. Reliable indexed shifting is a cooperative venture between rear derailleur, freewheel, chain, and shift lever. Shimano and SunTour have designed the various components of their indexed shifting packages to work as a unit. If you don't use the specified parts, you may not get top performance. (Such specialization of componentry has taken some of the fun out of gear freaking.)

The necessary parts of the indexed shifting packages are being sold as upgrade kits. These kits usually include indexed shift levers, front and rear derailleurs, freewheel, chain, cables, and casings. You may or may not be able to use your old freewheel, depending on its sprocket shape and spacing. Even if you end up with an extra freewheel, the upgrade kit is a much better buy than the separate parts. If you opt for indexed shifting, your choice is between the various Shimano and SunTour models, or a do-it-yourself approach with Campagnolo's Syncro levers. Out on the road, the differences between systems are relatively minor, though Shimano has two extra years of development and SIS is more forgiving of wear or misadjustment than the other systems.

Indexed shifting has separated the component makers into haves and have-nots, and the have-nots may not survive. Shimano, SunTour, and Campagnolo are survivors. Sachs-Huret has developed their ARIS package for the 1988 model bicycles. Sedis and Maillard are now part of Sachs-Huret. This allows Sachs-Huret to market a complete French gruppo. As I write this, Simplex has gone into bankruptcy and is merging with Ofmega. No Simplex or Ofmega indexed shifting package has been announced. I hesitate to predict the future for the rest of the derailleur makers.

Factors Affecting Rear Shifting

It has taken me a long time to sort out the reasons that make some gear trains shift more precisely than others. It's a complex multi-variable problem. There are more than a dozen factors involved and they interact with each other. In an ideal rear shift, the shift lever acts like a trigger. You move the lever to the shift point and the chain jumps to the next sprocket; it's precisely lined up, so no additional lever movement is necessary. Think about it and you'll realize that I've just described indexed shifting, which requires a nearly ideal gear train.

I've divided the factors that affect rear shifting into four main categories: rear derailleur, freewheel, chain, and shift levers. Some general factors don't fit neatly into the four categories, so I'll cover them first.

General Factors

There are a variety of general factors that affect the shifting on a bicycle. We will now examine them one by one.

Upshifts (Drops) and Downshifts (Climbs) Terminology time. *Upshift* and *downshift* are confusing terms. I use upshift to mean shifting up to a higher gear, so you can go faster. When you upshift on the rear derailler, the chain moves down from a larger to a smaller sprocket. In this chapter I'm going to call an upshift on the rear a "drop," and a downshift on the rear a "climb." To climb a hill, your rear derailleur causes the chain to climb onto a larger sprocket.

It's fairly easy to drop from a big sprocket to a smaller one. The jockey pulley levers the chain off the larger sprocket and it drops naturally to the next sprocket. It's much harder to climb from a small sprocket to a larger one. The jockey pulley and the rear derailleur cage bend the chain inward until the side of the chain meets the larger sprocket.

Like a blind date, the meeting of chain and sprocket can generate engagement or resistance. If the protruding pin or the corner of the chain runs into the teeth of the large sprocket, then the chain will climb smoothly onto the larger sprocket. On the other hand, if the flat side of the chain runs into the flat side of the larger sprocket, then the sprocket will act like a spoke protector and the chain will stay put. So you pull harder on the shift lever and the chain pushes harder against the big sprocket until the shift finally takes place, with much noisy mechanical sadism.

Shifting to the lowest gears takes extra skill because you're on a hill and you have to shift quickly before the bicycle slows down.

Hanger Drop The derailleur *hanger* is the tab of metal that hangs on the right hand rear dropout. It's also called the *tab* or the *dropout.* Inexpensive bicycles don't have a built-in hanger so inexpensive rear derailleurs come with a separate derailleur hanger. The derailleur designer assumes that the derailleur will be mounted in a given position relative to the rear axle. His design then locates the jockey pulley relative to the rear axle. If you use a different hanger than the one the designer used, your rear derailleur may perform differently than the designer intended.

There's quite a variation in hangers but they generally fall into racing and touring categories. A racing hanger has a drop of about 1 inch. A touring hanger has a drop of about 1¼ inches. If you mount a touring rear derailleur on a racing hanger, it may not be able to handle the largest freewheel sprocket. If you mount a racing rear derailleur on a touring hanger, it won't shift as crisply as it should on the small sprockets. (The differences between racing and touring dropouts are shown in figure 4-1.)

Chain Tension The top half of the chain is tensioned by your pedaling force. This affects front shifting, which is why you relax the pedaling force when you shift. The spring of the rear derailleur's cage pivot tensions the lower half of the chain, which has a modest effect on rear shifting.

Cable Stretch–Casing Compression Cable stretch, casing compression, binding, and friction all cause the derailleur to take a different position than that called for by the indexed shift lever. Each maker has come up with a different answer. Campagnolo uses an oversized wound cable for minimum stretch. Shimano uses an oversized braided cable. SunTour uses a smaller-diameter wound cable for minimum friction and binding. Casings should be made of square wire to minimize compression and they should be lined to minimize friction. The best liners are molded into the wire to increase rigidity.

Braze-On Bosses for Down Tube Levers Campagnolo-pattern braze-on bosses, with the flats parallel to the down tube, have become the industry standard. If the flats are at right angles to the tube, you'll have to use friction levers or Shimano 600 EX/SIS levers, which work with either alignment. Shimano makes a special "B-Type" braze-on adapter that lets you mount the shift levers on top of the down tube, rather than on the sides.

Rear Derailleur Design

Indexed shifting requires a precise-shifting rear derailleur. After the shift, the jockey pulley must be centered under the sprocket. You can move a friction

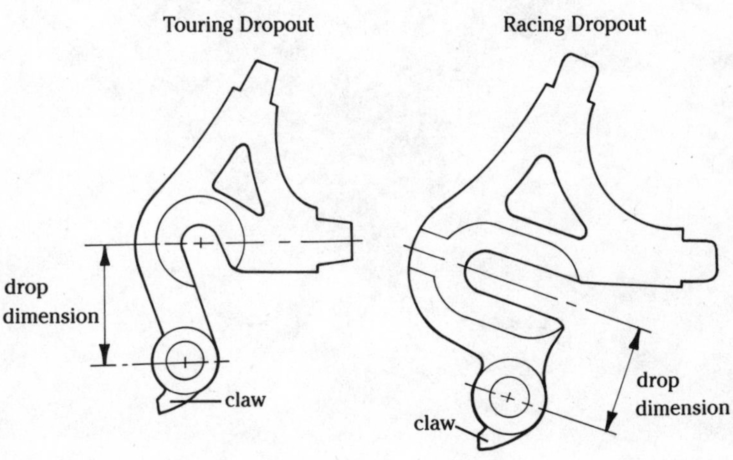

FIGURE 4-1 Rear derailleur hangers.

shift lever a tad to quiet the coffee grinding but the indexed lever can't do this fine-tuning. The following rear derailleur features affect shifting performance.

Jockey Pulley to Sprocket Distance (Chain Gap) The rear derailleur should maintain a *chain gap* of 1 to 2 inches—or two to four links of chain—between the jockey pulley and the sprockets in every gear. A longer chain gap will cause the jockey pulley to move more than one space before the chain derails to the next sprocket. I call this excessive movement "late" shifting. After each shift, you have to reverse the shift lever to center the jockey pulley and quiet the grinding at the back. Late shifting is an unpleasant derailleur characteristic. Late-shifting derailleurs sometimes shift two gears at once, or they shift back to the original gear when you reposition them. Late-shifting derailleurs are also reluctant to shift under load.

A short chain gap causes the shift to take place before the jockey pulley has moved far enough. You have to push the lever a bit farther after the shift. I call this "early" shifting. It's not nearly as unpleasant as late shifting. You often push the lever a bit too far anyway. There's a "quiet zone" about 1/32 inch wide on each side of the centered position. If the chain ends up in this zone, it will run quietly. For smooth, reliable indexed shifting, a rear derailleur should shift

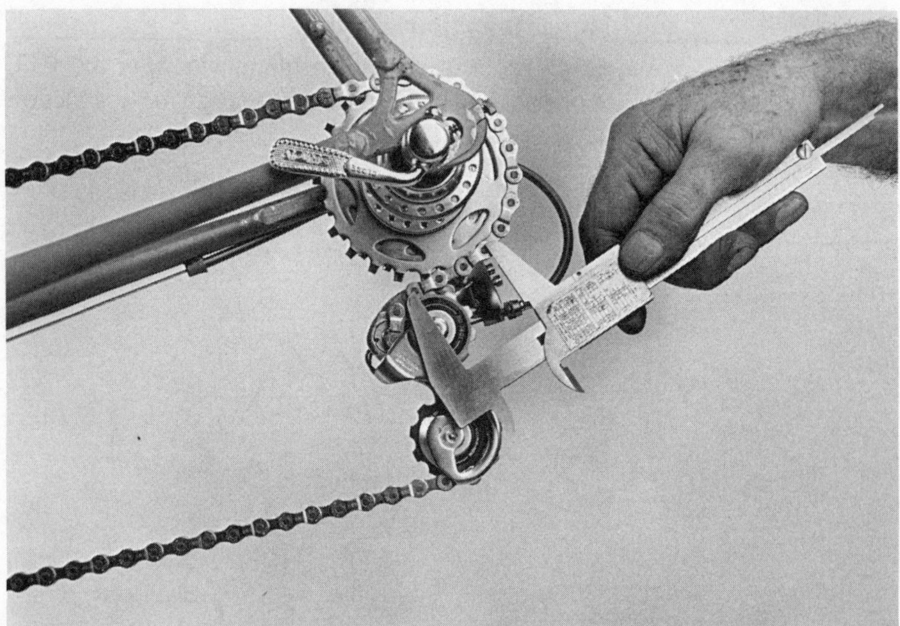

PHOTO 4-1 Chain gap on a Shimano Dura-Ace rear derailleur.

a bit early. When the shift lever moves to the detented position, it will center the jockey pulley.

Shimano, SunTour, and Huret have concluded that rear derailleurs with two spring-loaded pivots and a slanted parallelogram are the best design to provide a uniform chain gap. The new Shimano and SunTour indexed shifting rear derailleurs look the same, though they perform differently. Shimano designed for a very short chain gap to shift early in every gear. SunTour's derailleurs are more traditional and their chain gap is a bit greater. SunTour has designed their shift lever to compensate for late shifting.

Derailleur Rigidity Beefy derailleurs with rigid pivots and parallelograms bend less under the strain of shifting, so they shift more precisely. The current crop of mountain bike rear derailleurs is very rigid. They shift better and last longer than the old flexible touring rear derailleurs.

Floating Jockey Pulley Shimano designed the SIS rear derailleurs with a "Centeron" jockey pulley that can float back and forth so the chain can center itself in the quiet zone. Shimano can use a self-centering pulley because all the rest of the SIS gear train has very tight tolerances.

Freewheel Design

The following freewheel factors affect rear shifting:

Tooth Difference between Adjacent Sprockets When climbing to a lower gear, the jockey pulley bends the chain sideways until the chain runs into the larger sprocket. If there's less than a 3-tooth difference between the sprockets, the chain will encounter teeth. If there's more tooth difference, the chain will run into the flat side of the bigger sprocket, which looks like the spoke protector. This causes reluctant late shifting. Racing derailleurs have an easy task shifting over narrow-range racing freewheels. Any average design will work quite adequately. A touring, 13- to 34-tooth freewheel has a much more demanding task and only the best touring derailleurs climb well on the big sprockets. A 4-tooth difference is the break point between easy shifting and hard shifting.

Narrow- versus Wide-Sprocket Spacing Sprocket spacing is tricky. The problem with a narrow-spaced gear train isn't the narrow chain, it's the narrow spacing between the freewheel sprockets. The space is just wide enough for the narrow chain so that as soon as the chain bends, it runs into the side of the adjacent sprocket. If the tooth difference is four teeth or more, the chain is trapped in the valley. Now you know why your old narrow-spaced 18-speed touring bike shifts so badly.

A wide-spaced freewheel has more clearance, even with a wide chain. The extra clearance lets the chain bend at a sharper angle so that it can come to grips with the larger sprocket. Narrow chains usually shift a bit better than wide chains on wide-spaced freewheels because they can bend farther. Shimano and SunTour have both decided that narrow-spaced 7-speed freewheels are for racers and wide-spaced 6-speed freewheels are for tourists.

Freewheel Sprocket Cross Section For ten years, there's been a little Sino-European war going on. The Japanese freewheel companies made odd-shaped teeth that reached out and snagged the chain on climbs. Every other year, they made something a bit different, each time labeled with a new buzzword. The European freewheel companies made symmetrical, tapered teeth that avoided intimate physical contact with the chain. Maillard and Regina said that it didn't make any difference, and it didn't make very much difference on racing freewheels with small tooth differences. With wide-range freewheels, however, symmetrical teeth shift poorly. Indexed shifting was the modern version of the Battle of Tsushima and you war historians know who won.

Shimano's twist-tooth design twists each tooth so that the edge of the tooth sticks out waiting to snag any chain link that comes near. SunTour uses chisel-shaped teeth, flat on the outside and tapered on the inside on the middle sprockets. The large SunTour sprockets are "set" like a circular saw. Maillard and Regina started to provide chisel-shaped teeth on their larger sprockets in 1987. Maillard (Huret) developed a unique tooth profile for the 1988 ARIS freewheel. The teeth are narrower and higher at the rear. Shed a tear for the well-equipped pro bike shop with two or three sprocket boards full of expensive, obsolete sprockets.

PHOTO 4-2 Chain clearance: left, narrow Sedisport chain in a narrow-spaced freewheel; right, wide Uniglide chain in a wide-spaced freewheel.

Chain Design

The following chain features affect shifting performance.

Chain Flexibility The chain's flexibility works with the rear derailleur's chain gap distance to provide exact shifting. A stiff chain needs more distance. A flexible chain needs less distance. Narrow chains are usually more flexible than wide chains. With indexed shifting, the designer has to know the flexibility of the chain. That's why Shimano and SunTour recommend so few chains.

Chain Side Plate Shape Most of the current derailleur chains have bulged, flared, or cutaway side plates to improve shifting. Certain chain designs work better with certain freewheel sprocket profiles. Chain side plate design is discussed in detail in chapter 9, so I won't say anything more about it here.

Chain Width Wide chains have more pin protrusion than narrow chains, which helps shifting. Wide chains can't bend as much before they run into the adjacent sprocket, which hinders shifting.

Indexed Shift Levers

At this point, I can talk about the indexed shift levers. Writing this part of the indexed shifting story involved "reverse engineering." I sat in my workshop with the finished components and my calipers and tried to figure out what the designers had in mind. (Military intelligence officers do the same thing with captured enemy equipment.) Shimano, SunTour, and Campagnolo each took a different approach to indexed shifting, and each approach shows in the shift lever design.

Cable Travel A bicycle shifting system is a bit like the "Dry Bones" song. The shift lever's connected to the cable drum, the cable drum's connected to the derailleur cable, the derailleur cable's connected to the parallelogram, the parallelogram's connected to the derailleur cage, the derailleur cage's connected to the jockey pulley, the jockey pulley's connected to the chain, the chain's connected to the sprocket, and the sprocket's connected to . . . (I hear the word of the Lord).

Cable travel is the common denominator between the design of the indexed lever and the design of the rear derailleur. The cable travel required to shift over a 5-, 6-, or 7-speed freewheel varies between ½ and ¾ inch, depending on the width of the freewheel and the design of the rear derailleur.

In a perfect world, all rear derailleurs would shift early and there would be no friction, cable stretch, or casing compression. Leaving out these complicating factors, you could measure the components and calculate exactly how much cable travel is required to move the jockey pulley over the span of the freewheel. Then you could design the detents of the indexed shift lever to provide the necessary cable travel.

Campagnolo, Shimano, and SunTour designed their shift levers for a range of gear trains. I measured the cable travel of eight indexed shift levers and plotted the results in figure 4-2.

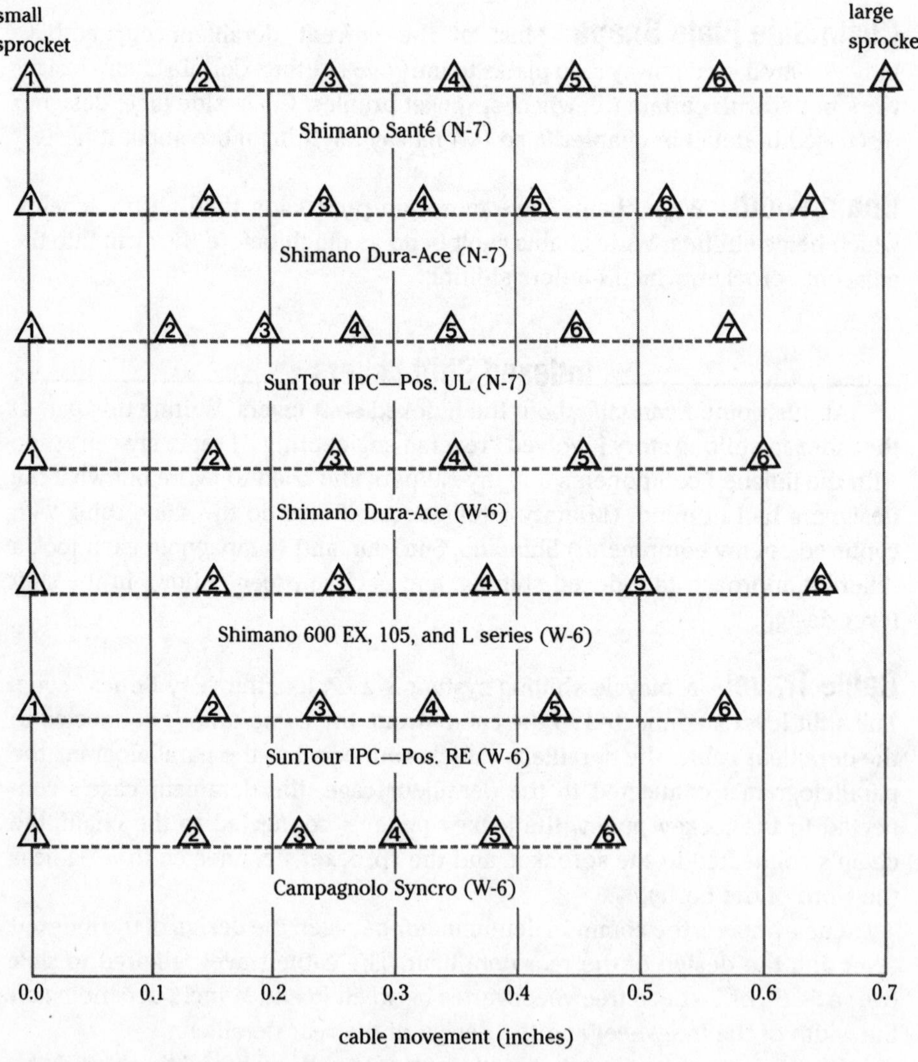

FIGURE 4-2 Indexed shift lever cable travel.

Looking at the levers for wide-spaced 6-speed freewheels, the cable travel varies from 0.47 inch for the Campagnolo Syncro lever to 0.66 inch for the Shimano 600 EX and 105 levers, and L-series levers. You shouldn't be surprised at the variation because there's so little standardization in the bicycle business. If you are thinking about adding indexed shift levers to your present gear train, your main problem will be matching the cable travel of the shift lever and the rear derailleur. Table 4-1 shows the total cable travel for eight of the ten indexed shift levers listed.

Look closely at figure 4-2, because it tells you a lot about indexed shifting. Position 1 is the smallest sprocket, position 2 is the next larger sprocket, and so on. All of the indexed levers provide an extra-large first step. This allows the cable to be slack in the first position, to make sure that the chain will drop onto the small sprocket. The derailleur high gear stop keeps the jockey pulley from moving too far out. The extra cable travel takes up the slack in the first climb.

Following the step from position 1 to position 2, there are three (or four) smaller steps, but they're not uniform, at least not on the Shimano and SunTour systems. The higher steps are a bit larger to compensate for cable stretch and for the nonlinearity of the rear derailleur. These intermediate steps are more critical than the end steps because the jockey pulley is located by the indexed lever, rather than by the derailleur stops. Table 4-1 shows the cable travel for the intermediate steps between the second smallest and the second largest sprockets.

Finally, there's an extra-large last step to haul the chain up onto the largest sprocket, which is often a difficult shift. The derailleur low gear stop keeps the jockey pulley from moving too far in.

Late Shifting–Overshifting Not all rear derailleurs have shifted when the jockey pulley arrives under the next sprocket. Sometimes, the chain is still grinding and grumbling away between the sprockets. With friction levers, you pull the lever a bit farther to finish the shift and push it back to re-center. This, of course, is the classic pull too far–push back drill for late-shifting derailleurs. The indexed shift lever can do the same thing with built-in lost motion. SunTour AccuShift levers move about 40 percent past the centered point before they click. The lever pops back when you release it. This technique only works on climbs. All indexed gear trains have to shift early on drops.

The original 6-speed Dura-Ace/SIS lever had about 25 percent built-in overshift, but the second generatiom SIS levers are different. They only overshift about 10 percent. The Campagnolo Syncro lever overshifts about 15 percent, but you can push it beyond the click point to finish the shift. I show the amount of built-in overshift in table 4-1.

TABLE 4-1.

Indexed Shifted Levers

Make and Model	Cost ($)	Weight (gr./pr.)	Design Free-wheel	Cable Travel (in.) Total Travel		Middle Sprocket Travel		Overshift (% of travel) Built-In		Manual	
				W-6	*N-7*	*W-6*	*N-7*	*W-6*	*N-7*	*W-6*	*N-7*
Campagnolo											
Syncro	90–120	72	W-6/N-7	0.48	—	0.27	—	15	—	50	—
Shimano											
Dura-Ace (SL-7401)	45–70	65	N-7	—	0.64	—	0.38	—	10	—	50
Dura-Ace (SL-7400)	40–60	65	W-6	0.60	—	0.31	—	25	—	60	—
Santé (SL-500)	40–60	70	N-7	—	0.71	—	0.42	—	5	—	40
600 EX (SL-6208)	25–40	69	W-6	0.65	—	0.35	—	10	—	30	—
105 (SL-1050)	20–30	68	W-6	0.65	—	0.35	—	5	—	30	—
L (SL-S434)	15–25	72	W-6	0.65	—	0.35	—	10	—	30	—
SunTour											
Superbe Pro/Sprint/IPC (SL-IP00)	30–50	82	W-6/N-7	0.57	0.58	0.28	0.33	35	40	60	60
Cyclone 7000/IFC (SL-CL10)	20–30	80	W-6	—	—	—	—	—	—	—	—
Alpha 5000/IFC (SL-5000)	18–25	82	W-6	—	—	—	—	—	—	—	—

Finally, if the lever clicks before the shift occurs, you can keep moving the lever until you feel the shift. I think this defeats the whole idea of foolproof indexed shifting. When this happened on my SIS-equipped bike, I stopped and tightened the cable tension. You can only move the lever past the click point on climbs. On drops, the lever will go to the next click point.

With SIS and AccuShift levers, there's a noticeable increase in lever effort just before you climb to the next position. I measured the amount of manual overshift before you feel this tactile stop and this is shown in table 4-1.

Built-in and manual overshift are significant differences between the different indexed levers, because they limit your options in rear derailleurs, freewheels, and chains. SIS allows you to push the lever to the next position with the pedals stationary and release it. The shift occurs when you pedal. This is a very severe test that reveals the inherent differences between the various indexed shifting systems.

Indexed Shifting Makers

A component company needs extensive resources to develop an indexed shifting package. Thus, it is no suprise that in 1987 only Shimano and SunTour made complete indexed shifting packages and Campagnolo had only Syncro shift levers. Sachs-Huret brought out their ARIS indexed package in 1988.

Shimano

Shimano spent the first five years of the 1980s getting ready for indexed shifting. By 1985, they had the pieces in place. Two outside ideas finalized their package: SunTour's slant parallelogram for the rear derailleur and Sedis's bushingless chain design for the Narrow Uniglide chain.

Shimano introduced indexed shifting with the top-of-the-line Dura-Ace because top-quality bicycles generally have better aligned dropouts and the riders generally take better care of their equipment. Shimano listened carefully to the feedback from the race teams and the bike shops and there were no serious problems. In 1986, Shimano moved down one price level with 600 EX/SIS. Again there were no major problems in a much broader market.

Shimano resisted narrow-spaced freewheels until 1987. Noting that most professional racers were using narrow-spaced 7-speed freewheels, Shimano developed 7-speed SIS prototypes and tested them on the Shimano-sponsored teams in 1986. By 1987, they had developed the following SIS models: the narrow-spaced 7-speed Dura-Ace for the racers, Santé for the sport tourers, and

Deore for the mountain bikers. At the same time, 105 and the SIS compatible freewheels in the L series made indexed shifting available at lower price levels.

All SIS versions are designed around early-shifting rear derailleurs, twist-tooth freewheel sprockets, flexible Narrow Uniglide or Sedisport chains, and either narrow-seven or wide-six freewheels.

SIS gear trains are designed to shift early in every gear. Even with friction and misadjustment, climbs and drops take place before the shift lever clicks. SIS levers have very little built-in overshift and you shouldn't have to push an SIS lever past the click point. Because of the early-shifting gear train and the minimum lost motion in the shift lever, Shimano ended up with a considerable tolerance in their SIS. They have used this tolerance to provide a self-centering Centeron jockey pulley. The Centeron pulley is the icing on the SIS cake.

Shimano makes six different down tube indexed levers, four wide-sixes and two narrow-sevens. The 600 EX, 105, and L-series levers are interchangeable. The old Dura-Ace wide-six, Dura-Ace narrow-seven, and Santé narrow-seven are unique. The 1988 600 Ultegra (replaces 600 EX) offers a choice of wide-six or narrow-seven.

SunTour

Through 1985, SunTour hoped that indexed shifting would be another Shimano fad. By early 1986, it was obvious that indexed shifting had caught on. When SunTour set out to develop AccuShift, they faced a nasty series of problems. Their freewheels had three different tooth profiles for the different sprocket positions and the small sprockets weren't evenly spaced. SunTour's old single-pivot rear derailleurs provided different chain gaps in the various gears so they shifted at different jockey pulley positions. These problems didn't matter in a nonindexed world—you just moved the lever a bit more or less, but they were critical with indexed shifting.

SunTour moved decisively. First, they discontinued their narrow-spaced 6-speed freewheel, which had the worst spacing variations. Next, they made the sprocket spacing uniform on their 5- and 6-speed freewheels. (You can tell the new SunTour freewheels with uniform spacing because they have four notches for a four-spline remover.) SunTour then redesigned all of their rear derailleurs to incorporate both slant parallelograms and top and bottom spring-loaded pivots. Finally, they designed the AccuShift levers to accommodate the redesigned SunTour gear train. By the end of 1986, everything was in production. Not a bad year's work.

Though the new SunTour rear derailleurs look like those of Shimano, they're not clones. The top spring isn't as powerful and they shift more like SunTour's old derailleurs. SunTour designed AccuShift around a more conventional rear derailleur, freewheel, and chain package than Shimano uses. The

AccuShift shift lever has built-in overshift so that even late shifts take place before the click. The overshift feature doesn't work on drops because you can't push the lever past the click point. AccuShift gear trains are designed to shift early on drops. The revised 1988 AccuShift levers have less overshift than the 1987 models.

SunTour makes three kinds of down tube levers for their AccuShift packages: *Indexed Power Control (IPC), Index Friction Control (IFC),* and *Index Control (IC).* The IPC lever goes with the Superbe Pro and Sprint gruppos and it includes SunTour's ratchet friction element. It has three positions: "UL" (Ultra) for narrow-spaced Winner Ultra-7 freewheels, "RE" (Regular) for wide-spaced 6-speed freewheels, and "P" (Power) for friction shifting.

The IFC levers go with the Cyclone 7000 and Alpha 5000 gruppos. They don't have the ratchet friction element and they have just two positions, Index and Friction. The IC lever is for economy packages and it doesn't have a friction position. The IFC and IC levers are designed for wide-spaced freewheels. My Cyclone 7000 upgrade kit included IPC levers; I haven't tested the IFC or IC levers.

Campagnolo

Campagnolo is different. There is no Campagnolo Syncro indexed shifting system. There's just the beautifully engineered Syncro shift levers. Campagnolo leaves the gear train choice up to the buyer. The Syncro lever is designed to work with a wide range of components. It uses a ratchet cam rather than a plate with holes. It has a smooth silky feel and it's designed to let you feel the shifts as they take place at the rear. On climbs, the click is quite soft, and if the shift hasn't happened, you move the lever past the click point until you feel the shift. On drops, Syncro feels like a trigger, you push hard and then it snaps to the next position. There's no feeling your way with drops. The rear derailleur, freewheel, and chain have to shift before the lever reaches the shift point.

Campagnolo plans to supply cams for wide-six, narrow-seven, and SunTour narrow-seven freewheels. So far, only the wide-six cam is available. The three combinations that I tested on the machine shifted just fine. I used a 13–23 wide-six Regina America freewheel, a Regina CX-S chain, and a C-Record or a Victory rear derailleur. The touring combination used a SunTour Winner 13–32 wide-six freewheel, a Regina CX-S chain, and a Campagnolo Victory Leisure rear derailleur. If I were building my own Syncro package, I'd worry a bit about the short cable travel of the wide-six cam, but I haven't undertaken a test program. Campagnolo has published a list of workable combinations that they've tested.

In my opinion, Campagnolo is swimming against the tide. I don't think that many OEM designers or gear freaks will spend $100 for an elegant set of shift levers to start a do-it-yourself project. Campagnolo's statement that indexed shifting is for "noncompetitive" cyclists tells it all. Serious (read competitive) cyclists and racers are Campagnolo's main customers. Campagnolo feels that these serious cyclists will continue to prefer friction shifting. Time will tell.

Conventional (Friction) Shift Levers

There are good reasons to stick with conventional (friction) shift levers. Probably the best reason for waiting is that indexed shifting is still in the shakedown period and we can expect performance to improve in the next few years. A gear train designed for indexed shifting shifts very sweetly with friction levers, it just doesn't click.

Almost everyone accepts the shift levers that come as a package with their new front and rear derailleurs. That's an excellent idea for indexed levers and a good idea for friction levers. However, all friction shift levers have about the same diameter cable drum so you can mix and match derailleurs and friction shift levers, if you have a particular favorite.

Shift Lever Location

Friction levers can be installed in four locations: on the stem, on the ends of the handlebars (bar ends), on the handlebars (thumb shifters), or on the down tube. Indexed levers are available in stem-mounted, handlebar, and down tube versions.

Stem-Mounted Shift Levers Like safety levers and counterweighted pedals, *stem-mounted* shift levers are a hallmark of gaspipe bicycles. The worst problem is that when you stand up on the pedals honking up a hill, your knee can hit the right lever and kick you out of low gear. Also, the long cable makes shifting a bit vague. If you like the levers up on the handlebars where you can see them, consider a set of indexed mountain bike thumb shifters. If you really like stem-mounted shift levers, there's just one quality model, SunTour's PUB-10 with a ratcheted right-hand lever. Shimano's SL-S431 and SunTour's Alpha 5000 provide indexed shifting and short lever arms but they're designed for the low-end OEM market.

Bar End-Mounted Shift Levers The tips of the handlebars is my favorite location for shift levers. With half-step plus granny gearing, I often double shift. With *bar end* levers, I make both shifts with my hands on the handlebars. Loaded tourists and tandems use bar end levers for the same reason. Bar ends make most sense for large riders and large bicycle frames because it's such a long reach down to down tube levers. I also like the sanitary look of a bicycle with the brake cables and the derailleur cables hidden under the handlebar

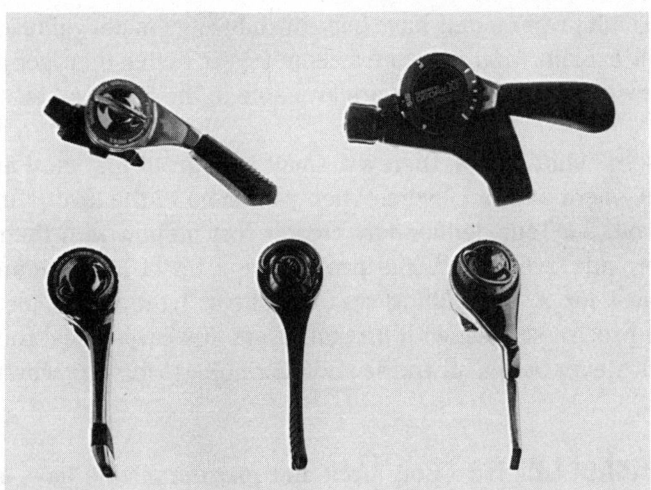

PHOTO 4-3

Indexed shift levers: top left and right, SunTour XC and Shimano Deore XT thumb shifters; bottom left to right, SunTour Superbe Pro, Shimano Dura-Ace, and Campagnolo Syncro indexed shift levers.

tape. Bar end levers have two disadvantages. The extra length of cable and casing causes spongy shifts and it's an extra chore to tape the handlebars.

SunTour's BarCon ratchet levers are the only ones to buy. At one time, Campagnolo, Huret, Simplex, and Shimano made bar end levers. But the SunTour BarCon shifts so much better than the rest that it's taken over the market. To date, no one makes indexed bar end levers.

Handlebar-Mounted Shift Levers Just because you have dropped handlebars doesn't mean that you can't use mountain bike thumb shifters mounted in the middle of the handlebars. If you have upright handlebars, thumb shifters are your best choice. They're available in friction shifting and indexed shifting versions.

Down Tube-Mounted Shift Levers Levers that mount on the down tube are the choice of all racers and of most serious riders. Top-of-the-line frames come with braze-on mounts for down tube shift levers. The cables are shortest so the shifting is crispest. If you ride a small frame on the drops, it's just a short reach down to the levers. If you ride a big frame mostly on the tops, you'll find that it's a long reach down to the levers. All of the indexed shifting gruppos provide indexed down tube shift levers. Most down tube levers are mounted on the sides of the down tube. Campagnolo and Shimano make down tube levers that mount on the top of the down tube, making it easier to double shift with one hand.

Features of Conventional Shift Levers

In 1980, I wrote a three-page article about shift levers. I rated 36 different models and expounded on all of the minor differences between them. Since then, another 50 or so shift lever models have been introduced. I'm not going to rate them. Instead, I'll explain what makes excellent levers better than good levers and I'll list a few of my favorites that are available in the aftermarket.

Lost Motion On some shift levers, there's a small amount of lost motion between the friction element and the levers. When you let go of the lever, the cable pulls it back a bit. SunTour deliberately creates lost motion with their AccuShift levers to provide overshift. Some people like a bit of lost motion because it compensates for a late-shifting rear derailleur. I think that lost motion works against precise shifting with friction levers. It's easy to feel the lost motion, just pull the lever back a bit and see how far it moves forward when you let go.

Friction versus Ratchet Levers Both front and rear derailleurs have a spring that pulls the cable against the shift lever. The lever pulls the derailleur in one direction and the spring pulls it in the opposite direction. Depending on the rear derailleur, it takes a 25- to 60-pound cable pull to climb. When the derailleur isn't shifting, the spring still exerts a 15- to 30-pound pull against the cable. You set the friction adjustment of the lever to counteract this pull so that the derailleur doesn't drop back to the smallest sprocket.

With a friction lever, the friction element works in both directions. With a ratchet lever, the friction element is uncoupled on the climbs. A typical friction lever needs a 12-pound pull to climb and a 1-pound push to drop. A typical ratchet lever needs only a 7-pound pull to climb and the same 1-pound push to drop.

The Simplex Retrofriction down tube shift levers are the racers' favorite. At the Coors Classic, I noticed several dozen professional racers' bicycles that were *tout Campagnolo* except for Simplex Retrofriction levers. The nonindex versions of SunTour's Superbe Pro and Sprint down tube shift levers have ratchets on both levers.

Shift Lever Return Springs SunTour calls their levers with return springs and ratchets *Power Shifters.* Shimano's Light Action derailleurs come with shift levers from the L economy component series, which have a ratchet and a return spring. As in brake lever return springs, to really get all the advantage, the derailleur return spring should have a lower tension.

Front Derailleur Levers You shift more often on the rear and you have to make finer adjustments of the shift lever. Sometimes the maker provides a fancy, ratcheted, spring-loaded right lever for the rear derailleur, and just a

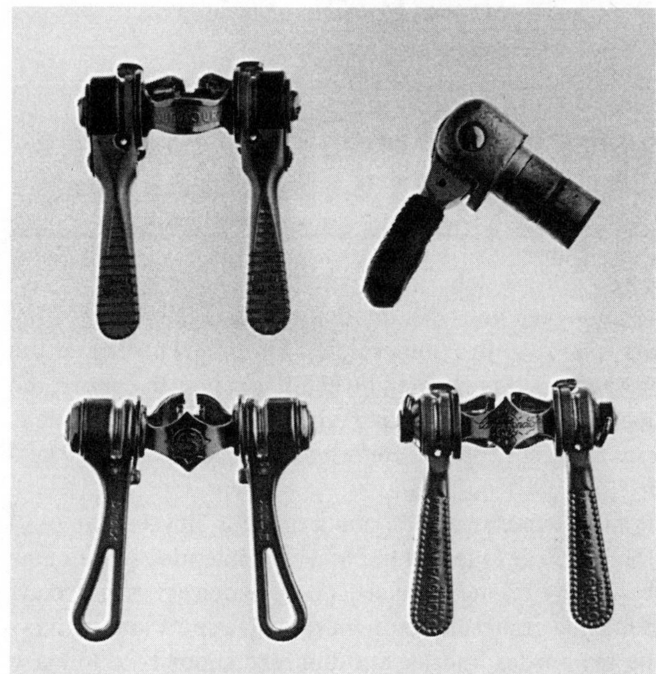

PHOTO 4-4

Conventional shift levers: top left and right, SunTour PUB-10 ratcheted stem levers and SunTour BarCon bar end shift lever; bottom left and right, Simplex Retrofriction shift levers and Campagnolo Nuovo Record shift levers.

plain, ordinary friction left lever for the front derailleur. With a triple crankset, or with a narrow-cage front derailleur, you do quite a lot of fussing with the left lever. Look for a set of levers with bells and whistles on both sides.

Frank's Favorite Shift Levers

After all of the hype on the benefits of indexed shifting, you would expect that all of my bikes would click. Sorry about that. I've got Dura-Ace/SIS on the Trek racer and SunTour BarCons on the other bicycles. I have used the 6-speed Dura-Ace/SIS for a year and a half. It's been pleasant and trouble-free. When I finished the chain tests, I put the 7-speed Dura-Ace/SIS gruppo on the Trek. It's been just as pleasant and reliable.

I'm scarcely an authority on the over-the-road performance of the various kinds of friction shift levers because I standardized on SunTour BarCon bar end shift levers ten years ago. As the quality of touring front and rear derailleurs has improved year by year, it takes less and less skill to shift precisely, even with mushy bar end levers. Although I've got all of the different index packages out in the workshop, I'm still waiting for indexed bar end levers.

CHAPTER 5

All about Cranksets

Earlier, in chapter 3, I presented you with the theoretical side of the gearing story and gave you two sets of teeth numbers: one for chainwheels and the other for freewheel sprockets. In this chapter, I will tell you how to convert the hypothetical chainwheel numbers into actual chainwheels and cranksets. (Chapter 6 will explain how to convert the freewheel numbers into sprockets and freewheels.)

The crankset is the most expensive component on your bicycle. The bicycle designer selected the crankset to match the bicycle's intended price range and its intended use. Expensive racing cranksets go on expensive racing bicycles. Inexpensive sport touring cranksets go on inexpensive sport touring bicycles. The importers, the mail-order houses, and the bike shops tend to carry expensive, top-of-the-line cranksets. Lower-priced versions are sold to the OEM bicycle makers. For these reasons, it may make more sense to replace an inexpensive bicycle rather than to replace the crankset.

Chainwheels are expensive too. They run from $10 to $40 each, while freewheel sprockets cost only $3 to $10 each. Plan your gearing modification to fit into your total upgrading budget.

Economic Choices

You have four options to choose from when upgrading your gearing:

- No crankset changes; freewheel changes only ($10 to $30).
- New inner chainwheel and freewheel changes ($20 to $40).
- Two new chainwheels and freewheel changes ($30 to $50).
- New crankset and freewheel changes ($100 to $200).

Each option will cost $20 to $50 more if you also replace the derailleur(s). Notice the big price jump when you replace the entire crankset. The usual reason for replacing cranksets is to get a lower Low by converting to a triple. Just make sure that you're going to be happy with the finished bicycle after you've spent all that money.

If you want a lower Low and your crankset has an intermediate bolt circle, which accepts a 32-, 34-, or 36-tooth minimum chainwheel, plan on a double with wide-range crossover gearing using the smallest available inner chainwheel. Don't even think about converting to a triple. A 34-tooth chainwheel combined with a 34-tooth freewheel cog gives you a 27-inch Low. When your Low is limited by a 32-, 34-, or 36-tooth inner chainwheel the complication of a triple just isn't worth it.

Crankset Terminology

Terminology time. The *bottom bracket* is really the shell that ties the seat tube, down tube, and chainstays together. The *bottom bracket set* is everything that fits into the bottom bracket: that is the *spindle, fixed cup, adjustable cup, lockring,* and *bearings.* However, many people, including yours truly, often call the bottom bracket set just "bottom bracket" to keep you alert. The *crankset* is the whole package: bottom bracket set, left- and right-hand cranks, chainwheels, chainwheel bolts, and dust caps. The crankset includes the bottom bracket set except when you see a low-ball price with the cryptic note "w/o bb."

Spider describes the arms on the right hand crank that hold the chainwheels. The words *chainwheel* and *chainring* are used interchangeably. In the prehistoric days of cottered "five-pin" cranks, chainwheels went on the outside and were bolted to the crank with five bolts called pins. Chainrings went on the inside and were bolted to the chainwheel with six bolts. Don't ask me why they're called "pins" and "bolts." It was probably a poor translation from French. The venerable TA Cyclotourist crankset still uses this arrangement.

Crankset Features

Although crankset prices vary widely, there's surprisingly little performance difference between a $50 melt-forged Sakae FXC and a $400 Campagnolo C-Record. ("Melt-forging" is the name of an improved aluminum casting method.) I judge cranksets by the following features, in order of importance.

Bolt Circle Diameter–Minimum Inner Chainwheel

The essential difference between racing and touring cranksets lies in the size of the bolt circle diameter and the corresponding size limitations on the inner chainwheel. A racing crankset with a large-diameter bolt circle is a bit more rigid, but the smallest inner chainwheel it can accept has either 39 or 42 teeth. A loaded touring crankset is less rigid, but its small-diameter bolt circle accepts inner chainwheels with 24, 26, or 28 teeth.

There's also a group of intermediate sport touring cranksets whose bolt circles take 32-, 34-, or 36-tooth minimum chainwheels. They rarely make sense if you're buying a new crankset. If you want a 32-, 34-, or 36-tooth inner chainwheel, buy a loaded touring crankset with a larger than minimum inner chainwheel. You can change your mind later.

There are more than 40 different bolt circles made. If your crankset uses 1 of the 6 standard bolt circles, you have multiple sources of replacement chainwheels. If your crankset uses 1 of the many bastard bolt circles, you'll have go to the importer and beg. Table 5-1 lists 20 fairly common bolt circles. You can find chainwheels for these bolt circles if you search hard enough. Measure the diameter of your bolt circle (or the distance between the bolt holes) and table 5-1 will tell you what chainwheels are available and where to look for them. Figure 5-1 shows how to measure bolt circles. I'll have more to say about bolt circle standardization further on.

The rigidity aspect of crankarm design is exaggerated. If your chainwheel rubs against the front derailleur when you stomp on the pedals, it's probably your frame that's deflecting, not the crankset. *Bicycling* magazine tested the rigidity of cranksets in the October 1984 issue. The basic conclusions were that the differences were small and not significant in pedaling efficiency. I show the results of their tests in the rigidity column of table 5-2.

Avocet/Ofmega and Sugino machine a notch at the base of the crankarms to provide chain clearance. This lets them install 41- and 38-tooth chainwheels

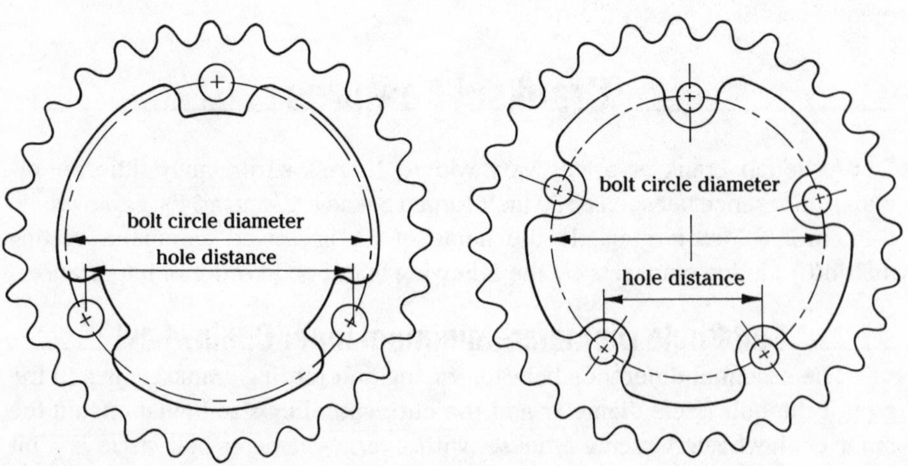

FIGURE 5-1 Measuring bolt circles.

TABLE 5-1.

Crankset Bolt Circles

No. of Arms	Bolt Circle Dia. (in.)	Bolt Circle Dia. (mm)	Hole Distance (in.)	Min. No. CW Teeth	Make and Model	Availability
Three	3.35	85	2.89	28	Sakae	P
Three	3.74	95	3.24	30	Shimano 600 (old)	P
Three	4.17	106	3.62	34	Sakae, Sugino, Takagi	P
Three	4.56	116	3.98	36	Nervar, Simplex, TA	F
Five	2.91	74	1.71	24	Sugino and many others	E*
Five	3.32	84.5	1.96	26	Shimano Deore (old)	F
Five	3.39	86	2.00	28	Sakae, Stronglight	G*
Five	3.74	95	2.20	30	Takagi	P
Five	3.94	100	2.31	36	Campagnolo (triple)	F
Five	4.01	102	2.36	32	Avocet, Ofmega	F
Five	4.33	110	2.55	34	Sugino and many others	E*
Five	4.57	116	2.69	35	Campagnolo Victory/ Triomphe, Chorus	F
Five	4.65	118	2.73	36	Sakae, Ofmega	F
Five	4.72	120	2.78	36	Zeus	P
Five	4.80	122	2.82	38	Nervar, Stronglight	P
Five	5.12	130	3.01	39(38)	Shimano and many others	E*
Five	5.31	135	3.11	39	Campagnolo C-Record	F
Five	5.67	144	3.33	42(41)	Campagnolo and many others	E*
Five	5.94	151	3.50	44	Campagnolo (pre-1972)	F
Six	3.15	80	—	26	TA Cyclotourist	G*

* One of the six standard bolt circles.

on 42- and 39-tooth bolt circles. If your crank doesn't have the notched spider, you may have problems with the 41- or 38-tooth chainwheels.

Crankarm Length

Before 1980, all stock bicycles came with 170mm cranks. Then Miyata began to offer crankarms and stems to match the frame size. This was a nifty sales feature and soon the rest of the industry caught up. In chapter 2, table 2-2,

(continued on page 76)

TABLE 5-2.

Cranksets

Make and Model	Cost[1] ($)	Weight[2] (gr.)	Type	Chainwheels Available[3] Outer	Middle	Inner	Crank Lengths[4] (mm)	Bolt Circle (mm) Outer
Campagnolo								
C-Record	275–400	870	R	57–39	N/A	57–39	165–180	135
Nuovo Record	225–300	930	R	57–42	N/A	57–42	165–180	144
Victory/ Triomphe	140–200	940	ST	53–50	N/A	42–35	170	116
Sakae								
FXC-200	55–80	950	R	53, 52, 50	N/A	42, 40, 39	165, 170	130
FXC-T-310	60–90	1000	LT	53, 52, 50 48, 46	46, 45 44–34 even	36–24 even	165, 170, 175, 180	110
Shimano								
Dura-Ace	160–240	950	R	54–48	N/A	46–39	165–175	130
600 EX	80–120	1000	R	53–48	N/A	45–39	165, 170–175	130
105	75–110	990	R	52-Biopace	N/A	42-Biopace	165, 170–175	130
Deore XT	140–200	1065	LT	50, 48, 46-Biopace	44, 38, 36-Biopace	28, 26-Biopace	165, 170 175, 180	110
Biopace	100–150	1050	LT	50, 48-Biopace	44, 38-Biopace	28-Biopace	170, 175	110
Specialized								
Racing	100–150	897	R	55–42	N/A	55–42	167.5–175, 180	144
Touring	100–150	—	LT	55–46	46–34	33–24	167.5–175, 180	110
Stronglight								
106/107	100–150	852	R	56–42	N/A	56–42	165, 170–180, 182	144
103/200	—	880	R	53, 52, 50, 48, 46, 45	N/A	46–44, 42, 40, 38	167.5–172.5	130
99/100	75–100	1010	LT	54–45	54–45	40–28 even	165, 170, 172.5	86
Sugino								
75	170–220	975	R	54–46	N/A	46–38	165–175, 180	130
GP-130	65-90	1220	R	54–46	N/A	45–38	160, 165 170, 175	130
Aero Tour	100–130	1010	LT	54–46	46–44, 42	40, 39, 36–24 even	170–180	110
SunTour								
Superbe Pro	150–200	940	R	53–48	N/A	43–38	165–175	130
Sprint	90–130	985	R	53–48	N/A	43–38	165–175	130
Cyclone 7000	75–110	1005	R	54–48	—	43–38	160, 165–175	130
TA								
Cyclotourist	80–120	1010	LT	69–40	50–26	50–26	150–185	80

1. The racing crankset prices are for doubles. The loaded touring crankset prices are for triples. The prices include the bottom bracket set. Where there are two bottom bracket sets available, it covers the lower-priced one.

2. The weights shown are for a racing crankset with 52/42 chainwheels and a touring triple crankset with 50/45 outer chainwheels and the smallest inner chainwheel. Both weights are for cranksets with 170mm cranks and they include the bottom bracket set.

Bolt Circle (mm) Inner	CW Hardness	Outer CW to Crank (in.)	Bearing Seal	Chain Stud	Material Processing	Chainwheel Availability	Rigidity	Appearance
—	B-88	0.385	part.	yes	Fg	F	E	E
—	B-88	0.385	part.	no	Fg	E	G	G
—	B-88	0.410	part.	no	Fg	F	VG	VG
—	B-75	0.440	no	yes	MFg	E	VG	G
74	B-75	0.500	no	yes	MFg	E	VG	G
—	B-86	0.375	yes	yes	Fg	E	E	E
—	B-80	0.375	yes	yes	Fg	E	E	VG
—	B-80	0.505	no	yes	MFg	E	VG	G
74	B-80	0.465	yes	yes	Fg	G	VG	VG
74	B-80	0.465	yes	yes	MFg	G	VG	G
—	B-75	0.415	yes	yes	Fg	E	VG	VG
74	B-75	0.415	yes	yes	Fg	E	VG	VG
—	N/A	0.385	no	no	Ca/Fg	E	G	VG
—	N/A	—	no	no	Ca/Fg	E	G	VG
86	B-80	0.425	no	no	—	G	G	VG
—	N/A	0.400	yes	yes	Fg	E	G	VG
—	B-70	0.390	no	no	Ca	E	G	VG
74	B-70	0.450	no	no	Fg	E	G	VG
—	B-95	0.395	yes	yes	Fg	E	VG	VG
—	B-95	0.435	yes	yes	Fg	E	VG	G
—	B-70	0.435	yes	yes	—	E	G	G
80	B-59	0.320	no	no	Fg	G	F	F

3. 57–39 means that chainwheels are available in 1-tooth steps from 57 to 39 teeth. 44–34 "even" means that only chainwheels with even-numbered teeth between 44 and 34 are available.

4. Inclusive numbers indicate the availability of lengths in increments of 2.5mm. Thus, 165–180 means the following lengths are available: 165, 167.5, 170, 172.5, 175, 177.5, and 180.

I correlated various crank lengths with leg lengths. The crank lengths listed there were chosen under the assumption that you pedal at a normal cadence. However, If you're a lightweight spinner, you may want to choose a shorter crank. On the other hand, If you're a heavyweight pedal masher, you may want to pick a longer crank. (Longer and shorter means, say, plus or minus 5mm.)

I use cranks 5mm longer than table 2-2 recommends. In theory, the bottom bracket should be raised to match the longer crank. In practice, bottom bracket heights are designed to allow racers to pedal around corners. Most of us don't fit that category and we can use lower bottom brackets or longer cranks and never drag a pedal. If you buy a new crankset, by all means buy the right crank length.

Crankset Design

Twenty years ago, there was a plethora of crankset designs. There were one-piece "Ashtabula" cranksets, steel-cottered cranksets, and alloy cotterless cranksets. The outer chainwheel was bolted or swaged onto the right-hand crank or the crank had a three- or five-arm spider to hold the chainwheels. The best-quality cranksets were forged from aluminum alloy with a five-arm spider to hold the alloy chainwheels. They had "cotterless" cranks that bolted onto square tapers at the end of the spindles. Best quality was usually spelled Campagnolo Record.

In the late 1960s, Sugino introduced the inexpensive Maxy crankset with an alloy three-arm spider swaged onto an alloy cotterless crank. The swaged Maxy looked a bit like a top-quality crankset. It sold for the price of an inexpensive steel-cottered crankset and it weighed two pounds less. Soon every bicycle selling for more than $100 sported cotterless alloy cranksets. Three-arm swaged Maxys begat five-arm swaged Super Maxys that begat forged five-arm Mighty Tours. Sakae, Shimano, Stronglight, SunTour, and Takagi were soon making Maxy-style cranksets. They've become the standard for standard-quality bicycles and all other designs are passé.

At the 1982 New York Bike Show, Campagnolo showed a prototype of a top-of-the-line crankset, which was to become the C-Record. I had to elbow the Japanese photographers out of the way to look at it. Instead of the right-hand crank sitting on top of the spider, it was nearly flush with the spider and the spider arms went back to the outer chainwheel. The crank came out at a slight angle and its cross section was rounded and oblong instead of square. The design was more rigid and it offered more ankle clearance than earlier designs. It used a shorter, stiffer spindle and it looked simply elegant. The Swiss company, Edco, showed a similar design at the same show. It took Campagnolo three years to get the C-Record to market, but the clever Japanese were much faster. Virtually all of today's cranksets show the influence of Campagnolo and Edco.

Bottom Bracket Spindles

Spindles come in three basic lengths: for single, for double, and for triple cranksets. Double and triple spindles also often come in both long and short lengths. The spindle length is designed to put the chainline in the middle of the freewheel. On a double, this means that a line drawn from the midpoint of the two chainwheels should fall on the middle cog of a freewheel. However, I don't think that this is the right way to set up a triple, because you never use the little chainwheel with the small sprockets. It's better to set the chainline of a triple so that the inner chainwheel just barely clears the chainstay.

You can often use a double spindle with a triple crankset. A 1/16-inch-thick spacer under the right-hand cup will sometimes provide the necessary clearance. Usually there will be enough threads to secure the locknut on the left-

PHOTO 5-1 Racing cranksets: top left to right, Campagnolo C-Record, Campagnolo Super Record, and Campagnolo Nuovo Victory; bottom left and right, Shimano Dura-Ace and SunTour Superbe Pro.

hand cup. The newest Shimano and Specialized triple cranksets are designed to use double spindles.

The Sugino Maxy used a square-tapered spindle with nuts to attach the cranks. Sakae, Takagi, and the Taiwanese crankset makers copied the Maxy spindle and it became a de facto standard. However, nut-type Maxy spindles didn't look as classy as bolt-type Campagnolo spindles, so before long Maxy-quality cranksets came with bolt-type spindles; this has become the new de facto standard.

There's an ISO Standard for the 2-degree taper found on the square end of bottom bracket spindles. Most manufacturers nominally comply with this standard, but a lot of variations exist, including the batch to batch variations that occur with low-priced Brand X spindles. Stronglight, TA, and the old swaged Maxy-style cranks are larger than standard so they'll bottom out if fitted on a standard spindle. The best-quality spindles are hollow to save weight.

Bottom Bracket Bearings

It doesn't cost very much to put a plastic seal inside the cups of the bottom bracket to keep water out of the bearings; in fact, most cranksets now come with semi-sealed bearings. This plastic seal removes one of the major advantages of bottom bracket sets that make use of sealed cartridge-type bearings. However, cartridge bearings have the additional advantage of allowing the chainline to be moved. Phil Wood makes the best quality bottom bracket set with sealed cartridge bearings. Specialized and SunTour also offer bottom bracket sets with sealed cartridge bearings. (Table 5-2 shows which cranksets come with seals. "Part." means "partial seal" and refers to the screw thread that Campagnolo provides in lieu of a seal on their cranksets to keep out road grit.)

I don't think that the industrial ball bearings used in cartridge-type bottom bracket sets are necessary for crankset service. Such bearings are designed to handle a constant high-speed load, whereas, bicycle cranks turn very slowly and the load placed on them varies. I believe that the cup-and-cone bearings that use eleven ¼-inch loose balls or nine caged balls are, in fact, ideal for crankset service. Incidentally, the load capacity increases directly with the number of balls, so eleven loose balls have 22 percent more capacity than nine caged balls.

Chainwheel Hardness

Top-quality cranksets come with chainwheels made from hard aluminum alloys. They bend less than inexpensive chainwheels and their teeth wear much longer. Table 5-2 shows chainwheel hardness where I could find the information. Chainwheel hardness is measured on the Rockwell B scale. (B-90 is a very hard aluminum alloy; B-60 is the soft annealed condition.) Top-quality chainwheels are usually thicker and made to tighter tolerances than chainwheels of lesser quality, so they run truer.

Spacing Between the Outer Chainwheel and the Crankarm

The distance between the outer chainwheel and the crankarm may seem like a trivial little dimension, but it has a major effect on front shifting. The early Huret, Simplex, and Campagnolo front derailleurs had cage sides that were parallel and fairly close together. These narrow cages allowed about two shifts on the rear and then you had to adjust the front derailleur because the chain was rubbing on the cage. In the 1970s, Shimano and SunTour widened the rear of their front derailleur cages so that you could make four or five shifts on the rear before you had to fine-tune the front derailleur. Now, just about everybody makes front derailleurs with wide cages. When these wide-cage front derailleurs are properly set up, the tail of the cage extends out beyond the outer chainwheel.

The gap between the outer chainwheel and the crank on 1970 cranksets was designed for the 1970 narrow-cage front derailleurs. Unfortunately, even though the old narrow-cage front derailleurs are obsolete, many cranksets still have narrow gaps between the crank and outer chainwheel. The TA Cyclotourist is the worst offender. If you have a crankset with a narrow gap, you have two options. You can either set up the front derailleur incorrectly so the cage just misses the crank and put up with poor shifting, or you can buy a properly designed crankset with a wide gap.

In theory, the narrow gap prevents the chain from wedging between the crank and the chainwheel if you overshift. In practice, a small stud on the outer chainwheel or on the crank works much better to prevent wedging, even with narrow chains. Table 5-2 shows chainwheel to crank spacing. Anything over 0.375 inch is adequate for a double. A triple should have 0.425 or so.

Chainwheel Spacing

The spacing between chainwheels is rarely a problem on double cranksets. The front derailleur is simply adjusted to push the chain firmly from one chainwheel to the next. But triples are different. On a triple you have to feel your way from the outer chainwheel to the middle chainwheel, and it's possible for the chain to "freewheel" on top of the middle chainwheel until you "kick" it over with the front derailleur. This problem is worse with narrow chains and with half-step gearing. With crossover gearing, the chain has farther to drop down to the middle chainwheel, so the problem is less likely to arise.

The solution to this problem is slightly narrower spacing between the two outer chainwheels on half-step setups. The magic spacing for trouble-free half-step shifting is about 0.275 inch. The crankset makers have trouble providing this because they have to design their chainwheels to please us gear freaks who often mix and match outer and middle chainwheels.

The spacing on many Stronglight cranksets is on the wide side. On the other hand, spacing is not terribly critical on cranksets that use Shimano Biopace chainwheels, because these elliptical chainwheels are free from the chain freewheeling problem. Variations exist between brands in spider thickness, chainwheel thickness, and where the teeth are centered in the chainwheel cross section. You may encounter spacing problems if you mix and match different brands of chainwheels. Sorry about that!

Crankset Standardization

You would do well to consider the standardization issue before you buy a new crankset, because cranksets spotlight the worst features of the bicycle's lack of standardization. There are two different bottom bracket widths: 68mm and 70mm. There are five different threads: English, Italian, French, and two kinds of Swiss. Each crankset comes with six to ten different spindle lengths to accommodate the two bottom bracket widths as well as single, double, and triple cranksets. The spacing between the bearing races on the spindles varies depending on the thickness of the cups. The taper of the spindles varies from maker to maker. There are even three different dust cap thread sizes, so bike shops have to have three different crank removers. The ISO thread standard is 22mm dia. × 1 pitch. The old Stronglight size was 23.5mm dia. × 1 pitch. TA is 23mm dia. × 1 pitch.

To complete the frustration, there's just a smidgeon of commonality. Almost everyone uses eleven ¼-inch ball bearings. On a good day, Shimano cranks might fit onto a Campagnolo spindle, which might fit into Sugino cups, and the chainwheels might fall on the proper chainline. But on most average days, nothing interchanges properly. Even if you buy an all-Shimano bottom bracket set, you've got to properly specify the bottom bracket width and threading and pick the right spindle length. *Sutherland's Handbook for Bicycle Mechanics* (4th ed.) devotes roughly 20 pages to the subject of bottom bracket interchangeability. (When it takes 20 pages, it's really noninterchangeability.)

Where does all of this leave you if you want to replace your crankset with minimum hassle? First, buy your crankset complete with bottom bracket set. Second, buy your crankset from a pro bike shop and have them do the installation. Third, buy an English-threaded frame, if you can, to avoid about half of the frustration. If you want to keep your costs down and reuse your existing bottom bracket, just accept the fact that you won't know if your new crankset will fit until you try it.

Bolt Circle Standardization

Here comes the second verse of the crankset standardization song. The bolt circle diameter determines which chainwheels fit on which cranks. Over the last decade, six bolt circles have gained wide acceptance and have become de facto standards. With the exception of the Campagnolo C-Record, Victory, and Triomphe cranksets, all of the racing and touring cranksets shown in table 5-2 use the six standard bolt circles listed in table 5-3.

All of the standard bolt circles have more than one maker and they're widely distributed. Everything else is bastard. If you buy a bastard bolt circle, you're at the mercy of the maker and the importer for replacement chainwheels. If your crankset uses a bastard bolt circle and the maker goes out of business, as Takagi recently did, you may have no source of replacement chainwheels. To help you make your decision about a new crankset, let's talk about the six standard bolt circles.

Campagnolo Record (144mm) In 1968, Campagnolo reduced the size of the bolt circle on their Record crankset from 151mm to 144mm to allow the use of 42- instead of 45-tooth inner chainwheels. Such was Campagnolo's power in those days that 144mm promptly became the new racing standard. More

TABLE 5-3.

Standard Bolt Circles

Name	Dia. (mm)	Min. No. CW Teeth	Service	Other Makers
Campagnolo Record	144	42(41)	R	Avocet, Galli, Mavic, Nervar, Ofmega, Sakae, Specialized, Stronglight, Sugino, SunTour, others
Shimano Dura-Ace	130	39(38)	R	Sakae, Stronglight, Sugino, Takagi
Sugino Maxy	110	34	I	Sakae, Shimano, Specialized, Takagi
Stronglight 99/100	86	28	T	Sakae
TA Cyclotourist	80	26	T	Sugino
Sugino Aero Tour	74	24	T	Avocet, Ofmega, Sakae, Shimano, Specialized, Takagi

than a dozen makers now use the 144mm bolt circle. It's an excellent choice if you race and if a 42-tooth inner chainwheel isn't too big for you.

Shimano Dura-Ace (130mm) About five years ago, it became apparent that 42 teeth was a bit big for a racing inner chainwheel. The widespread use of 12-tooth sprockets allowed racers to produce their desired High gear with smaller outer chainwheels, so proportionately smaller inner chainwheels and freewheel sprockets could be used to produce the desired Low. A smaller bolt circle was thus needed to permit the use of a smaller inner chainwheel. To meet this new demand, Sakae, Stronglight, Sugino, SunTour, and Takagi have all adopted the 130mm bolt circle, which Shimano has used on their racing cranksets since the early 1970s. When Campagnolo developed two new cranksets to meet the same need they assumed that it was still 1968. They chose to introduce two new bastard bolt circles, 135mm and 116mm. Reducing the size of chainwheels and sprockets saves weight, but more importantly, it provides more 1-tooth jumps on the freewheel.

Sugino Maxy (110mm) The Sugino Maxy 110mm bolt circle, which takes a 34-tooth minimum chainwheel, is the only intermediate bolt circle that makes any sense. Five years ago, when it was used on Sugino's five-arm Maxy and Mighty Tour cranksets, it was just one of three fairly common intermediate bolt circles competing in the low-price sport touring market. Then in 1982, Sugino introduced the Aero Tour triple crankset, which used 110mm for the outer and middle chainwheels and 74mm for the inner chainwheel. It became the favorite of the mountain bikers. I waxed enthusiastic about this combination in the May 1983 issue of *Bicycling.* Soon Sakae, Takagi, and Specialized were making Aero Tour clones. The real breakthrough came in 1984 when Shimano adopted 110- and 74-mm bolt circles for their triple cranksets. Now there's de facto standardization with five different makers.

Stronglight 99/100 (86mm) Stronglight and Sakae make cranksets using the 86mm bolt circle, which takes 28-tooth minimum chainwheels. It makes a nice triple that has all three chainwheels attached with long bolts. It also makes doubles for gear freaks who like wide-range combinations like 44/28. Stronglight is maintaining this bolt circle in production. Sakae is now emphasizing the 110mm and 74mm combination.

TA Cyclotourist (80mm) The 80mm bolt circle is a link with the past. I include it as one of the six standards for sentimental reasons and because there are so many in use. It's a six-hole bolt circle that has been around since the 1930s. It goes with a five-pin bolt circle that attaches the outer chainwheel to the crank. There used to be a dozen manufacturers making five-pin cranksets. Now only TA survives with their Cyclotourist touring triple crankset.

Sugino Aero Tour (74mm) I first saw 74mm bolt circles on Avocet and Ofmega triple cranksets in 1981. Five holes were drilled and tapped in the spider arms and inner chainwheels as small as 24 teeth could be bolted onto studs. I immediately made up a 50/45/24 triple and dropped my low to 19 inches. The problem with these two cranksets was the 144mm outer bolt circle. Few mountain bikes would accept a 42-tooth middle chainwheel. When Sugino picked the 74mm bolt circle for the Aero Tour crankset, its future was assured.

Crankset Makers

We will complete our discussion of cranksets with a look at the major crankset manufacturers.

PHOTO 5-2 Six standard bolt circles shown on cranksets fitted with the smallest usable inner chainwheel: top left to right, Campagnolo Record with 52/42 chainwheels (144mm), Shimano Dura-Ace with 50/39 chainwheels (130mm), and Sugino Aero Tour with 52/47/34 chainwheels (110mm); bottom left to right, Sugino Aero Tour with 52/47/24 chainwheels (74mm), Stronglight 100 with 50/45/28 chainwheels (86mm), and TA Cyclotourist with 50/45/26 chainwheels (80mm).

Campagnolo

Campagnolo's crankset terminology is tricky. It isn't easy to master all of the subtleties and impress your bike freak friends. Campagnolo is determined to call their top crankset "Record" regardless of the confusion. Virtually everyone else calls it "C-Record."

Prior to 1985, Campagnolo used different model names for cranks, chainwheels, and bottom bracket sets. The old cranks were called "Record" in all models, until Campagnolo renamed them "Nuovo Record" in 1986. Nuovo Record (née Record) chainwheels have an inner ring of metal. Super Record chainwheels have the ring removed to save weight.

There were three bottom bracket sets for Nuovo Record cranksets: Record, Nuovo Record, and Super Record. (You can feel for Campy's renaming problems here—Nuovo Record and Nuovo-Nuovo Record? I remember when Chevron introduced a super premium gasoline and the old premium was called "Supreme." Same kind of problem.)

The old Record bottom bracket uses plain cups. The Nuovo Record cups have spiral grooves to keep out water, which requires different spindles, since the cups are thicker. Super Record uses a titanium spindle and special cups with small-diameter ball bearings. Nothing interchanges between the three versions. If I read the catalogs correctly, there are two new bottom bracket sets for C-Record and Triomphe/Victory.

Campagnolo Nuovo Record cranks with Nuovo Record or Super Record chainrings make a splendid racing crankset. It's used by more than half of today's professional racers. It has been copied by a dozen makers, the sincerest form of flattery. If you're buying a new Campagnolo crankset, I recommend Nouvo Record.

The C-Record is an absolutely gorgeous crankset and it's very rigid. Just realize that when you purchase it you're buying a bastard 135mm bolt circle. The new Triomphe and Victory cranksets have a different bastard 116mm bolt circle. (Actually, Campagnolo perpetrated the foul deed a few years earlier with the Gran Sport crankset.) If you buy a C-Record, Victory, or Triomphe, you'll be forced to buy your chainwheels from Campagnolo. I'm not paranoid about this. If the super bike of your dreams needs C-Record, go for it. (At $400 a copy, who needs a second source of chainrings?) Victory and Triomphe are another matter. With their 35-tooth minimum chainwheels, they're not suitable for loaded touring. The sport tourer can get more for his money elsewhere.

Sakae

Sakae is the volume supplier of standard-quality cranksets. They make a vast range of cranksets for bicycles in the $150 to $300 price range. Sakae was the first major user of melt-forging. They make top-quality racing cranksets in both of the standard racing bolt circles, but they haven't been too successful competing with Campagnolo and Shimano for the premium market. Sakae makes touring triple cranksets in both the Stronglight 99/100 and the Sugino Aero Tour bolt circles, with the emphasis on the latter. They've concentrated on the OEM bicycle makers rather than the mail-order houses or the bike shops. They're making a major effort to sell their FXC series in the aftermarket. The FXC-200 double uses the 130mm bolt circle. The FXC-T310 triple uses the 110mm/74mm bolt circles. Both are available with oval chainrings.

Specialized

The Specialized racing crankset is made by Sugino. It uses the latest recessed crank design, which allows a shorter, stiffer spindle. It has very hard chainwheels for longer wear. The Specialized touring crankset is a Sugino Aero Tour clone. The bottom bracket sets include O-ring seals.

Shimano

Until about ten years ago, Shimano made only top-of-the-line Dura-Ace cranksets to compete with Campagnolo. They left the lower-priced market to

PHOTO 5-3 Touring cranksets: top left to right, Sakae FX with 48/38/28 chainwheels, Shimano Biopace with 48/44/26 chainwheels, and Specialized Touring with 50/45/24 chainwheels; bottom left to right, Stronglight 100 with 50/45/28 chainwheels, Sugino Aero Tour with 52/47/24 chainwheels, and TA Cyclotourist with 50/45/26 chainwheels.

Takagi. As derailleurs and chains became more sophisticated, Shimano felt they had to make the entire drivetrain. They now have a complete line of cranksets. Shimano concentrates on innovation. Five years ago they introduced a whole range of aerodynamic AX cranksets featuring "dropped" Dyna-Drive pedals. This enjoyed a brief spurt of popularity and then Shimano moved on to other designs.

There are six Shimano lines in the replacement market: Dura-Ace, Santé, 600 Ultegra, and 105 for the racers and Deore XT and Biopace for the tourists and mountain bikers. Shimano has decided that racers want conventional equipment, so Dura-Ace is a conventional crankset with all of the current features. The Santé and 600 Ultegra cranksets are nearly identical to Dura-Ace, but with a bit less polish. The 105 is Shimano's economy melt-forged crankset.

Shimano's two touring triples, Deore XT and Biopace are built around Biopace chainwheels. There are now two versions of Biopace. The newer Biopace II is a bit closer to round than the original Biopace. I've pedaled Biopace chainwheels for three years or so. They make a small, positive difference, especially if you pedal in the saddle all of the time and at a fairly low cadence. If you stand up to pedal an old Biopace, it feels a bit like walking down a staircase. I've got round chainwheels on three bicycles and the two versions of Biopace on the other two. There's not a great difference among them.

The elliptical shape of the Biopace chainwheels does have a positive effect on shifting. Biopace triple cranksets shift beautifully. The chain never rides on the middle chainwheel.

Stronglight

Five years ago, Stronglight was another sleepy French company resting quietly in the sun, waiting for the Japanese to eat their lunch. They printed a new catalog every few years even if it was the same as the old one. Then Stronglight woke up and reacted to the competition. They restyled their entire line and introduced handsome new models with new model numbers. Models 106 and 107 use the 144mm bolt circle. Models 103 and 200 use the 130mm bolt circle. Models 106 and 103 are cast; models 107 and 200 are forged. Model 100 is the updated version of the old model 99 triple crankset. It uses the 86mm bolt circle, which is the smallest that mounts all of the chainwheels on one bolt circle.

Sugino

Sugino and Sakae are similar Japanese companies. They make a complete line of cranksets with the major emphasis on the lower-priced OEM market. Over the years, Sugino has made excellent copies of virtually all of the popular premium cranksets: Campagnolo Record, Shimano Dura-Ace, Stronglight 99, and TA Cyclotourist. This is a good thing because it provides a reasonably priced second source. The Maxy was Sugino's first breakthrough and the Aero Tour was their second. The Sugino 75 is a special top-of-the-line model to celebrate their 75th anniversary. Sugino cranksets are available with a nice feature called "Autex," which is a combination attaching bolt, dust cap, and crank remover. All you need is a 6mm Allen wrench to remove your cranks. Shimano has a similar feature that they call "One-Key Release."

SunTour

SunTour decided that they had to market a complete gruppo to compete with Shimano. SunTour's cranksets are made by Sugino. SunTour makes a top-quality sealed-cartridge bottom bracket set. The Superbe Pro, Sprint, and the Cyclone are all excellent values.

TA

TA stands for Specialities TA. They're the sleepy French company that hasn't yet reacted to the Japanese competition. TA makes a range of cranksets but the Cyclotourist is the only model that is widely distributed in the USA. Twenty years ago, if you wanted a wide-range triple crankset, you bought a Cyclotourist. Today, you'll get exactly the same crankset, complete with the softest chainwheels available, the narrowest gap between the crank and the outer chainwheel, and 11 bolts to hold the whole assembly together. In TA's favor, they have the widest range of crankarm lengths (from 150mm all the way to 185mm) and chainwheel sizes (from 69 to 26 teeth). The Cyclotourist bolt circle is unique, but Nervar, Shimano, Stronglight, Sugino, and many other companies make (or made) chainwheels that bolt onto the five-pin TA crank.

Everybody Else

Edco, Galli, Gipiemme, Mavic, Nervar, Ofmega, Omas, and Zeus all make good-quality racing cranksets. All, except Zeus, use the Campagnolo 144mm bolt circle. They all also face a Catch-22 situation. The bicycle makers and bike stores won't handle their products until they are widely used and they can't become widely used until they are fitted by the OEMs and are carried in the stores.

Frank's Favorite Cranksets

This one is close. My favorite racing crankset is the new Shimano Dura-Ace. It's got the right bolt circle, a sealed bottom bracket set, and it's beautifully finished. My favorite touring triple crankset is the Sugino Aero Tour, however, the copies from Shimano and Specialized are so close that you can buy the one that catches your eye.

CHAPTER 6

All about Freewheels

The most economical way to upgrade your gearing is to change freewheel sprockets. Freewheel changes are inexpensive, since sprockets cost only $3 to $10 each. If your freewheel is an old model and sprockets are hard to find, you can replace it with a new one for around $20. If you have a racing rear derailleur and you want a significantly lower Low, you can buy a new touring derailleur and a new wide-range freewheel for less than $50.

It's easy to change freewheel sprockets. Professional racers change sprockets before every race, to match their gearing to the race course. If you're a serious racer or triathlete, you can do the same. Some freewheels make the task easier than others.

Status of the Freewheel Market

While there are a dozen crankset makers and a hundred or so different cranksets, freewheels are more straightforward. There are only four major makers—Maillard, Regina, Shimano, and SunTour—and they make only two or three models each, at least for the aftermarket. The Japanese companies, Shimano and SunTour, have done more basic research into freewheel design in the past decade than had been previously done since the freewheel was invented at the turn of the century. At first, they concentrated on tooth shape and we saw innovations like alternate teeth and zigzag teeth and different tooth profiles for the different sprocket positions.

Starting about five years ago, some really significant improvements in freewheel design have occurred. In 1979, Shimano introduced the Freehub and Maillard introduced the Helicomatic. Both combine the freewheel with the rear hub, resulting in greater strength and easier sprocket changes. SunTour's Winner Pro and Regina's CX and CX-S allow you to build wide- or narrow-spaced, 5-,

6-, or 7-speed freewheels with the same body. In the last two years, freewheel research has concentrated on the interaction between chains, sprockets, and rear derailleurs.

Leaving out all of the new developments, the most important thing the Japanese did was to upgrade freewheel quality. Twenty years ago, low-priced freewheels were unreliable. Stories abounded of freewheels locking up solid, or freewheeling in both directions, 20 miles from the nearest bike shop. The companies that made those rotten old freewheels have either improved their product or gone out of business. Today, you can't buy a bad freewheel. Any of the listed freewheels will take all of the punishment that you can dish out.

Freewheels for Indexed Shifting

Indexed shifting has created a major change in the freewheel market. Today's freewheel is part of a total system—like Shimano's SIS, SunTour's AccuShift, or Huret's ARIS. Each of these companies makes their own freewheels. (Sachs-Huret now owns Maillard.) These manufacturers have designed and calibrated their indexing systems around specific freewheel–chain–rear derailleur combinations. You can't mix and match gear train components any more, as gear freaks have done since the time of the Wright Brothers. If you use "foreign" components, the onus is on you if the indexing doesn't index.

The freewheel is a critical part of the indexing system. The freewheel market has thus been divided into "have" freewheels that are suitable for indexed shifting and "have-not" freewheels that aren't suitable. The indexed shifting freewheels have the following features:

- Two basic configurations: narrow-spaced 7-speed freewheels for racing, and wide-spaced 6-speed freewheels for touring. Both are mounted on a 126mm wide rear hub. The old standard wide-spaced 5-speed freewheel on a 120mm rear hub is now used only on the lowest-priced bicycles.
- Even spacing between sprockets. SunTour's narrow-spaced 7-speed freewheels are unevenly spaced but SunTour's indexed lever is designed to match.
- Wide spacing on touring freewheels. The narrow-spaced 6-speed touring freewheel is history. You'll still be able to get sprockets and spacers but the makers have removed the freewheels from the catalogs.
- Sprocket tooth profiles designed for easy shifting. Maillard, Shimano, and SunTour have special tooth profiles. Regina has introduced chisel-shaped teeth on their larger sprockets.

- Fewer sprocket sizes. Indexed rear derailleurs can't shift over very small or very large sprockets. Shimano doesn't make an 11-tooth narrow-spaced sprocket for 7-speed Dura-Ace Freehubs. None of the indexed rear derailleurs are advertised for 34-tooth sprockets, let alone SunTour's 38-tooth sprocket.

If you're thinking about a new freewheel, think about indexed shifting at the same time. You may decide to buy the freewheel that goes with your future indexed shifting package.

Standardization

There's no freewheel standardization, but that doesn't matter very much. The only thing to worry about is the four different threads that screw onto the hub: ISO, English, Italian, and French. You want English or ISO threads, 1.375 inches in diameter by 24 tpi. The Italian thread is close to the English standard and you can mate English and Italian in a pinch. (Of course you can, that's my ethnic background.) The new ISO standard thread is a compromise between English and Italian. If you have a French-threaded hub, sell it cheap, complete with freewheel, to someone you don't like very much.

Everything else about freewheels is unique. It's as if there's a Freewheel Designers Politburo that requires a unique new remover and unique new threaded and splined sprockets on every new freewheel, so you can't use your old ones. There are so many varieties that every now and then they blunder and a Shimano sprocket fits on a Regina freewheel. (I'm sorry Commissar, I'll never do it again.)

Important Freewheel Features

The many freewheel models available on the market today can be distinguished one from the other by comparing several basic features. Below is a discussion of these features in the order of their importance.

Ease of Rear Shifting

Two freewheel factors enter into shifting: the shape of the sprocket tooth and narrow versus wide sprocket spacing. The freewheel interacts with the chain and the rear derailleur so it's not quite that straightforward.

Narrow versus Wide Spacing

A narrow-spaced freewheel requires a narrow chain. (I'll talk about narrow spacing here rather than in the chain chapter because the freewheel is more

PHOTO 6-1 SunTour Winner Pro freewheels: left to right, narrow-spaced 7-speed, wide-spaced 6-speed, wide-spaced 5-speed, and narrow-spaced 6-speed.

important than the chain.) Narrow spacing is basically a simple idea. By reducing the width of the spacers between the freewheel sprockets, it's possible to install six narrow-spaced sprockets in the same width as five wide-spaced sprockets, or seven narrow-spaced sprockets in the same width as six wide-spaced sprockets.

Width is critical because wide freewheels require an asymmetrical "dished" wheel. A dished wheel has the hub offset to make room for the freewheel. The way this is done is described in chapter 11. The width of the rear dropout and the width of the rear hub have to be the same. The two common widths are 120mm and 126mm. Today, most quality bicycles use the 126mm width. You can comfortably use a wide-spaced 5-speed freewheel or a narrow-spaced 6-speed freewheel with a 120mm width. You can use a wide-spaced 6-speed freewheel or a narrow-spaced 7-speed freewheel with a 126mm width. If you go beyond this, you'll end up with excessive dishing and a weak rear wheel. Thus the number of sprockets and the sprocket spacing that you can use is intimately tied to the rear dropout width of your bicycle.

I've never liked narrow-spaced freewheels and narrow chains, because they don't shift very well. It's taken me ten years to be able to properly explain my objections. At first I blamed the narrow chains, and I kept testing one narrow chain after another seeking the holy grail, a narrow chain that shifted as well as a wide chain. I didn't succeed because the problem isn't the chain, it's the narrow spacing between the freewheel sprockets.

When you shift to a larger sprocket, the derailleur jockey pulley pushes the chain over against the larger sprocket until the teeth engage the side of the chain and it climbs up. With wide spacing, the chain can bend 3 to 6 degrees before it runs into the next sprocket. With narrow spacing, there's so little clearance between the chain and the sprocket that the chain can only bend about one-third of a degree. Then it contacts the side of the larger sprocket. Because the chain is essentially parallel to the sprocket, the teeth can't find anything to embrace, especially since the rivets on narrow chains are nearly flush. So you pull harder on the shift lever and the flat side of the sprocket pushes back harder against the chain. Finally, with much grinding and mechanical sadism, the upshift takes place. It's a complex mechanism since it depends simultaneously on the design of the rear derailleur, the shape and flexibility of the chain, and the shape of the sprocket teeth.

Smooth upshifting especially depends on the tooth difference between adjacent sprockets. Narrow spacing works quite well on a racing freewheel, known as a "corncob" or "straight block," because of the single-tooth differences that exist between adjacent sprockets. A touring freewheel has much larger tooth differences and the flat sides of the big sprockets act like spoke protectors. If narrow chains and narrow spacing had started out as a racing innovation, we might have sorted out the problems when tourists started to fool with wide-range, narrow-spaced 18-speeds. Instead, it started out as a Fuji-SunTour-HKK marketing gimmick for sport touring bikes: 12 speeds for the price of 10.

Then the racers realized that narrow spacing provided one more gear and one more one-tooth step, for the same wheel dish. The racers switched over to narrow-spaced seven-sprocket freewheels while we technical experts argued about the merits of the various narrow chains. We wrote about HKK's Z-chain versus Sedis's Sedisport versus Daido's DID Lanner versus Shimano's Narrow Uniglide until we finally sorted out what was really happening with the rear shifts. Narrow chains also shift a bit worse up front because they don't settle onto the next chainwheel as readily as wide chains.

Shimano never played the narrow-spaced game. Instead they designed their Freehubs with wide spacing and minimum wheel dish. In 1987, Shimano finally introduced a narrow-spaced 7-speed indexed shifting racing package.

After flirting with narrow spacing, most of the mountain bike makers have switched back to wide-spaced 15-speeds, or they've widened the rear dropouts to 130mm to provide less wheel dish with wide-spaced 6-speed freewheels. Some sport touring bike makers still make poor-shifting bicycles with narrow-spaced 6-speed freewheels. That's a sign of an old model (or an ossified designer). By 1987, the industry had pretty much standardized on wide-spaced 6-speed freewheels for touring bikes and narrow-spaced 7-speed freewheels for racers.

The final critical aspect of sprocket spacing is uniformity. If a freewheel is going to be used for indexed shifting, the sprockets have to be uniformly spaced. The new Regina Synchro and the SunTour Alpha freewheels correct the uneven spacing in the previous models.

Sprocket Tooth Shape

When I say "tooth shape," I'm talking about the cross section of the tooth. In this area, Shimano and SunTour are miles ahead of Regina. The Maillard (Huret) ARIS is too new for me to evaluate. The European makers concentrated on racing freewheels and they didn't seem to like or understand wide-range touring freewheels. As long as you don't use a sprocket larger than 28 teeth, tooth shape isn't too critical. When you use 32-, 34-, or 38-tooth sprockets, you need a proper tooth shape to help the rear derailleur shift.

Shimano does this by twisting the teeth so that the tooth corners snag the chain when you shift up. It works just beautifully. It works so well, in fact, that I don't use Shimano twist-tooth freewheels in my rear derailleur tests because their eager shifting masks the small differences between derailleurs.

Shimano has done a lot of experimenting over the last decade. First, they left out every other tooth on their largest sprockets ("alternate teeth"). Then, they cut off the tops of one tooth on the large sprockets ("cross cut teeth"). Neither of these innovations seemed to make any difference. Then, they chamfered the teeth on the inside only ("chamfered sprocket"), which helped. Then, they twisted the teeth ("twist-tooth"), which really helped. Finally, they carved away the back of their twist-tooth sprockets ("super shift"), which shifted so quickly that you sometimes got two shifts instead of one. By the time Shimano introduced the SIS package, they knew what was needed for predictable shifts that matched the calibration of the SIS shift lever. Twist-tooth is their standard.

SunTour has played a similar game and their tooth profiles have changed over the years. They now have three different tooth profiles: symmetrical teeth for the smallest sprockets, asymmetrical teeth that are flat on the outside for the middle positions, and asymmetrical teeth with a set for the largest sprockets ("zig-zag teeth"). You have to be very careful assembling a SunTour freewheel. If you install the sprockets backwards, or if you install an outer sprocket in a middle position, the shifting is dreadful.

Until 1987, Maillard and Regina used symmetrical teeth chamfered on both sides with a flat top and a little groove. You can flop them over and get twice the wear but that's their only advantage. Shifting deteriorates with more than a two-tooth difference between adjacent sprockets. This is particularly noticeable with narrow spacing. As a further insult, the flat top of the teeth sometimes allows the chain to ride on top of the sprocket until you kick it over with the rear derailleur. This doesn't happen with Japanese freewheels. In 1987, both companies introduced new freewheels with a chisel-shaped tooth profile on the larger sprockets. Regina calls this Synchro. In 1988, Maillard (Huret) introduced a new ARIS tooth profile. On all makes of freewheels, the smallest sprocket (the one on the outside) usually has a different, more symmetrical profile, because you don't shift up onto the smallest sprocket.

Neither Maillard nor Regina actively market a 34-tooth sprocket, which tells you something about their view of the touring freewheel market. (Figure 6-1 shows the various tooth profiles and table 6-1 indicates the profile found on each freewheel model described.)

There's a third reason that freewheels may shift poorly. The sprockets may be worn. Small sprockets wear out much faster than the larger ones. If you can see that the shape of the leading edge of the teeth on a sprocket is significantly different from the trailing edge, it's time to replace that sprocket. Many people change the small sprockets whenever they buy a new chain.

Number of Speeds

The proper combination of chainwheels and freewheel sprockets was covered in the discussion on gear selection found in chapter 3. Before you pick out a favorite arrangement, measure the dropout width of your bicycle. If you're building a loaded touring gear train, stick with wide-spaced freewheels, five sprockets with a 120mm dropout and six sprockets with a 126mm dropout. A narrow-spaced, wide-range 18- or 21-speed triple is a dumb idea. If you're building a racing gear train, use a narrow-spaced freewheel, six sprockets on a 120mm dropout and seven sprockets on a 126mm. If you're building an intermediate gear train for a sport tourer, establish your priorities. Do you want smooth

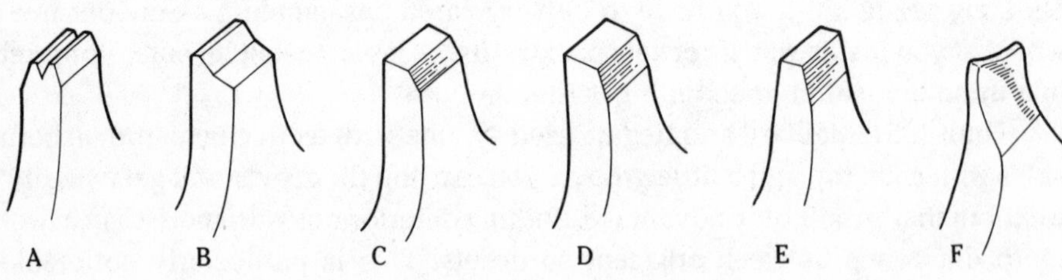

FIGURE 6-1 Freewheel sprocket tooth profiles.

shifting or two extra gears? It depends a bit on your gear patterns. Crossover patterns, which waste gears, need the extra two gears.

For a minimum cost upgrade, don't change the number of speeds. Just buy new sprockets for your present freewheel. Sometimes you can convert a 5-speed freewheel to a 6-speed. SunTour Winners and Regina CXs are designed with this in mind. You can replace the outer sprocket with a two-sprocket pair on some Regina and Maillard freewheels. The easy way to revise a freewheel is with the help of your nearest pro bike shop. Freewheel sprocket boards are a hallmark of a pro bike shop. Before you spend a lot of money on a worn-out freewheel, check the cost of a new one. It's easy to spend more on sprockets than on a whole new freewheel.

Smallest Small Sprocket

There used to be a standard for the size of the smallest sprocket. Regular touring freewheels had five sprockets, and the smallest sprocket had 14 teeth. Deluxe racing freewheels had six sprockets and the smallest sprocket had 13 teeth. SunTour and Shimano changed the pattern. Your small sprocket can now be as small as 11 teeth with a Shimano Dura-Ace Freehub or 12 teeth with Maillard, Regina, or SunTour freewheels. You can use the smallest sprocket with either racing or touring gearing arrangements. So in today's multiple-choice world, you have to decide which small sprocket is right for you. You can get a 100-inch High gear with a 52-tooth chainwheel and a 14-tooth sprocket, or with 48 × 13, or 44 × 12, or 41 × 11, or even 55 × 15. To help you with your decision, I'll explain the factors involved.

Higher Highs

A small fraction of the bicycling population needs a High higher than 100 inches. An even tinier group needs a High higher than the 108 inches you get with a 52-tooth chainwheel and a 13-tooth sprocket. Still, racing chainwheels with 56 and 58 teeth are made, and 115-inch gears are used by very strong time trialists. An 11-tooth Shimano Dura-Ace Freehub sprocket and a 52-tooth chainwheel give a high of 128 inches. For most people, the proper response is "So what?" If you like to pedal downhill at 45 mph or you have long cranks or a slow cadence, you might occasionally use an "overdrive" gear of 110 or so. Most riders are better advised to save their knees and speed up their cadence. I have a 118-inch High and a 108-inch 17th gear on my loaded touring bike, but I use them only about 5 percent of the time. Shimano sells a few 11-tooth sprockets to racers for the downhill side of hilly stages. The 12-tooth sprocket has become the racing standard since it became readily available.

(continued on page 98)

TABLE 6-1.

Freewheels

Make and Model	Cost ($)	Weight[1] (gr.)	No. of Sprockets	Spacing	Smallest Sprocket	Largest Sprocket
Maillard						
700 Course	20–30	455	5	W	14	32
700 Course	21–31	520	6	W	13	32
700 Compact	23–34	500	6	N	13	32
700 Compact	24–36	355	7	N	12	32
700 Helicomatic	85–125	710	5	W	14	32
700 Helicomatic	85–125	630	6	N	13	32
700 Helicomatic	85–125	650	7	N	12	32
Regina						
Extra/Oro	15–22	410	5	W	13	31
Extra/Oro Scalare	17–25	240	5	W	13	31
Extra/Oro	17–25	285	6	W	13	31
Extra/Oro Synchro	20–30	405	5	W	13	32
Extra/Oro Synchro	20–30	455	6	W	13	32
America (CX)	35–50	400	5	W	13	31
America (CX)	40–55	435	6	W	12	31
America (CX-S)	50–65	290	6	N	13	31
America (CX-S)	50–65	315	7	N	12	31
Shimano						
MF-Z	17–25	360	5	W	13	34
MF-Z (Z-012)	17–25	445	6	W	13	34
600 EX (MF-6208)	20–30	460	6	W	13	34
Santé (MF-5000)	35–50	355	7	N	12	28
Dura-Ace (MF-7400-6)	35–50	430	6	W	13	28
Dura-Ace (MF-7400-7)	40–60	355	7	N	12	28
Deore XT Freehub (FH-M730)	45–70	730	6	W	12	34

Tooth Profile[2]	Re-mover[3]	Tooth Hardness	Bear-ing Seal	Ease of Changing	Sprocket Versa-tility	Mech. Const.
Sym	2N	C-15	no	VG	VG	VG
Sym	2N	C-15	no	G	G	VG
Sym	2N	C-15	no	G	G	VG
Sym	2N	C-15	no	F	F	VG
Sym	N/A	—	no	E	E	E
Sym	N/A	—	no	G	VG	E
Sym	N/A	—	no	G	G	E
Sym	Sp	C-35	no	P	P	F
Sym	Sp	C-35	no	P	P	F
Sym	Sp	C-35	no	P	P	F
Asy	Sp	—	no	VG	G	VG
Asy	Sp	—	no	G	G	VG
Sym	Sp	—	yes	G	G	VG
Sym	Sp	—	yes	F	F	VG
Sym	Sp	—	yes	F	F	VG
Sym	Sp	—	yes	F	F	VG
Tw	Sp	C-40	no	E	VG	VG
Tw	Sp	C-40	no	E	VG	VG
Tw	Sp	C-40	yes	E	VG	VG
Tw	Sp	C-40	yes	G	G	VG
Tw	Sp	C-40	yes	E	VG	VG
Tw	Sp	C-40	yes	G	G	VG
Tw	N/A	C-40	yes	E	E	E

(continued)

Freewheels—*Continued*

Make and Model	Cost ($)	Weight[1] (gr.)	No. of Sprockets	Spacing	Smallest Sprocket	Largest Sprocket
Shimano—*continued*						
Dura-Ace Freehub (FH-7400-6)	125–190	730	6	W	11	28
Dura-Ace/SIS Freehub (FH-7400-7)	130–200	630	7	N	12	28
SunTour						
Perfect	12–18	425	5	W	14	38
Alpha	15–21	—	6	W	13	34
Winner	15–22	420	5	W	13	34
Winner	18–27	480	6	W	13	34
Winner Pro	22–30	420	5	W	13	34
Winner Pro	27–36	480	6	W	13	34
Winner Pro	28–40	295	6	N	13	34
Winner Pro	30–44	325	7	N	12	34

1. The weights shown are for 14-17-20-24-28 sprockets on the 5-speed freewheels, 14-16-18-21-24-28 sprockets on the wide-spaced 6-speed freewheels, 13-14-15-16-17-18 sprockets on the narrow-spaced 6-speed freewheels, and 12-13-14-15-16-17-18 sprockets on the narrow-spaced 7-speed freewheels. The Shimano Freehub and Maillard Helicomatic weights include the weight of a small-flange, 126mm hub. Subtract about 330 grams to compare these weights with those of conventional freewheels.

Less Weight

The weight saving possible with small sprockets and chainwheels appeals to me. It makes more sense than drilling holes in highly stressed components. An alpine gear train using a 52/40 crankset and a 14-17-20-24-28 freewheel weighs about 1 pound, 13 ounces (810 grams). The same gear train using a 41/32 crankset and an 11-13-15-18-22 freewheel weighs about 1 pound, 4 ounces (570 grams). You save more than ½ pound, and you save even more if you use a racing instead of a touring rear derailleur.

My wife doesn't like triple shifting but she wants a low Low. Her bike is an ultra-wide 12-speed using a 40/28 crankset and an 11-13-15-18-24-34 Shimano Freehub. The biggest problem we had with this setup was finding a front

Tooth Profile[2]	Re-mover[3]	Tooth Hardness	Bear-ing Seal	Ease of Changing	Sprocket Versa-tility	Mech. Const.
Tw	N/A	C-40	yes	E	E	E
Tw	N/A	C-40	yes	E	E	E
AsyZ	2N	C-45	no	VG	E	VG
AsyZ	4N	C-45	no	G	VG	VG
AsyZ	4N	C-45	yes	VG	VG	VG
AsyZ	4N	C-45	yes	G	G	VG
AsyZ	4N	C-45	yes	VG	VG	VG
AsyZ	4N	C-45	yes	G	G	VG
AsyZ	4N	C-45	yes	VG	G	VG
AsyZ	4N	C-45	yes	G	F	VG

2. See figure 6-1 on page 94 for the tooth profiles. Sym = symmetrical, or teeth with a chamfer on both sides and a flat top; Asy = asymmetrical, or teeth on the small sprockets have a chamfer on both sides, while teeth on the large sprockets have a chisel profile with the chamfer on the inside. Tw = twist-tooth, or teeth chamfered on the inside and twisted clockwise; AsyZ = asymmetrical zigzag, which is the same as asymmetrical except that the teeth on the largest sprockets are set alternately left and right.
3. Remover symbols: Sp = splined; 2N = two notches; 4N = 4 notches.

derailleur that mounted low enough and cleared the chainstay. Her gear train has been in service for five years.

Chordal Action

The mechanical engineering textbooks recommend 16-tooth minimum sprockets for maximum efficiency and chain life. At 400 rpm, a 14-tooth sprocket can transmit 50 percent more horsepower than an 11-tooth sprocket. However, bicycle gear trains are not industrial chain drives and sound engineering principles don't necessarily apply. The main problem with very small sprockets is "chordal action." The sprocket isn't completely round so the chain moves with a jerky action. The uneven movement amounts to 2 percent for a 16-

tooth sprocket, 3 percent for a 13-tooth and 4½ percent for an 11-tooth sprocket. I can't detect the chordal action in my 11-tooth gear trains. Small-wheel bicycles like the Moulton AM-7 use tiny sprockets to avoid monster chainwheels. At the International Human Powered Vehicle Association finals, the Moulton entry used a 10-tooth sprocket to go 50 mph at a cadence of 120. They had a 9-tooth sprocket in reserve, if the rider had needed it.

High Chain Force and High Tooth Wear

As you reduce the diameters of the sprockets and the chainwheels, the chain tension must increase to transmit the same power. An 11-tooth drivetrain stresses the chain 27 percent more than a 14-tooth drivetrain. The answer seems to be to make stronger chains. The Sedisport Pro, Regina CX, and Shimano Dura-Ace racing chains are among the strongest made.

The higher chain forces work against fewer teeth. Without question, smaller sprockets wear out faster. The response has been to make the small sprockets out of very hard alloy steels. I've been using 11-tooth sprockets for more than six years and I've only worn a small hook in one or two. However, I'm more of a spinner than a masher and only use my highest gears to pedal down hills.

Tooth Jump

Tooth jump is the most severe problem that you encounter with tiny sprockets. I suspect it's the main reason that so few professional racers or tandems use 11-tooth sprockets. It's unpleasant when you're really stomping on the pedals to have the chain jump a tooth or two and the pedal fall a couple of inches. To avoid tooth jump, the rear derailleur should position the jockey pulley close to the sprocket and well forward. This provides more chain wrap.

Summing up, if you have a 14-tooth freewheel and you're happy with your High, stick with it. If you're buying a new crankset and a new freewheel for loaded touring or for sport touring, you might as well order a freewheel with a 13-tooth small sprocket. The benefits exceed the demerits. If you're buying a racing freewheel, buy a 12- or 13-tooth small sprocket depending on how high you want your High (11-tooth sprockets are still pretty much a gear freak's specialty item). Keep the size of your large chainwheel between 45 and 52 teeth. If you find that you never use your High, install a 15-tooth sprocket to give you a useful High.

Largest Large Sprocket

Choosing the largest freewheel sprocket is more straightforward than choosing the smallest. The economical way to get a lower Low is to install the largest sprocket that your freewheel (or rear derailleur) will handle. Regina makes a 31-tooth sprocket, Maillard a 32-tooth sprocket. (The Maillard sprocket board has a place for a 34, but they are very rare.) Shimano makes a 34-tooth sprocket for both Freehubs and regular freewheels. Dura-Ace and 600 EX sprockets top out at 28 teeth, but the lower-priced sprockets are completely interchangeable except for color.

SunTour is special. They make a 38-tooth AG (alpine gear) sprocket that requires a special AG rear derailleur. It's most useful for economy Lows on bicycles like the Schwinn Varsity, which has a 39-tooth inner chainwheel. No smaller chainwheel is available and it doesn't make economic sense to install a new crankset. You can get a 31-inch Low with a 34-tooth sprocket. If that isn't low enough, you can get 28-inch Low with the 38-tooth sprocket. Shifting with the AG rear derailleur is good but not excellent.

SunTour now makes 34-tooth sprockets for all of their freewheels. They used to play games with the gear freaks. They made 34s for their low-priced Perfect/Pro-Compe freewheels but only 32s for their top-quality Winners. The Perfect splined sprockets had slightly deeper splines, so you had to file them a bit to use them on a Winner. Old SunTour Perfect large sprockets had an excessive amount of set on their zig-zag teeth and they worked poorly with narrow chains.

The main reason not to use a 34-tooth sprocket is indexed shifting. So far, both Shimano and SunTour are limiting their rear derailleurs to 32-tooth sprockets in the index mode. In the nonindex mode, today's touring rear derailleurs shift like gangbusters on the "buzz saws." If your gear scheme only involves a 31- or 32-tooth large sprocket, buy a Shimano or SunTour freewheel anyway because the Japanese wide-range freewheels shift the best and you may want a lower Low in the future.

Mechanical Construction

The best mechanical design for freewheels calls for both a strong rear hub and a strong freewheel body. The two requirements often conflict (I talk about hub construction in chapter 11). The Shimano Freehub and the Maillard Helicomatic take a different approach. They integrate the hub and the free-wheel, which allows them to locate the hub bearings next to the dropout. This puts the load right next to the dropout and results in fewer broken axles. The integrated design requires that the hole in the smallest splined sprocket be bigger than the freewheel body. Shimano's 11-tooth No. 1 sprocket and 12-tooth splined No. 2 sprocket means that the Freehub's freewheel body is only 1.35 inches in diameter. Shimano has to go to special lengths to provide an adequate ratchet in this small diameter. The Helicomatic uses a more conventional freewheel design and its sprocket arrangement isn't quite as flexible.

Designers of conventional freewheels face a different set of problems. As long as the smallest sprocket had 14 teeth, the freewheel body diameter could be designed to fit inside the 15-tooth splined No. 2 sprocket. When the market demanded 11-, 12-, and 13-tooth sprockets, there were problems. The makers solve these problems in different ways.

Some makers use a narrow 4-speed freewheel body and screw one or two of the outer sprockets onto the fourth sprocket. The small outer sprockets hang outboard of the large-diameter body. This stresses the outboard freewheel bearings and makes it harder to change sprockets. Other makers step the freewheel body and thread the small outer sprockets onto the small-diameter outer section. The larger-diameter middle sprockets thread or spline onto the larger-diameter section, which holds pawls, ratchet, and inboard bearings. Some bodies have three steps.

Ease of Changing Sprockets

The ease with which sprockets can be changed has two aspects. First, how easy is it to take off the old sprockets and install new ones? Second, how many sprockets do you have to own to cover your needs? Shimano Freehubs and Maillard Helicomatics win hands down on both points.

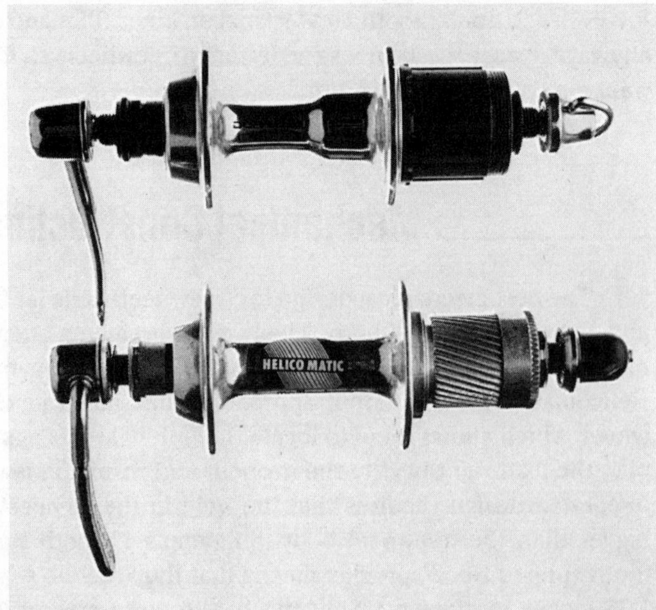

PHOTO 6-2

Freewheel-hub combinations: Shimano Freehub (top) and Maillard Helicomatic (bottom).

Ease of Sprocket Removal

The most convenient design for easy sprocket changing has a threaded sprocket on the outside and splined inner sprockets. That's how the Shimano Freehub works. You unscrew the small sprocket, zip on a stack of spacers and splined sprockets, and screw the small sprocket back on. The Maillard Helicomatic is similar. Both Maillard and Shimano let you pre-assemble the sprockets into a cassette, but this hasn't been a big advantage.

The freewheels that pair the two small sprockets together are harder to work on. Basically, the more threaded sprockets and the more different thread diameters and spline diameters you have to deal with, the more difficult it is to change sprockets. If you're buying a freewheel to incorporate your ultimate gear scheme, easy sprocket changes don't matter very much. If you plan to change your sprockets every few months (or every race), then ease of changing sprockets is important. (Table 6-1 rates this feature.)

Number of Sprockets Needed

If your freewheel has threaded pairs, different thread diameters, different spline diameters, and different tooth profiles for different positions on the freewheel, then few, if any, sprockets can be used in more than one position. Thus, if you want to be able to change sprockets for different events or different types of riding, you will have to purchase a range of sprockets for each position.

Sprocket Versatility

Sprocket versatility involves four questions concerning the sprockets that are available for each particular freewheel. How small a smallest sprocket is available? How large a smallest sprocket is available? (This second concern is important to Junior racers who are limited to a 90-inch High or to people who want Highs in the 80s.) How large is the largest sprocket? What intermediate sprockets are available in what positions?

SunTour offers six 15-tooth sprockets and four 16-tooth sprockets for use on the Winner Pro. (However, you can't make a Winner Pro with a 16-tooth outer sprocket.) There are seven 15-tooth sprockets and six 16-tooth sprockets available for use on the Regina CX. By contrast, the Shimano Freehub has one threaded sprocket and one splined sprocket in each size and you can even make up a Freehub with an 18-tooth outer sprocket. (Table 6-1 lists the number of sprockets found on each freewheel model, while table 6-2 describes the type of sprockets used and the choices available for each position.)

Making a custom-built freewheel used to be harder because the widely available freewheels had limited sprocket versatility. Now you can make up

(continued on page 106)

TABLE 6-2.

Sprocket Versatility

Make and Model	Sprockets Available[1] Pos. 1	Pos. 2	Pos. 3	Pos. 4	Pos. 5	Pos. 6	Pos. 7	Sprocket Types[2]
Maillard								
700 Course	14–16	15–23 →		17–26, 28, 30, 32 →				1-STh, 2-SSp, 2-LSp
700 Course	13–16	14–18	15–23 →		17–26, 28, 30, 32 →			1-P, 1-STh, 2-SSp, 2-LSp
700 Compact	13–17 →		15–23	16–21	17–26, 28, 30, 32 →			2-STh, 1-SSp, 1-LTh, 2-LSp
700 Compact	12–13	13–15	13–17	15–23	16–21	17–26, 28, 30, 32 →		1-P, 2-STh, 1-SSp, 1-LTh, 2-LSp
700 Helicomatic	14–20	14–26, 28, 30, 32 →						1-STh, 4-SSp
700 Helicomatic	13–16	14–18	14–26, 28, 30, 32 →					1-P, 1-STh, 4-SSp
700 Helicomatic	12–14	13–15	14–18	14–26, 28, 30, 32 →				1-P, 2-STh, 4-SSp
Regina								
Extra/Oro	13–18	14–22	16–24	17–31 →				1-P, 1-STh, 1-LTh, 2-LHTh
Extra/Oro Scalare	13–17	14	14–18	16–24	17–31 →			1-P, 1-STh, 1-LTh, 1-LHTh
Extra/Oro	13–17	14–20	15–22	16–24	17–31 →			1-T, 1-LTh, 2-LHTh
Extra/Oro Synchro	13–18	15–19	16–26, 28, 31, 32 →					1-STh, 1-SSp, 3-LSp
Extra/Oro Synchro	13–16	14–17	15–19	16–26, 28, 31, 32 →				1-P, 1-STh, 1-SSp, 3-LSp
America (CX)	13–18	14–19	15–21	16–26, 28, 31 →				1-STh, 1-SSp, 1-LTh, 2-LSp
America (CX)	12–16	13–17	14–19	15–21	16–26, 28, 31 →			1-P, 1-STh, 1-SSp, 1-LTh, 2-LSp
America (CX-S)	13–15	14–19 →		15–21	16–26, 28, 31 →			1-STh, 2-SSp, 1-LTh, 2-LSp
America (CX-S)	12–16	13–15	14-19 →		15–21	16–26, 28, 31 →		1-P, 1-STh, 2-SSp, 1-LTh, 1-LSp
Shimano								
MF-Z	13–16	14–20	17–21, 26, 28, 30, 32, 34 →					1-STh, 2-SSp, 2-LSp
MF-Z (Z-012)	13–16	14–20 →		17–24, 26, 28, 30, 32, 34 →				1-STh, 2-SSp, 3-LSp

600 EX (MF-6208)	13–17 →	→	15–20	16–26, 28, 30, 32, 34 →	→		1-STh, 2-SSp, 3-LSp
Santé (MF-5000)	12–14	13–15	14–20	16–26, 28 →	→	→	1-ITh, 1-STh, 2-SSp, 3-LSp
Dura-Ace (MF-7400-6)	13–18	14–22 →	→	16–26, 28 →	→		1-STh, 2-SSp, 3-LSp
Dura-Ace (MF-7400-7)	12–14	13–15	14–22 →	→	16–26, 28 →	→	1-ITh, 1-STh, 2-SSp, 3-LSp
Deore XT Freehub (FH-M730)	12–15	13–24, 26, 28, 30, 32, 34 →	→	→	→		1-STh, 5-SSp
Dura-Ace Freehub (FH-7400-6)	11–16	12–26, 28 →	→	→	→		1-STh, 5-SSp
Dura-Ace/ SIS Freehub (FH-7400-7)	12–14	13–26, 28 →	→	→	→	→	1-STh, 6-SSp
SunTour							
Perfect	14–18 →	→	16–28, 30, 32, 34, 38 →	→			2-LTh, 3-LSp
Alpha	13–15	14–22	15–23 →	→	17–28, 30, 32, 34 →		1-STh, 1-LTh, 2-SSp, 2-LSp
Winner	13–15	14–22	15–23	16–26, 28, 30, 32, 34 →			1-STh, 2-SSp, 2-LSp
Winner	13–15	14–16	15–23 →	→	17–26, 28, 30, 32, 34 →		1-P, 1-STh, 2-SSp, 2-LSp
Winner Pro	13–15	14–16	15–23	16–26, 28, 30, 32, 34 →			1-STh, 2-SSp, 2-LSp
Winner Pro	13–15	14–16	15–23 →	→	17–26, 28, 30, 32, 34 →		1-P, 1-STh, 2-SSp, 2-LSp
Winner Pro	13–15	14–22	15–23 →	→	17–26, 28, 30, 32, 34 →		1-STh, 1-SSp, 2-MSp, 2-LSp
Winner Pro	12–14	13–16	14–22	15–23 →	→	17–26, 28, 30, 32, 34 →	1-P, 1-STh, 1-SSp, 2-MSp, 2-LSp

1. The sprockets are numbered from the outside to the inside, so Pos. 1 refers to the outer, smallest sprocket. The designation 17–26, 28, 30, 32 means that 17-, 18-, 19-, 20-, 21-, 22-, 23-, 24-, 25-, 26-, 28-, 30-, and 32-tooth sprockets are available for these positions.

2. Sprocket types indicate the sprocket arrangement from smallest to largest. P = pair, a small, externally threaded sprocket mating with a larger, internally threaded sprocket; T = triple, three sprockets threaded together. STh = small thread; LTh = large thread; SSp = small spline; MSp = medium spline; LSp = large spline; ITh = internal thread; LHTh = left-hand thread (found only on Regina Oro large sprockets). 1-STh, 2-SSp, 2-LSp means one small-threaded sprocket, two small-splined sprockets, and two large-splined sprockets.

almost any reasonable sprocket combination. However, only SunTour and Regina make 27-tooth sprockets. At 28 teeth and higher, you have to pick even numbers. And not all freewheels can be made up into a straight block.

Weight

The freewheel is a big, heavy lump of metal, so its weight is important to the weight fanatics. As discussed earlier, one way to save weight is to use smaller sprockets and smaller chainwheels for the same gears. The other alternative is to make the freewheel body and the sprockets out of aluminum or titanium.

Currently, there are four alloy freewheels available: the Campagnolo C-Record, the Maillard 700 Course, the SunTour MicroLite, and the Zeus. The C-Record is very expensive. The Maillard and the SunTour are expensive and the Zeus is a bargain. If you buy an alloy freewheel, expect to change sprockets

PHOTO 6-3 Range of freewheel sprockets: Shimano Dura-Ace Freehub, 11 to 16 teeth (upper left); Maillard 700, 12 to 17 teeth (lower left); SunTour Perfect, 14 to 38 teeth (right).

frequently because aluminum sprockets wear faster than steel sprockets. Of course if you can afford an alloy freewheel, you probably won't worry about sprocket expense.

Bearing Seals

Conventional folklore says that you shouldn't grease freewheels because the grease will harden and cause the pawls to hang up. Then along comes Phil Wood with his ingenious freewheel greaser. Phil assures me that Phil grease will not harden in a normal freewheel lifetime. I believe him, but I haven't bought one of Phil's grease guns yet. All four major freewheel makers say to oil and not to grease their freewheels.

I still treat my freewheels in the time-honored fashion. Every six months or so, I flush them out with kerosene and then I pour oil in the front until it comes out the back. Since oil doesn't do much to keep water out of the freewheel body if you ride in the wet or in the outback, mountain bikers demand something better. Fortunately, the best of today's freewheels include labyrinth seals to keep the oil inside and the water and dirt outside. This feature is shown in table 6-1.

Tooth Hardness

The harder the teeth, the longer a sprocket will last before it develops a hook and has to be replaced. Worn sprockets and stretched chains cause poor shifting and chain jump. The small sprockets wear out first. Sprocket wear is the main argument against using freewheels with aluminum or titanium sprockets. You save weight but you have to replace the sprockets regularly. In Table 6-1, the numbers used to describe tooth hardness are taken from the C scale of the Rockwell hardness test. Teeth rated C-20 and below are relatively soft and short-lived, while those rated C-40 and above are relatively hard and long-lived.

Type of Remover

There are two general kinds of removers, *splined* and *notched.* With a splined remover, there is less chance of gouging up the face of the freewheel body. There are two kinds of splined removers, *solid* and *shell* types. The solid models require you to completely disassemble the hub before you can remove the freewheel. The shell models fit around the outside of the axle cones, but they're more delicate. Phil Wood makes a series of shell removers for those models that come only in solid versions. With a notched remover, use the quick-release skewer to make sure that the remover is securely locked into the notches. I try to have a remover for every freewheel that I've tested. At last count, I was up to sixteen. And you wonder that I'm just a bit paranoid about standardization.

Freewheel Makers

In the other component chapters, I cover only the components that are currently in production and are widely available in the aftermarket. Freewheels are an exception because you can still buy sprockets for obsolete freewheels. To help you decide between revising your present freewheel or buying a new one, I list both current and obsolete freewheels in tables 6-1 and 6-2, and also describe them below.

Maillard

Maillard makes three different brands of freewheels: Atom, Normandy, and Maillard. The Atom is the lower-priced model for the OEM market. The Normandy uses a 4-speed body and an outer two-sprocket pair. It has a large-diameter bore and is the lightest model. The top-of-the-line Maillard 700 won 11 straight Tour de France victories. The various models that bear this name are usually carried by the mail-order houses and bike shops. The Maillard 700 comes with an expensive all-alloy body or with a steel body. The 700 Course body can be made into wide-spaced 5- and 6-speed freewheels and the 700 Compact can be made into narrow-spaced 6- and 7-speed freewheels.

Maillard's Helicomatic hub-freewheel has almost the same sprocket versatility as Shimano's Freehub and in some ways (larger-diameter bearings and ratchet) it's a superior piece of mechanical engineering. In the past, my main objection to Maillard was their old-fashioned sprocket tooth profile. Wide-range Maillard freewheels simply didn't shift as well as their Japanese competition. I observed this on my derailleur testing machine and I could feel the difference out on the road. I once talked about this to their director general at the Long Beach Bike Show. He said that Maillard had built asymmetrical sprockets á la SunTour, but they couldn't detect any difference and the European buyers preferred symmetrical sprockets.

Maillard freewheels and Sedis chains are now owned by Sachs-Huret, and the Huret ARIS indexed shifting system will use Maillard and Sedis. In 1987,

Maillard provided chisel-shaped teeth on their largest sprockets. In 1988, they introduced a brand-new ARIS tooth profile.

Regina

There are three series of Regina freewheels: Extra/Oro, Extra-BX/Oro-BX, and CX/CX-S. *Extra* and *Oro* are quality designations. They're essentially the same except that Oro sprockets are brass plated. I recall an apochryphal story about the Regina inspector standing in front of two boxes spinning freewheels. The extra-smooth ones went into the Oro box and the rest went into the Extra box.

Extra/Oro is out of production. It's an antique design that's been around for 40 years. Milremo and Atom used to make lower-priced Oro clones but they've passed away. It's very hard to change sprockets on these freewheels because all of the sprockets are threaded. The two largest sprockets have left-hand threads and you have to remove the freewheel and lock the body with a special tool to change the big sprockets.

The main reason that this freewheel survives is that there are so many of them (and Atoms and Milremos) still in service and so many bike stores have sprocket boards. That's a considerable investment since there are 59 different sprockets on a full board. There's even a special "Scalare" body to allow making up a 13-14-15-16-17 straight block. The 6-speed Oro uses a triplet. The little sprocket screws into the second sprocket, which screws into the third sprocket, which (finally) screws on to the body. Today, there's no good reason to buy an old Extra/Oro freewheel, but if you have one, you might decide to change the sprockets.

Regina replaced the old Extra/Oro series with the Extra-BX and the Oro-BX. In 1987, the BX models were upgraded for indexed shifting. The upgraded version, called Synchro, has chisel-shaped teeth and uniform sprocket spacing. These are modern designs with one threaded sprocket and two sizes of splined sprockets in the 5-speed model and a two-sprocket pair in the 6-speed model. Synchro is made only in wide-spaced versions. This is the freewheel to use if you build a do-it-yourself indexed system with Campagnolo's Syncro levers.

The CX and CX-S are Regina's modern, top-of-the-line freewheels. They're very similar to the SunTour Winner. One body lets you make up wide and narrow 5-, 6-, and 7-speed freewheels. The wide-spaced 5- and 6-speed versions are called CX and the narrow-spaced 6- and 7-speed versions are called CX-S. They have all of the complexity of the Winner and then some. Regina added an extra threaded sprocket in the middle. There are 47 different sprockets and five different spacers on the sprocket board. The CX and CX-S use symmetrical sprockets in all sizes. The America is a special version of the CX and CX-S with a plastic bearing seal. It comes in a neat can that you use for cleaning and oiling.

Shimano

Shimano makes freewheels in four different price-quality levels for the aftermarket: Dura-Ace, Santé, 600 EX, and the Z series. Shimano currently imports Dura-Ace and Deore XT Freehubs into the USA. Shimano avoided narrow-spacing until 1987. Now racers can get indexed shifting, narrow-spaced 7-speed Santé and Dura-Ace freewheels with sprockets available from 12 to 28 teeth. The Santé and Dura-Ace freewheels are identical except for the finish of the sprockets. Shimano does not believe in sprocket pairs. On the Dura-Ace and Santé freewheels, the small outer sprocket threads into the body rather than into the No. 2 sprocket.

Thanks to their twist-tooth profile, all of Shimano's freewheels and Freehubs are superior shifting, particularly with Uniglide chains. Shimano freewheels and Freehubs have a minimum number of different kinds of sprockets. It's easy to change sprockets and it requires a minimum number of sprockets.

Shimano Freehubs are the gear freak's favorite because of the ease of changing sprockets and their sprocket versatility, from an 11-tooth (Dura-Ace) or 12-tooth (all other models) smallest sprocket all the way to a 34-tooth largest sprocket. There are five or six different Freehub models but Shimano is currently only importing Dura-Ace and Deore XT. Until 1987, all Freehubs were wide-spaced 5- or 6-speeds. (Shimano made a wide-spaced 7-speed Dura-Ace AX Freehub in the aerodynamic age. Now it's a collector's item.)

In 1987, Shimano decided that the racers wanted 7-speed SIS. So they came out with narrow spacers and narrower threaded small sprockets. You can now make the Dura-Ace Freehub into either a wide-spaced 6-speed or a narrow-spaced 7-speed. The early (1981) Freehubs had mechanical reliability problems. Over the years, Shimano has made frequent modifications so that the Freehub is now one of the most reliable units available.

SunTour

SunTour currently makes four freewheel models: Winner Pro, Winner, Alpha, and Perfect. SunTour dominates the low-priced freewheel market. There

PHOTO 6-4

Narrow-spaced 7-speed freewheel bodies: left to right, Regina CX-S, Shimano Dura-Ace, and SunTour Winner Pro.

are probably more low-priced Perfect and Pro-Compe freewheels in use than everything else combined. (These two models are the same except for the Pro-Compe's gold-plated sprockets.) Over the years, the Perfect and Pro-Compe have improved in quality, but they haven't changed in essential detail since SunTour entered the U.S. market in the early 1970s. There are two threaded sprockets and three splined sprockets on the 5-speed model. There used to be a variety of wide- and narrow-spaced 6-speed models as well.

Right from the start, SunTour used a symmetrical tooth profile on the threaded sprockets and an asymmetrical profile on the large splined sprockets. In the late 1970s, they provided zigzag teeth with a distinct set—one left, one right—on the largest sprockets. This interfered with the shifting of narrow-spaced chains and SunTour reduced the amount of set. SunTour makes a 38-tooth sprocket for the Perfect series. It gives you an idea of the impact of the indexed shifting revolution, that SunTour is replacing Perfect and Pro-Compe with a new Alpha series. Alpha is a low-priced, wide-spaced 6-speed freewheel similar to the old Pro-Compe.

SunTour made substantial revisions to their freewheels in 1987 to accommodate AccuShift. You can tell the AccuShift-compatible models because they have four notches for a four-notch remover. SunTour's top freewheels, Winner Pro and Winner, were little changed, but the narrow-spaced 6-speed versions will no longer be sold. Narrow-spaced 7-speed Winner freewheels have uneven spacing: The smaller sprockets are wider-spaced than the larger ones. SunTour designed the AccuShift shift levers to match the uneven spacing.

SunTour developed and marketed the first narrow-spaced freewheels, known as "Ultra" type. SunTour Ultra-6, wide-range freewheels shift better with narrow spacing and narrow chains than any others. SunTour's top-of-the-line freewheel has progressed from Winner to New Winner and back to Winner and Winner Pro. The Winner Pro has an excellent labyrinth seal to keep out water.

The current Winner series was designed to let the bike shops build up wide and narrow, 5-, 6-, and 7-speed freewheels with just one body. It's a complicated system. There are 41 sprockets and seven spacers on the Winner sprocket board. It's absolutely essential that you use SunTour's chart when you assemble a Winner. I've answered dozens of letters from people who have misassembled their Winners, turning them into losers. I once calculated that there are 534,287 wrong ways to assemble a 6-speed Winner, and only 1 right way.

SunTour tries to keep some sprocket interchangeability between their different models and between new and old models. In the 1986 metamorphosis from New Winner to Winner/Winner Pro, the second set of threaded sprockets went from large-threaded to small-splined. SunTour both threaded and splined the Winner Pro body so the shops could use up their old stocks. You can use the

PHOTO 6-5 Wide-spaced freewheel bodies: left to right, Maillard 700 Course (5- or 6-speed); Regina Oro BX (5- or 6-speed); Regina America (6-speed); Shimano MF-Z (6-speed); and Maillard Helicomatic (5-speed).

Perfect/Pro-Compe splined sprockets, including the 38-tooth "buzz saw," on the Winner bodies.

Everybody Else

Everybody else consists of two aluminum-bodied freewheels made by Campagnolo and Zeus. Campagnolo introduced their ultra-light, 6- or 7-speed C-Record freewheel in 1983. Symmetrical profile sprockets are available in sizes ranging from 12 to 28 teeth. Cost for this freewheel runs around $200 for the 13-tooth version. The 12-tooth version uses two titanium sprockets, which adds an extra $100 to the price. Campagnolo provides a $500 tool kit in a plushly lined hardwood box to properly service their freewheel. Campagnolo replacement sprockets are priced accordingly.

At the other end of the alphabet and the price spectrum, Zeus makes the least expensive alloy freewheel. It comes in wide-spaced 5- and 6-speed and narrow-spaced 7-speed versions. The small sprockets are steel. Sprockets are available from 13 to 30 teeth. The 5-speed model's smallest sprocket has 14 teeth. Prices run in the $75 to $100 range.

Frank's Favorite Freewheel

Picking my favorite freewheel is easy. It's the Shimano Dura-Ace Freehub hands down for both racing and loaded touring. It has the best shifting tooth profile, and it's strong and reliable because of the wide-spaced hub bearings. It's also adequately sealed against water. The sprocket versatility and the ease of changing sprockets on this freewheel is the best available. I have eight Freehubs on the Berto bicycle fleet.

CHAPTER 7

All about Rear Derailleurs

If your present rear derailleur is more than five years old, you have a treat in store for you. Today's rear derailleurs are so much better behaved than their parents that they make shifting almost second nature; in addition, they're rugged and reliable. If you install one of the new indexed shifting packages, you'll find that you can shift on the rear just by pushing the shift lever to the next indexed setting. You can also downshift to a lower gear on a hill with a lot more certainty.

In the past decade, I've tested more than 100 rear derailleurs and written seven articles about them. During that period, derailleurs multiplied like amoebas. There are now a dozen derailleur companies and some of them make more than a dozen different models. Two recent developments, mountain bikes and indexed shifting, have dramatically changed the derailleur market.

Mountain bikers demand bulletproof, wide-range equipment. The old touring components weren't good enough and Shimano and SunTour rushed in to fill the demand. If you're touring with an old wide-range rear derailleur, you'll be impressed with the superior performance of the new mountain bike models.

Indexed Shifting Rear Derailleurs

Indexed shifting is a litmus test for rear derailleur quality. A rear derailleur that works well with indexed shift levers will shift splendidly with friction levers.

Indexed shifting has caused a major shakeout in the derailleur business. In 1987, Shimano and SunTour dropped about 30 derailleurs from their catalogs because they weren't suitable for indexed shifting. Huret and the other small makers still make their old models, but the market is drying up. Campagnolo's

TABLE 7-1.

Racing Rear Derailleurs

Make and Model	Cost ($)	Weight[1] (gr.)	Largest FW Sprocket (teeth)[2] Advert.	Largest FW Sprocket (teeth)[2] Meas.	Chain Wrap-Up Capacity (teeth)	Cable Travel[3] (in.)	Lever Force (lb.)	Suitable for Indexed Shifting[4]
Campagnolo								
C-Record (102050)	140–190	215	28	30	26	0.53	6	maybe
Super Record (102018)	120–170	195	28	30	28	0.56	7	maybe
Nuovo Record (1020A)	80–120	200	26	28	26	0.56	7	no
Nuovo Victory (102045)	50–65	195	30	30	26	0.54	6	maybe
Nuovo Triomphe (102055)	30–40	200	30	30	26	0.55	6	maybe
Huret								
Jubilee (AR 44.1D)	40–60	145	28	28	30	0.73	6	no
Shimano								
Dura-Ace/SIS (RD-7401)	70–90	205	26	28	26	0.61	4	yes
Santé/SIS (RD-5000)	50–70	190	24	24	24	0.72	3	yes
600 EX/SIS (RD-6208)	35–50	200	28	28	28	0.72	4	yes
105/SIS (RD-1050)	25–35	255	28	30	28	0.76	4	yes
SunTour								
Superbe Pro (RD-SB00)	85–120	195	23 (26)	24	26	0.59	5	yes
Sprint 9000 (RD-SP10)	30–45	205	23 (26)	24	26	0.61	5	yes
Cyclone 7000 (RD-CL10-SS)	25–35	220	26	26	30	0.64	6	yes

1. I weighed rear derailleurs without hangers.
2. See the text under Maximum Freewheel Sprocket on page 124. The maximum sprocket is different depending on the drop of the derailleur hanger. I measured the racing rear derailleur using a hanger with a 1-inch drop. SunTour's catalog shows two maximum sprocket ratings: a larger sprocket for normal shifting, and a smaller sprocket for indexed shifting. I show the normal-shifting sprocket in parentheses.
3. I tested the racing rear derailleurs with a narrow-spaced seven-sprocket freewheel. The cable travel shown is the amount required to shift the derailleur from the smallest sprocket to the largest.

Syncro indexed shift levers work adequately with the newest Campy rear derailleurs, but the company is betting that serious bikers will continue to use friction levers.

Today, there are two kinds of rear derailleurs: current models that are suitable for indexed shifting and obsolete models that may or may not shift

No. of Spring-Loaded Pivots	Design Features: Cage Pivot Location[5]	Slant Parallelogram	Angle Adjust. Screw	Cable Length Adjuster	Chain Gap (in.) Min.	Max.	Rigidity and Longevity	Indexed Shifting Performance	Friction Shifting Performance
1	Frw	no	no	no	2.1	3.3	E	G	G
1	Frw	no	no	no	1.9	3.1	VG	P	P
1	Frw	no	no	no	1.6	3.4	VG	P	P
1	Frw	no	3 pos.[6]	no	1.3	2.6	VG	G	G
1	Frw	no	no	no	1.8	3.2	E	P	F
1	Cnt	no	yes	no	1.7	2.2	F	P	VG
2	Frw	yes	yes	yes	1.4	2.0	VG	E	E
2	Frw	yes	no	yes	1.5	1.8	VG	E	E
2	Frw	yes	no	yes	1.1	2.4	G	E	E
2	Frw	yes	yes	yes	1.0	1.7	G	E	E
2	Frw	yes	yes	yes	1.4	2.2	VG	VG	VG
2	Frw	yes	yes	yes	1.4	2.2	G	VG	VG
2	Frw	yes	yes	yes	1.6	2.1	G	VG	VG

4. Huret, Shimano, and SunTour make complete indexed systems. The models shown as "yes" are those that they say are suitable. Campagnolo says that their Syncro indexed shift lever works with the C-Record, Super Record, Nuovo Victory, and Nuovo Triomphe rear derailleurs. It does, after a fashion. I show a "maybe" in these cases.

5. Cnt means that the cage pivot and the jockey pulley are on the same axis. Frw means that the cage pivot is located forward of the centerline of the two pulleys.

6. The Nuovo Victory uses a three-position bushing instead of a screw for adjusting the mounting angle.

precisely enough for indexed shift levers. As I explained in chapter 4, indexed shifting works best with a completely coordinated gear train: rear derailleur, freewheel, chain, and shift levers. Thus, if you plan to buy a new rear derailleur, it makes sense to buy a model that's suitable for indexed shifting, in case you decide to complete the conversion later.

TABLE 7-2.

Touring Rear Derailleurs

Make and Model	Cost ($)	Weight[1] (gr.)	Largest FW Sprocket (teeth)[2] Advert.	Largest FW Sprocket (teeth)[2] Meas.	Chain Wrap-Up Capacity (teeth)	Cable Travel[3] (in.)	Lever Force (lb.)	Suitable for Indexed Shifting[4]
Campagnolo								
Victory LX (102047)	55–70	200	32	32	38	0.50	5	maybe
Huret								
Eco Duopar (AR-401T)	30–40	285	36	36	36	0.56	5	no
Shimano								
Deore XT (RD-M730)	35–50	260	32	32	38	0.58	4	yes
Deore (RD-M760)	25–35	310	32	32	38	0.58	4	yes
SunTour								
XC-9000 (RD-XC00)	40–50	255	32(34)	34	39	0.58	4	yes
XC-Sport 7000 (RD-XS00)	35–40	290	32(34)	34	39	0.58	4	yes

1. I weighed rear derailleurs without hangers.

2. See the text under Maximum Freewheel Sprocket on page 124. The maximum sprocket is different depending on the drop of the derailleur hanger. I measured the touring rear derailleurs using a hanger with a 1.3-inch drop. SunTour's catalog shows two maximum sprocket ratings: a larger sprocket for normal shifting, and a smaller sprocket for indexed shifting. I show the normal-shifting sprocket in parentheses.

3. I tested the touring rear derailleurs with a wide-spaced six-sprocket freewheel. The cable travel shown is the amount required to shift the derailleur from the smallest sprocket to the largest.

Derailleur Testing

In 1979, I built a derailleur testing machine. It's simply a gear motor installed on an old bicycle frame to turn the crank at a steady 70 rpm. A pointer attached to the shift lever and a protractor let me read exactly where each shift takes place. I run each rear derailleur up and down the scale on each chainwheel. After each shift, I adjust the shift lever until the chain is exactly centered on the freewheel sprocket. This is just what you do when you quiet the "coffee grinding" at the rear. The difference between the shift point and the recentered point measures the derailleur's shifting precision.

A precise-shifting rear derailleur requires minimum lever movement after each shift. A sloppy-shifting rear derailleur requires large adjustments after most shifts. I measure how much the derailleur shifts "early" or "late" on each

Design Features					Chain Gap (in.)		Rigidity and Longevity	Indexed Shifting Performance	Friction Shifting Performance
No. of Spring-Loaded Pivots	Cage Pivot Location[5]	Slant Parallelogram	Angle Adjust. Screw	Cable Length Adjuster	Min.	Max.			
1	Cnt	no	3 pos.[6]	no	1.4	3.0	VG	F	F
1	Cnt	no	yes	no	1.7	2.0	F	P	G
2	Frw	yes	yes	yes	1.1	2.4	G	E	E
2	Frw	yes	yes	yes	1.1	2.4	G	E	E
2	Frw	yes	yes	yes	1.8	2.3	G	G	VG
2	Frw	yes	yes	yes	1.8	2.3	G	G	VG

4. Huret, Shimano, and SunTour make complete indexed systems. The models shown as "yes" are those that they say are suitable. Campagnolo says that their Syncro indexed shift lever works with the Victory LX rear derailleur. It does, after a fashion. I show a "maybe" in this case.

5. Cnt means that the cage pivot and the jockey pulley are on the same axis. Frw means that the cage pivot is located forward of the centerline of the two pulleys.

6. The Victory LX uses a three-position bushing instead of a screw for adjusting the mounting angle.

gear and I use the measurements to calculate the "shifting performance." (Chapter 4 talks about the reasons that rear derailleurs shift early or late.) In the calculations, I score late shifting much more harshly than early shifting. The shifting performance score is included among the ratings in tables 7-1 and 7-2.

Over the years, I've also installed 50 or so different rear derailleurs on my bicycles to check their performance. The road tests have corroborated the machine's results. Interestingly, when designers from Shimano and SunTour visited my home workshop, they knew exactly what I was doing because they use sophisticated versions of my testing machine to design better derailleurs.

Indexed shifting requires rear derailleurs that shift precisely, so that after the indexed shift the jockey pulley is centered under the sprocket. All of the new Shimano and SunTour rear derailleurs that are designed for indexed shifting are very precise. They would all have scored "excellent" or "very good"

PHOTO 7-1

Derailleur testing machine.

with my old tests. Indexed shifting also works best with early-shifting rear derailleurs.

I still use the testing machine to test the new rear derailleurs designed for indexed shifting, but I run the tests differently. I used to test all rear derailleurs with a standard wide-spaced 5-speed freewheel and a standard chain. Now I use a narrow-spaced 7-speed, 12-13-14-15-16-17-18 freewheel for the racing rear derailleurs, and a wide-spaced 6-speed, 13-15-18-22-26-32 freewheel for the touring rear derailleurs.

I use the maker's recommended freewheel and chain for each system so I'm testing the performance of the total system, not just the rear derailleur. I used the following freewheels and chains for the rear derailleur tests:

- Campagnolo: Regina America freewheel and Regina CX-S chain.
- Huret: Maillard freewheel and Sedisport chain.
- Shimano: Dura-Ace twist-tooth freewheel and Narrow Uniglide chain.
- SunTour: Winner Pro freewheel and SunTour Pro chain.

In my old tests of racing rear derailleurs, I used a freewheel with the maker's maximum recommended sprocket. Shimano pointed out that the 1-tooth steps of a "straight block" freewheel are harder on rear derailleurs than 2- or even 3-tooth steps. I checked and they were right. That's why I used a 12- to 18-tooth freewheel to test the racing rear derailleurs.

The tests take four steps. First, I confirm that the total package shifts precisely with its indexed lever. Second, I disconnect the derailleur from its indexed lever and measure exactly where the shifts take place with a calibrated friction lever. Third, I measure the indexed lever's shift points. (The results of this test are shown in figure 4-2 on page 60.) Finally, I compare the fit between the rear derailleur's shift points and the indexed lever's shift points. This measures how much wear and misadjustment the system can tolerate. This new rating, indexed shifting performance, is shown in tables 7-1 and 7-2.

Major Rear Derailleur Design Features

Chapter 4 lists a number of factors that affect rear shifting performance. Most of them involve freewheels, chains, cables and casings, and rear hangers. These factors interact in various perverse and barely predictable ways. No wonder it took so long to invent better rear derailleurs! (The principal parts of a rear derailleur are identified in figure 7-1.)

The ideal rear derailleur moves the jockey pulley in a precise path just in front of the sprockets, regardless of the size of the sprockets or the chainwheels. The designer has four main options available to accomplish this objective.

Number of Pivots

Rear derailleurs can have one or two spring-loaded pivots. Most of today's single-pivot derailleurs are based on Tullio Campagnolo's classic, simple, rugged Gran Sport, which was introduced in 1950. The top pivot doesn't have a spring. It just allows you to pull the derailleur back to remove the back wheel. The lower spring-loaded pivot rotates the cage and wraps up chain. Campagnolo's single-pivot design was copied by SunTour, Huret, Galli, Mavic, Ofmega, Zeus, and many other manufacturers. It's basically a narrow-range design and it has serious limitations for wide-range shifting.

The double-pivot design is based on the Simplex LJ model invented by Lucien Juy 50 years ago. Two spring-loaded pivots are used. The spring in the top pivot pulls the derailleur backwards. The spring in the bottom pivot rotates the cage, winding up chain and pulling the derailleur forward. The two springs and the geometry of the cage keep the jockey pulley close to the sprockets. When Shimano copied the Simplex design, they improved performance by dropping the parallelogram under the top pivot, making it more nearly horizontal. Shimano calls this the "Servo-Panta" mechanism. Most Simplex rear derailleurs now have a horizontal parallelogram. The new SunTour and Huret indexed shifting rear derailleurs incorporate double pivots and dropped parallelograms.

Shimano seems to understand the spring interactions of double-pivot derailleurs better than anyone. Shimano SIS rear derailleurs have more tension in the top springs than Huret, Simplex, or SunTour double-pivot models.

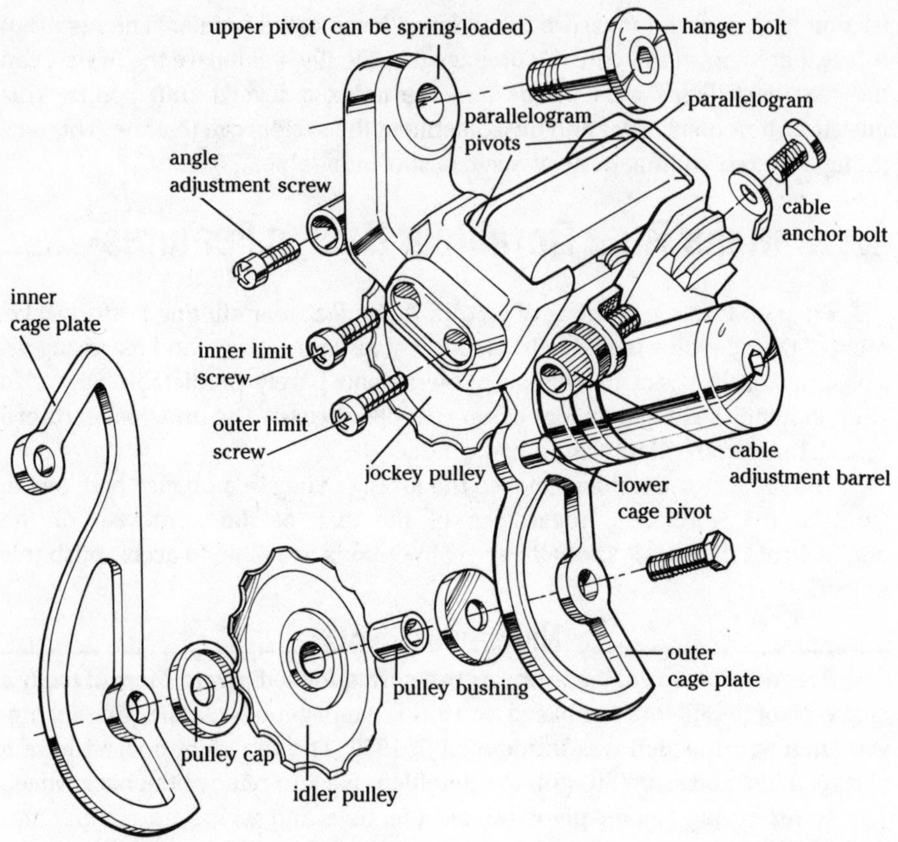

FIGURE 7-1 Rear derailleur nomenclature.

Cage Pivot Location

The pivot for the derailleur cage can be located on the centerline between the two pulleys, or in front of the pulley centerline, or right at the jockey pulley. The original Campagnolo Gran Sport rear derailleur had the cage pivot halfway between the two pulleys. The first Campagnolo Record rear derailleur, introduced in the early 1960s, moved the pivot in front of the jockey pulley. This allows the jockey pulley to swing in an arc back and down as it climbs onto larger sprockets. Almost all current rear derailleurs use this design. The location of the pivot significantly affects the shifting character of the derailleur.

The Huret Jubilee and the Campagnolo Victory touring derailleurs mount the cage pivot on the same axis as the jockey pulley. The jockey pulley moves straight in and out, so it has to be positioned well forward and just low enough to clear the largest freewheel sprockets. The advantage is that rear shifting isn't affected by front shifts. The disadvantage is that the jockey pulley is mounted too low for the small sprockets. The old SunTour VGT was a fixed jockey pulley derailleur. It shifted as well as it did because of the slant parallelogram. Because the jockey pulley has to be mounted so low (to clear the large sprockets), this class of derailleur tends to shift late on the small sprockets.

Slant Parallelograms

SunTour patented the slant parallelogram in the early 1950s. By mounting the parallelogram pivots at an angle, the jockey pulley moves down a ½ inch as it moves inward. All SunTour rear derailleurs have slant parallelograms. It's the basic technical reason for their fine performance. Because of SunTour's patent, the other makers had to use straight parallelograms. When the patent expired in the mid-1980s, Shimano quietly incorporated slant parallelograms into their new derailleurs. The 1988 Huret ARIS and Campagnolo Chorus derailleurs have slant parallelograms. (Tables 7-1 and 7-2 indicate which derailleurs have slant parallelograms.)

Angle Adjustment Screw

When you bolt the rear derailleur onto the hanger, a tab on the derailleur engages the claw of the hanger. This sets the mounting angle, which in turn locates the jockey pulley. This angle is very important to single-pivot rear derailleurs and important to double-pivot rear derailleurs, because it determines the chain gap. If the derailleur has an angle adjustment screw, then you can raise or lower the jockey pulley to match the largest sprocket.

You can also compensate for variations in the claw angle of the hanger. Claw angles aren't standardized. The other makers of rear dropouts kind of copy Campagnolo's rear hangers, but they don't do a very good job. Even Campagnolo doesn't do a very good job of copying Campagnolo because the different Campagnolo rear dropouts and separate hangers have different claw angles.

Shimano provides an angle adjustment screw on all of their indexed shifting rear derailleurs. SunTour provides what looks like an angle adjustment screw on their new rear derailleurs, but it's actually a stop rather than an angle adjuster. Huret provides an accessory adjuster for the Jubilee and the Duopar.

The Campagnolo Nuovo Victory and Victory LX rear derailleurs have a three-position bushing that lets you adjust the mounting angle. No other Campagnolo derailleur has an angle adjuster. If you want to change the angle, you have to file the claw on the hanger. Even if your bicycle has a proper Campagnolo hanger, the angle that's right for a 28-tooth sprocket isn't right for a 12- to 18-tooth straight block. (Table 7-1 and 7-2 show which rear derailleurs have an angle adjustment screw.)

Chain Gap

An ideal rear derailleur has a chain gap between 1 and 2 inches in every gear. Within this range the derailleur will shift precisely and predictably. Tables 7-1 and 7-2 show the minimum and maximum chain gap measured with the extreme combinations of chainwheels and freewheels. (I discussed chain gap at greater length in chapter 4 because it's so important to indexed shifting.)

The indexed shifting rear derailleurs from Shimano, SunTour, and Huret are very similar. Either they read each other's mail, or their design packages are giving the same answer. Their new rear derailleurs all have two spring-loaded pivots, slanted parallelograms, and cage pivots about an inch in front of the jockey pulley.

Minor Design Features

In addition to the four major features, the designer has several other design options.

Cage Pusher Plate

The early rear derailleurs depended entirely on the jockey pulley to lead the chain from sprocket to sprocket. Then, the makers discovered that a larger outer cage would help the chain to climb to the larger sprockets, much like a front derailleur cage. Notice how the outer cages of Campagnolo's rear derailleurs have grown year by year from Nuovo Record to Super Record to C-Record.

Cable Length Adjuster

Some rear derailleurs provide a threaded sleeve where the casing enters the derailleur body. This allows you to set the angle of the shift lever. Otherwise, you have to loosen the cable. Such an adjuster is required for indexed shifting. Campagnolo makes an accessory threaded sleeve that comes as part of the Syncro shift levers. Tables 7-1 and 7-2 show which rear derailleurs have cable adjusters.

Lever Force

Every rear derailleur has a spring to pull the jockey pulley back to the small sprocket. A strong spring requires more lever force to climb and more lever friction to prevent automatic shifting. It's more pleasant to shift with a light lever pull. Shimano "Light Action" rear derailleurs have light springs.

To measure lever pull, I released the friction adjustment on the shift lever. Then I measured how much pull is needed at the end of the shift lever to climb onto the largest sprocket. This measures both the parallelogram spring force and the reluctance of the rear derailleur to shift onto the largest sprocket. Tables 7-1 and 7-2 show the required lever force.

Cable Travel

I used the calibrated shift lever as a caliper to measure the cable travel required to stroke the racing rear derailleurs over a narrow-spaced 7-speed freewheel and to stroke the touring derailleurs over a wide-spaced 6-speed freewheel. (Cable travel is shown in tables 7-1 and 7-2.) There's quite a variation. This gives you some idea of the problems involved in building your own indexed shifting system.

Jockey Pulley Travel

I used to measure the total travel of the jockey pulley with the limit stops all the way out. I don't list this dimension anymore because all modern rear derailleurs have more than 1.65 inches of travel, which will handle a wide-spaced 7-speed freewheel.

Chain Wrap-Up

The derailleur design should position the jockey pulley high enough that the chain wraps around the sprocket for nearly 180 degrees. This is particularly important on the small sprockets. If there is less than, say, six teeth of wrap, the chain may jump forward when you stomp on the pedals, especially with worn chains or worn sprockets.

Moveable Jockey Pulley

The Huret Duopar provided the archetype for the moveable jockey pulley. In 1976, Huret invented and patented a rear derailleur with the jockey pulley mounted on a separate unsprung parallelogram. The jockey pulley on this derailleur floats freely up and down 1½ inches, which is the difference in radius between a 14-tooth and 34-tooth sprocket. The jockey pulley is just the right distance from the sprockets in every gear, so the Duopar shifts a bit early in every gear. SunTour and Shimano responded with their own moveable jockey pulley rear derailleurs, the MounTech and the Super Plate. They had to install a spring in the second parallelogram to get around Huret's patent. Moveable jockey pulley derailleurs have extra pivots and extra parts so they're inherently less rugged than conventional rear derailleurs. Mountain bikers want strong equipment, so the MounTech and the Super Plate were dropped. The Duopar is the only survivor of the genre.

Derailleur Capacity

There are two rear derailleur capacity specifications: the largest freewheel sprocket that the derailleur can climb onto, and the total amount of chain that it can wind up. Tables 7-1 and 7-2 show these capacities.

Maximum Freewheel Sprocket

Today's derailleurs fall into two categories: racing and touring. The only mid-range derailleurs still available are low-end steel models. The top-of-the-line racing derailleurs can handle at least a 24-tooth maximum sprocket. The less expensive models can handle 28- or 30-tooth sprockets.

Today's touring derailleurs can handle 32- or 34-tooth sprockets. However, most of today's touring derailleurs need to be mounted on a touring hanger to handle a 34-tooth sprocket. If your bicycle has a racing dropout, you may have to restrict yourself to 30- or 32-tooth sprockets. The old wide-range touring derailleurs used to be able to handle 36- or 38-tooth sprockets.

There's a sub-species of gear freaks who constantly seek lower Lows. (I don't consider myself a member since I limit myself to a Low of 19 inches.) These people use SunTour's 38-tooth alpine sprocket or they buy custom-made sprockets as large as 42-tooth. With the demise of Shimano's Super Plate and SunTour's AG, the Huret Duopar is the only surviving rear derailleur that can shift over these "buzz saw" sprockets.

Tables 7-1 and 7-2 show two maximum freewheel sprockets: the advertised size and the tested size. The makers underrate their capacities a little, partly in fear of the trial lawyers and partly to make sure that indexed shifting will work, even in the worst case. I tested the racing rear derailleurs with a narrow-spaced freewheel and a racing derailleur hanger with a 1-inch drop. I tested the touring rear derailleurs with a wide-spaced freewheel and a touring hanger with a 1.1-inch drop. They shifted well in both the friction and the indexed mode with the maximum sprocket shown.

Maximum Chain Wrap-Up Capacity

The *wrap-up capacity* is determined by the distance between the jockey pulley and the tension pulley. When the cage is fully extended, the chain must reach around the large chainwheel–large sprocket combination. When the cage is fully wound back, the chain shouldn't hang loose in the small chainwheel–small sprocket combination. Even if you never plan to use the large chainwheel–large sprocket gear, you must size your chain length to handle it. Otherwise, you could wreck your derailleur or worse with a missed shift.

You measure wrap-up capacity by adding the number of teeth on the largest chainwheel and the largest sprocket and subtracting the number of teeth on the smallest chainwheel and the smallest sprocket. Double-pivot derailleurs can often wrap up more chain than advertised. However, if you take advantage of this extra wrap-up capacity, they shift poorly.

I used to advise readers to exceed the advertised wrap-up capacities and I listed larger numbers based on my own tests. However, I don't think that you can take much liberty with the advertised capacity of the current Shimano and SunTour rear derailleurs and still expect good indexed shifting.

There's one exception. Triple-chainwheel bikes shouldn't use the inner chainwheel with the small freewheel sprockets because the gears are duplicates and the chain may rub on the middle chainwheel. For triples, calculate the wrap-up by adding together the big chainwheel and the biggest sprocket, but subtract the small chainwheel and the smallest middle sprocket that you plan to use, rather than the smallest one on the freewheel. If you ever accidentally shift into one of the little-little combinations, the chain will hang loose, but it doesn't matter.

Rigidity and Longevity

With rear derailleurs, as with most things, you get pretty much what you pay for. The more expensive rear derailleurs have better bearings for the pulleys and the parallelogram. The spring-loaded pivot(s) is sealed to keep out moisture. The parallelogram pivots use stainless steel pins and brass bushings. All of these features increase the rigidity of the derailleur and they lengthen the life until wear causes shifting to get sloppy. I inspected each of the derailleurs and my judgment of their rigidity and longevity is shown in tables 7-1 and 7-2.

Racing Rear Derailleurs

An ideal racing rear derailleur has the following characteristics:

- Quick positive shifting from one sprocket to the next, under load, without hanging up or skipping the desired sprocket.
- Precise, predictable shifting response to lever movement.
- Light, uniform lever pressure when shifting.
- Enough chain wrapped around the sprockets to avoid chain jump under load in any gear.
- Capacity to shift over the largest sprocket normally used by racers (24 teeth).

- Ability to shift over narrow-spaced 7-speed freewheels.
- Rugged, reliable, long-wearing construction.
- Lightweight.

In selecting a racing rear derailleur you have two basic choices: conventional or indexed shifting.

Conventional Shifting

If you opt for conventional shifting, you can still use a Shimano or SunTour indexed shifting rear derailleur. That's what I would buy. The indexed SunTours will shift much like the older models. The indexed Shimanos will shift early so that you'll have to revise your shifting technique. However, most people who buy a conventional rear derailleur and friction shift levers in today's market will be buying either a Campagnolo single-pivot derailleur or one of the clones from Galli, Mavic, Ofmega, and Zeus. These traditional derailleurs have won thousands of races. They're rugged, reliable, and completely proven. They also shift imprecisely. Most racers grew up with Campagnolo Nuovo Records, learning to snap the lever too far and then pull back. Many racers think derailleurs are supposed to shift that way.

Indexed Shifting

If you opt for an indexed shifting racing derailleur, your choice is definitely between the various Shimano and SunTour models. The differences between them are subtle. The main difference is that Shimano gear trains always shift early, which makes Shimano more forgiving of wear or misadjustment. Also, Shimano has had two extra years of development to iron out the bugs. Campagnolo doesn't expect many serious racers to opt for Syncro levers and I agree with them on that count.

Touring Rear Derailleurs

Touring rear derailleurs need all of the features of racing rear derailleurs. In addition, they have to shift over wide-range gearing, which might consist of a triple crankset with a total tooth difference of 24 teeth and a wide-range freewheel with a 20-tooth difference between the sprockets. Touring derailleurs don't need to be light or quick-shifting; they need to be rugged. As long as the wide-range market was a small fraction of the racing–sport touring market, touring rear derailleurs were step-children—simply conventional derailleurs with longer cages.

When the mountain bike appeared on the scene in the early 1980s, the builders used whatever touring, BMX, or motorcycle equipment worked best. I remember Gary Fisher giving me a wheel in exchange for a Huret Duopar and a Simplex front derailleur to be installed on mountain bike number five. I used to say that you could do a mountain bike census by counting the total sales of SunTour thumb shifters and dividing by two. Touring components weren't designed to be pedaled over branches and boulders or to shift under water.

SunTour and Shimano had the good sense to recognize a growing market. SunTour's president, Junzo Kawai, attended the 1982 Pearl Pass Tour. The next year SunTour introduced MounTech, the first derailleur specifically designed for mountain bikes. From then on, SunTour and Shimano leap-frogged each other to provide the most rugged and best-shifting gear trains for the burgeoning mountain bike market. They sponsored teams and listened to feedback from the mountain bike builders. Wide-range mountain bike derailleurs became rugged, reliable, and able to shift under load.

By 1987, mountain bike rear derailleurs were so good that they could use indexed shift levers. Huret and Simplex made belated attempts to catch the market, but so far, they've been competing with last year's Japanese models. Campagnolo chose not to compete. Thus, it's a choice between Shimano and SunTour when you upgrade the gear train on your touring bicycle. I think that Shimano is the clear favorite, though for 1988, SunTour has come out with significantly revised mountain bike rear derailleurs.

Rear Derailleur Makers

The business of making and selling rear derailleurs has become a shootout between Shimano, SunTour, and Campagnolo. Sachs-Huret is still competing but the clock is ticking.

Campagnolo

Either Valentino Campagnolo or Frank Berto is misjudging the future market for rear derailleurs. Campagnolo has never actively competed in the touring market and they're completely out of mountain bikes. Their strength is the serious bicycle racer. They're operating on the basis that serious racers don't want indexed shifting. On the off chance that Campagnolo may have misread the market, they've produced the Syncro indexed shift lever for "noncompetitive cyclists." Campagnolo's rear derailleurs are only marginally suitable for indexed shifting.

Campagnolo's model philosophy is unique. They never really make anything obsolete. They keep old models in production as long as anyone will buy them. They introduce new models and let them compete with the old models to see what sells. I limited my tests to the four racing models that are widely distributed. I also tested the Victory LX, which is their latest touring rear derailleur.

The C-Record, introduced in 1985, is the ultimate single-pivot rear derailleur—strong, reliable, and handsome. It shifts better than any previous Campagnolo rear derailleur. However, the Nuovo Victory is the best Campagnolo rear derailleur because you can adjust the mounting angle. Both the C-Record and the Nuovo Victory require you to master the push-pull shifting technique. The Nuovo Triomphe lacks the angle adjustment, which is why it scores so much worse than the Nuovo Victory on a straight block freewheel.

The Super Record, introduced in 1982, is a minor upgrade of the Nuovo Record with slightly more capacity. Campagnolo has made small improvements over the years but current parts will still fit a 20-year-old model. I've tested the Nuovo Record four times since 1979. Compared to the competition, it has scored worse each time.

Today's racers are using wider chainwheel differences, like 53/39, and smaller freewheel differences, like 12–20. This works against the old single-

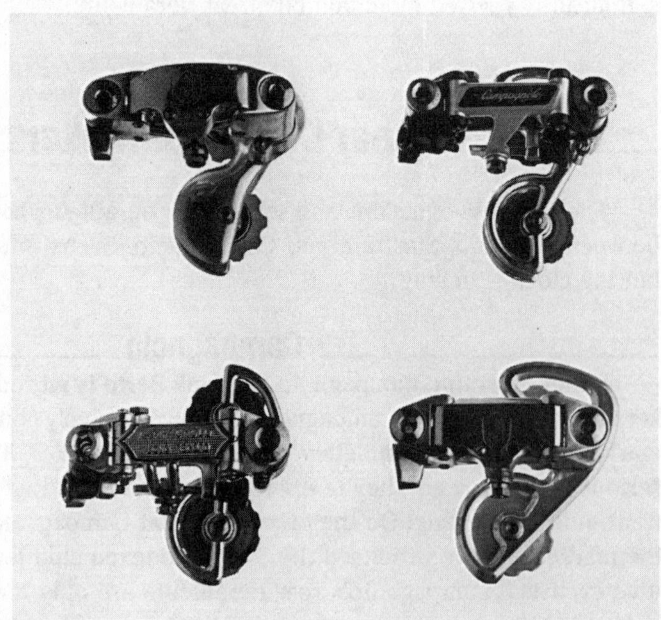

PHOTO 7-2

Campagnolo racing rear derailleurs: top left and right, C-Record and Super Record; bottom left and right, Nuovo Record and Nuovo Victory.

pivot rear derailleurs like the Nuovo Record and the Super Record. They shift much better with an 8-tooth difference on the front and a 14-tooth difference on the rear. I can't think of any reason, except nostalgia, for buying a Nuovo Record or a Super Record rather than a Nuovo Victory.

If you measure the key dimensions of the Campagnolo Victory LX (or Leisure) touring rear derailleur, you'll find that it's a SunTour VGT without the slant parallelogram. It's for the cyclist who wants to be *tout Campagnolo* and also wants a lower gear. The best thing that I can say about its shifting is that it's better than Campagnolo's previous touring rear derailleurs.

Huret

The 1983 marriage between Mlle. Huret and Herr Sachs gave birth to greatly improved derailleurs. The Sachs-Huret New Success, Rival, and Rider models are sturdy, good-shifting, double-pivot rear derailleurs. The Rival is the best-shifting, inexpensive, European rear derailleur. However, Huret suffers from limited distribution in the aftermarket. You rarely see a New Success or a Rival derailleur in a bicycle store or a mail-order catalog.

The rear derailleurs that you do see, the Jubilee and the Duopar, are from the period prior to Sachs-Huret. The Jubilee is an elegant, ultralight little jewel that shifts very nicely on narrow-range freewheels. It doesn't have a whole lot of metal and it works best if you don't abuse it. When it was introduced in 1976, the Duopar was unique—the only precise-shifting touring rear derailleur on the market. It's a bit fragile, especially the titanium version. However, it shifts so well that it doesn't need to be rugged. The market has changed and the competition has improved. The current steel model, called the Eco Duopar, is sturdier and has a loyal following.

ARIS, Huret's entry into the indexed shifting derby, got a late start. I've only seen the prototype. Its success will probably depend on the ability of Peugeot, Motobecane, and Gitane to prove that French bicycles with French components have a future.

Shimano

Shimano has a two-year lead in the indexed shifting derby. Shimano's top racing rear derailleurs are 7-speed Dura-Ace, Santé, 600 EX and 105. The top mountain bike or touring rear derailleurs are Deore XT and Deore. All six of these models are now found on the aftermarket as SIS models. Shimano also makes a range of L series (Light Action) and Z series rear derailleurs for the lower-priced OEM market. Not all of the L-series models and none of the Z-series models are suitable for indexed shifting. Shimano changes models frequently but they keep the same names for a few years, so you can't always

PHOTO 7-3

Huret rear derailleurs: top left and right, New Success and Jubilee; bottom left and right, Rival and Eco Duopar.

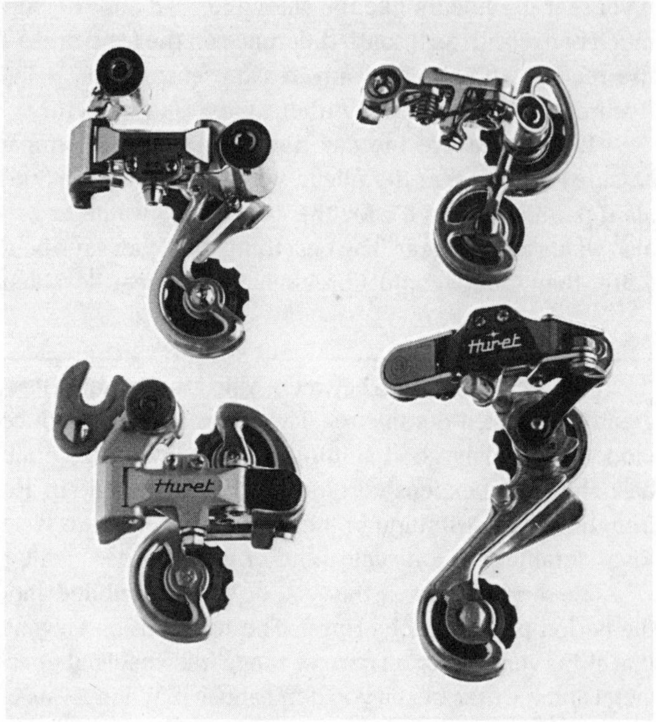

identify the latest models. I show 1987 model numbers, which were the models that I tested. For 1988, Shimano replaced 600 EX with 600 Ultegra. They also introduced Exage, a new gruppo priced below the 105.

The top-of-the-line models are all alloy and they have stainless steel pins and brass bushings for the parallelograms, sealed bearings in the pivots, and high-quality bearings in the pulleys. As you move down in price, some of the forged alloy parts become stamped alloy and then steel and the bearing quality goes down. The top models are long-lived.

All of Shimano's current SIS derailleurs shift early. They've increased the tension of the top spring and changed the cage geometry to achieve this. Shimano uses words like "ballistic" and "aggressive" to describe shifting performance. What they mean is that the jockey pulley is very close to the sprockets in all gears. All shifts take place well before the jockey pulley gets to the next sprocket. When you use SIS rear derailleurs with friction levers, you have to forget your old shifting patterns. You push the lever till the shift takes place and then a bit more for good measure.

You can't play games with advertised capacity any more. If you do, you may find that your jockey pulley rattles against the big sprocket, even with the angle adjustment screw turned all the way in.

The choice between Shimano and SunTour racing rear derailleurs is close, especially if you use friction levers. With indexed levers, SIS is a bit better. Deore and Deore XT are clearly better for loaded touring and mountain bikes, because SIS shifts better under load.

SunTour

SunTour's top four indexed shifting racing rear derailleurs are Superbe Pro, Sprint 9000, Cyclone 7000, and Alpha 5000. The top three indexed mountain bike, or touring, rear derailleurs are XC-9000, XC-Sport 7000, and Alpha 5000-GX. The OEM models are SVX, Alpha 3000, Seven, and Honor. All of the old names like Superbe, Cyclone, Cyclone Mark II, LePree, AR-X, AR, Moun-

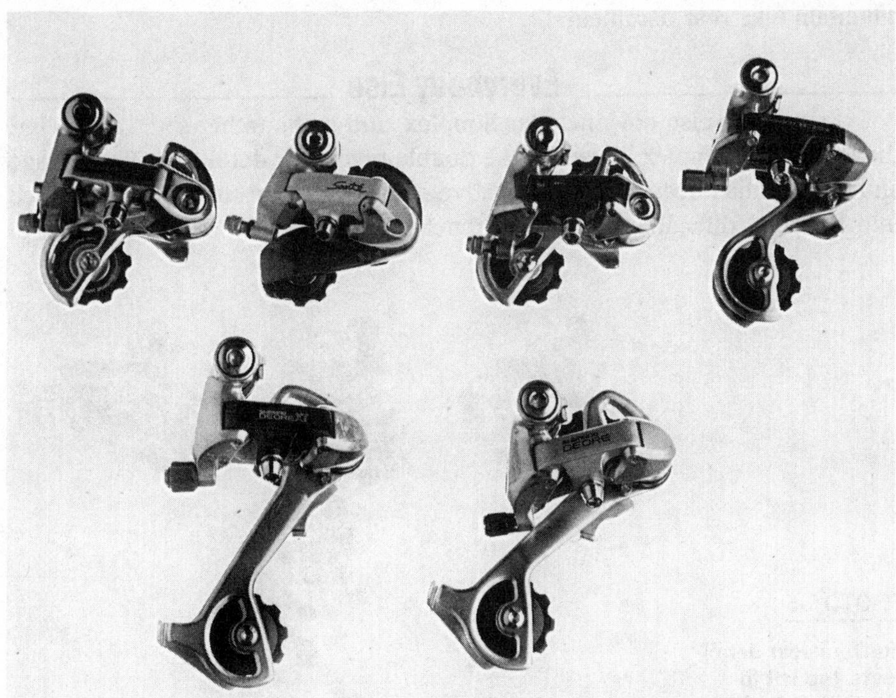

PHOTO 7-4 Shimano rear derailleurs: top left to right, Dura-Ace (racing), Santé (racing), 600 EX (racing), 105 (racing); bottom left and right, Deore XT (touring) and Deore (touring).

Tech, LeTech, and AG Tech are attached to old models. If you find them in a store or a catalog, they should be priced accordingly.

When SunTour upgraded their rear derailleurs for AccuShift, they added double-pivots, but they didn't copy Shimano. Compared to Shimano, the top pivot spring isn't as strong and the jockey pulley is closer to the cage pivot. There isn't an angle adjustment screw, so you can't match the mounting angle to the largest sprocket. As a result, the AccuShift rear derailleurs don't shift as early as SIS rear derailleurs.

SunTour designed the AccuShift levers to match the AccuShift rear derailleurs. If you use an AccuShift rear derailleur with friction levers, it will feel very much like an old pre-index SunTour rear derailleur.

SunTour's mountain bike rear derailleurs still have lots of capacity, especially in the friction mode. SunTour lists a larger maximum sprocket for friction shifting. If you want to stick with extra wide-range gearing, SunTour is a good choice.

For 1988, SunTour has significantly upgraded the performance of the mountain bike rear derailleurs.

Everybody Else

Everybody else now includes Simplex, and that's rather sad. Lucien Juy, the founder of Simplex, invented the double-pivot rear derailleur 50 years ago and Simplex has been a very innovative company. Unfortunately, Simplex fell into financial difficulties in 1985. French labor laws made it impossible to

PHOTO 7-5

SunTour rear derailleurs: top left to right, Superbe Pro (racing), Sprint (racing), and Cyclone (racing); bottom, XC-9000 (touring).

reduce their staff, so they went into bankruptcy. All of the disruption has limited their ability to develop an indexed shifting package. The reorganized Simplex is in the process of merging with Ofmega. Everybody else also includes Galli, Mavic, Ofmega, and Zeus. They all make Campagnolo-copy, single-pivot, racing rear derailleurs. It seems to me that if you're going to put up with imprecise Campagnolo shifting, you ought to get the Campagnolo mystique.

Frank's Favorite Rear Derailleurs

I had a 6-speed Shimano Dura-Ace/SIS rear derailleur on my Trek 2000 racing bicycle for more than a year and more than 2,000 miles. I set it up with a 28-tooth large sprocket rather than Shimano's recommended 26. It was still shifting flawlessly, with very little tinkering or adjustment, when I replaced it with the 7-speed version. I can't give a better recommendation than that.

I'm using a Shimano Deore XT rear derailleur on one of my touring bicycles, a Shimano Light Action on the second and a SunTour XC-9000 on the third. I use bar-end shift levers with all three, so I can't talk about their indexed shifting. The XC-9000 and the Shimano Light Action handle 44 teeth of wrap-up, and 11–34 freewheels. The Deore XT handles 40 teeth of wrap-up and a 12–32 tooth freewheel. These capacities are way outside of the makers' recommendations. All three derailleurs shift very well, under load, on a hill, but the two Shimano touring rear derailleurs shift better.

CHAPTER 8

All about Front Derailleurs

I have a book about bicycles, published in 1935, that pictures a front derailleur—on a triple crankset, yet. The book shows half a dozen rear derailleurs, so they must have been invented somewhat before that time. The inventor of the front derailleur was probably a strong-willed Frenchman. He certainly didn't read the mechanical engineering textbooks, because they all say that the sprockets of a chain drive must be exactly aligned. Rear derailleurs also violate that rule, but at least they operate on the unloaded half of the chain. The front derailleur works on the loaded half of the chain, so front derailleurs have to use a cage instead of a jockey pulley to derail the chain.

A bicycle front derailleur is not only confronted with the challenge of a chain under load, it must also deal with the tooth differences between chainwheels, which are much greater than those between sprockets on a freewheel. In short, a front derailleur poses a nasty design problem. Nevertheless, the inventor persisted and the first front derailleurs worked, after a fashion. The next models worked a bit better, and the next ones a bit better yet.

Current front derailleur models continue the evolutionary process, both by finesse and by brute force. I've been testing derailleurs for a decade and there's clearly been substantial progress. The makers have learned that front derailleurs must be rigid. If the cage deflects under load, upshifts will be hesitant and unreliable. Similarly, there's been a lot of ingenious metal bending applied to the cage contours to help seduce the chain from one chainwheel to the next.

There haven't been any dramatic breakthroughs in front derailleur design similar to indexed shifting. However, the demands of mountain bikers have had a very salutory effect on wide-range front derailleur performance. My front derailleur tests for this chapter revealed major improvements in the newer models. If you're struggling along with an old, worn-out front derailleur, be advised that the latest models shift much more pleasantly.

Today's front derailleurs are designed for three specific gear trains: racing, half-step touring, and crossover touring. Buy the model that suits your gear train. If you do that, front derailleur selection isn't a big deal anymore. Indeed, front derailleurs are often bought as an afterthought. You buy a fancy new rear derailleur and you take the front derailleur that matches it. Actually, that's not a bad approach, since the same companies that make top-rated rear derailleurs also make top-rated front derailleurs. The indexed shifting shakeout that dramatically reduced the number of rear derailleurs on the market also reduced the number of front derailleurs.

Hurrah for that! I tested 81 different models for my 1986 *Bicycling* front derailleur articles and each test took more than an hour. About half of those 1986 models are still available. However, I only show the best-performing 10 of them. I also tested 16 new front derailleurs from Shimano and SunTour for this chapter. They were measurably better than anything you could have bought two years ago.

Since there's no standard definition of what constitutes a "racing" or a "touring" front derailleur, I developed my own. A touring derailleur should be able to handle a 52×X×28 triple crankset (the size of the middle chainwheel will vary according to the gearing system). Anything with less capacity than that is, by my definition, a racing derailleur. Note that the same front derailleurs are used for both racing and sport touring. In fact, most racing front derailleurs have enough capacity to handle a triple crankset. They just don't shift as well as a purpose-built touring front derailleur. Similarly, a touring front derailleur would think that it had died and gone to heaven if you installed it on a racing crankset. Of course if you did that, your bald-legged racing buddies might sneer at you.

Racing Front Derailleurs

Racing is an easy derailleur service, since the chainwheel difference on a racing crankset is usually about 12 teeth. The standard racing crankset used to be 52/42. Today 53/39 is the closest thing to a standard. The 39-tooth inner chainwheel allows smaller big sprockets to be used on the freewheel. Every front derailleur shown in table 8-1 will shift well on a 53/39 racing crankset. Racing front derailleurs have narrower cages to make sure that the chain doesn't come off at a crucial time.

Over the past 20 years, racing front derailleurs have improved with each succeeding model. The Campagnolo Nuovo Record is the exception. It worked right when it was introduced in the late 1960s, so Campagnolo never fixed it. But

TABLE 8-1.

Racing Front Derailleurs

Make and Model	Cost ($)	Weight (gr.)	Shifting Performance			Capacity Measurements				
			Double 52×36	Triple 52×47×34	Smallest Good-Shifting CW (teeth)	Smallest Inner CW (teeth) *Advert.*	*Meas. Double*	*Meas. Triple*	Largest Middle CW (teeth)	Smallest Outer CW (teeth)
Campagnolo										
C-Record (104018)	45–60	103	E	VG	32	34	32	28	48	47
Super Record (104010)	40–55	92	G	VG	36	41	36	32	49	45
Nuovo Record (104007)	35–50	98	G	VG	36	41	36	32	49	45
Victory (104020)	30–40	102	VG	VG	32	44	32	30	49	46
Huret										
Jubilee (AV66.1D)	15–25	82	VG	G	36	36	32	28	50	48
New Success (AV66.3D)	12–18	110	VG	VG	32	36	32	28	48	46
Rival (AV62.1D)	8–12	110	VG	VG	32	36	32	28	48	46
Shimano										
Dura-Ace (FD-7400)	33–48	94	VG	E	32	37	34	32	49	41
Santé (FD-5000)	27–40	97	E	E	32	38	30	28	47	46
600 EX (FD-6207)	13–20	115	E	VG	32	34	30	26	49	46
105 (FD-1050)	11–16	105	E	E	30	38	30	28	48	45
SunTour										
Superbe Pro (FD-SB00)	42–60	93	E	E	32	36	30	28	50	46
Sprint 9000 (FD-SP00)	18–25	97	E	E	34	34	30	28	50	48
Cyclone 7000 (FD-CL10)	15–22	105	E	E	32	34	30	28	50	48

1. See text discussion of cable attachment on page 148.
2. The overall quality rating is my best judgment, summing up all of the factors evaluated. You don't see any F or P ratings because all of the derailleurs that I've listed are pretty darn good.

the tide has come in around the Nuovo Record. Now it's merely good in a field of very good and excellent front derailleurs.

Touring Front Derailleurs

It's much harder to shift over a wide-range triple touring crankset than over a racing double crankset. Fortunately, today's touring front derailleurs are five times better than their ten-year-old parents. Both mountain bikers and

Cage Rigidity (in. of deflec.)		Rear Shifts with No Re-adjustment	Cage Dimensions (in.)					Cable Attach[1]	Overall Quality[2]
1-lb. Force	10-lb. Force		Width		Length	Travel			
			Rear	Front		Min.	Max.		
0.035	0.165	3+	0.46	0.40	3.3	0.60	1.50	cable	E
0.015	0.115	3	0.48	0.43	3.3	0.60	1.35	cable	G
0.015	0.115	3	0.48	0.43	3.3	0.60	1.35	cable	G
0.025	0.155	4+	0.50	0.40	3.5	0.55	1.55	cable	VG
0.050	0.220	3+	0.47	0.43	3.8	0.55	1.30	cable	G
0.030	0.115	3+	0.51	0.47	3.4	0.50	1.35	cable	VG
0.025	0.125	3+	0.50	0.47	3.4	0.45	1.40	cable	VG
0.020	0.105	4+	0.46	0.46	3.4	0.60	1.50	cable	E
0.035	0.120	6	0.51	0.40	2.8	0.70	1.40	cable	E
0.020	0.100	5+	0.53	0.45	3.4	0.51	1.40	both	VG
0.015	0.100	6	0.50	0.40	3.2	0.70	1.35	cable	E
0.010	0.100	5	0.47	0.46	3.2	0.60	1.50	cable	E
0.015	0.110	5+	0.51	0.43	3.5	0.60	1.50	both	E
0.010	0.070	5+	0.49	0.48	3.5	0.60	1.50	both	E

cross-country tourists can appreciate the improvements. The touring front derailleurs listed in table 8-2 can reliably shift over any sensibly selected triple crankset that you care to use. The old books that advised you to shift before you reached the hill are as obsolete as the old front derailleurs that they described. With just a modest bit of technique, today's front derailleurs will shift on a hill under load.

There are now two distinct types of touring front derailleurs, one for half-step gearing and the other for crossover gearing. (I wrote about the difference

TABLE 8-2.

Touring Front Derailleurs

Make and Model	Cost ($)	Weight (gr.)	Shifting Performance[1]			Capacity Measurements		
			Double 52×X	Triple 52×X×X	Smallest Good-Shifting CW (teeth)	Smallest Inner CW (teeth) Advert.	Meas. Double	Meas. Triple
Campagnolo								
Victory LX (104024)	30–40	107	F	G	36	29	26	24
Huret								
Duopar Half-Step (AV67.1T)	15–20	116	G	G	32	26	32	28
New Success (AV66.3T)	15–20	120	G	G	32	26	32	28
Shimano								
Deore XT Alpine (FD-M730AL)	20–30	112	E	E	28	26	<24	<24
Deore XT Half-Step (FD-M730HS)	20–30	112	E	E	28	26	<24	<24
Deore Alpine (FD-MT60AL)	15–22	113	E	E	28	26	<24	<24
Deore Half-Step (FD-MT60HS)	15–22	113	E	E	28	26	<24	<24
Z (FD-Z206GS)	12–18	123	VG	G	28	25	26	24
SunTour								
XC-9000 (FD-XC00)	27–40	110	G	VG	30	28	<24	<24
XC-Sport 7000-GT (FD-XS00-GT)	19–28	119	E	E	28	30	26	24
XC-Sport 7000-GX (FD-XS00-GX)	19–28	126	G	VG	30	28	<24	<24

1. See the text on page 145 for a description of the crankset combinations used in the tests.
2. See the text discussion of cable attachment on page 148.
3. The overall quality rating is my best judgment, summing up all of the factors evaluated. You don't see any F or P ratings because all of the derailleurs that I've listed are pretty darn good.

between these two types of gearing in chapter 3.) First decide which type of gearing you prefer, then choose the front derailleur to match. Half-step front derailleurs are for cranksets like 50/45/28. Crossover front derailleurs are for cranksets like 48/38/28. Crossover front derailleurs can't be mounted correctly on cranksets with half-step chainwheels because the deep inner cage hits the middle chainwheel. A half-step front derailleur can be used on a crossover crankset, but it won't shift as well as a good crossover front derailleur.

Capacity Measurements		Cage Rigidity (in. of deflec.)		Rear Shifts with No Readjustment	Cage Dimensions (in.)					Cable Attach.[2]	Overall Quality[3]
Largest Middle CW (teeth)	Smallest Outer CW (teeth)	1-lb. Force	10-lb. Force		Width		Length	Travel			
					Rear	*Front*		*Min.*	*Max.*		
44	40	0.035	0.240	3	0.49	0.41	3.6	0.52	1.53	cable	G
46	46	0.030	0.105	3+	0.51	0.47	3.5	0.50	1.36	both	G
44	46	0.025	0.105	3+	0.51	0.47	3.5	0.50	1.36	both	G
44	50	0.010	0.090	6	0.59	0.48	3.5	0.55	1.50	cable	E
47	50	0.010	0.090	6	0.60	0.48	3.5	0.55	1.50	cable	E
44	50	0.010	0.085	6	0.60	0.48	3.5	0.55	1.50	cable	E
47	50	0.010	0.085	6	0.60	0.48	3.5	0.55	1.50	cable	E
46	45	0.035	0.175	5	0.53	0.46	3.7	0.50	1.45	both	VG
46	50	0.020	0.140	4	0.56	0.53	3.4	0.55	1.45	cable	VG
48	47	0.010	0.110	4	0.56	0.53	3.4	0.55	1.45	both	E
46	50	0.010	0.080	4	0.56	0.53	3.4	0.55	1.45	both	VG

Crossover Front Derailleurs

Many people think that a "split-the-difference" crossover crankset like 52/40/28 is easier on the front derailleur than a 52/47/28 half-step, with a little step and a humongous one. Many people are wrong. In fact, a 52/28 double is easier on the front derailleur than a 52/40/28 triple.

Why is that, Doctor Derailleur?

After observing 10,000 or so front shifts, I finally figured it out (maybe I'm just a slow learner). The 28 to 40 upshift is poor because the front derailleur is mounted an inch too high for the 40-tooth chainwheel. If you remove the outer chainwheel, it becomes obvious. There's your derailleur way up on the seat tube. The tail of the cage gently massages the chain about 3 inches behind the chainwheel. No wonder the upshift is so poor!

You have to force the upshift by pushing the chain way past the middle chainwheel. When it finally shifts, it may climb onto the middle chainwheel, or it may go farther over onto the outer chainwheel, or go even farther off into the wild blue yonder. The whole performance is accompanied by much grinding, chattering, and mechanical sadism. I used to say that the middle chainwheel was "hiding in the shadow" of the outer chainwheel. That's true, but the real problem is the 12-tooth difference between the middle and the outer chainwheels, which forces you to mount the derailleur too high.

The way to make a 52/40/28 triple shift better is to convert it to a 48/40/28, or to a 52/44/28. You either lower the derailleur down to the middle chainwheel, or raise the middle chainwheel up to the derailleur. Raising the little chainwheel doesn't help at all. Yet many people decide that God intended them to walk their bikes up steep hills, so they convert to something silly like a 52/40/34.

Mountain bikes use crossover gearing. To meet the demand for bulletproof front derailleurs, the makers developed a new class of crossover superderailleurs. These new crossover derailleurs have an extra-deep inner cage that just clears the middle chainwheel. Given the magnitude of the task, they shift very well. However, you can overpower even the best of them by using a triple crankset with too much difference between the middle and the outer chainwheel. Ten teeth is a practical limit. With a 10-tooth difference, the front derailleur is mounted about an inch too high for the middle chainwheel. Go to a 12-tooth difference (say a 50/38/28 crankset) and the 28/38 upshift will be marginal.

Half-Step Front Derailleurs

I'm a wee bit biased toward half-step gear trains. I've been using half-step plus granny gearing for a decade. I didn't invent the arrangement, but I named it. I think it's the only way to set up triples for over-the-road use.

A half-step front derailleur has to have a shallow inner cage so that it doesn't run into the middle chainwheel when you shift to the outer chainwheel. Even though mountain bikers outnumber loaded tourists about a zillion to one, Huret, Shimano, and SunTour (bless their hearts) still make pure half-step front derailleurs. SunTour's crossover front derailleurs require only a six-tooth chainwheel difference. They can be mounted just a bit high and they'll work on half-step cranksets. However, SunTour's half-step front derailleur works better.

PHOTO 8-1 A 52/40/28 crankset with the outer chainwheel removed to show a high-mounted front derailleur.

Shimano's half-step looks just like their crossover, but the inner cage has a wide chamfer so that it clears the middle chainwheel. You can even use a racing front derailleur on a triple crankset if you'll forgo using the granny chainwheel with the smallest cogs.

Front Derailleur Tests and Measurements

I tested front derailleurs for capacity, rigidity, and shifting performance. The capacity and rigidity tests were the same for racing, half-step, and crossover front derailleurs. I used different performance tests for the three different kinds of front derailleurs.

Capacity Measurements

The capacity measurements are simple geometry. I measured the various dimensions with a ruler or a vernier caliper. Some of the front derailleurs have appetites that are bigger than their stomachs. They can clear wider range cranksets than they can shift over. Tables 8-1 and 8-2 show five different capacity numbers.

The capacities list the middle or inner chainwheels that go with a 52-tooth outer chainwheel. I used a 52-tooth outer chainwheel for all my measurements and tests. If you use a different outer chainwheel, just add or subtract the appropriate number of teeth from the middle and inner chainwheels listed in the tables. For example, table 8-1 states that the Campagnolo C-Record shifts well on a 52/32 double crankset. If you're using a 50-tooth outer chainwheel (2 teeth smaller), then the inner chainwheel can be a 30-tooth (also 2 teeth smaller). I could have shown a 20-tooth chainwheel difference, but I think that using actual chainwheel sizes is more straightforward.

If you are using Shimano Biopace or oval chainwheels, treat them like round chainwheels. If you are mixing oval and round chainwheels, add 2 teeth to the size of the oval chainwheel, because a 50-tooth Biopace has the same outer diameter as a 52-tooth round chainwheel.

Advertised Smallest Inner Chainwheel The numbers in the "advertised" column are taken right from the catalogs. Each maker decides whether to list the mechanical capacity based on dimensions and clearances, or the shifting capacity based on some performance criteria.

Measured Smallest Inner Chainwheel (Double) Based on my measurements, the "measured double" number identifies the smallest inner chainwheel that can be combined with a 52-tooth outer chainwheel without the chain rubbing on the spacer at the rear of the derailleur cage. For this measurement, I set the chain on the 14-tooth freewheel sprocket. If the spacer had a "step" in it, I positioned the derailleur for maximum chain clearance. This number depends a bit on chainstay length and seat tube angle. Note that this is a mechanical measurement, not the results of my shifting tests.

Measured Smallest Inner Chainwheel (Triple) The "measured triple" numbers were obtained in the same way as the measured doubled numbers, but with the chain set on a 20-tooth middle freewheel sprocket. If you set up a triple crankset with the listed inner chainwheel and you tried to use that inner chainwheel with the smallest freewheel sprocket, the chain would rub on the back of the derailleur. By giving up 2 or 3 of your 15 (or 18) speeds, you can stretch the capacity of your front derailleur. On my Redcay, I use an old Dura-Ace EX racing front derailleur with a 48/44/24 crankset and an 11–34 freewheel, but I only use the 24-tooth chainwheel with the 26- and 34-tooth freewheel sprockets.

Largest Middle Chainwheel You need the information in the "largest middle chainwheel" column in order to buy a front derailleur for a half-step plus granny triple. The measurement is based on the depth of the derailleur's inner cage. Racing front derailleurs have shallow inner cages that can pass over a 49- or 50-tooth middle chainwheel. Half-step front derailleurs can usually pass over a 48-tooth middle chainwheel. Crossover front derailleurs have deep inner cages. To use one on a half-step crankset, you have to mount it too high. Note that this is a maximum size. With a 49-tooth limit you can use a 52/48 half-step with no problem.

Smallest Outer Chainwheel There's a very modest trend towards smaller outer chainwheels. With 11-, 12-, or 13-tooth freewheel sprockets, you can get the high gear you need with smaller chainwheels. For example, a 41-tooth chainwheel and an 11-tooth sprocket gives the same High as a 52 and a 14.

The front derailleur is mounted lower with a smaller outer chainwheel. Mount it low enough and it will foul the rear derailleur cable. The number shown is the smallest outer chainwheel that lets the front derailleur clear a cable that runs ⅜ inch above the chainstay. If the rear derailleur cable runs under the chainstay, subtract six teeth from the listing.

Rigidity Testing

Rigid front derailleurs shift better than flexible models. That's why worn-out front derailleurs with loose bushings shift so poorly. To test rigidity, I made a simple test jig with a dial gauge and a spring balance. I pull on the end of the cage, first with a one-pound force and then with a ten-pound force. The one-pound deflection is a rough measure of the slop in the derailleur's mechanical construction. The ten-pound deflection measures the overall strength of the front derailleur's cage and parallelogram. (I arrived at the ten-pound figure by multiplying a normal lever pull by the mechanical advantage of the shift lever and the front derailleur.) The results of both types of rigidity test are recorded in tables 8-1 and 8-2. More deflection indicates a flimsier front derailleur.

Shifting Performance of Front Derailleurs

I measured front derailleur shifting performance with the same derailleur testing machine that I used for rear derailleurs. The machine is a bicycle frame with the crank driven by a gear motor. The shift levers have pointers so I can see where each shift takes place. (This machine is shown in photo 7-1 on page 118.) The shifting performance ratings shown in tables 8-1 and 8-2 are more than test results; they also serve as predictions of how the derailleurs will perform on the road. I consider these ratings to be the most important data recorded in these two tables.

PHOTO 8-2

The rigidity tester.

Racing Front Derailleurs The latest model racing front derailleurs have a curved bulge on the inner cage that lifts the chain from the small to the large chainwheel. This bulge makes a major improvement in shifting compared to the old-style, flat inner cages. This is the main reason that the Campagnolo Nuovo Record has seen its best days.

To test racing front derailleurs, I used a 52/36 crankset and a Shimano Narrow Uniglide chain. I carefully adjusted the derailleur height, the cage angle, and the travel stops. Then I started the machine with the crank turning at 60 rpm. With the chain on a middle freewheel spocket, I made repeated up and down front shifts. First, I snapped the lever from one position to the next and then I slowly moved the lever and observed how the shifts took place. High-scoring derailleurs pop the chain right up onto the big chainwheel with no chattering or vibration, even when I move the lever quite slowly. Low-scoring derailleurs shift reluctantly with much vibration. On downshifts, high-scoring models shift with a light lever force and the chain drops cleanly onto the small chainwheel.

You might wonder why I tested racing front derailleurs with a 52/36 chainwheel combination. That's a 16-tooth difference and racers rarely use more than a 12- or 14-tooth difference between the chainwheels. I tried testing with 52/42 chainwheels, but it was just too easy. Even the worst front derailleurs shifted so well that I couldn't measure significant differences. The 52/36 crankset provided a severer test.

I've ridden with most of these derailleurs and confirmed that the tests correlate with over-the-road performance. I could feel the large differences, but not the small ones. Basically, all of the listed racing front derailleurs shift very competently. Cranksets like 52/42 or even 52/36 aren't much of a challenge.

I also tested the racing front derailleurs with a 52/47/34 triple crankset. I don't think much of the Low that you get with a 34-tooth granny gear, but many sport touring bikes use this kind of triple. Again, this wasn't a severe test and all of the derailleurs handled it well. The upshift from the 34-tooth to the 47-tooth chainwheel was the hardest part. Narrow chains make the test a bit more severe, but the best derailleurs just pop the chain over. The triple crankset score is a composite of the two upshifts and the two downshifts.

I added up the results of the two tests and the rigidity measurements and developed an overall shifting performance rating. (Table 8-1 shows separate ratings for the tests on double and triple cranksets.) Finally, I installed a series of double cranksets with ever smaller inner chainwheels and checked shifting performance. The wider the chainwheel difference, the worse the shift. Table 8-1 shows the widest range double crankset that still gave a reliable shift, a G score. The best front derailleurs handled a 52/32 crankset quite comfortably, and they're "racing" derailleurs, mind you.

Touring Front Derailleurs The tests on touring front derailleurs were much more severe than the tests on racing front derailleurs. I used one set of double and triple chainwheels to test the half-step front derailleurs and a different set to test the crossover front derailleurs. Sugino provided me with five Aero Tour triple cranksets and a full complement of chainwheels to do these tests.

I tested the half-step front derailleurs with a 52/32 double and a 52/47/24 triple. I used five different cranksets to test the crossover front derailleurs: a 52/28 double and 52/44/28, 52/42/26, 52/40/26, and 52/38/24 triples. Each triple crankset was a more severe test than the previous one. The 52/38/24 was a real rock crusher. In my 1986 tests, none of the front derailleurs shifted well on that crankset. Some of them couldn't shift at all from the 24 to the 38.

I was impressed with the performance of the new Shimano Deore and Deore XT alpine front derailleurs. They shifted competently on the 52/38/24 crankset, better than any previous front derailleur. Before the tests, I had been using a Deore XT with a 46/36/26 Biopace crankset and I'd attributed its smooth shifting to the Biopace chainrings. The SunTour XC-9000 and XC-Sport 7000 were improved over the previous models, but they weren't quite up to Shimano's performance. We're seeing the benefits of Shimano's and SunTour's support of mountain bike racing. These are mountain bike derailleurs that also work splendidly on touring bikes.

In spite of the improvement in front derailleurs, there's a lesson in my test experience. If you want to use crossover gearing, keep the difference between the middle and the outer chainwheels as small as you can.

The best crossover front derailleurs handled the 52/28 double quite comfortably. It's easy to test front derailleurs on double cranksets. All I do is evaluate how well they upshift from the inner to the outer chainwheel. It's much harder to rate front derailleurs on triple cranksets. The shifts onto the middle chainwheel are more difficult, both on the testing machine and on the road. I rated the following factors, in order of importance:

- Smooth upshifting from the inner to the middle chainwheel, without the need to overshift too far and then recenter.
- Smooth downshifting from the outer to the middle chainwheel, without early or late shifting. Early shifts can let the chain ride on the middle chainwheel, making you nudge it over with another jog of the shift lever. This is more severe with narrow chains. Late shifting requires you to recenter after you shift. Sometimes a late-shifting front derailleur kicks the chain all the way over onto the inner chainwheel.
- Smooth upshifting from the middle to the outer chainwheel. This is an easy shift on a half-step crankset and a harder shift on a crossover crankset. If the derailleur overshifts at all, or if it has a wide cage, it's harder to adjust properly on an older crankset with a narrow gap between the crankarm and the chainwheel. (I talked about that in chapter 5.)
- Reliable downshifting from the middle to the inner chainwheel. None of the derailleurs had any problem with this shift. I've concluded that if you have a problem with the chain dropping off on the inside, your front derailleur is probably set up wrong.

I added up all of these factors and converted the sum into an overall shifting performance rating. (Table 8-2 shows separate ratings for double and triple cranksets.)

Other Measurements

I took a set of calipers to the front derailleurs and measured their key dimensions. I also measured how far they moved in and out. Finally, I measured how many rear shifts you can make without having to readjust the front derailleur. These measurements, along with a few others, are detailed below and listed in tables 8-1 and 8-2.

Weight The listed weight is for a clamp-on model. Lighter isn't better for front derailleurs. More rigid is better. That's why the less expensive models sometimes shift better than their highly polished and lighter siblings. If the bearings are the same, the heavier models shift better. If the weight differs a bit from the advertised weight, it just means that my test front derailleur weighed a bit more or less.

Cable Travel I used to laboriously measure the amount of cable travel required to shift a front derailleur over a double and a triple crankset. I don't bother to do this any more. All current front derailleurs take about 0.4 inch of cable movement to shift over a double and about 0.6 inch to shift over a triple. Rear derailleurs require more cable movement than front derailleurs. All shift levers provide at least an inch of cable movement. Basically, you can mix or match front derailleurs, rear derailleurs, and shift levers. Huret front derailleurs take a bit less lever movement than most and SunTours take a bit more. If the makers go to indexed shifting for triple cranksets, cable travel will become an important measurement.

Rear Shifts with No Readjustment This tells you how many shifts you can make with the rear derailleur before the chain moves over far enough to rub against the cage of the front derailleur. This depends mostly on the cage width at the rear, which is also listed. Wide cages let you make five or six rear shifts. Narrow cages limit you to only three shifts before you have to readjust the front derailleur. This is an approximate number because chain rubbing also depends on chain width, chainstay length, and the size of the chainwheel.

Racing front derailleurs have narrower cages because there's less chance of the chain coming off the chainwheel with a narrow cage. Shimano and SunTour touring derailleur cages are quite wide at the rear. Most of them can shift over a six-cog, wide-spaced freewheel without adjusting the front derailleur. You can't set up these wide cages properly with old cranksets that have a narrow gap between the crankarm and the outer chainwheel. Don't blame the front derailleur if it shifts poorly because it's misaligned.

Derailleur Cage Width I measured the width at the rear of the cage and at the middle, opposite the seat tube. I talked about the rear width above. The cage width at the middle varies very little between derailleurs. Cage width was easy to measure on the old derailleurs with flat cages. It's harder to measure on the current models because the cages now have all kinds of grooves and bulges to help the shifting. Some people bend the front part of the cage to improve downshifting from the big chainwheel. I leave it alone.

Cage Length This is the distance from the centerline of the down tube to the rear cage spacer measured along the cage. Long-cage derailleurs can mechanically span larger chainwheel differences. This is the key difference between touring and racing derailleurs.

Cage Travel (Minimum) This is the distance between the inner derailleur cage and the seat tube with the adjustment screw backed all the way out. For a normal double chainwheel, 0.80 inch gives lots of clearance. For a triple with a triple spindle, 0.70 inch will suffice. When you install a triple crankset on a double spindle, the inner chainwheel will be right against the chainstay. This requires 0.60 inch of clearance. Wide-cage derailleurs require a bit less clearance than those with narrow cages. If your front derailleur doesn't have quite enough adjustment to drop the chain onto the inner chainwheel, you can sometimes do a bit of judicious persuasion with a file.

Cage Travel (Maximum) This is the maximum distance between the seat tube and the inner cage with the adjustment screw all the way out. Triple chainwheels on triple spindles need 1.25 inches. If you find your derailleur won't shift out far enough, it probably means you have a bad combination of spindles and cranksets, one which locates your chainwheels too far out. Both of the cage travel dimensions concern only triple cranksets.

Cable Attachment Many lower-priced bicycles have a casing stopper on the down tube rather than a cable guide on the bottom bracket. These bicycles require a front derailleur with a casing stopper. Some derailleurs can handle both a bare cable or a casing. In tables 8-1 and 8-2, models that can handle a bare cable are identified by "cable" and those that can handle either a bare cable or casing are identified by "both."

Front Derailleur Mounting

Most top-of-the-line racing front derailleurs are available in braze-on or clamp-on versions. There isn't an industry standard for the braze-on mounting. The Shimano and SunTour fittings are similar to Campagnolo and their braze-on front derailleurs will mount on the Campagnolo fitting. Both my Trek 2000 and my Redcay sport touring bicycles have braze-on fittings. It's prettier and there's no clamp to scratch the paint.

However, there are disadvantages to the braze-on method of mounting. There's limited vertical adjustment, so you have to pick your chainwheel size range and tell the builder before he brazes on the fitting. Since there's no standardization in braze-on height, don't expect to switch derailleurs once you select a braze-on model. When I had my Columbine made to order, I didn't order a braze-on.

You can't get the best shifting from your front derailleur unless it's properly mounted. Generally speaking, I mount the front derailleur so that its outer cage is just high enough to clear the outer chainwheel. With half-step cranksets, I mount it so that the inner cage just clears the middle chainwheel. In either case, I allow only 1/16 inch of clearance.

The next part is trickier. All of the instruction sheets tell you to mount the derailleur so that the cage is parallel to the chainwheels. Fine, but which side of the cage? The inner and the outer cages aren't parallel, since most derailleurs are wider at the rear. With the inner cage parallel, upshifting will be better. With the outer cage parallel, downshifting will be better. I tend to mount the inner cage a bit nearer to parallel, because upshifts are harder. This angles the derailleur out a bit. With many cranksets, you can't go very far because the heel of the cage will hit the inside of the crankarm. This is a particular problem with TA Cyclotourist cranksets, which have a rather narrow gap. You have to fiddle with the angle adjustment, because the angle changes as you tighten the clamp. It's a bit like adjusting a crank spindle.

Front Derailleur Makers

There's a shakeout taking place in the business as described in chapter 7. The surviving companies are making fewer and better models. What follows is a brief overview of the major makers of front derailleurs and their current line of products.

Campagnolo

I talked about Campagnolo's model names in chapter 7. There's a front derailleur to go with each of the rear derailleurs. The new Campagnolo C-Record, Victory, Triomphe, and 980 front derailleurs share an improved cage design that shifts much better than the older cage on the Nuovo Record and Super Record front derailleurs. These two old front derailleurs must hold the record for unchanged design; they're both old enough to vote. The two little pieces of black-anodized aluminum in the parallelogram of the Super Record cost an extra ten bucks. (Don't say Mrs. Campagnolo raised any dumb children.) Campagnolo makes just one touring front derailleur, the Victory LX. It's shifting performance isn't up to the competition and its deep inner cage isn't suitable for half-step cranksets.

PHOTO 8-3

Campagnolo front derailleurs: top left and right, C-Record and Nuovo Record/ Super Record; bottom left and right, Nuovo Victory/ Nuovo Triomphe and Victory LX.

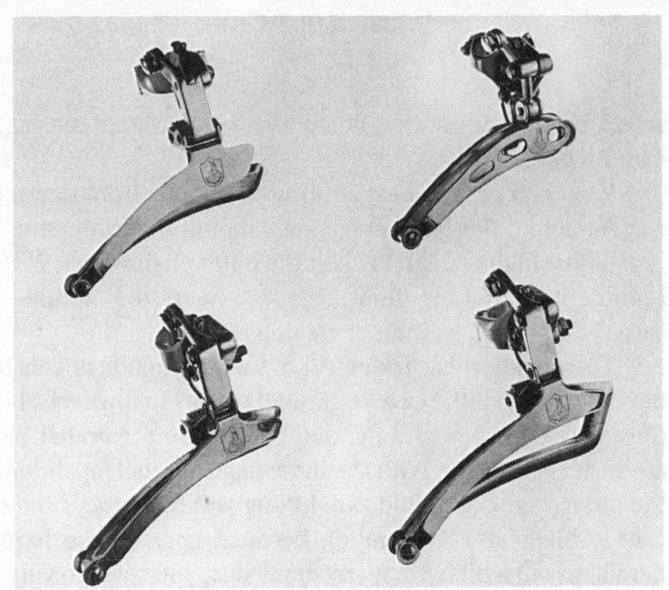

Huret

Huret's New Success, Rival, and Duopar front derailleurs were introduced in 1985. They were a major improvement over the old models. So far, distribution in the aftermarket is limited. Huret shows racing, half-step touring, and crossover touring front derailleurs in their catalog. I've tested a dozen Huret front derailleurs, but I just show the five models that have the best availability. The Huret Jubilee is the lightest front derailleur made but it's more for time trial records than for serious racers. It's an old Huret design. The old Hurets had long, skinny cages and flexible parallelograms. They would chatter and vibrate and refuse to shift, especially after they wore a bit. If you have an old Huret front derailleur on your bicycle, any modern front derailleur will be a major improvement.

Shimano

Shimano introduces about four new front derailleurs every year so they've improved their products by evolution. The Dura-Ace is light and beautifully sculptured. The inner cage has an embossed ridge to aid upshifts. The 600 EX has more capacity than the Dura-Ace and it shifts nearly as well. The Santé and 105 are new models with the parallelogram slanted forward. The cage moves forward as it moves out. They shifted smoothly on a 52/32 crankset, six teeth wider than Shimano's rating.

Shimano makes both half-step and crossover models for mountain bikers and tourists. They are the best shifting available. All Shimano front derailleurs have wide rear cages so you can shift over five- or six-sprocket freewheels without readjusting the front derailleurs. The only weakness of Shimano front

PHOTO 8-4

Huret front derailleurs: top left and right, New Success (racing) and Rival (racing); bottom left and right, New Success (half-step touring) and Duopar (crossover touring).

derailleurs is that they will occasionally drop narrow chains off the inside or the outside. I think that this is caused by a cage width that's designed for wide rather than narrow chains. Now that Shimano is promoting the Narrow Uniglide chain, I expect to see their cage widths become a bit narrower.

I used to limit the top scores of front derailleurs because even the best of them didn't shift well compared to rear derailleurs. The Santé, 105, Deore XT, and Deore front derailleurs deserve their excellent score.

SunTour

SunTour, like Campagnolo and Shimano, reissues old names on new derailleurs. Most of SunTour's front derailleurs were brand new in 1987 to match their new indexed shifting rear derailleurs. The racing front derailleurs are Superbe Pro, Sprint 9000, Cyclone 7000, and Alpha 5000. SunTour and Shimano racing front derailleurs look alike. They also shift alike, which is definitely top-notch.

SunTour's mountain bike or touring front derailleurs are XC-9000, XC-Sport 7000 and Alpha 5000. They shift better than anything SunTour has made previously. The half-step models (called GT) shift as well as the Shimano Deore half-steps. The crossover models (called GX) weren't quite up to Shimano's standard.

Some old SunTour front derailleurs have reverse lever movement. On most derailleurs, pulling back on the lever causes a shift up onto the big chainwheel. On the old SunTours, pulling back drops the chain onto the little chainwheel.

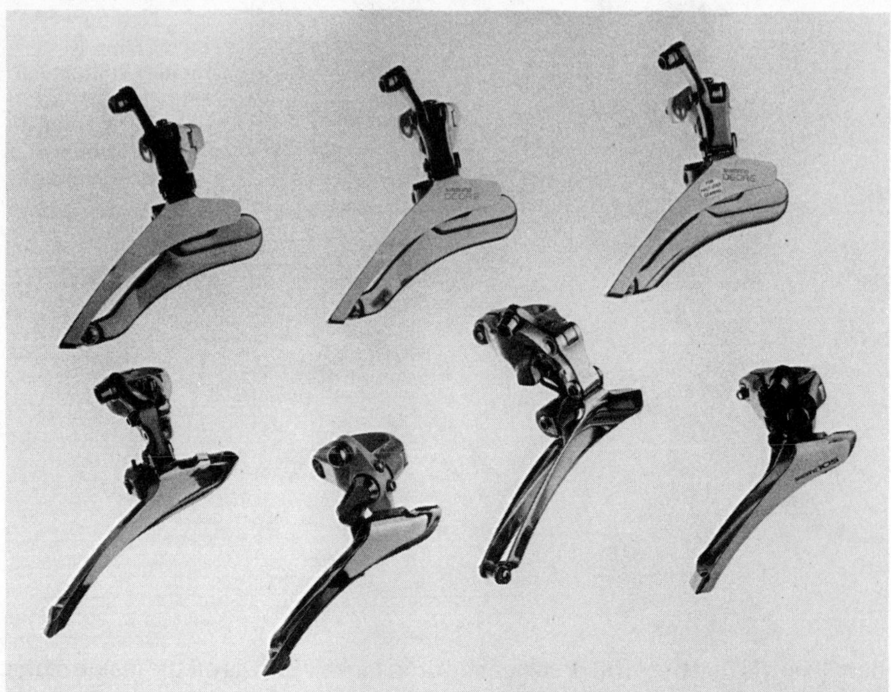

PHOTO 8-5 Shimano front derailleurs: top left to right, Deore XT (crossover touring), Deore (crossover touring), and Deore (half-step touring); bottom left to right, Dura-Ace (racing), Santé (racing), 600 EX (racing), and 105 (racing).

Once you get used to it, the reverse action makes a lot of sense. Both levers produce the same shift response. Many tandem riders prefer the "backwards" SunTours because they shift down onto the little chainwheel more positively. In 1987, SunTour surrendered to the common practice. All SunTour front derailleurs except the lowest-priced Spirt now have normal lever response.

Everybody Else

Everybody else is the same for both front and rear derailleurs. Galli, Ofmega, and Zeus make copies of the Campagnolo Nuovo Record front derailleurs to match their Campy-copy rear derailleurs. Simplex used to make excellent front derailleurs, but they're now almost out of business. Mavic makes a powerful and well-built racing front derailleur.

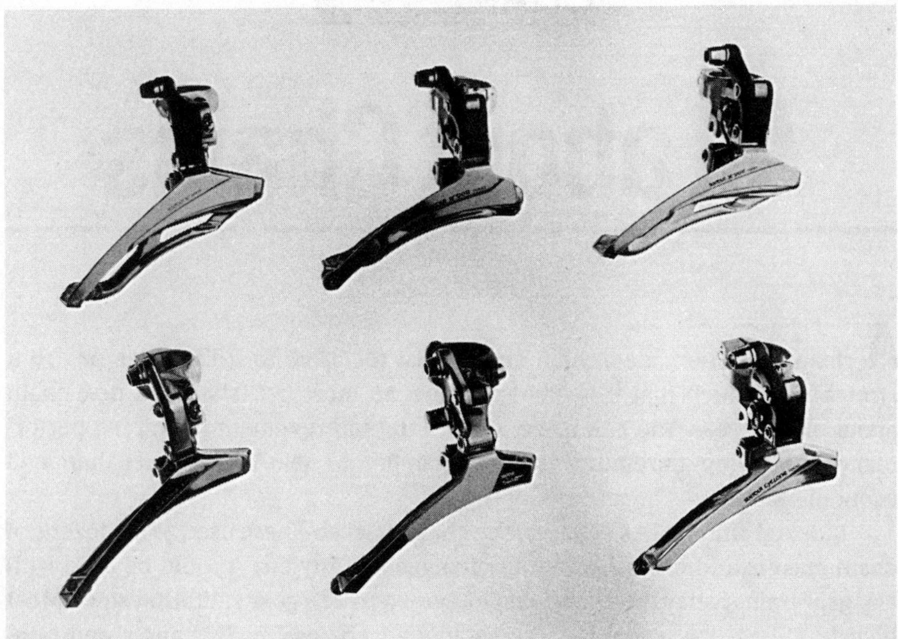

PHOTO 8-6 SunTour front derailleurs: top left to right, XC-9000 (crossover touring), XC-Sport 7000-GT (half-step touring), and XC-Sport 7000-GX (crossover touring); bottom left to right, Superbe Pro (racing), Sprint 9000 (racing), and Cyclone 7000 (racing).

Frank's Favorite Front Derailleurs

For the past few years, it's been a toss-up between Shimano and SunTour front derailleurs. The SunTours were usually slightly better shifting but I often mounted a Shimano to match the rear derailleur. Currently, I have a Dura-Ace and a Santé on the two racing bikes. I have a Deore XT crossover on one touring bike. The other touring bike has a braze-on front mount and I use an old model Dura-Ace racing derailleur. The commute bike serves as a test bed for whatever I'm currently playing with.

CHAPTER 9

All about Chains

A clean, well-lubricated chain should last for 3,000 to 5,000 miles before it stretches so much that it needs replacing, so most cyclists buy a new chain about once a year. You can make a nice little improvement in shifting performance by buying a premium chain to match your gear train, rather than a $3 economy model.

Indexed shifting has changed the chain market. There used to be dozens of chain makers and chains were interchangeable. Any chain could be used with any gear train. Today the chain is an integral part of a gear shifting system. Most bicycle stores now carry the recommended chains for Shimano's and SunTour's indexed gear trains and perhaps Sedisport and Regina CX-S chains for the racers. There's hardly any market left for the little old chain makers.

Chain Development

Hans Renold invented the roller chain in the first bicycle engineering boom of the 1880s. The addition of a free-turning roller to the older pin-and-bushing chain greatly reduced noise and power losses. A well-lubricated roller chain wastes only about 1½ percent of the power transmitted. Chain drives are efficient, reliable, and economical—which is why they've survived for so long.

Chain design stagnated as long as bicycles had only one gear. You could use a century-old chain on a current 1-speed bicycle and never tell the difference. Derailleurs added two special requirements. The chainwheels and sprockets weren't aligned in most gears, so derailleur chains had to bend or deflect sideways, and chains had to be derailled from sprocket to sprocket and from chainwheel to chainwheel.

The first major design change took place in the 1950s when narrow 3/32-inch "derailleur" chains were developed to replace standard 1/8-inch 1-speed chains. The 3/32-inch chain was more flexible and it allowed the use of five-sprocket freewheels. Three sprockets were the limit for 1/8-inch chains.

Chains changed significantly in the late 1970s. Narrow-spaced freewheels were developed along with narrow chains. At the same time, Shimano and Sedis introduced the Uniglide and Sedisport chains with their funny-looking bulged side plates. The Sedisport chain also used special inner plates to get rid of the bushings. (Figures 9-1 and 9-2 show the difference between a conventional and a bushingless chain.) These three changes kicked off the current generation of modern derailleur chains. Now different chains are designed for different gear trains and few cyclists interchange chains any more.

Terminology time. I call the standard-width 3/32-inch derailleur chain a "wide" chain, and the narrow 3/32-inch derailleur chain a "narrow" chain. I won't talk any more about extra-wide, 1/8-inch, 1-speed chains.

Chains for Indexed Shifting

When Shimano and SunTour set out to design indexed shifting, repeatability was the overriding requirement. The indexed shift lever moves the cable, and the cable moves the rear derailleur jockey pulley a constant distance for each click. Therefore, the rear shift has to occur at the same place each time. An indexed shifting gear train is designed around a specific rear derailleur–freewheel–chain combination.

Each maker came up with a different design. Shimano designed SIS for flexible, early-shifting narrow chains. SunTour designed AccuShift for stiffer, late-shifting narrow chains. Campagnolo provides indexed shift levers and you pick the chain to match the rear derailleur and freewheel. You don't have to use the chains that Shimano, SunTour, or Campagnolo recommend, but if you use a different chain, then the shifting performance is your responsibility.

A chain that shifts very well with friction shift levers may not shift properly with the same freewheel and rear derailleur using indexed shift levers. This is particularly true with AccuShift. Sedisport and Narrow Uniglide chains shift well with current SunTour gear trains using friction levers, but not with AccuShift levers.

How the Chain Affects Shifting

In chapter 4 on indexed shifting, I told you about the rear derailleur, freewheel, chain, and shift lever interactions, so I won't repeat that information again. Instead, let's look at how chain design affects shifting, with or without indexed shift levers. The chain is involved in both front and rear shifting. You shift on the rear more frequently and chain design affects rear shifts more than front shifts.

In order of importance, crisp, positive rear shifting depends upon the following factors:

- The design of the rear derailleur.
- The shape of the freewheel sprockets.
- The spacing between freewheel sprockets.
- The tooth difference between adjacent freewheel sprockets.
- The design of the chain.

In order of importance, smooth, positive front shifting depends upon these factors:

- The design of the front derailleur.
- The tooth difference between the chainwheels.
- The spacing between the chainwheels.
- The design of the chain.

This suggests that chains don't matter very much, which isn't quite true. The chain is an essential part of the shifting system. The wrong chain can make a good gear train shift less crisply. The right chain is like icing on the cake, making a good gear train shift beautifully. However, even the best chain can't salvage a gear train with poor derailleurs and freewheels. Incidentally, good chains and poor chains cost about the same.

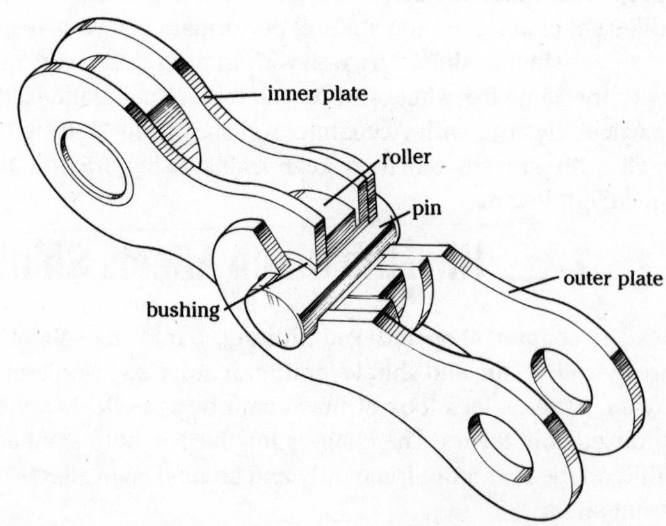

FIGURE 9-1

Parts of a conventional chain.

Chain Performance Testing

I've been mucking about with gear trains for more than ten years. It's taken me that long to put chains into perspective. In 1980, I had to stay home for three weeks while recovering from an operation. I couldn't ride my bicycle or do anything strenuous so I amused myself by using the derailleur testing machine to investigate differences between chains. I spent about 150 hours testing various permutations of chains, rear derailleurs, and freewheels. Then I spent about 20 hours writing my first chain article. The sweat-to-intellect ratio was higher than anything before or since. I gave some general recommendations in that article, but I didn't completely understand the chain's role in the complex rear-shifting mechanism. I could see what was happening, but I couldn't explain why it was happening.

I ran a similar series of tests for this chapter. This time, I understood the interactions better so my goals were better defined. Basically, I checked the performance of six integrated gear trains: Shimano narrow-range, Shimano wide-range, SunTour narrow-range, SunTour wide-range, Campagnolo narrow-range, and Campagnolo wide-range. The Campagnolo wide-range is typical of old-fashioned (pre-mountain bike) touring gear trains. The Campagnolo narrow-range is typical of old (pre-indexed shifting) racing gear trains. These six gear trains make up about 90 percent of all the applications.

I used the 11 chains listed in table 9-1. They include the 6 chains recommended by Shimano, SunTour, and Campagnolo for their indexed shifting gear

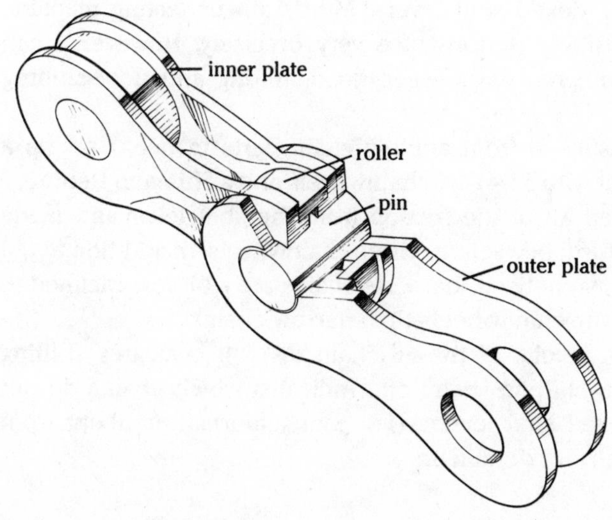

FIGURE 9-2

Parts of a bushingless chain.

TABLE 9-1.

Test Chains

Maker	Model	Model No.	Width	Maker's Recommendation
Regina	CX-S	50	N	racing, Syncro–W & N
Sedis	Sedisport	PRO, GT7	N	racing, SIS–W & N
Shimano	Narrow Uniglide	CN-7400, CN-6208	N	general, SIS–W & N
SunTour	SunTour Pro	SP-6200	N	racing, AccuShift–W & N
SunTour	Superbe Pro	SP-6000, SP-6100	N	general, AccuShift–W & N
HKK	Z-Chain	TZ-6000	I	general, AccuShift–W
HKK	Blue	H-1480	W	general
Regina	Oro	50	W	general
Regina	Record	50	W	racing
Sedis	Sedistraveler	DST	W	general, mountain bike
Shimano	Uniglide II	CN-6100, CN-UG20	W	general, SIS–W

trains, 4 popular and widely available premium chains, plus the HKK H-1480 chain, which is a conventional, low-priced derailleur chain.

I tested the chains in the same fashion that I test front and rear derailleurs. For the rear shifting chain tests, I used the gear trains listed in table 9-2. I tested all of the gear trains, except the Campagnolo racing, with both conventional friction shift levers and indexed shift levers. My derailleur testing machine doesn't measure front shifting performance very precisely. However, I can observe the significant differences between good-shifting and poor-shifting chains.

To get a rough measure of front shifting chain performance, I set up a Sugino Aero Tour crankset with 52/47/24 chainwheels and a Shimano Deore XT front derailleur. I removed all of the friction from the shift lever and made repeated shifts back and forth beween the three chainwheels. In addition to the machine measurements, I've noticed that wide chains are a bit less inclined to ride on the gap between the chainwheels than narrow chains.

Table 9-3 shows the results of the 66 chain tests. It evaluates shifting performance with friction shifting levers and indicates which chains do not work properly with indexed shift levers. (For more information about front shifting, see chapter 8 on front derailleurs.)

Chain Features

All of the differences in chain performance result from three design features: flexibility, width, and sideplate shape.

Chain Flexibility

A 1-speed chain is always perfectly aligned, so it doesn't have to be flexible. A derailleur chain must bend sideways (deflect) in most of the gears. In the cross-chain gears (big sprocket–big chainwheel or little sprocket–little chainwheel) the deflection is about an inch. The chain is noisy and inefficient in the cross-chain gears and most riders avoid them, especially on racing bicycles with short chainstays. A flexible chain gives less problem with deflection.

Flexibility can be either good or bad, depending on the rear derailleur. Chain flexibility works with the rear derailleur's chain gap (jockey pulley-to-sprocket distance) to provide precise shifting. A stiff chain needs more distance. A flexible chain needs less distance.

The Sedisport and the Shimano Narrow Uniglide chain have a unique bushingless construction that's very flexible. In general, worn chains are more flexible than new chains, which is why new chains often shift differently than worn chains.

With indexed shifting, the designer has to know the flexibility of the chain. I measured flexibility by laying a brand-new chain on its side on a ⅛-inch-thick plate and pushing it over the edge one link at a time. A flexible chain could only be pushed out three links (1½ inches) before it sagged ⅛ inch. A stiff chain

TABLE 9-2.

Chain Test Equipment

Gear Train	Rear Derailleur	Freewheel	Width	Sprockets
Campagnolo racing	C-Record	Regina CX	N	12-13-14-15-16-17-18
Campagnolo touring	Victory LX	Winner Pro	W	13-15-18-22-26-32
Shimano racing	Dura-Ace/SIS	Dura-Ace	N	12-13-14-15-16-17-18
Shimano touring	Deore XT/SIS	600 EX	W	13-15-18-22-26-32
SunTour racing	Superbe Pro AccuShift	Winner Pro	N	12-13-14-15-16-17-18
SunTour touring	XC-9000 AccuShift	Winner Pro	W	13-15-18-22-26-34

TABLE 9-3.

Chains

Make and Model	Cost ($)	Weight (gr.)	Width	Rear Shifting Performance						Front Shifting Performance
				Campy Narrow	Campy Wide	Shimano Narrow	Shimano Wide	SunTour Narrow	SunTour Wide	
HKK										
Z-Chain	6–10	340	W	—	VG	—	E	—	VG	G
Standard (H-1480)	4–6	340	W	—	G	—	P	—	G	P
Regina										
CX-S	25–35	350	N	G	G	VG	VG	VG	VG	E
Record	17–25	355	W	—	P	—	P	—	P*	F
Oro	7–10	390	W	—	F	—	P	—	F*	VG
Sedis										
Sedisport Pro	25–35	335	N	VG	F	VG	VG	G*	F*	VG
Sedisport Gold	8–12	330	N	VG	F	VG	VG	G*	F*	VG
Sedisport	5–8	330	N	VG	F	VG	VG	G*	F*	VG
Sedistraveler	8–12	350	W	—	G	—	P*	—	G*	F
Shimano										
Dura-Ace Narrow UG (CN-7400)	30–40	345	N	F	VG	E	E	G	VG*	VG
600 Narrow UG (CN-6208)	12–18	340	N	F	VG	E	E	G	VG*	VG
600 Uniglide (CN-6120)	12–18	375	W	—	P	—	G	—	P	VG
Uniglide II (CN-UG20)	8–12	375	W	—	P	—	G	—	P	VG
SunTour										
Superbe Pro (SP-6000)	15–22	350	N	VG	P	F	F*	VG	G	VG
SunTour Pro (SP-6200)	10–15	330	N	VG	G	F	F*	VG	VG	E
Cyclone (SP-6100)	8–12	350	N	G	P	F	F*	VG	G	VG

*This combination does not work with indexed shift levers.

could be pushed out six links. I show three ratings in table 9-3: flexible, intermediate, and stiff.

Chain Width

If your bike has a wide-spaced freewheel, you can use either a wide or a narrow chain, but best shifting performance usually comes from a narrow chain. If you have a narrow-spaced freewheel, you must use a narrow chain. Both wide and narrow derailleur chains have a 3/32-inch gap between the inner

Noise	Flexibility	Dimensions (mm)							Plate Shape		Color
		Pin Length	Outer Pl Width	Outer Pl Bulge	Outer Pl Gap	Inner Pl Width	Inner Pl Bulge	Inner Pl Gap	Outer	Inner	
avg.	int	7.6	6.8	—	4.8	4.3	—	2.5	Chmf	Chmf	silver, blue
avg.	int	8.0	6.8	—	4.9	4.5	—	2.6	—	—	blue
quiet	stf	7.3	6.9	—	4.9	4.6	—	2.5	—	cut	black, silver
avg.	flx	7.9	6.8	—	4.9	4.4	—	2.6	—	Chmf	gold, black
avg.	stf	8.1	7.2	—	5.1	4.5	—	2.5	—	—	gold, black
quiet	flx	7.5	6.8	—	4.8	4.5	5.4	2.6	—	Flr	silver
quiet	flx	7.4	6.8	—	4.8	4.5	5.4	2.6	—	Flr	gold
quiet	flx	7.4	6.8	—	4.8	4.5	5.5	2.6	—	Flr	black
avg.	stf	8.1	6.9	—	4.9	4.5	—	2.6	—	—	black, silver
quiet	flx	7.4	6.7	7.3	5.3	4.5	—	2.6	Bul	—	silver
quiet	flx	7.4	6.7	7.3	5.3	4.5	—	2.6	Bul	—	silver, black
noisy	int	8.0	6.9	7.9	5.8	4.5	—	2.8	Bul	—	silver, black
noisy	int	8.0	6.9	7.9	5.8	4.6	—	2.8	Bul	—	black
quiet	stf	7.4	6.6	7.0	4.8	4.3	—	2.6	Flr	Chmf	silver
avg.	int	7.4	6.5	—	4.8	4.4	—	2.7	—	cut	silver, black
quiet	stf	7.4	6.6	7.0	4.8	4.3	—	2.6	Flr	—	silver, black

plates. The wide and narrow categories are determined by the length of the pins. Narrow chains are less than 10 percent narrower than wide chains, but the spacing between the sprockets of a typical narrow-spaced freewheel is reduced from 3.5mm to 2.7mm, or 23 percent. Most of the narrowing comes from reducing the clearance between the chain and the sprockets.

You can tell quite a lot about a chain with a caliper. The key widths listed below are shown in figure 9-3 and are listed for each chain in table 9-3.

Pin Length The pin length tells you if the chain can fit in a narrow-spaced freewheel. It also tells you how far the chain can bend before the pins hit the adjacent freewheel sprocket. Narrow chain pins are 7.4mm long, or less. Wide chain pins are typically about 8mm long.

Outer Plate Width The width of the outer plate is most important when subtracted from the pin length, because protruding pins catch onto the teeth of chainwheels or sprockets and help shifting. Wide-spaced outer plates make the chain stiffer. Many of the better-shifting chains have bulged or flared outer plates. Flaring the outer plates exposes a wider gap to the teeeth, but it also shields the protruding pins.

Outer Plate Gap Wide outer plate gaps have more room to catch the corners of the sprocket or chainwheel teeth.

Inner Plate Width The width of the inner plate affects flexibility. The difference between the outer plate gap and the inner plate width also affects flexibility. The bulged inner plate is a unique feature of the Sedisport chain. The inner plate is flared out, which helps shifting.

Inner Plate Gap The width of the gap between inner plates measures how readily the chain will fall onto a smaller chainwheel when you shift on the front.

Chain Sideplate Design

Until 1977, all chains looked very much the same. The inner and outer plates were flat little dumbbells. With the introduction of narrow chains, the makers got the idea of widening the center of the plates to improve the chain's shifting ability. Now almost all of the premium chains have some kind of special plate shape. I think this is a bit like tire treads. It looks more important than it is. The key items are still width and flexibility. However, widened outer plates do improve front shifting. They also tend to marry certain chains to certain free-

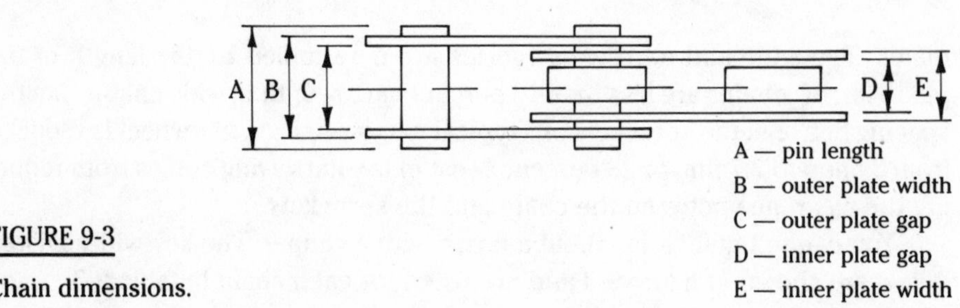

FIGURE 9-3

Chain dimensions.

wheel tooth profiles. The most obvious example is Shimano's twist-tooth freewheel sprockets and their Uniglide chains.

Four sideplate variations can be found among the chains listed in table 9-3. The outer plates can be bulged out, the inner or the outer plates can be flared out, the inside of the plates can be chamfered, or the bottom of the plates can be cut away.

Chain Tensile Strength

For my 1980 chain article, I tore the chains apart with a tensile test machine. I haven't run tensile tests on the new chains and I don't show the old test results. I think all chains, even the least expensive, are more than strong enough. For example, assume that a strong racer can push on the pedals with a 250-pound force. That's a 500-pound tension on the chain. The weakest chain that I tested in 1980 had an ultimate strength of 1,600 pounds. Chains don't stretch from tension. They get longer because of the wear of the pins, bushings, and rollers.

Chain Lubrication and Longevity

I've generally avoided maintenance topics in this book, but I can't resist this one. I didn't test chain longevity, but I'm convinced that chains wear out because of dirt and rust. Cleanliness and lubrication are the keys to long chain life. The definitive article on chain wear was written by Don Pruden in the February 1977 issue of *Bike World.* Don measured chain stretch after pedaling a series of chains 1,000 miles or so, using 11 different chain lubricants. He concluded that the best lubricant is paraffin wax. I agree and I've been touting wax since I read the article. You heat it up to about 300°F on top of your stove. Wax has about the same flash point as cooking oil, so take the same fire precautions as you do making french fries.

The hot wax gets in between the pins, bushings, and rollers, which are the only places where lubrication is needed. Once the chain cools off, the wax on the outside is hard. In fact, it quickly flakes off, so the chain doesn't attract dirt. I wax my chains every 300 miles or so, more often in wet weather.

Chain Makers

Just half a dozen makers sell quality chains in the aftermarket. There are another dozen or so makers of standard bulk bicycle chains.

HKK

HKK (Hokoku Chain Sales Co.) cooperated with SunTour and Fuji in the development of the narrow-spaced freewheel and the companion narrow chain. HKK made SunTour's early narrow Ultra-6 chains. The current HKK Z-Chain is a bit wider than a narrow chain and it's designed for wide-spaced freewheels. It has deep chamfers on the outer plates. The Z-Chain and HKK's Spirit chain are included in SunTour's list of recommended chains for wide-spaced 5- and 6-speed AccuShifts. The HKK H-1480 is a typical conventional derailleur chain. I used the HKK H-1480 for all of my old front and rear derailleur tests because I wanted a completely average chain. I include it to give you a "standard" chain for comparison.

Regina

Regina is the old favorite of the racers. They make eight different chains but only three or four are widely distributed. I ran the full series of tests on the wide Oro and Record and the narrow CX-S. I ran a few tests on the wide CX and the narrow BX chains.

Regina was late to develop a chain for narrow-spaced freewheels. By the time they introduced their top-of-the-line CX-S, virtually all of the racers were using Sedisports. The CX-S is an excellent-shifting chain. It's the only chain that shifts well on both AccuShift and SIS gear trains. The CX-S is asymmetrical and it has to be installed correctly. The inner and outer plates on the inside, and the

PHOTO 9-1

Narrow chains: top to bottom, Shimano Narrow Uniglide (bulged outer plates), Sedisport (flared inner plates), SunTour Superbe Pro (flared outer and chamfered inner plates), SunTour Pro (cutaway inner plates), and Regina CX (cutaway inner plates).

inner plates on the outside have a deep notch on the bottom to facilitate shifting onto larger sprockets. Regina's other narrow chains, the BX, Silver BX, and Oro BX look like conventional wide chains with short pins. They don't shift nearly as well as the CX-S.

The Regina Oro and Record are classic old designs. They both have oversized inner plates with a narrow gap between the inner plates and a large clearance between the inner and the outer plates. The Record has small outer plates that are drilled for lightness. Neither shifts very well on modern gear trains. The CX is the modern version of the Record.

Sedis

Sedis is now a part of Sachs-Huret, so that the Huret ARIS indexed shifting system will be calibrated around Sedis chains. Sedis introduced the narrow Sedisport chain in the late 1970s at the same time that Shimano introduced the wide Uniglide chain. The Sedisport was the first bushingless chain, with inner plates punched and upset to form bushings. This construction gives a very flexible chain. The Sedisport has flat parallel outer plates and bulged inner plates. It's one of the strongest chains made. It really excels on close-ratio, narrow-spaced seven-sprocket racing freewheels.

The Sedisport has completely taken over the professional racing circuit. It's strong, reliable, and cheap. The professional team mechanics can't be

PHOTO 9-2

Standard-width chains: top to bottom, Regina Oro BX (oversize plates), Sedistraveler (conventional chain), Shimano Uniglide II (bulged outer plates), Regina CX (oversize inner plates), and DID Lanner (flared outer and chamfered inner plates).

bothered cleaning and lubricating chains. They buy low-priced, gray Sedisports by the gross and install a new chain before every race.

Shimano designed their indexed system around two flexible narrow chains: the Narrow Uniglide and the Sedisport. On SIS gear trains, the two chains perform almost the same with a slight edge to the Narrow Uniglide. Sedisports may or may not work well with wide-range touring gearing. It depends on the rear derailleur and the freewheel. The combination of a Sedisport chain, a SunTour freewheel, and an old SunTour single-pivot GT derailleur is a sure loser. The Sedisport chain does not index well with SunTour AccuShift; it shifts too early, but it works fine in the friction mode.

Sedis is delighted to sell you higher-priced Sedisports. The silver or the gold models are identical to the gray model except for color and price. The Sedisport Pro is a nickle-plated super chain with selected links, extra-hard rollers, and extra-strong riveting.

The Sedistraveler is a conventional wide chain with special corrosion protection for mountain bike service. Conventional chains don't shift well with Shimano or SunTour indexed systems. The pins on all Sedis chains are "Delta-treated," which is their proprietary surface-hardening process.

Shimano

Shimano introduced the Uniglide chain with its characteristic bulged outer plates in 1977. I liked it then and I still like it. When Shimano developed the twist-tooth freewheel sprockets to go with the Uniglide chain, the shifting got even better. For a decade I've been recommending the wide Uniglide chain to people with problem gear trains. If it doesn't help, the gear train probably requires major surgery. The wide Uniglide chain is noisy. Nobody seems to know just why, not even Shimano.

As part of the SIS program, Shimano developed the Narrow Uniglide chain. I call it the "Shimanosport" because it combines Uniglide's bulged outer plates with the Sedisport's bushingless design. The Narrow Uniglide shifts better than the wide Uniglide both front and rear and it's silent.

Shimano now makes Narrow Uniglides in the Dura-Ace and 600 models and wide Uniglides in 600 and UG II models. The Dura-Ace is made from chrome-moly steel and has boron-treated pins.

SunTour

SunTour, Fuji, and HKK invented the narrow-spaced freewheel. (They brought it on themselves, Mrs. Twiddle.) For the first five years, SunTour recommended HKK Z-Chains or the very similar SunTour Ultra chain. The early Z-Chains shifted rather miserably. However, narrow-spaced, wide-range gear trains shift poorly regardless of what chain you use. I must have answered 50

TABLE 9-4.

Chain Recommendations

Gear Train	Index	Service	Recommended Chains
Shimano SIS	yes	R,T	Narrow UG, Sedisport, CX-S
SunTour AccuShift	yes	R,T	SunTour Pro, Superbe Pro, CX-S
Shimano, Simplex (pre-indexed)	no	R	Narrow UG, Sedisport, CX-S
Shimano, Simplex (pre-indexed)	no	T	Narrow UG, Wide UG
Suntour, Huret (pre-indexed)	no	R	Narrow UG, CX-S, Z-Chain
Suntour, Huret (pre-indexed)	no	T	Narrow UG, SunTour Pro, CX-S, Z-Chain
Campagnolo, Galli, Mavic, Ofmega, Zeus	no	R	Sedisport, SunTour Pro, CX-S

letters on that theme. The Daido DID Lanner chain, which appeared in about 1984, was a better chain for narrow-spaced, wide-range gear trains. The Daido company has never had good distribution in the U.S. aftermarket. All SunTour chains are now made by Daido.

SunTour now sells three fairly stiff narrow chains. The Superbe Pro (SP-6000) and the Cyclone (SP-6100) have similar flared outer plates. The Superbe Pro has chamfered corners on the inside of the inner plate.

The SunTour Pro (SP-6200) has cutaway inner plates, like the Regina CX-S, to allow the sprocket teeth to engage the chain. These two chains are called "Lone Rangers" because the cutaway plate looks like his mask. The SunTour Pro has fewer cutaway plates than the CX-S. The SunTour Pro shifts better on the front and a tiny bit better on the rear than the Superbe Pro. All three SunTour chains have Daido's "Dai-hard" surface treatment.

Frank's Favorite Chain

Table 9-3 records the results of many hours spent testing chains. There's a lot of data in that table. To help make your chain selection simpler, I have prepared table 9-4, which offers recommendations on which chains are best suited to different gear trains and different types of riding.

All of my bicycles have Shimano Dura-Ace Freehubs with twist-tooth sprockets. The Shimano Narrow Uniglide chain makes beautiful music with this freewheel and it's on all of the bikes.

CHAPTER 10

All about Pedals

More has happened to pedals in the past 5 years than in the previous 50. The big change is the strapless pedal systems that were introduced in 1986. A second significant change is the inclusion of pedals in most component gruppos. Before 1986, most serious riders used quill pedals made by either Campagnolo or by one of the small pedal companies. (The name "quill" comes from the turned up tab on the outside of the cage that keeps your shoe from slipping off. This tab resembles the nib of a goose quill pen. Quill pedals date back to the days when people still used goose quill pens.) Today, many serious riders are thinking about using something different. This chapter will outline your current options.

More good-quality 10-speeds use quill pedals than all of the other kinds of pedals put together. Quill pedals are used in three ways:

- With toe clips, tight straps, and cleated racing shoes.
- With toe clips, loose straps, and rubber-soled touring shoes.
- Without toe clips and with rubber-soled cycling shoes or running shoes.

If you're using one of the above combinations, you shouldn't be using quill pedals. (Now there's a controversial statement.) If you're in the first category, you should be using one of the new strapless pedal systems. If you're in the second category, you should be using platform pedals. If you're in the third category, you should be moving up to the second category, or you should be using double-sided rat-trap or mountain bike pedals. I'll expand on the rationale for each of these assertions later on.

Anchoring Feet to Pedals

For efficient pedaling, your feet have to be anchored to the pedals, and traditionally this has been done by means of toe clips and straps. Getting used to toe clips and straps is a difficult experience for most cyclists, who encounter them as adults rather than as part of the childhood process of learning to ride a bicycle. Perhaps a quarter of the adult riders who have mastered all of the subtleties of efficient bicycling still can't hack toe clips and straps. If you're in that category, all I can say is keep trying, the benefits are worth the effort.

Getting used to having your feet nailed to the pedals is mostly psychological. Some people start off with mini-clips and then move up to uncleated shoes and loose straps. Finally, they begin to tighten their straps. My observations are that only about 10 percent of adult riders ever progress to the point of using cleated shoes.

You can anchor your feet to the pedals with toe clips and straps or you can adopt one of the new strapless pedal systems. Either way, you improve your efficiency by spinning faster and applying power through more of the pedal circle. Only the short distance rider or city commuter should be without one system or the other. Let's look at the advantages and disadvantages of the two systems.

Conventional Pedals with Toe Clips and Straps

Toe clips and straps keep your feet in place on the pedals. There are two levels of rigidity, depending on whether or not you use cleated shoes. Prior to 1986, really serious riders used deep-cleated racing shoes with tight straps. With such shoes, you're nailed to the pedals and your feet can't rotate or pull out when you pull backwards at the bottom of the stroke. Cleated shoes keep your feet in place when you go over bumps. Because of the more rigid attachment, cleated shoes provide more pedaling efficiency than do toe clips and straps alone. You can spin faster and more smoothly and get more power out of your legs. Despite their advantages, there are four things wrong with cleated shoes:

- It's a chore to lock onto the pedals and tighten the straps when you start off.
- You have to remember to loosen the toe straps before you try to get out of the pedals.
- The tight toe straps act like tourniquets and cut off the flow of blood to your feet.
- Finally, cleated shoes aren't made for walking, so as soon as you get off your bike, you have to change shoes.

In addition to the above disadvantages, many riders feel acute mental distress at the thought of being nailed to the bicycle, especially at low speeds. To avoid some of the disadvantages and to reduce the terror, many riders use uncleated touring shoes and ride with loose straps. This way you get about half of the efficiency benefits and a tenth of the terror. You put up with lower pedaling efficiency because it's easy to get in and out of loose straps and because touring shoes are comfortable to walk on.

Strapless Pedal Systems

The strapless pedal is an idea whose time has come. I think that most racers will be using strapless pedals within 2 years. The great mass of serious cyclists will use them as the costs come down and the best overall designs become accepted. With hindsight, it's surprising that it took so long to improve on the old familiar shoe–pedal–toe clip–strap combination. Skis have used safety bindings for more than 20 years, but until now nobody thought to apply that technology to the much larger bicycle market.

All of the strapless pedal systems provide the efficiency of deep cleated shoes and they don't cut off the blood to your feet. All of the systems are easier to get into and out of than conventional pedals with cleated shoes. Still, they're for the kind of experienced riders who are comfortable with toe clips and straps. You're rigidly attached to the pedals and you have to remember the release drill and practice it until it becomes automatic.

I've tested five current strapless shoe-pedal systems made by Adidas, AeroLite, CycleBinding, Look, and Pedalmaster. Each system has a different entry and exit drill. CycleBinding and Look are the easiest to enter and exit. They're about the same as toe clips, straps, and touring shoes. All of the systems except CycleBinding are unpleasant to walk on. You can easily walk on CycleBinding shoes, though they are still not as comfortable for walking as touring shoes. Unfortunately, strapless pedal systems are expensive. They cost anywhere from $40 to $200, so you want to buy the right one the first time.

Basic Pedal Features

Before going into a more detailed discussion of the different pedal types and specific makes and models, let's review the principle features of a bicycle pedal system. Take these features into account when you make your choice as to which system is right for you.

Ease of Entry and Exit

I think that ease of entry and exist are the decisive factors in making the choice between the various strapless pedal systems, so I cover the differences at length in the writeups and in table 10-1. If you don't feel comfortable getting in and out of your pedals, you won't be happy with strapless pedals (nor with toe clips and straps).

TABLE 10-1.

Ease of Entry and Exit versus Pedaling Efficiency

Shoe-Pedal System	Ease of Entry	Ease of Exit	Pedaling Efficiency
Platform pedals, toe clips, loose straps, touring shoes	G	VG	G
Quill pedals, toe clips, tight straps, cleated racing shoes	P	P	E
Rat-trap or MB pedals, no toe clips	E	E	P
Strapless pedal systems	*	*	E

*See table 10-2.

Cost

In any pedal system there are actually three costs: pedals, shoes, and connecting hardware. If you have to throw away both your present pedals and shoes, it's going to cost more to upgrade. The cost column in table 10-2 shows shoe and pedal prices for Adidas and CycleBinding, pedal and cleat prices for Look and AeroLite, and cleat and pedal adapter prices for Pedalmaster. Clearly I'm comparing apples and oranges since the prices reflect the different amounts of equipment. But, in each case, what is shown is the total cost of the components required to make the conversion to strapless pedals. Table 10-3 shows the cost of conventional pedals only.

Weight

Pedals, toe clips, and straps are part of the bicycle weight. Weight freaks measure that in milligrams. Shoe and cleat weights are different because they're worn. (Instead of worrying about a few ounces of shoes, maybe you should worry about those extra pounds of lard that are standing on top of the shoes.) Table 10-2 shows four weights: pedals, cleats, shoes, and total. I assume a 600-gram racing shoe for the systems that don't include shoes. Table 10-3 shows the weight of just the pedals. To be comparable to the total weight in table 10-2, you should add about 130 grams for toe clips and straps, and 650

Table 10-2.

Strapless Shoe-Pedal Systems

Make and Model	Cost ($)	Type	Weight (gr.) Total	Pedals	Cleats	Shoes	Body Material	Drag Angle (deg.)	Height (in.)
Adidas									
System 3 Super Pro	180–200	P + Sh	1130	440	N/A	690	Fbrgl	29	1.5
AeroLite									
Titanium	120–150	P + Cl	740	96	40	600	Ttnm	33	0.7
Standard	70–80	P + Cl	790	150	40	600	Al	33	0.7
CycleBinding									
Racing	210–230	P + Sh	1230	480	—	750	Al	30	0.6
Sport	130–150	P + Sh	1380	480	—	850	Al	30	0.6
Look									
Competition	130–160	P + Cl	1190	480	110	600	Al	30	1.3
Sport	90–120	P + Cl	1230	520	110	600	Al	29	1.3
ATB/Leisure	65–90	P + Cl	1140	430	110	600	Fbrgl	28	1.3
Pedalmaster	40–60	Cl + Ad	1220	470	140	610	N/A	N/A	1.4

grams for cleated racing shoes, or 700 grams for touring shoes. The shoe weights are typical for a size 10½.

Drag Angle

Larger drag angles let you pedal around corners leaning your bike farther over without dragging a pedal. Since this is critical for criterium racers, their bicycles have extra-high bottom brackets. Quill pedals and racing platform pedals are made as narrow as possible and the underside is cut away to improve the drag angle.

Drag angle isn't nearly as critical for tourists as it is for racers. I've installed triple cranksets and 175mm cranks on all of my bicycles. Both changes worsen the drag angle. I surprise myself and scrape a pedal once a year or so, but it's no big deal.

There's a break point at about 25 degrees. With less than that, you'll find your pedals scraping in normal cornering. Campagnolo quill pedals have a 30-degree drag angle. Most riders can live very comfortably with that. The new racing platform pedals and AeroLite have even better drag angles. But, bear in mind that most of us feel quite nervous with a bike leaned over as much as 35 degrees, Avocet tire advertisements notwithstanding.

Drag angle is affected both by pedal dimensions and by bicycle design. Bottom bracket height, crank length, and spindle length all determine how far

Bearing Type	Bearing Seal	Ease of Entry	Ease of Exit	Ease of Walking	Ease of Adjust.	Rotation (deg.)	Release Torque (in.-lb.)	Over-stress Release	Service	Overall Rating
CB	yes	VG	F	VG	VG	2	200–400	G	R, ST	F
SCN	yes	F	G	P	P	0	N/A	P	R, ST, LT	G
SCN	yes	F	G	P	P	0	N/A	P	R, ST, LT	G
SCB	yes	E	VG	G	G	0	150	E	R, ST	E
SCB	yes	E	VG	VG	G	0	150	E	ST, LT	E
SCB	yes	VG	VG	F	E	4	90	F	R, ST	VG
SCB	yes	VG	E	F	E	6	60–100	F	R, ST, LT	VG
SCB	yes	VG	E	F	E	6	60	F	ST, LT	G
N/A	N/A	G	G	F	VG	0	—	P	R, ST, LT	G

you can lean over before you drag a pedal. Because the right crank is further outboard, the right drag angle is about 2 degrees smaller than the left. In countries where you drive on the right, the chain should be on the right in order to place the better drag angle on the left. However, the British, who invented the chain-driven bicycle, put the chain on the right side even though they drive on the left.

If you use a triple crankset and the longer triple spindle, the right-side drag angle will be about 1 degree smaller. If you use 175mm cranks instead of 170mm, the drag angle will be about 1½ degrees smaller. Conversely, 165mm cranks will increase the drag angle about 1½ degrees.

I built a jig to measure drag angle. I assumed a 10¾-inch bottom bracket height and I used a 170mm Campagnolo Record crankset with a Campagnolo 68-SS-120 double spindle. (The drag angle listed in tables 10-2 and 10-3 is the average of the left and right side drag angles.)

Height

Height is the distance from the inside of the shoe sole to the centerline of the pedal spindle. The greater the height, the higher you have to raise your

(continued on page 176)

TABLE 10-3.

Conventional Pedals

Make and Model	Cost ($)	Type	Weight (gr./pr.)	Spindle	Material Body	Cage	Drag Angle (deg.)	Dimensions (in.) Shoe Width	Rear Width
Campagnolo									
C-Record	160–220	track	370	CrMo	Al	Al	30	—	3.2
C-Record (305)	160–220	R. plat.	365	CrMo	Al	Al	30	—	3.2
Super Record (4021)	225–300	quill	259	Ttnm	Al	Al	30	3.6	—
Super Light (1037A)	130–170	quill	320	CrMo	Al	Al	30	3.6	—
Victory (405)	100–130	R. plat.	—	CrMo	Al	Al	30	—	3.2
Record Strada (1037)	100–130	quill	397	CrMo	Al	Al	30	3.6	—
Galli									
Criterium/ Maillard 700	60–90	quill	339	Stl	Al	Al	29	4.0	—
Lyotard									
Berthet (ref. 23)	15–25	T. plat.	365	Stl	Stl	—	31	—	3.2
Rat-Trap (ref. 136R)	12–20	rat-trap	330	Stl	Stl	Stl	27	—	3.5
MKS									
RX-1 (1014)	50–70	track	255	CrMo	Al	Al	—	—	—
Unique Custom (1002)	30–50	quill	361	CrMo	Al	Al	30	3.6	—
Grafight-2000 (5808)	15–25	ATB	500	CrMo	Fbrgl	Fbrgl	—	—	4.1
Grafight-X (5802)	15–25	ATB	426	CrMo	Fbrgl	Fbrgl	—	—	4.0
Sylvan Road (2021)	12–20	quill	360	Stl	Al	Al	29	3.6	—
Sakae									
Silstar (SP-11)	20–30	T. plat.	375	Stl	Al	—	30	—	2.8
Silstar (SP-100)	15–25	quill	345	Stl	Al	Al	30	3.7	—
Mountain (SP-518)	12–20	ATB	375	Stl	Plst	Plst	—	—	—

Dimensions (in.)			Height (in.)	Bearing		Features	Service
Front Width	Gap	Cage Thickness		Type	Seal		
2.0	2.3	0.10	1.2	C&C	spiral	includes toe clips and straps	R, ST
2.0	2.6	0.10	1.2	C&C	spiral	includes toe clips and straps	ST, LT
—	2.4	0.10	1.2	C&C	spiral	titanium spindle	R, ST
—	2.4	0.10	1.2	C&C	spiral	aluminum cage	R, ST
2.0	2.6	0.10	1.2	C&C	spiral	includes toe clips and straps	R, ST
—	2.4	0.10	1.2	C&C	spiral	steel cage	R, ST
—	2.3	0.10	1.2	C&C	laby	wide quill	R, ST
3.2	N/A	0.07	1.0	C&C	none	flat platform	LT
3.5	2.5	0.11	1.1	C&C	none		City
—	—	—	—	SCB	plst. bush		R, ST
—	2.6	0.10	1.2	C&C	spiral		R, ST
4.1	3.5	N/A	—	C&C	plst. bush		City
4.0	3.5	N/A	—	C&C	plst. bush		City
—	2.4	0.11	1.1	C&C	plst. bush		R, ST
2.8	N/A	0.11	1.1	C&C	plst. bush	flat platform	LT
—	2.5	0.10	1.1	C&C	plst. bush		R, ST
—	—	—	—	—		—	City

(continued)

Conventional Pedals—*Continued*

Make and Model	Cost ($)	Type	Weight (gr./pr.)	Spindle	Material Body	Cage	Drag Angle (deg.)	Dimensions (in.) Shoe Width	Rear Width
Shimano									
Dura-Ace (PD-7400)	95–140	R. plat.	310	CrMo	Al	Al	34	—	3.1
Deore XT (PD-M730)	45–65	ATB	415	CrMo	Al	Al	26	—	3.5
105 (PD-1050)	35–50	R. plat.	287	CrMo	Al	Al	33	—	2.9
600 EX (PD-6207)	35–50	R. plat.	370	CrMo	Al	Stl	31	—	3.2
Triathlon (PD-T100)	20–30	T. plat.	362	CrMo	Al	Al	31	—	2.9
Specialized									
Racing (PL-R)	60–90	track	335	CrMo	Al	Al	31	—	3.0
Touring (PL-T)	60–90	T. plat.	372	CrMo	Al	Al	30	4.4	3.6
SunTour									
Superbe Pro (PL-5800)	60–90	quill	290	CrMo	Al	Al	32	3.4	—
XC-Compe (PL-5700)	40–60	ATB	320	CrMo	Al	Al	27	—	3.2
Sprint (PL-5600)	30–45	track	345	CrMo	Al	Al	29	—	3.2
Cyclone (PL-5300)	30–40	track	398	CrMo	Al	Al	29	—	3.2

*This model has a conventional cup-and-cone inner bearing, but a sealed cartridge needle outer bearing.

saddle and the higher your center of gravity. To measure height, I used the total distance rather than measuring from the outside of the shoe sole, because Adidas System 3 and CycleBinding require you to use their specific shoes. With conventional pedals and shoes, there's more variation in the shoes than in the pedals. A thick-soled shoe and a cleat with extra material above the slot increases the height.

Bicycling's August 1986 issue rated cleated racing shoes. The distance from the inside of the sole to the top of the cleat slot varied from 0.25 to 0.75 inch between the different shoes. I used 0.5 inch (0.4 inch sole thickness and 0.1 inch cleat thickness) in table 10-3 for measuring height on the conventional quill pedals.

Dimensions (in.)			Height (in.)	Bearing		Features	Service
Front Width	Gap	Cage Thickness		Type	Seal		
2.0	1.5	0.09	1.1	*	laby		R, ST
3.5	3.1	0.11	1.1	C&C	laby		City
2.3	1.8	0.10	1.2	C&C	plst. bush		R, ST
2.0	1.7	0.09	1.2	C&C	O-rings		R, ST
2.5	N/A	0.10	1.1	C&C	O-rings		ST, LT
2.5	2.5	0.10	1.1	C&C	plst. bush		R, ST
3.6	N/A	0.10	1.2	C&C	plst. bush		LT
—	2.3	0.10	1.1	SCB	yes		R, ST
3.2	2.3	0.10	1.1	SCB	yes		City
2.5	2.3	0.10	1.1	C&C	O-rings		R, ST
2.5	2.3	0.10	1.1	C&C	plast. bush		R, ST

Bicycling's October 1986 issue rated rubber-soled touring shoes. The sole thickness varied from 0.3 to 0.5 inch between the different shoes. I allowed 0.4 inch for sole thickness in table 10-3 when measuring height for platform, rat-trap, and mountain bike pedals. I also used a 0.4-inch sole thickness in my table 10-2 height measurements for AeroLite, Look, and Pedalmaster systems.

Service

Each kind of conventional pedal and each of the strapless pedal systems was designed for a particular kind of bicycling service. Tables 10-2 and 10-3 show my judgment of this service, whether it be racing, sport touring, loaded touring, or city riding.

Bearings

Pedal bearings are smaller and more highly stressed than hub or crankset bearings. Pedal rpm is too slow for good lubrication and pedal bearing loading is cyclic because you push only on the downstroke. Moreover, pedal bearings take a lot of abuse from the water and grit splashed up by the front wheel. Adding insult to injury, most cyclists neglect pedal lubrication. Considering all of these factors, it's amazing that conventional cup-and-cone ball bearings hold up as well as they do.

Pedals are the one place on a bike where sealed cartridge bearings make sense. All of the strapless pedal systems use high-quality sealed cartridge

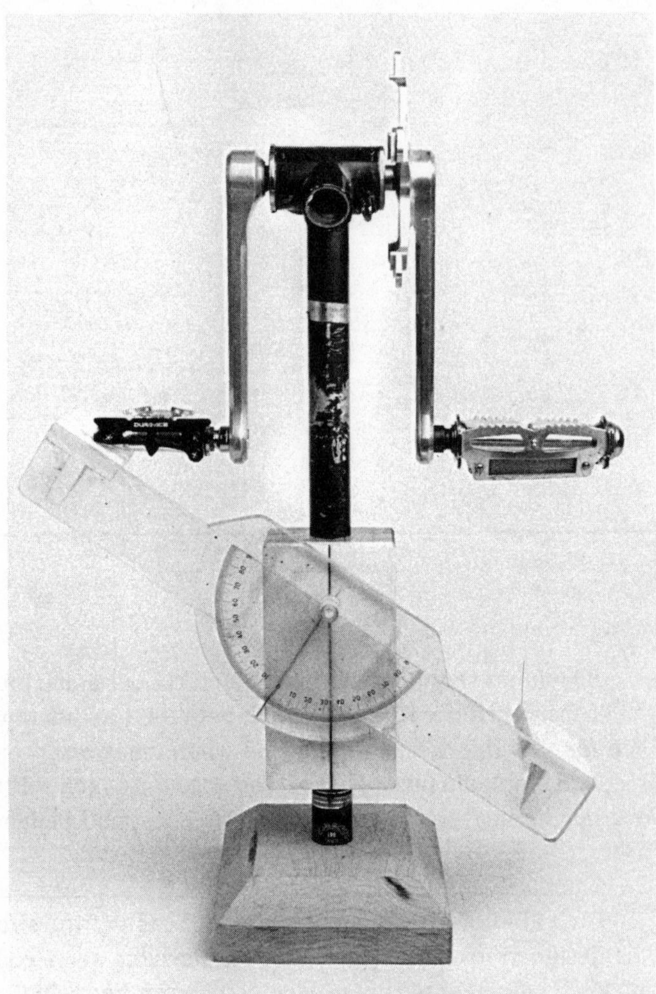

PHOTO 10-1

Drag angle measurement jig: left, Dura-Ace pedal (34-degree drag angle); right, counterweighted pedal (23-degree drag angle).

bearings of one kind or another. Adidas, CycleBinding, Look, and Shimano combine roller and ball bearings. AeroLite uses two cartridge roller bearings.

All good-quality conventional pedals either use cartridge bearings or cup-and-cone bearings with a seal to keep moisture out of the inboard bearing. Campagnolo and the Japanese Campy-copies use a spiral on the spindle. As the pedal revolves, the spiral grooves "screw" dirt and moisture away from the bearings. This works surprisingly well if you use lots of grease. The other top-quality pedals use close-clearance plastic bushings or labyrinth seals.

You get what you pay for with pedal bearings. Top-of-the-line pedals have hardened and ground races and cones, and you can feel the quality when you spin them. Lower-priced pedals use cruder manufacturing techniques, however, even poor-quality cup-and-cone bearings work adequately. *Sutherland's Handbook for Bicycle Mechanics* (4th ed.) says that most pedals have ten to twelve 5⁄32-inch balls per race. Campagnolo Super Record and Sakae use 1⁄8-inch balls, but everyone else uses 5⁄32-inch balls.

For some strange reason, some pedal makers install one less ball than it takes to fill the race. I can't believe this is an economy measure, so I suspect they're anticipating that the bearings will never be serviced. When I was disassembling and inspecting pedals, I had to restrain myself to keep from popping an extra ball into the obvious gap.

Tables 10-2 and 10-3 show the type of bearings used and whether or not they have seals. The type of seal for most models is indicated in table 10-3.

Walkability

Walkability depends entirely on the shoes. There's a basic conflict between pedaling efficiency and walking comfort. Stiff soles protect your feet from pedal pressure, but they're less comfortable to walk on. When you attach cleats to the bottom of your cycling shoes, walking becomes uncomfortable. If you walk on your cleats, they'll wear out in short order.

The inverted cleat of the CycleBinding system is unique. You can walk on CycleBinding shoes. However, the slots fill up if you walk on soft dirt. (Table 10-2 shows my personal rating of the walkability of the five strapless pedal systems.)

Adjustability

With conventional pedals, you adjust the shoe-pedal fit when you install the cleats. Most good-quality racing shoes have some adjustability with their built-in cleats. There are two different adjustments with the strapless pedal systems. One is the ability to correct the alignment of a pedal-cleat system after you've attached the cleats to the shoes. With Adidas and CycleBinding, the shoe attachment is fixed, but you can modify the alignment of the pedal attachment.(Ease of adjustment for the different systems is rated in table 10-2.)

Rigidity

The experts agree that for maximum pedaling efficiency, the shoe should be fixed to the pedal. There should be no back and forth, up and down, or side to side movement. However, there's disagreement about rotation. Some experts think a small amount of rotation is desirable. When only toe clips and straps are used, there's quite a bit of movement in all directions except forward. With cleated shoes, you're fixed in all directions except up and down, which is why the racers cinch their straps so tightly. All of the strapless pedals are rigid in all three directions. They vary in the amount of rotation (table 10-2 shows the approximate rotation).

Release Torque

Release torque is the amount of twist that your ankle applies to rotate out of Adidas, CycleBinding, Look, and Pedalmaster pedals. Force times lever arm equals torque. It's about 7 inches from a size 10½ ankle to the pedal spindle. Thus, a 10-pound release force produces a 70 inch-pound torque. Release torque is shown for most models in table 10-2. I don't show the AeroLite release torque because it's applied in a different plane and the forces aren't comparable. AeroLite torque varies significantly, depending on the tightness of the screws.

Overstress Release

I think overstress or "safety" release is more important on the ski slopes than on the road. And with 60,000 trial lawyers waiting for the next Corvair, you won't be reading much about the safety aspect of the new strapless pedal systems. However, there are significant differences between systems. CycleBinding provides the most complete overstress release. The Adidas literature talks about quick release in the event of an obstacle or fall. The other strapless systems only release in the designed direction. There's precious little overstress release with deep cleats and tight straps, but there aren't many broken ankles, even in the Category 4 demolition derbies.

I didn't test overstress release in a formal way. Proper testing would have required comprehensive laboratory equipment and I'm not sure that it's worth the effort. The ratings provided in table 10-2 are thus based on my informal observations.

Dimensions

With conventional pedals, you have to match the pedal's dimensions to dimensions of your feet and your shoes. In table 10-3, I list "shoe width" for the quill models, where your shoe has to fit between the shoe stop on the inside and the quill on the outside of the pedal (as shown in figure 10-1). I list the "front width" and "rear width" for the other kinds of pedals. The "gap" figures found in the table are measurements of the space between the cage rails on quill or track pedals and between the back rail and the front platform on platform pedals. (It is this space between rails that makes so many pedals uncomfortable with soft-soled shoes.) The "cage thickness" figures tell you how wide your shoe cleat must be, and are thus relevant only on models made to be used with cleated shoes.

Strapless Shoe-Pedal Systems

Since the first strapless pedals appeared in 1985, five makes of strapless pedals have achieved significant distribution in the aftermarket: Adidas, Aero-Lite, CycleBinding, Look, and Pedalmaster. I've tested each system and assembled relevant data into table 10-2.

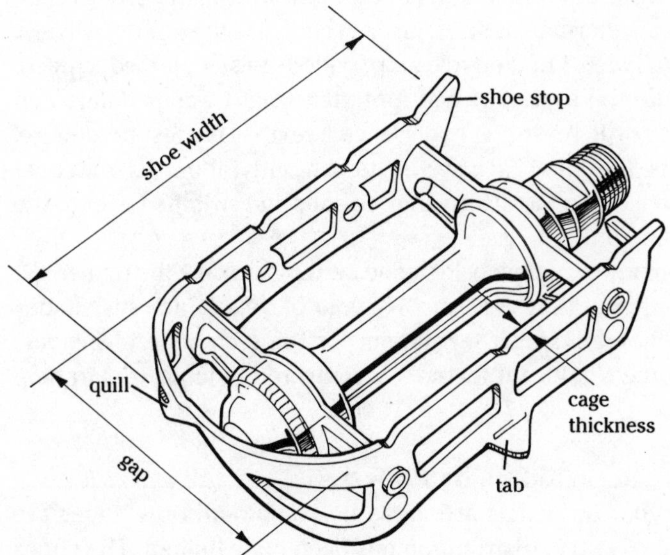

FIGURE 10-1

Dimensions of quill pedals.

Adidas and Look are major companies who make other products besides pedals. Their pedals are imported from France. AeroLite, CycleBinding, and Pedalmaster are small American companies. Shimano has a license to use the Look cleat design. You'll be seeing Shimano "Look-alike" pedals soon, but they were not available to me for testing at the time of this writing.

Adidas, CycleBinding, and Look use ski-binding technology. AeroLite and Pedalmaster have their own unique concepts. Adidas and CycleBinding come as shoe-cleat-pedal systems with shoes specifically designed for strapless pedals. AeroLite and Look provide pedals and cleats that you install on your own racing shoes. Pedalmaster provides clamps that bolt onto conventional pedals and adapter plates that bolt onto regular racing shoes.

Pre-1986 racing shoes were designed for toe clips and straps. "Animals" who really pull up may pull the uppers from the soles if they use their old shoes with AeroLite, Look, or CycleBinding strapless pedals. The new strapless pedal systems have caught on so well that most of today's racing shoes are designed for strapless pedal service, and many of them are pre-drilled for Look cleats.

It would be wonderful if there were an American Bicycle Standards Association to develop a standard for strapless shoe-pedal systems. Our industry doesn't work that way, so we have five different systems with five different entry-exit drills. I've pedaled all five and compared them, both in my workshop and out on the road. I used Look pedals on my 1986 summer tour of the Pacific Northwest.

I tested Look and AeroLite first. I installed them on two different bikes, planning to test them on alternate outings, just as I compare tires or derailleurs. That was a dumb idea. Twice, I braked to a stop, pulled, twisted, jerked, cursed, and toppled softly onto the asphalt. I had forgotten what I was pedaling and used the wrong release drill. After that experience, I revised my test procedure. For the rest of the tests, I pedaled each system for a month (about 300 miles) to get completely used to it. Then I wrote my impressions and switched over to the next system.

Take a lesson from my experience. Pick one system and take the time to get fully used to it. Install the same system on all of your bicycles. Each system has its own entry-exit technique, and it takes time for the technique to become second nature. All of the significant features are covered in table 10-2 to help you make your choice.

Adidas System 3

System 3 is French. The pedals are made by Manolo and the shoes are made by Adidas. Until now, U.S. distribution has been quite limited. The shoes have ridges on the sides of the sole that engage with grooves in the fiberglass-reinforced pedals. According to the advertising, the pedal grooves are designed to release under excessive stress in all three positions. I didn't test the overstress release.

System 3 is a combination of the very popular Adidas cross-country ski binding and the old Cinelli M 71 strapless pedal system. Cinelli M 71s were often called "death cleats" because there were just two positions: "lock" and "release." You used a little tab to make the selection. In the "release" position, you could slide your shoe in and out of the pedal, but it was awkward to pedal because the shoe would pull out coming around the bottom. In the "lock" position, you were nailed to the pedals. The only way to get out was to push in the little tab. Track racers were the major users of these pedals.

Currently, there is only one System 3 model available, the Super Pro. The Super Pro pedal adds an intermediate position and overstress release to the M 71 design. A three-position lever on the pedal raises a stud partly in the second position and completely in the third position. The positions are called "town," "road," and "sprint."

In the "road" position, you're supposed to be able to rotate your foot out of the pedals, but the release torque varied and I couldn't always jerk my foot out. With the pedal at the six o'clock position, I could usually get out with a combined twist and pull up. After a dozen or so false attempts, I always put the lever into the "town" position before pulling out. I treated System 3 like racing shoes with deep cleats. (It's easier to turn the little lever than to loosen a tight toe strap on a conventional pedal.) I never used the "sprint" position because I never came close to a false release in the "road" position.

It's easy to get into the System 3 pedals, much like a conventional pedal with toe clips. I also liked the Adidas STi shoes. They use Velcro closures and straps instead of laces; they were very comfortable pedaling and fairly comfortable walking. There's no cleat but there's also no heel. Adidas now makes three System 3 shoes: one for road racing, one for track racing, and one for touring.

AeroLite

AeroLite is a small American company started by inventor Roger Sanders. The AeroLite system isn't based on a ski binding; it's uniquely designed for bicycles. The other four systems all have a rotate-to-release drill, in which you push your heel out. AeroLite has a roll-to-release drill, in which you push your knee out.

The AeroLite pedal will be controversial because it's unique. Riders will either love it or hate it. Look at table 10-2. This pedal system rates at the top or the bottom in almost every category—for example, it's lightest in weight and offers the best drag angle, but it's the poorest for walking. The AeroLite system is elegantly simple. The pedal is a spindle with a roller, and the cleat is a wide, plastic C-clip attached to the sole of the shoes with four screws.

You attach yourself to an AeroLite pedal by placing the cleat on the spindle and pushing down hard. You release by rolling your foot sideways and pulling free. I found that this worked best at the 12 o'clock and 6 o'clock positions. I developed a roll-and-jerk action to counteract the cleat's tendency to hang on to the end of the roller. There's only one adjustment—the tightness of the four screws that attach the cleat. Tightening the screws squeezes the cleat together, making it harder to clamp onto the pedal and harder to pull free. It's more pleasant to ride with loose screws. However, if they're too loose and you're a strong rider, you may pull out of the pedal on the upstroke. So the adjustment is critical. I got them just right after I took a Phillips screwdriver with me on a ride and tightened the screws a quarter of a turn at a time.

AeroLite had startup problems with the cleats sliding sideways on the roller pedal. They went through three different fixes before they finally licked the problem. The current cleat has a stop on both ends. With more and more shoes coming pre-drilled for Look cleats, AeroLite developed an adapter plate that bolts onto the three Look holes and is pre-drilled for AeroLite cleats. AeroLite is the favorite of serious triathletes. I expect to see AeroLite pedals on ultra-light bicycles. AeroLite recognizes the weight-freak market and they make a special super-light titanium model.

AeroLite is the least expensive and lightest of the five strapless systems, and has the best drag angle. You're solidly attached to the pedal. There's no overstress release on ankle rotation. In fact, your shoes don't rotate at all. You "wear" your bicycle just like you do with deep cleats and tight straps. The difference is that there's no strap to restrict your circulation and there's a no-hands release drill.

The AeroLite pedal is a roller, so it's difficult to start out or to pedal when you're not clamped on, because your shoe tends to slip off. I learned to put the cleat behind the roller and not push too hard. I also learned to clamp one pedal before I swung onto the saddle. Finally, the shoes are hard to walk on, just like racing shoes with deep cleats.

CycleBinding

CycleBinding is a new company founded by Rick Howell, who used to work for the Geze ski-binding company. CycleBinding makes racing, triathlete, and sport shoes, as well as racing and sport pedals. The CycleBinding and Look systems are quite similar. CycleBinding is closer to Geze ski bindings, while Look is closer to Look ski bindings. Skiers might find it useful to select a pedal system to match their ski bindings. The key difference between them is that

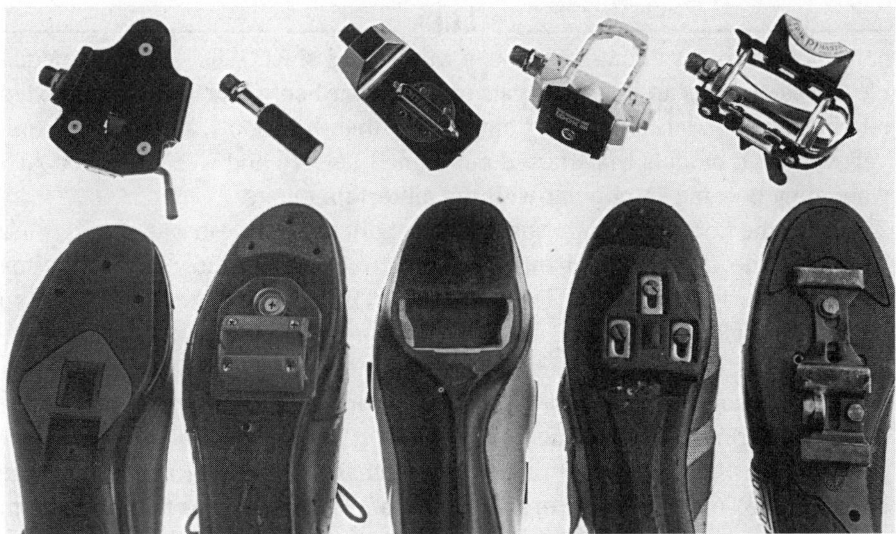

PHOTO 10-2 Strapless shoe-pedal systems: left to right, Adidas System 3 pedal and shoe, AeroLite Pedal and Diadora shoe, CycleBinding Competition pedal and shoe, Look Sport pedal and shoe, and Pedalmaster adapters on Galli pedals and Vittoria shoes.

CycleBinding is a shoe-pedal-cleat system with the female element molded into the shoe sole. Look is a pedal-cleat system and the male cleat protrudes from the shoe sole. The flat-soled CycleBinding shoes are much more comfortable to walk on.

The CycleBinding pedal is dropped like the old Shimano Dyna-Drive. Rick Howell set out to improve on what he saw as limitations of Shimano's design. The pedal is elegantly engineered with top-quality bearings and seals. The pedal is self-righting so that the male element, called the powerhead, always faces up. You lock in with an easy push and twist motion. In fact, it's so easy that I sometimes locked in unintentionally when I rested my foot on the pedal after releasing. The shoe is rigidly locked onto the pedal in all directions.

You release from the CycleBinding pedal by rotating your foot sideways. The release torque is more than Look and less than Adidas. The shoe is restrained against rotation until you exceed the release torque and then it releases with a snap action. I could easily get out at any crank position. The CycleBinding system has overstress release in other directions when the torque or the force approaches a critical level. My test setup used a 50-pound scale. The overstress releases took more than 50 pounds, so I only measured the release torque.

Look

Look strapless pedals have been race-tested since 1984. Look is a pedal-cleat system. You can bolt the cleats onto any hard-soled racing shoes. I tested all three Look pedals: the black Competition, the white Sport, and the black and yellow plastic models that started out named Leisure and were renamed ATB when they became so popular with the all-terrain bikers.

All of the Look pedals are substantially built using industrial ball and roller bearings. The locking mechanism on all three hangs below the centerline giving an average drag angle. The Sport and ATB (Leisure) models are wider so their drag angles are worse.

The Look cleat is substantial, though not too thick. It's easier to walk on Look cleats than on AeroLites, Pedalmasters, or racing shoes with deep cleats, but you wouldn't enjoy walking up a long hill. (On my 500-mile tour, I carried a pair of Hush Puppies in my panniers and changed as soon as I got off the bicycle.) Look makes a range of shoes. All feature Velcro straps that make them very easy to slip on and off.

The Look pedal hangs with the back down. Locking in is easy. You push the front of the cleat forward against the pedal and push down. Getting out is even easier. I'm most comfortable with the adjustment set at the minimum. But even with the adjustment turned to maximum, you can rotate your foot out in any crank position. I'm comfortable braking to a stop and pulling out at the last moment. The Look binding is rigid in all directions except rotation. Your shoes can rotate on the pedals about 5 degrees. If you rotate beyond that, you release. Depending on the advertising you believe, freedom of rotation may or may not be ergonomically desirable.

Pedalmaster

Bicycle Parts Pacific (BPP) is an importer whose lines include Galli pedals and Vittoria shoes. After the first strapless pedals had been on the market for two years, Darek Barefoot of BPP got a brilliant idea. Many cyclists were going to want strapless pedals, but they wouldn't want to throw away their perfectly good quill pedals. As new bicyle customers bought strapless pedals, the bicycle stores were going to be swamped with brand-new nonstrapless pedals. The Pedalmaster system was designed to fill that need.

For $40, you get a set of front and rear clamps to bolt onto your quill or platform pedals and a set of shoe plates to bolt onto your racing shoes. You fasten shoe to pedal by pushing the front of the shoe plate into the front pedal clamp. Then you swing your heel inward so that the loop at the back of the shoe plate engages the hook on the back of the pedal. You swing your heel outward to exit. I pedaled a Pedalmaster set for 300 miles or so. I found this system harder to enter and exit than the Look or CycleBinding systems and easier than the AeroLite system. Once locked in, you're rigid in all directions. Your shoe is about ⅛ inch higher than it would be with conventional cleats. The pedal dimensions and features depend on the pedal that you adapt in this way.

Overall Comparison

With strapless pedals, you're dealing with a new product and the players in the marketplace are still learning their roles. Now that Shimano is making Look-licensed pedals, the Look system is the one to beat—widely advertised and widely available. You can expect Shimano to introduce lower-priced versions year by year. The present Look pedals are solidly built. Entry and exit are easy and reliable and your shoes can rotate a bit.

The CycleBinding system appeals to the person who wants all of the features and is willing to pay for them. CycleBinding's comfortable walking shoes are very appealing, but you have to buy the complete shoe-pedal package from CycleBinding, and they don't come cheap.

Pedalmaster appeals to the other end of the price spectrum. It's not as convenient to enter and exit as most of the others but it lets you use your present shoes and pedals.

AeroLite will find a major market because of it's low weight, splendid drag angle, and low price. It's unique entry/exit drill takes some getting used to. For racers and triathletes, it has all of the advantages of racing shoes with deep cleats and it beats them hands down.

"Looking" at the competition, I don't think Adidas System 3 will survive in the USA. The lack of a completely predictable exit in this system and the limited distribution is too much of a handicap.

Types of Conventional Pedals

If you stick with conventional pedals, be aware that there are important differences between the various types. Pick the type that suits you. There are two main categories: single-sided and double-sided. When I wrote my first pedal article in 1983, I weighed, disassembled, and measured 60 different pairs of conventional pedals. For this chapter, I picked the best of the 60 and added 20 conventional pedals that have appeared on the market since 1983.

Single-Sided Pedals

Single-sided pedals are designed for toe-clips and straps. Toe clips come in three or four lengths: short, medium, large, and sometimes extra large. Lengths aren't standardized, and the French sizes are a bit larger than the Japanese. Buy a toe clip length that positions the ball of your foot over the pedal spindle. You can now buy reinforced plastic toe clips from Specialized. That's a nice idea. They don't rust and they don't chew up your shoes as quickly.

If you don't use toe clips, you still have to kick the pedals right side up every time. The three types are: quill, track, and platform. Each type matches a different kind of rider and a different usage. Let's look at each one in turn.

Quill Pedals If your bicycle is more than two years old and it cost more than $300 new, it's probably equipped with quill pedals. They may be the right choice for you, but you should take a serious look at your riding style. The quill is a racing pedal designed for toe clips, straps, and cleated shoes. If you use cleats, then one of the strapless systems may be a better choice for you, because they offer easier entry and exit and there's no tight strap to cut the blood circulation to your feet.

When you buy cleats, check that the cleat slot is wider than the thickness of the pedal cage. Occasionally, narrow cleat slots will have trouble fitting onto pedals with thick cages. A few file strokes through the slot will "open" your cleats to fit a fat cage. (Table 10-3 shows cage thickness.)

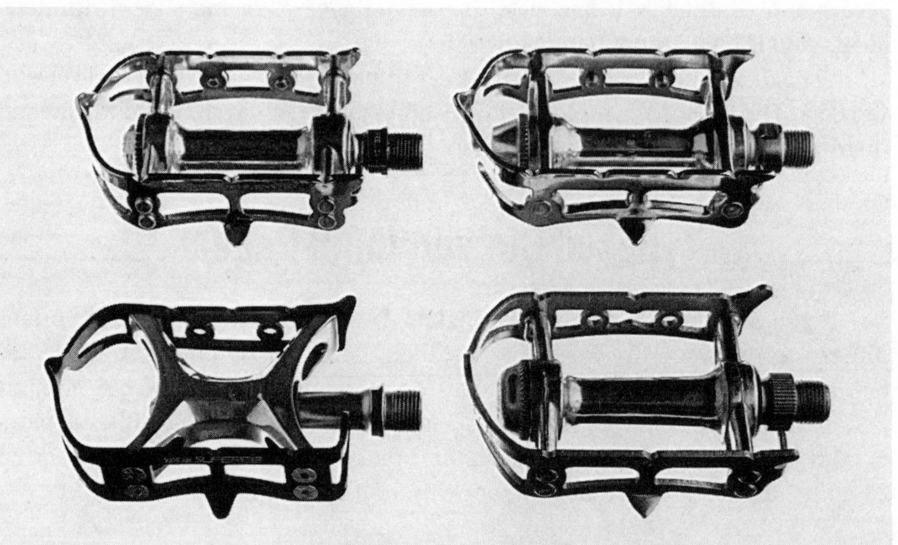

PHOTO 10-3 Quill pedal quality levels: top left and right, Campagnolo Nuovo Record (top-quality) and Maillard Spidel (top-quality); bottom left and right, SunTour Superbe Pro (medium-quality) and MKS Sylvan (economy-quality).

If you pedal in uncleated shoes, you'll be more comfortable with a platform pedal that provides a broader surface to support your shoes. However, it's not a big improvement and you may decide to stick with your quill pedals. If you don't use toe clips and straps, you're much better off with a double-sided pedal.

Quill pedals are made as narrow as possible and the underside is cut away to improve the drag angle. If you wear a wide shoe, you'll be in trouble with quill pedals because they're designed to match narrow European racing shoes. Wide shoes ride on the inside shoe stop and the quill instead of the flat cage. This is particularly uncomfortable on the quill pedals with high inside stops. Most quill pedals have an inner shoe stop in addition to the outer quill. The stop and the quill keep your feet from slipping sideways on the pedals.

I call the spacing between the two stops the "shoe width" and it's listed in table 10-3. It varies from 3.4 to 4.0 inches for quill pedals, although some models omit the inner shoe stop. You could grind or file it off the other pedals without too much trouble, which lets you use a wider shoe. If you find that your quill pedals are gouging crevices in your wide shoes, consider switching to strapless, track, or platform pedals.

Because quill pedals are so universal, they come in four price/quality levels: super-quality, top-quality, medium-quality, and economy. Campagnolo's $300 Super Record, which has titanium spindles and their $200 C-Record make up the super-quality class.

Top-quality quill pedals are either Campagnolo or something that looks very much like a Campagnolo quill. They have forged, one-piece aluminum alloy bodies, aluminum or steel cages, precision ground bearings with effective inside bearing seals, and chrome-moly spindles. There's usually considerable hand polishing. They weigh 300 to 350 grams with aluminum alloy cages, and 400 grams with steel cages. Prices run in the $100 to $150 range. Aluminum cages get chewed up in 10,000 miles or so, but steel cages last forever.

Medium-quality quill pedals costing $30 to $60 are very adequate pedals. The aluminum alloy body may be cast instead of forged. It certainly won't be hand polished. The cage will be steel or aluminum. The MKS Unique Custom Campy-copy is the bargain in this price range. The SunTour Superbe Pro is the top performer.

Economy quill pedals sell for about $15 per pair. There are two kinds. One has a body swaged together from separate pieces of steel and aluminum. The other has a melt-forged, one-piece body and cage.

All quill pedals are drilled for toe clips. On the higher-quality pedals, the toe clip mounting holes are threaded and the bolts and washers are included. Many of the newest models have bodies shaped like a letter X rather than the usual letter H. This moves in the outer bearing and improves the drag angle.

Track Pedals Every top-quality quill pedal has a track brother. The spindles and bodies are identical, but the track pedal has two separate cage plates instead of the wrap-around quill cage. Track racers don't use quill pedals in order to avoid sharp projections that might gouge an adjacent racer. Also, since the strap doesn't pass outside the quill frame, it holds the shoe more securely (and cuts off circulation to the feet more completely). The average pair of track pedals weighs 10 to 20 grams less than the comparable quill pedals. Most track pedals don't have an inner shoe stop so they depend on the straps to keep your feet from sliding sideways. Not all track pedals have a shoe pickup tab, but even so, they're not reversible. They have a top and a bottom, and they're designed for use with toe clips and straps.

I don't show the companion track pedals in table 10-3. I do show the new breed of road-track pedals that came on the market when road racers started to use track pedals. These new "track" pedals have narrower front cages, lighter weight, and better drag angles. Since there is no outer shoe stop (quill), you can use wider shoes.

Platform Pedals For many riders, platform pedals make more sense than quills and there's a wide assortment of sexy-looking models to choose from. However, since both quill and platform pedals are designed for toe clips and straps, the real competition is the strapless pedal. There are two kinds of platform pedals: racing and touring.

Racing platform pedals have a triangular shape with the front rail replaced by a platform for the front of the shoe. They have the following advantages over quill pedals:

- There's no outer quill or inner shoe stop so you can use wider shoes.
- It's easier to lock into the toe clips since platform pedals hang straight down instead of upside down. Many models have effective shoe pickup tabs.
- They're lighter than quill pedals.
- They have a better drag angle than quill pedals.
- Many have adjustable toe clips so you can fine-tune the toe clip length and the toe clip angle. Standard toe clips don't fit these new platform pedals and each requires its own unique toe clips. If you wear large shoes, you'll need XL toe clips, and these aren't always available. Make sure you buy the right length toe clip when you buy the pedals. With most toe clips, the amount of adjustment is typically limited to the difference between toe clip sizes.

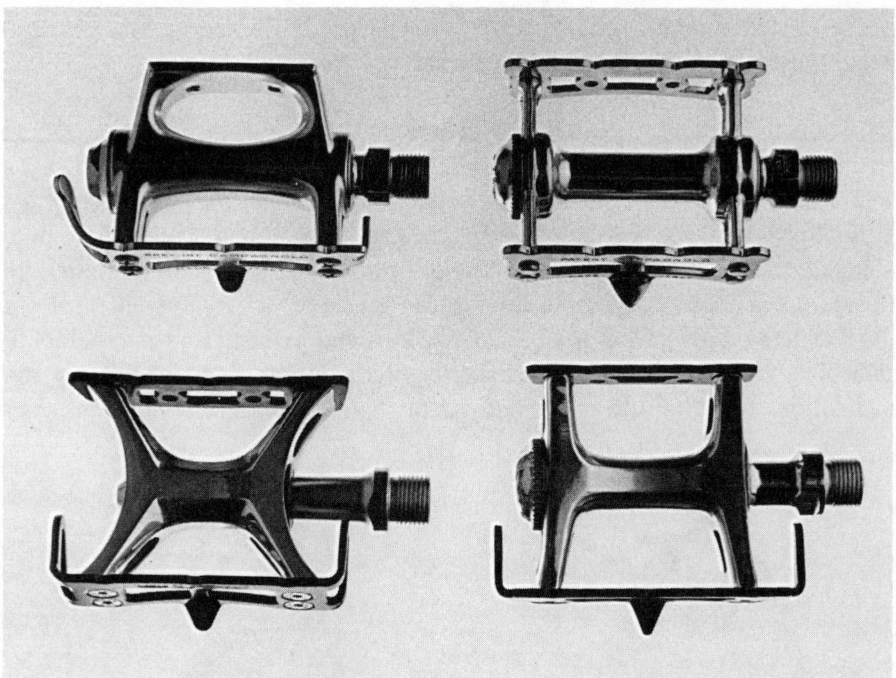

PHOTO 10-4 Track and track-style road pedals: top left and right, Campagnolo C-Record (road racing) and Campagnolo Nuovo Record (track); bottom left and right, SunTour Superbe Pro (track) and Specialized Racing (road racing).

- Many platform pedals are streamlined. This seems like a dubious benefit, since the turbulence generated by the front wheel, the leg, and the foot overwhelms the benefit of streamlined pedals.

There's a small group of *touring platform pedals* that really provides a flat platform to support your shoes. Buy these pedals if you use rubber-soled touring shoes. Touring shoes compromise sole rigidity to provide flexibility for walking. These pedals usually have a vestigial rear rail, but it's designed for slotted shoe soles rather than deep cleats. If you use quill pedals, your feet are supported on the two cage rails 2¼ inches apart and you can feel the rails through the soles. Racing platform pedals have a 2-inch gap between the front platform and the projecting rear cage. Your toes rest on a platform, but that's all. The Lyotard Berthet was the first touring platform and the Sakae SP-11 is similar. The Specialized Touring looks like a quill pedal at first glance. Then you notice that the end frames provide a flat support for your soles. The Shimano Triathlon has a plastic insert to fill the gap.

Double-Sided Pedals

Many users of quill or platform pedals don't use toe clips and straps. That's a poor pedal selection, unless you're planning to install toe clips and straps later. If you don't use toe clips and straps, you're much better off with double-sided pedals. They have a better gripping surface for your shoes and there is no upside-down position. Why put up with the hassle of kicking the pedal over to get it right side up. The four kinds of double-sided pedals are: rat-trap, mountain bike, rubber block, and counterweighted. Double-sided pedals are designed for use without toe clips and straps. You can install toe clips on many

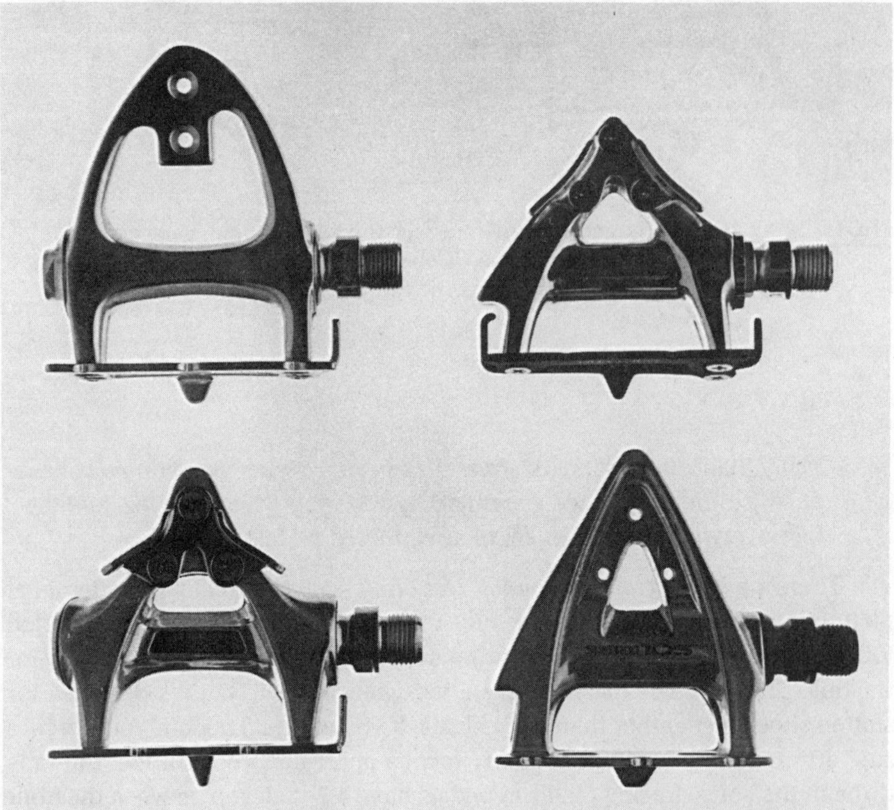

PHOTO 10-5 Racing platform pedals: top left and right, Campagnolo C-Record and Shimano Dura-Ace; bottom left and right, Shimano 600 EX and Shimano 105.

double-sided pedals, but that converts them to single-sided pedals with a poor drag angle.

Rat-Trap Pedals Ten years ago, most low-priced 10-speeds used rat-trap pedals. Today, counterweighted or economy quill pedals have largely replaced rat-traps. This is a retrograde step for the beginning bicyclist. A rat-trap pedal is basically a wide track pedal with no pedigree. The main advantage is that it's reversible. If you don't use toe clips and straps, you should use double-sided pedals. Rat-trap pedals have an uncouth image. They're only used on inexpensive bicycles, and the name sounds antisocial. The pedal catalogs show a range of widths and quality levels, but most bike stores carry only the $5, bottom-of-the-line replacement rat-trap. These "bargain-basement" rat-traps are fairly wide, and their bearings can't be disassembled. When they start to creak, you throw them away. The cage of the standard rat-trap is about 3¾ inches wide and they drag at about 25 degrees.

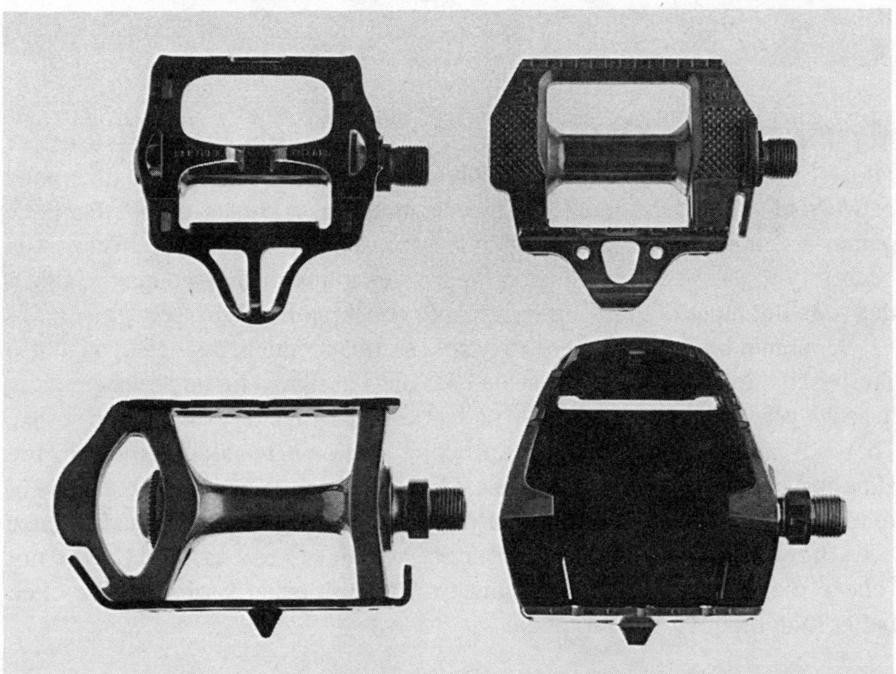

PHOTO 10-6 Touring platform pedals: top left and right, Lyotard Berthet and Sakae SP-11; bottom left and right, Specialized Touring and Shimano Triathlon.

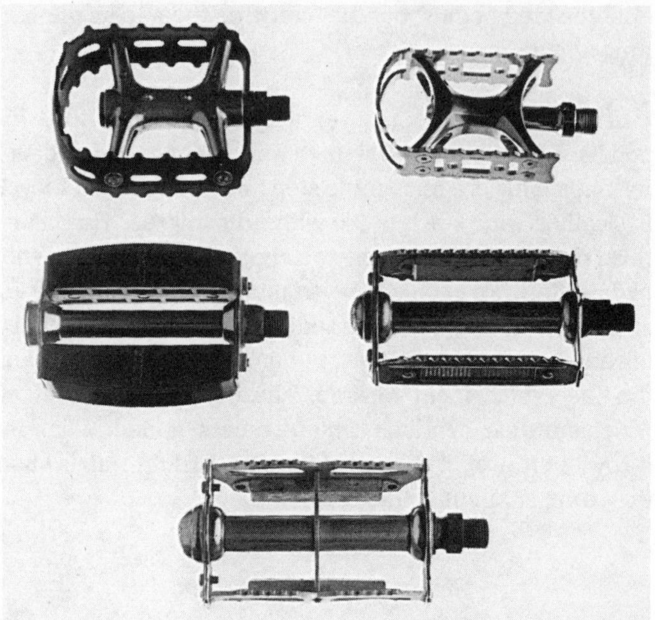

PHOTO 10-7

Double-sided pedals: top left and right, Shimano Deore XT (mountain bike) and SunTour XC-Compe (mountain bike); middle left and right, Lyotard rubber block and a rat-trap pedal; bottom, a counterweighted pedal (with bent frame).

Mountain Bike or BMX Pedals If you want a high-quality, hell-for-stout rat-trap pedal, ask for a mountain bike pedal. (There's no basic difference between mountain bike and BMX (bicycle motocross) pedals, except that BMX pedals are often anodized in flamboyant colors.) Some mountain bike pedals have very aggressive serrations on their cages to retain shoe contact in gonzo descents but most of them are reasonably conservative.

Mountain bike pedals are widely sold so they come in a range of qualities. The best models have excellent sealed bearings designed for underwater biking in scuba gear. Many mountain bike pedals are designed for toe clips and straps. That may make sense for mountain biking but a single-sided pedal with toe clips and straps is better for road use. Many mountain bike pedals are made of reinforced plastic for lightness and corrosion resistance. These pedals have been thoroughly tested in off-road service so you can rest assured they're not "cheap plastic" imitations. Drag angle on these pedals varies but it's often better than that of a rat-trap pedal.

Rubber Block Pedals Rubber block pedals share most of the advantages and disadvantages of rat-trap and mountain pedals. They don't accept toe clips and straps. The significant difference is the surface your shoe rests on. The cage of a rat-trap or mountain bike pedal is serrated to grip soft shoe soles. The serrations press uncomfortably through thin soles and they do a poor job of gripping leather soles. By contrast, rubber block pedals are designed for thin-soled or leather-soled shoes. The pedal catalogs show a wide range of rubber block pedals, but the typical bike store stocks only the bottom-of-the-line replacement models.

Counterweighted Pedals I mention counterweighted pedals last because they're a rotten design with no redeeming virtues. If your bicycle has counterweighted pedals, replace them with a type that suits your needs.

In theory, the counterweighted pedal is a reflectorized rat-trap that accepts toe clips without removing the reflectors. The reflectors on a counterweighted pedal hang below the spindle frame and act as counterweights to keep the pedal right side up. If you install toe clips, a counterweighted pedal hangs upside down like any other pedal. If you don't install toe clips, the counterweights don't always work. When you stomp on the bottom of the pedal, the cage bends, rendering the reflectors useless. The counterweighted pedal has the worst (and least safe) drag angle of any pedal. Today, few new bicycles use counterweighted pedals and I use them as a litmus test for sloppy bicycle design.

Conventional Pedal Makers

The pedal market is shaking out. As more and more bicycle makers buy their pedals as part of Shimano, SunTour, or Campagnolo gruppos and the replacement buyers opt for strapless pedals, there's very little business left for the small maker of conventional pedals. Here's the current market situation.

Campagnolo

Campagnolo dominates the quill pedal market. They make models at four price levels. Each quill has a companion track model. The Super Record pedal is an exotic model with a titanium spindle and ⅛-inch ball bearings to bring the weight down to 259 grams. Titanium is inherently weaker than steel, and the racing scene abounds with stories of failed titanium pedals. Super Leggeri (Super Light) is the pedal that you get in most Super Record gruppos. It has a black aluminum frame. Record Strada (Road) has a chrome-plated steel cage. All three are equally polished. Gran Sport is the middle-priced model and it's not widely available. Since they were introduced in 1985, Campagnolo has been struggling with their C-Record, Victory, and Triomphe platform pedals. They're things of beauty but the racers keep buying the old quill pedals. Campagnolo introduced a new C-Record road-track pedal in 1987 that looks more like a quill pedal and repositions the foot support point.

Lyotard

Lyotard was making pedals in France before I was born. The Lyotard Berthet platform pedal is a classic design and a bargain, if you can locate a pair. Lyotard makes good-quality rat-trap and rubber block pedals, but these designs are no longer fashionable, so they're hard to find.

Maillard (Galli)

Maillard, the quality French pedal maker, is now part of Sachs-Huret. Galli sells the Maillard 700 quill pedal as the Galli Criterium. There's no inner stop on Maillard quill pedals, so you can use a bit wider shoe. Both companies make a whole range of pedals, but distribution is spotty.

MKS

MKS (Mikashima Industrial Co.) is Japan's largest pedal manufacturer. They make a complete range of pedals, and U.S. distribution is fairly good. MKS makes SunTour's and Specialized's pedals. The Unique Custom is the middle-priced Campy-copy quill and the Sylvan Road is the lower-priced model. The 255-gram MKS RX-1 (217 grams with titanium spindles) is the lightest conventional pedal that I know of. The Grafight-2000 and the Grafight-X are the reinforced fiberglass mountain bike pedals.

Sakae

Sakae Ringyo (SR) has used their Silstar aluminum casting skills to make a very complete line of low-to-middle priced pedals with one-piece die-cast bodies. Most of them are sold in the OEM market. The SP-11 is a touring platform modeled after the Lyotard Berthet.

Shimano

Shimano broadened its line to include pedals, but it's been one area where they haven't made a great impact. I suspect that this is what led to the decision to make a Look-based strapless pedal. (If you can't beat 'em, join 'em.)

Part of Shimano's problem was their Dyna-Drive concept, which never caught on. Dyna-Drive pedals featured a unique dropped platform design that minimized height. Shimano installed both bearings at the crank end and cantilevered the pedals outward. The top of the platform was right at the bearing centerline, rather than ½- to ¾-inch above the centerline. Shimano claimed all sorts of ergonomic advantages for Dyna-Drive, but after three years of advertising, they quietly dropped the design. I never noticed any pedaling improvement with the dropped design, but it was easy to get into the toe clips.

Although it's not shown in the catalogs, you can still buy Dyna-Drive pedals and cranks. They use a special oversized pedal thread and Shimano doesn't want to leave the old users high and dry. The dropped platform idea has resurfaced in the CycleBinding strapless pedal.

Shimano's Dura-Ace, 600 EX, and 105 pedals are very similar aerodynamic platform models with excellent bearing seals and drag angles. Shimano's Triathlon pedal is great for touring in touring shoes. The Deore XT is their mountain bike pedal.

Specialized

Specialized went to MKS and ordered two pedals to their specifications. The racing model was one of the first road racing "track" pedals. The touring pedal is the best of the breed in my opinion. It offers good support for soft-soled shoes.

SunTour

SunTour now has pedals made by MKS for each of the SunTour gruppos: Superbe Pro, Sprint, Cyclone, and XC-9000 and XC-Sport 7000. The Superbe Pro quill pedal shows up the weakness of Campagnolo's old quill pedal design. The Superbe Pro has less weight, a better drag angle, sealed cartridge bearings, and a replaceable cage. Before the yen went through the roof, it sold for about half the price of the Campagnolo Super Light. The XC-Compe, which serves both XC gruppos, is SunTour's top-quality mountain bike pedal.

Everybody Else

There are a lot of everybody elses. Competition came late to the pedal business. KKT, a major Japanese maker, is now bankrupt. Excell, Gipiemme, Mavic, Stronglight, and Zeus all make very good racing pedals. The market is shrinking and their U.S. distribution is spotty.

Frank's Favorite Pedals

I have Shimano-Look strapless pedals on one racing bike and Look Sports on the other. I like them and I think they improve my pedaling efficiency. I adjust the release setting of the Looks as low as it will go. I have CycleBinding pedals on my two touring bicycles. CycleBinding and Look have a similar release drill. I have Specialized touring pedals with toe clips and straps on my commuting bike so that I can use regular street shoes.

CHAPTER 11

All about Wheels

A second set of wheels is the best way to give your bicycle a split personality. You can have heavy-duty, soft-riding wheels with nice fat tires for touring, commuting, and wet-weather riding. You can also have lightweight, easy-rolling wheels with narrow, high-performance tires for racing or fast sport touring. You might decide to put a wide-range freewheel on the touring wheels and a narrow-range freewheel on the racing wheels, but that's optional. Select your second set of wheels to complement your present wheels. If you have narrow racing wheels with high-pressure tires, pick wide touring wheels with lower-pressure tires, or the reverse.

Most likely your present wheels are the in-between sport touring type. If so, pick a second set to match the kind of riding that you do most often. Wheel selection is tied in with tire selection. Therefore, I suggest that you read both this chapter and chapter 12 on tires before making a wheel decision.

I'm not a wheel expert, and since I don't race, I've never bothered with tubular tires and rims. I build my own wheels because I enjoy wheel building, but I doubt if I've built more than 20 all together. However, I have some very knowledgeable friends who helped me with this chapter. Jobst Brandt, in his book, *The Bicycle Wheel,* applied science to the former black art of wheel building. Eric and Jon Hjertberg are the proprietors of Wheelsmith and they've made tens of thousands of wheels, albeit many of those Wheelsmith wheels were produced by sophisticated computer-controlled machines. (Interestingly, the machines require more consistent rims and spokes than human wheel builders.) Both Eric and Jobst reviewed this chapter and made major contributions.

A wheel is made of three parts: hubs, rims, and spokes. We'll look at the separate parts first, then we'll put them all together and talk about the wheel as a unit.

Hubs

There are significant differences between different makes of rear hubs, but front hubs are almost all the same. When you select your rear hub, you normally take the front hub that comes with the hubset. You can buy front and rear hubs separately, but they're normally sold as a hubset. There are more than a dozen top-quality brands to choose from in the aftermarket and another 20 or so standard-quality brands in the OEM marketplace. If you restrict yourself to the name brands, there's surprisingly little performance difference between the best and the worst hubs.

Today's hubs look very much like the turn-of-the-century models in my old books. Tullio Campagnolo's invention of the quick-release 60 years ago was a major innovation. The next major innovation was Shimano's combining of the hub and freewheel in the Freehub.

You'll have to decide right up front if you like the idea of combining the freewheel and the hub into a single unit. It has advantages in both hub strength and freewheel versatility. The Maillard Helicomatic and the Mavic MRL freewheel-hub packages are as strong as the Freehub, but their freewheel sprockets use a symmetrical tooth profile and that's a disadvantage. Also, Maillard and Mavic aren't nearly as widely distributed as the Shimano Freehub.

I talked about the Freehub's freewheel features back in chapter 6, so I won't repeat that here. If you decide to forget about the combination units and use conventional hubs, you've got lots of options and features to reflect upon. I have arranged the following features in rough order of importance.

Over-Locknut Width

The width of the hub is called the "over-locknut width," which refers to the fact that the measurement is made from outside to outside of the two axle locknuts. Front hubs come in 90mm, 100mm, and 110mm widths. Pick the width that matches the width of your front fork. (Since the hub locknuts fit inside the fork blades, the over-locknut width should be the same as the space between the fork blades.) The 100mm width is far and away the most common for front hubs. There are three fairly standard rear hub widths from which to choose: 120/122mm, 126mm, and 130mm. Pick the rear hub over-locknut width that matches the rear dropout width of your bicycle.

The new ISO standard 5-speed rear hub width is 122mm. Most nominal 120mm hubs are closer to 121mm or 122mm when you actually measure them. There was a move to an in-between 124mm width in the early 1980s; narrow-spaced 6-speed, 120mm wheels were a tad weak. Fortunately for standarization, the 124mm width didn't catch on. If your bicycle measures 124mm, you can still

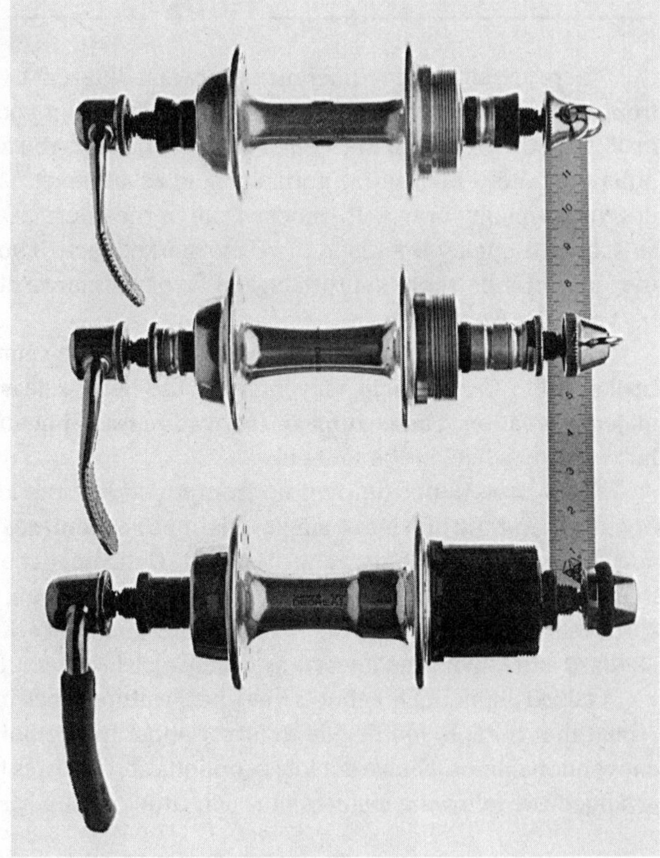

PHOTO 11-1

Hub over-locknut widths: top to bottom, Campagnolo Nuovo Record rear hub (122mm), SunTour Superbe Pro rear hub (126mm), and Shimano Deore XT Freehub (130mm).

find 124mm rear hubs, or you can take a couple of spacers out of a 126mm hub. However, my advice is to take the easy way out and have your frame spread 2mm (about $\frac{1}{12}$ of an inch) wider so that you can use a standard 126mm hub. Some of the latest professional racing bikes are using 130mm hubs, but the mountain bikers are the main users. In fact there's a trend to 135mm for mountain bikes.

The trend is from narrow hubs to wide hubs. The main advantage of wider rear hubs is that they require less rear wheel "dish." Dishing is the process that centers the wheel rim between the frame dropouts even though the hub flanges are not in the center of the hub. The flanges are moved to the left to make room for the freewheel. To dish a wheel, the left side spokes are inclined inward and have less tension. The right side spokes are more nearly vertical and have more tension. Because of the imbalance in spoke tension, dishing results in weaker wheels. Installing spacers on the left side of the hub reduces dishing and makes the hub wider.

The main disadvantage of wider rear hubs is that the rear axle is more highly stressed. The rear axle is a beam supported by the dropouts. It transmits the load to the wheel through the hub bearings. The right side hub bearing is well inboard of the dropout. The hub width determines the length of the beam. The freewheel width determines the lever arm for the load. The longer the beam and the lever arm, the higher the stress on the rear axle. Rear hubs would be stronger if the bearings were closer to the dropouts. However, wider dropout widths and wider freewheels locate the right side bearing nearer to the center of the axle. When the axle breaks, it's almost always just inside the right cone. The bike store's usual response is to replace it with a Campagnolo axle and cones. Most mountain bikes use solid rear axles with their 130mm widths.

The Shimano Freehub, the Maillard Helicomatic, and the Mavic MRL take a different approach. They locate the right side hub bearing next to the dropout, where it ought to be. Shimano locates the freewheel bearings inboard of the hub bearing. Maillard uses large-diameter freewheel bearings and locates them in the same plane as the hub bearings.

You might benefit from the history of my Redcay sport tourer. It came as a wide-spaced 15-speed with 120mm dropouts. To maintain my standing in the gear freaks fraternity, I had to have at least 18 speeds, which I wanted to obtain by means of a wide-spaced 6-speed freewheel. First, I tried a 6-speed Shimano Freehub, which was available in a 120mm width. The wheel was steeply dished. I didn't like the looks of it, so I added spacers on the left side to reduce the dish. I had to pull the rear dropouts apart a bit to insert the wheel.

My next two bikes had 126mm dropouts and I wanted to be able to switch wheels between bikes. So I widened the rear dropout width of the Redcay to 126mm. This adjustment, bending the stays, is often called "cold setting." It isn't as gruesome as it sounds, especially for bicycles with long chainstays. I put a rear axle between the dropouts and turned the cones outward ⅛ inch at a time, measuring after each increment. Then I used a "Campagnolo H-tool" to make the dropouts parallel. You might decide to do something similar or have it done by your bike shop.

Basically, 126mm has become the new standard dropout width for wide-spaced 6-speed touring freewheels and narrow-spaced 7-speed racing freewheels. A 126mm, 5-speed wheel has almost no dish. Table 11-1 shows the widths that are available for the various hubs.

Sealed Bearings and Bearing Seals

Deep in my heart of hearts, I believe that the bicycle is primarily a means to multiply the distance that you can travel and the load that you can carry. It should remain a simple tool. This principle certainly applies to hub bearings.

(continued on page 204)

TABLE 11-1.

Hubsets

Make and Model	Cost ($)	Weight (gr.)	Over-Locknut Widths (mm)		Bearing	
			Front	Rear	Type	Size
Campagnolo						
C-Record	200–300	510	100	122–126	C&C	9 × 3/16 (Fr.) std (Rr.)
Nuovo Record	130–200	510	100	122–126	C&C	9 × 7/32 (Fr.) std (Rr.)
Maillard						
700	65–100	635	100	120, 126	C&C or SCB	std
700 Helicomatic	60–90	540	100	120, 126	C&C or SCB	std
Mavic						
RD 550	75–100	505	100	126	SCB	—
MRL 570	65–100	—	100	126	SCB	—
Phil Wood	80–120	550	100, 108	120, 125	SCB	—
Shimano						
Dura-Ace Freehub	95–135	666	100	126.5	C&C	std
Dura-Ace	75–110	543	100	126	C&C	std
Deore XT Freehub	40–60	682	100	130	C&C	std
600 EX	35–55	531	100	126	C&C	std
105	30–50	545	100	126	C&C	std
Specialized	50–75	575	100	120, 126, 130	SCB	—
SunTour						
Superbe Pro	70–100	537	100	120, 126	SCB	—
Sprint	50–75	557	100	120, 126	SCB	—
Cyclone	45–65	555	100	120, 126	SCB	—
Cyclone 7000	40–60	550	100	120, 126	C&C	std

1. The inclusive numbers indicate that spoke holes are available in 4-hole increments.
2. Hubs that are 1⅜ to 1¾ inches in diameter are called small flange. Hubs that are approximately 2⅝ inches in diameter are called high flange. The rare models that fall somewhere in between can thus be called medium flange.

Bearing Seals	Spoke Holes Available[1]	Flange Height[2]	Threads FW	Threads Axle	Quick-Release	Finish	Overall Rating
part.	24–40	SF, HF	ISO	Itl	yes	E	E
no	24–40	SF, HF	ISO	Itl	yes	VG	E
part.	28–36	SF, HF	ISO	Eng	yes	VG	VG
part.	28–36	SF, HF	—	Eng	yes	VG	VG
yes	24–40	SF	—	—	yes	VG	VG
yes	24–36	SF	—	—	yes	VG	VG
yes	20–48	MF	ISO	Eng	QR or bolt	VG	E
yes	28–36	SF	—	Eng	yes	E	E
yes	28–36	SF	ISO	Eng	yes	E	E
yes	36	SF	—	Eng	QR or nut	VG	E
yes	32, 36	SF	ISO	Eng	yes	VG	VG
yes	32, 36	SF	ISO	Eng	yes	VG	VG
yes	24–40	SF	ISO	Eng	QR or nut	VG	E
yes	20–36	SF	ISO	Eng	yes	VG	E
yes	28–36	SF	ISO	Eng	yes	VG	VG
yes	28–36	SF	ISO	Eng	yes	VG	VG
yes	28–36	SF	ISO	Eng	yes	VG	VG

Cup-and-cone hub bearings, using nine ¼-inch balls in the rear races and ten 3⁄16-inch balls in the front races, have been around since the safety bicycle was invented nearly 100 years ago, long enough to qualify as the standard for hub bearings. In table 11-1, where this arrangement is found, it is marked "std." Only where the bearing count is different from this is it shown.

Cup-and-cone ball bearings are inherently self-adjusting. If they're properly adjusted, the work lost in bearing friction is trivial compared to the other pedaling losses. They work splendidly in spite of minor misalignment. They have one major disadvantage. They aren't waterproof. If water or dirt gets in the bearings, the balls and the races will rapidly corrode. You have to clean and regrease your hubs every year or so, more frequently if you ride in the wet.

The hub makers can improve bearing longevity in two ways: by providing a lip seal on the dust cap to keep water out and grease in, or by redesigning the hub to use sealed, cartridge-type ball bearings instead of cup-and-cone bearings. Very roughly, the load capacity of a ball bearing increases directly with the number of balls and with the square of the ball diameter. If everything is designed just right (larger-diameter axle, Conrad-type ball bearings, precise bearing alignment, parallel dropouts, and a bunch of *et ceteras* that I don't know about), a hub using cartridge-type ball bearings has about the same capacity as one using cup-and-cone bearings.

Many sealed-bearing hubs advertise that you can replace the bearings yourself. Given the amount of precision required to avoid side loads, I'm not sure that this is such a good idea. In short, I like hubs that use cup-and-cone bearings with a lip seal. (Table 11-1 shows the type of bearings and seals used in the various hubs.)

Number of Spokes

There is no 11th commandment that says, "Thou shalt use 36 spokes." In fact, the classic Raleigh Roadster, which is the model for most of the bicycles in the third world, uses 32 spokes on the front and 40 spokes on the rear. Moreover, there are hubs and rims drilled for 24, 28, and 48 spokes. However, the vast majority of hubs and rims are drilled for 36 spokes and that's a good choice for almost everyone. If you pick something other than 36 holes, you'll often be forced to special order. In the esoteric special-order world, only 28- and 32-hole models are normally carried.

The strength of a wheel depends on the number of spokes, the strength of the spokes, the strength of the rim, and the skill of the wheel builder. Racers use fewer spokes in order to reduce wind resistance. That's also the reason for disc wheels and flat-bladed spokes. Spoke wind resistance is significant because the top spokes are going twice as fast as the bicycle, and wind resistance goes up directly with the number of spokes. Fewer spokes also weigh less, but there are better ways to reduce wheel weight.

If you're a deadly serious racer, you may find yourself building wheels with fewer than 36 spokes. The less you weigh and the smoother the road and your pedaling style, the fewer spokes you can get away with. Just be aware that racing wheels are generally built to a very high standard and that wheels with 28 or 24 spokes are intended for special applications, not long life.

The loaded tourist has a different problem. A 40- or 48-spoke rear wheel is unquestionably stronger than a 36-spoke wheel. But, if you do crunch a 48-spoke rim, you won't be able to replace it except at a very large, well-equipped bicycle shop. I use 36 straight-gauge spokes on my loaded touring wheels with good, heavy-duty rims and tires. The main users of 48-spoke rims are tandems. Table 11-1 shows the numbers of spoke holes available on the various hubs. These are the numbers that are shown in the catalogs. Most stores stock only the 36-hole models. Table 11-2 is my conservative recommendation on the number of spokes appropriate for various riders and services.

Flange Height

There are two basic hub heights: *high-flange* and *low-flange* (a.k.a. large-flange and small-flange). Ten years ago, macho racers used high-flange hubs and wimpy tourists used low-flange hubs; so every bottom-of-the-line, 10-speed racer came with high-flange hubs. The bicycling books told us that high-flange wheels were stiffer and stronger because of the shorter spokes. Low-flange wheels were softer riding.

Recent calculations and tests indicate that these assumptions about strength are just barely true for lateral (sideways) and radial (potholes) loads, but the difference between hub types is very minor. With low-flange hubs, the

TABLE 11-2.

Recommended Number of Spokes

Service	**Weight of Rider and Load**					
	100–125 lb.		**130–175 lb.**		**180–225 lb.**	
	Front	***Rear***	***Front***	***Rear***	***Front***	***Rear***
Time trials	24	28	28	32	32	36
Road races	28	32	32	32	36	36
Sport touring	32	36	36	36	36	36
Loaded touring	36	36	36	36	36	36 or 40

tangential (pedaling) load stresses the rear spokes about twice as much. However, the pedaling load is a small part of the total spoke tension and low-flange hubs are more than strong enough. The main reason to use low-flange hubs is because they're lighter. Most professional racers now use low-flange hubs. However, if you are going to use more than 36 spokes in a wheel, you should use a high-flange hub to provide enough metal between the spoke holes.

Some hubs slant the flanges inward so that the outer spokes don't have to bend as much. Phil Wood and SunTour advertise this feature. (Table 11-1 shows the flange heights available for the various hubs.)

There are no standard hub diameters. This becomes a nuisance when you buy spokes. You have to know which hub and which rim you will be using, and how many spoke crosses. Then you can look up the appropriate spoke length. If your front and rear hubs are the same diameter, then you can use the same size spokes on both.

Threads

There are four threads available for the rear hub–freewheel thread: ISO, English, Italian, and French. However, you almost have to special order a hub to get anything other than ISO or English (1.37 × 24 tpi). There's no reason to do this unless you have a collection of bastard-threaded freewheels or you're a masochist.

There are still four threads in use for axles. However, there's a trend to the standard ISO thread. That's what you'll find in most replacement hubsets except Campagnolo. The ISO (9mm × 1mm pitch) thread for the hollow front axles is the same as the old French thread. The ISO (10mm × 1mm pitch) thread for the hollow rear axle will mate with most of the older English and French axle threads. You don't have to worry too much about axle thread standardization because it isn't a great expense to replace an axle along with its cones and locknuts. Table 11-1 shows the type of thread listed in the manufacturer's catalog.

Quick-Release

Your replacement hubs will almost certainly come with hollow axles and quick-release skewers. There's a modest case to be made for solid axles with nuts. They're quite a bit stronger, a bit lighter, and they make it harder to steal the wheels from a parked and locked bicycle. For most people, however, the convenience of a quick-release is worth these disadvantages. The trial lawyers who take cases on contingency are all in favor of quick-releases. At any given time, there are a dozen or so lawsuits involving dumbhead cyclists who failed to tighten the quick-release on their front wheels. Table 11-1 shows which hubset models are available with a fastening system other than the quick-release.

Weight

The old rule that a pound off the wheels equals two pounds off the frame is really talking about the weight of the rims and the tires. They are on the outside of the flywheel and they contribute to the rotational inertia of the wheel. That's fancy engineering talk to say that heavy tires and rims accelerate slowly. The hub doesn't contribute very much to the rotational inertia so that it's weight is more like frame or component weight. The lightest hubs have low flanges, and nuts in place of quick-releases. The sealed-bearing hubs that use large-diameter, hollow axles and built-up bodies are quite light. Finally, it should be noted that the weight of a Shimano Freehub compares very well with the combined weight of a conventional hub and freewheel.

Table 11-1 shows the weight of a low-flange hubset with quick-release. The rear hub is 126mm. The weight for the two Shimano Freehub models includes the freewheel body but no sprockets. Subtract about 175 grams to make the weight comparable to conventional hubsets.

Hubset Makers

The trend is toward including hubs in the gruppo. However, the small hub makers are surviving because so many bicycles have more than one pair of wheels.

Campagnolo Campagnolo's hubsets set the standards for conventional cup- and-cone designs. Only the two top lines, C-Record and Nuovo Record, are widely available in the replacement market. The C-Record has a fancy new dust cover that requires a special remover. Campagnolo uses nine 7/32-inch balls instead of ten 3/16-inch balls in their Nuovo Record front hubs. C-Record uses nine 3/16-inch balls. Campagnolo measures the balls to a micron and installs matched sets. If you wear out the cups on a Campagnolo hub, you can press them out and replace them. A good pro bike shop will carry replacement Campagnolo cups.

Maillard Maillard makes three lines of hubs: Maillard, Normandy, and Atom. Their conventional hubs are available with cup-and-cone bearings with seals or with sealed cartridge bearings. In the old days, Normandy was high-flange and Atom was low-flange. Now, Normandy is the middle line and Atom is the low-priced line. Trek and Peugeot bicycles often use Maillard hubs, so their dealers tend to carry Maillard. Otherwise, distribution is very sparse. The Helicomatic design is available in all three lines. The Helicomatic hub is as strong or stronger than the Shimano Freehub, but the Helicomatic freewheel is less suitable for touring.

Mavic Mavic hubs are racing favorites. They use sealed cartridge ball bearings with large-diameter, hollow aluminum axles. The bearings are user-replaceable, but it takes special tools. The 7-speed Mavic MRL freewheel-hub was introduced in 1987. All of the sprockets are narrow-spaced and they use the identical coarse thread. Sprockets from 12 to 28 teeth are available.

Phil Wood Phil Wood is the father of the sealed-bearing hub. He has done more to popularize the use of sealed-bearing hubsets than anyone. His quality control includes individual inspection of every cartridge bearing. When your Phil Wood hub finally needs service after many thousands of miles, you send it back to the factory. If you believe what Phil says about the care and feeding of cartridge ball bearings, then you won't buy hubsets with user-replaceable, sealed bearings. The Phil hub uses a big hollow axle. It isn't particularly handsome, compared to most of the competition, but it's stronger than all get out.

Shimano Shimano makes conventional hubs in eight or nine price levels for the OEM market. Dura-Ace, Santé, 600 Ultegra, 105, and Deore XT are the hubs that you'll find in the replacement market. All versions come in either Freehub or conventional versions. Shimano hubs have cup-and-cone bearings with an effective lip seal. There is a little hole in the dustcap that allows you to inject a dollop of grease without taking everything apart.

Freehubs used to be available at six different price levels. Then Shimano only imported Dura-Ace and Deore XT Freehubs. In 1988, they started to import the whole range of Freehubs. I've already raved about the Freehub in chapter 6 on freewheels. It's the most versatile freewheel available and it comes with one of the strongest hubs.

Specialized Specialized hubsets are made in Japan to their specifications. They have user-replaceable, sealed cartridge bearings. The Specialized 126mm hub is available as a 5-speed and the 130mm hub is available as a 6-speed. With the extra spacers on the left side, these allow you to build almost dishless wheels.

SunTour SunTour hubs come in four versions: Superbe Pro, Sprint, Cyclone 7000, and Cyclone. The Cyclone 7000 has cup-and-cone bearings. The remainder have user-replaceable, sealed cartridge bearings. SunTour and Specialized hubs are very similar. They're both made by Sanshin.

Everybody Else Edco, Excell-Rino, Galli, Gipiemme, Miche, Ofmega, Omas, and Zeus all make Campagnolo-like hubs for the European racing market. American Classic, Durham (Bullseye), and Hi-E Engineering are American makers of sealed-bearing hubs. Arai, Sakae Ringyo, Sanshin, and Suzue are major

Japanese suppliers to the OEM market. These 15 companies make very good hubs but you won't often see them in the aftermarket.

Rims

The rim business is a jungle. Most of the major gruppo makers don't bother with rims, so the small companies have survived. I found 20 different rim makers in my review of the catalogs and each company makes ten or more different models in a wide range of sizes. I picked the dozen companies that have the widest distribution.

There are two main considerations in rim selection: size and weight. The rim should match the tires that you plan to use and the rim should be heavy enough (or light enough) for your proposed use. Let's look at these important considerations first and then get into the less important items.

Rim Selection: Matching Rims with Tires

Rim selection and tire selection go hand in hand. Your rim selection limits your tire selection. Your first decision is tubular tires and rims versus clincher tires and rims. If you have a deep inner craving for tubular tires, it might be a good idea at this point for you to read what I have to say about tubulars in chapter 12. After that, if you're still convinced that tubulars are a good idea, you'll find a section on tubular rims further on. Table 11-3 has four columns covering tire-rim compatability: inside width, edge type, service, and tire compatability.

Rim Width

Assuming that you opt for the flag, motherhood, and clinchers, you then have to make a basic narrow tire versus wide tire decision. There are five sizes of tires and three sizes of rims. Tire size labeling is a mess and it's covered in detail in chapter 12. First, decide on the range of tire sizes that you plan to use, then select rims to match. The key rim dimension is the inside width between the rim flanges. The outside width is tied into the inside width so it's not important by itself. Rims that have an inside width of 13mm or 14mm (a bit more than ½ inch) are designed for narrow tires. Rims with an inside width of 15mm or 16mm are designed for medium-width tires. Rims with an inside width of 16.5mm or more are designed for wide touring tires. (The basic parts and dimensions of a rim are shown in figure 11-1.)

Rim Edge Type

The second important feature of clincher rims is the shape of the rim flange. There are three types: straight-side, hooked-edge, and an intermediate

(continued on page 212)

TABLE 11-3.

Clincher Rims

Make and Model	Cost ($)	Weight (gr.)	Service	Width (mm) Inside	Width (mm) Outside	Depth (mm)	Cross Section	Edge Type	Spoke Holes Available*
Ambrosio									
Aero Elite Durex	40–60	425(450)	R	14	18.5	19.5	aero	hooked	32, 36
Super Elite Durex	40–60	510(500)	ST	14.5	20.5	13.5	box	hooked	32, 36
Araya									
ADX-1W	60–90	490(530)	ST	14	19.5	17	aero	hooked	36
20A	50–70	435(450)	ST	14	19.5	14.5	box	hooked	36
16A (3)	30–50	560	LT	19	25	14	M-58	bulged	36
16A (5)	30–50	480	LT	16	22	14	M-58	bulged	36
Matrix									
ISO C	65–100	475(500)	R	13	19	21	aero	hooked	28–36
Titan	50–75	455(470)	R	13	19	15	box	hooked	32, 36
Titan T	50–75	550	LT	16	22	12	M-58	bulged	36, 40, 48
Mavic									
MA-50	—	430	ST	13	20.5	14	box	hooked	28–36
MA-40	50–65	430(470)	ST	13.5	20.5	14	box	hooked	32–40
M3-CD	40–60	530	LT	15	22	14	box	hooked	36, 40
Module 4	40–60	550	LT	19	26	14	box	hooked	36, 40
Mistral									
M 14A	55–75	511	ST	14	19	17	aero	hooked	36
M 13L	35–50	430(480)	ST	13	19	14	box	hooked	36
M 17	35–50	496	LT	17.5	22.5	14	M-58	bulged	36
M 20	35–50	585	LT	20	25.5	14.5	M-58	bulged	36
Rigida									
HLC-2000	70–100	485	ST	13	19.5	18	aero	hooked	24–40
AL-1320	25–40	390(400)	ST	13	19	14.5	box	hooked	24–40
AL-1622	25–40	520	LT	16	22	13	M-58	straight	36
Specialized									
Saturae HC 20	40–60	450	ST	14.5	19	13.5	box	hooked	28–36
Weinmann									
Concave A-124	35–55	534	ST	14	20	13	Cncv	bulged	36
Concave A-129	35–55	557(580)	LT	16	20	13	Cncv	bulged	36, 40, 48
Wolber									
Model 430	50–80	430	ST	13	19	13	box	hooked	32, 36
Model 59	40–60	550	LT	16	23	14	M-58	bulged	36, 40, 48
Gentleman, GTA, GTX	28–40	430	ST	14	19	13	box	hooked	32, 36
Model 58	28–40	520(540)	LT	16	23	14	M-58	bulged	36, 40, 48

* The inclusive numbers indicate that rims are available in 4-hole increments.

Surface Finish	Aluminum Alloy	Heat-Treated	Joint		Eyelets	Tire Compatibility (ETRTO section width)		Strength-to-Weight
			Type	Uniformity		27-inch	700C	
An, HAn	3000	no	pin	VG	none	⅞–1⅛	19–28	VG
C, An, HAn	3000	no	pin	VG	double	⅞–1⅛	20–28	VG
P, An, HAn	3000	no	welded	G	none	⅞–1⅛	19–28	VG
P, C, HAn	3000	no	welded	VG	none/ double	⅞–1⅛	19–28	VG
An	3000	no	welded	VG	none	1¼–1⅜	32–35	VG
An	3000	no	welded	VG	none	1⅛–1⅜	28–35	VG
HAn	6000	yes	pin	G	none	⅞–1	19–25	E
HAn	6000	yes	pin	G	single	⅞–1⅛	19–25	VG
HAn	6000	yes	pin	G	single	1⅛–1⅜	25–35	E
HAn	3000	no	pin	VG	double	⅞–1⅛	19–25	VG
HAn	3000	no	pin	VG	double	⅞–1⅛	19–25	VG
HAn	3000	no	pin	VG	double	1–1⅛	20–28	VG
P	3000	no	pin	VG	double	1⅛–1⅜	28–35	VG
HAn	6000	yes	pin-glue	G	none	⅞–1⅛	19–28	VG
HAn	6000	yes	pin-glue	G	single	⅞–1	19–25	E
HAn	6000	yes	pin-glue	G	single	1⅛–1⅜	28–35	E
HAn	6000	yes	pin-glue	G	single	1⅛–1⅜	28–35	E
HAn	6000	yes	pin	G	double	⅞–1	19–25	E
P, C, An	3000	no	pin	G	single	⅞–1	19–25	VG
P	3000	no	pin	G	single	1¼–1⅜	32–35	E
HAn	3000	no	welded	VG	double	⅞–1⅛	20–28	VG
P, An	3000	no	welded	G	single	1–1⅛	23–28	F
P, An	3000	no	welded	G	single	1¼–1⅜	32–35	F
HAn	6000	yes	welded	VG	double	⅞–1	19–25	E
HAn	6000	yes	welded	VG	single	1⅛–1⅜	28–35	E
P	3000	no	pin	VG	double	⅞–1	19–25	VG
P	3000	no	pin	VG	single	1⅛–1⅜	28–35	VG

FIGURE 11-1

Clincher rim nomenclature.

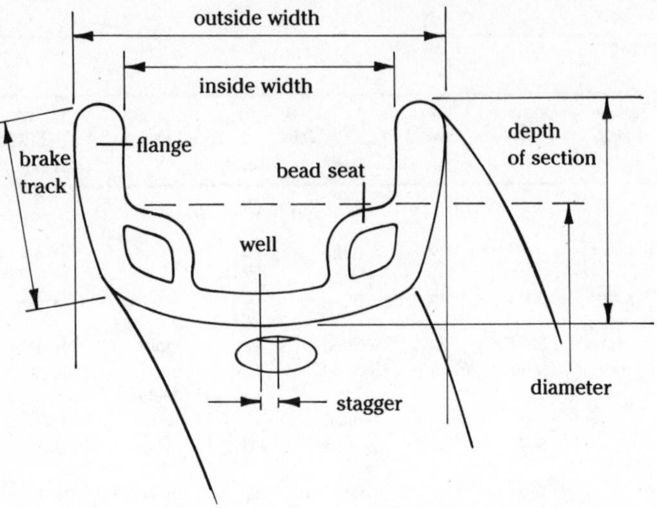

type with a vestigial hook that I call "bulged." Straight-side rims have bead seats and dropped centers. The bead seat mates with the bead of a wired-on tire to keep it on the rim. The dropped center makes it possible to mount the tire. A hooked-edge rim is designed to mate with a hook-bead tire. In 700C and 27-inch sizes, hooked-edge rims are hybrids. They have both hooked edges and bead seats. Sometimes the dropped center is just a concave inner bed, but there's still a bead seat that centers the tire. In the smaller diameters, there are "pure" hooked-edge rims that don't have bead seats and they rely entirely on the hooked-edge to center and retain the tire. (See figure 11-2 for a depiction of a pure hooked-edge rim.)

If you plan to use narrow, high-performance, skinwall tires and to inflate them to maximum pressure, you need a hooked-edge rim. Rigida calls this a "crotchet" edge. Foldable tires use Kevlar beads, and hooked-edge rims are mandatory. If you install cheap gumwall tires on hooked-edge rims, the tire sidewall may fail just above the bead because the hook has such a sharp radius. Usually the tire wears out before this happens. Finally, straight-side rims give a poorer ride because the part of the tire's sidewall that's inside the rim can't soak up road shocks.

For any given tire width, construction, and inflation pressure, tubular rims and tires perform best. Hooked-edge rims and tires are next and straight-side rims and tires are worst. There's no good reason to buy straight-side rims today. You can get hooked-edge rims in all three widths and they're inherently superior to straight-side rims.

Tire Compatibility

Table 11-3 shows tire compatibility. Based on ETRTO (European Tire and Rim Technical Organization) recommendations, I took the rim inside width and multiplied by 1.45 to get the smallest tire size and by 2.0 to get the largest tire size. ETRTO suggests that hooked-edge rims can retain tires up to 2.25 times the rim inside width. The tire sizes shown in this column are the actual ETRTO section widths, not the labeled tire sizes.

Rim Weight

It's more fun to pedal a bicycle with light wheels. It accelerates faster and it feels alive beneath you. Light wheels and tires don't cost that much extra. If it weren't for flat tires and bent wheels, we'd all be riding on ultra-light wheels. The rim, tire, and tube are located at the outside of the wheel diameter. They're the important elements in tire weight. The basic problem is building a pair of light wheels that are exactly light enough for your particular combination of rider weight, road roughness, and riding style.

Jeff Davis of Campagnolo shared his formula with me. Multiply your weight in pounds by 1.75 to get the absolutely lightest tubular rim weight in grams that you can use on a smooth surface for a few races. Multiply your weight by 2.75 to get the weight of the lightest rim that you can use in normal service on normal roads. There's probably no substitute for trial and error. Build a pair of wheels that are too light and when they fall apart, build another pair using rims that are just a tad heavier and stronger. If you go this route, you'll have lots of flats and

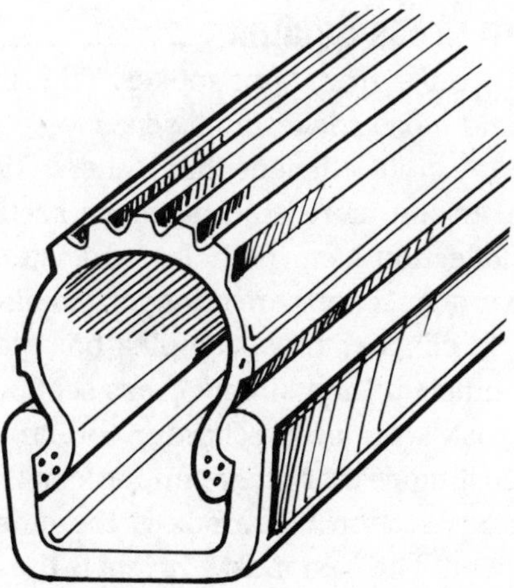

FIGURE 11-2

A hook-bead tire mounted on a hooked-edge rim.

you may crunch one or two rear wheels before you find your personal limits. Lightweight wheels are a bit addictive. It's always tempting to go too far.

I have an analogy. In my wild youth, I used to race boats powered by souped-up, flathead, Ford V-8 engines. The engines were built to class rules so most of the top boats had the same power. We burned a mixture of alcohol and nitromethane. Nitromethane releases oxygen as it burns so it acts like a liquid supercharger. It also releases a lot of heat and too much heat burns holes in the pistons. There wasn't any magic formula to tell us when to stop. In the last heat of a close championship race, there were lots of blown engines. Light tires and light rims with a minimum number of spokes are like nitromethane.

Lightweight clincher rims are made from thin-walled aluminum extrusions. (Tubular rims are often made from an aluminum alloy strip.) Extruding is a process that squeezes the metal through a die under very high pressure, like toothpaste from a tube. It's hard to extrude uniform thin-wall cross sections. That's why lightweight rims cost so much. As the die wears, the walls become a bit thicker. A rim extruded from a worn die will weigh more than one from a new die. It will also be stronger. The makers don't deliberately lie about rim weight but they weigh rims made with new dies.

There's a significant sample-to-sample variation in rim weight. Table 11-3 shows two weights for several rim models. The first is the maker's advertised weight. The second (in parentheses) is the weight of a typical run-of-the-mill rim. The weight is for a 700C rim. A 27-inch rim weighs a bit more.

Wide rims take more metal, so they naturally weigh more than narrow rims. I don't worry about the weight of my heavy-duty touring wheels. When I want to go fast, I use the bike with light wheels.

Rim Cross Section

Much of a wheel's strength comes from tight spokes. The rim distributes the shock loads to the spokes and loose spokes impose a severe stress on the rim. Some rim cross sections are more efficient than others. Two rims may weigh the same, but the one with the more efficient cross section will do a better job of resisting radial deflection from potholes and lateral deflection from skidding in a corner. Deep cross sections are stronger radially. Wide cross sections are stronger laterally. In clincher rims, complex box-type cross sections with thin walls are more efficient than simple cross sections with thick walls. Unfortunately, hollow cross sections are harder to extrude, so light, strong, efficient clincher rims cost more than their simpler cousins.

The clincher rim with a cross section like a box is the most efficient. It copies the tubular box cross section. The next most efficient is the aerodynamic cross section, which is stronger against radial loads because it's deeper. Next comes the Super Champion Model 58, then the Weinmann Concave cross section. The least efficient cross section is the wide, straight-side rim that's used in standard-quality bicycles. Rim dimensions and cross section types are shown in tables 11-3 and 11-4.

Rim Material

Steel rims have no place on a bicycle that's ridden for fun. For any given weight, a steel rim is weaker than an aluminum rim. A steel rim is also more likely to dent if you hit a pothole. Moreover, chrome-plated steel rims stop very poorly when wet.

Until about five years ago, most alloy rims were made from a 3000 series aluminum alloy that uses about 1 percent of manganese and magnesium. This alloy attains its strength by cold working in the extruding and forming processes. Sometimes these rims are annealed after cold working to increase their ductility and fatigue resistance. Sometimes the advertisers call the annealing process "heat treating." That's misleading since the rim actually loses strength in the annealing process.

Recently, there's been a move to make rims out of aluminum alloys that can be made harder and stronger by heat treating. Matrix, Mistral, and some Rigida rims use a 6000 series aluminum alloy that employs silicon and magnesium as the alloying elements. Campagnolo rims use 7000 series aluminum alloy, which employs zinc. After heat treating, rims made from 6000 or 7000 series alloys are stronger and/or more ductile than rims made from 3000 series alloy. They can legitimately be called "heat-treated." Tables 11-3 and 11-4 indicate the particular aluminum alloy used in each rim model.

Surface Finish

The surface of an alloy rim can be left in its natural polished condition or it can be anodized. An anodized rim is placed in a hot conducting bath and a current is passed through it. This forms a protective aluminum oxide layer on the surface. "Soft" anodizing makes the rims prettier and reduces corrosion and pitting. Dyes in the solution can add color. "Hard" anodizing is a longer, more expensive process. The current density is higher and the solution is chilled. This results in a much thicker oxide layer. A hard-anodized rim is somewhat stronger than a soft-anodized rim and the thick oxide layer reduces wear on the brake track. Hard-anodized rims also cost more. A hard-anodized rim is dark gray, but not all dark gray rims are hard anodized.

Some inexpensive steel rims have serrations or dimples on the brake track. This doesn't help wet-weather stopping. It makes it worse. Tables 11-3 and 11-4 show the various surface finishes that are listed in the makers' catalogs. Sometimes a different surface finish has a different model name. I don't show all of

(continued on page 218)

TABLE 11-4.

Tubular Rims

Make and Model	Cost ($)	Weight (gr.)	Width (mm)	Depth (mm)	Cross Section
Ambrosio					
Metamorphosis	90–130	420	21.5	12	box
Synthesis Durex	50–80	430	21.5	12	box
Montreal Crono	30–50	340(400)	21.5	12	box
Araya					
Aero ADX-4	75–100	340	18.7	18.5	aero
Assos					
AS-16	150–200	290	16	—	aero
AS-18	150–200	320	18	—	aero
Campagnolo					
Sigma Pave	160–240	410	22	11	box
Sigma Strada	120–180	380	22	11	box
Sigma Crono	100–150	330	20	11	box
Lambda Strada XL	50–80	405	20	11	box
Lambda Strada	40–70	445	20	11	box
Fiamme					
Ergal	35–60	290	20.4	—	box
Red Label	25–40	360	21.5	—	box
Matrix					
ISO	70–100	355	20	—	aero
Mavic					
SSC	150–200	400	21.5	11	box
Gel-280	60–80	280	20	11	box
GL-330	50–65	330	20	11	box
GP-4	45–60	395	20	11	box
Mistral					
M 19A	50–75	314	19	18.5	aero
Wolber					
Aubisque AS-40	50–75	400	20	—	box
Aspin AS-33	40–60	330	20	—	box
Arc en Ciel C-35	25–40	350	20	—	box
Profil 18	—	300	17.6	15.5	aero
Profil 20	—	430	18.8	20.0	aero

*The inclusive numbers indicate that rims are available in 4-hole increments.

Spoke Holes Available*	Surface Finish	Aluminum Alloy	Heat-Treated	Joint		Eyelets	Service
				Type	Uniformity		
24–36	HAn	—	no	pin	G	double	R
28–36	An, HAn	3000	no	pin	G	double	R
28–36	HAn	3000	no	pin	G	double	TT
24–36	P, HAn	3000	no	pin	G	none	TT
24–32	HAn	—	yes	pin	E	none	TT
32	HAn	—	yes	pin	E	none	TT
24–40	HAn	7000	yes	pin	E	double	R
24–40	HAn	7000	yes	pin	E	double	R
24–40	An	7000	yes	pin	E	double	TT
32–36	P	5000	no	pin	E	double	R
32–36	P	5000	no	pin	E	double	R
32–36	P	7000	no	pin	G	double	TT
36	P	3000	no	pin	G	double	R
28–36	HAn	6000	yes	pin	G	none	R
24–40	HAn	3000	no	pin	E	double	R
28–36	HAn	3000	no	pin	G	double	TT
24–36	HAn	3000	no	pin	G	double	R
24–40	HAn	3000	no	pin	G	double	R
36	HAn	6000	yes	pin	G	none	TT
32–36	HAn	3000	no	pin	G	double	R
32–36	HAn	3000	no	pin	G	double	R
32–36	Silver	3000	no	pin	G	double	R
28–32	HAn	3000	no	pin	G	none	TT
28–32	HAn	3000	no	pin	G	none	R

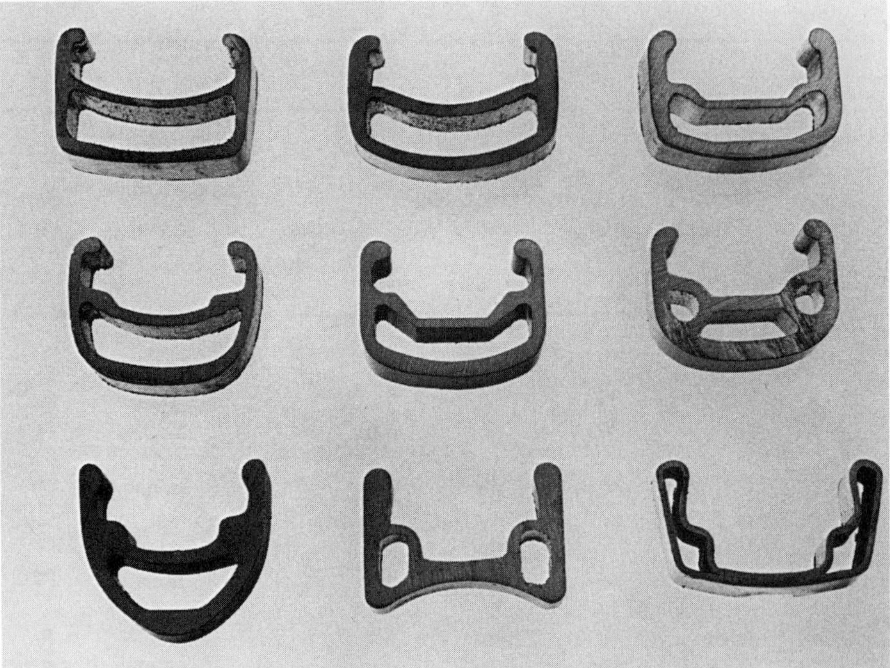

PHOTO 11-2 Cross sections of narrow clincher rims (widths in parentheses): top left to right, Mavic MA-2 or MA-40 (13.5mm), Mavic Module C or Module 3-CD (15mm), and Wolber Super Champion Gentleman (14mm); center left to right, Rigida AL 1320 (13mm), Mistral M 13L (12.5mm), and Mistral M 13 (13mm); bottom left to right, Mistral Aero M 14A (14mm), Weinmann Concave A-124 (14mm), and an economy steel rim (14mm).

the different models, just the top-quality one. Where more than one symbol is shown, it means that the rim is available with different finishes.

Rim Diameter

There are two main choices for rim diameter, 27-inch and 700C. The difference between them is found neither in the actual outside or inside rim diameter. The difference lies in the "bead seat diameter" where the bead of the tire rides on a ledge in the rim: 700C rims have a 622mm bead seat diameter, while 27-inch rims have a 630mm bead seat diameter. Size 700C wheels can be interchanged with tubular wheels without moving the brake pads. However, tire availability is the main factor to consider when making the choice. (I'll have more to say about this in chapter 12.) Brake reach and fender clearance are other factors to consider. All good-quality clincher rims are available in both 27-inch and 700C diameters, so I don't show this in table 11-3.

Number of Spoke Holes

I discussed the reasons for using more or less than 36 spokes earlier in the chapter when talking about hubs, so I won't repeat them all here. But I will point out that reducing the rim weight and the number of spokes works at cross purposes. A 24-spoke rim needs more weight to spread the higher spoke forces than does a 36-spoke rim. You have to compromise either weight or wind resistance.

Tables 11-3 and 11-4 show the number of spoke holes listed in the rim makers' catalogs. Rim availability is a different story. You can find narrow, lightweight, racing rims with 28, 32, and 36 holes. You can find wide, tandem, or loaded touring rims with 36, 40, and 48 holes. Everything else is special order and wait. Good-quality rims stagger the spoke holes. This lets the spoke leave the rim tangentially and it anchors the rim to resist torsional deflection.

Spoke Eyelets

Good-quality rims have spoke eyelets to distribute the spoke force over a wider area and to reduce friction of the spoke nipple when you true a wheel. Eyelets are essential for lightweight rims. Box-section rims have a choice between single eyelets on the bottom of the box or sockets (double eyelets) that

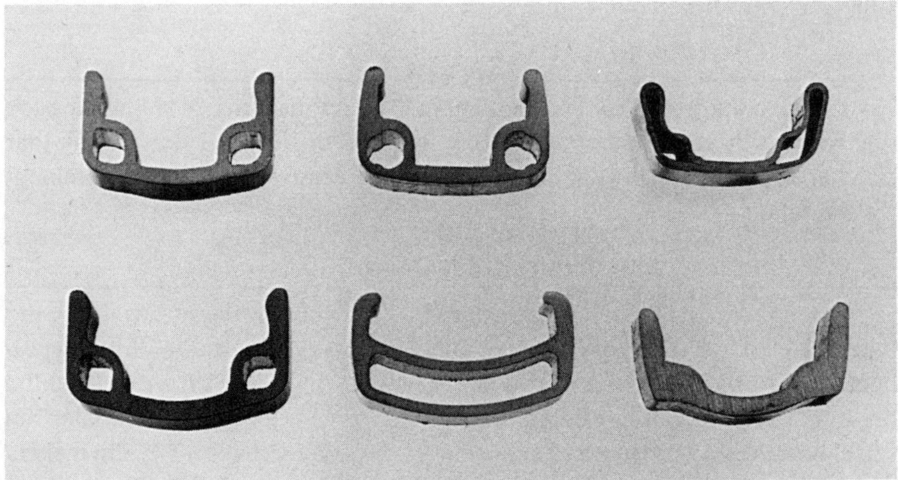

PHOTO 11-3 Cross sections of medium and wide clincher rims (widths in parentheses): top left to right, Mistral M 17 (18mm), Wolber Super Champion Model 58 (17mm), and an economy steel rim (16mm); bottom left to right, Mistral M 20 bulged-edge (20mm), Mavic Module 4 hooked-edge (19mm), and Araya 16A(1) straight-side (19mm).

extend through to the top of the box and tie the rim together. Sockets are better and they always cost more. Tables 11-3 and 11-4 indicate the type of eyelets found on different rims.

Joint Type

The joint is a critical part of the rim. If the joint bulges at all, it will cause the brakes to grab. If the rim isn't completely round at the joint, the wheel won't be completely true. When you buy rims at a bike store, pick the ones that have the smoothest joints. Most rims are rolled into a circle and then joined with either pins in the holes or sleeves. Mistral uses an epoxy glue to hold the pins. Everyone else relies on a press fit. There's no problem with the joint separating because the compressive force of the spokes pulls the joint together. A few of the heavier rims have flash-welded joints that are ground smooth after the welding. This gives a stronger, more uniform joint provided the grinding is properly done. Wheelsmith inspects thousands of rims and rejects the ones with poor joints. The level of joint uniformity is shown in tables 11-3 and 11-4. The tables also show the type of joint.

Valve Hole

Picking the best type of valve hole is easy. Buy Presta valve tubes and use Presta valve rims. The Presta valve hole is smaller than the Schrader valve hole and it weakens the rim less. Besides, tubes with Presta valves are easier to inflate.

Service

I made a judgement in table 11-3 about the normal kind of riding for each rim: whether it is racing, sport touring, or loaded touring. I don't think that clincher rims are suitable at all for time trials, where speed is the dominant consideration.

Tubular Rims

The tubular rim's box cross section has a higher strength-to-weight ratio than any clincher rim cross section. Tubular rims can be welded from aluminum alloy strips, rather than extruded. A tubular rim doesn't have to keep the tire from expanding under inflation pressure. For these reasons, a tubular rim will always weigh less than a clincher rim of the same strength. The rim makers make a range of weights. The lighter rims have thinner walls. It's as simple as that. Many users have the idea that their favorite lightweight rim is somehow stronger than Brand X's middle-weight model because of heat treating, hard anodizing, better joints, or just plain virtue. Maybe so, but the strength differences are less critical than weight.

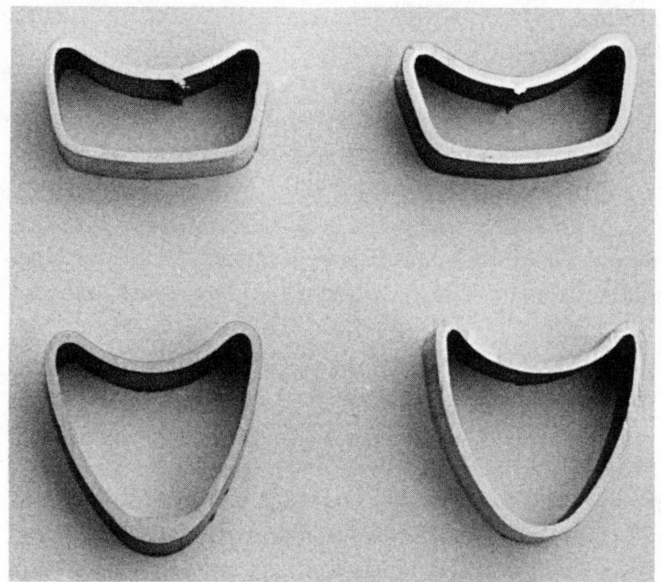

PHOTO 11-4

Cross sections of tubular rims: top left and right, Fiamme Ergal (lightweight) and Fiamme Silver (team weight); bottom left and right, Mistral M 19A Aerodynamic and Araya Aero 1 (washers required).

Wheelsmith co-owner Eric Hjertberg divides tubular rims into three classes:

- *Extra-light*, 280 to 320 grams, for limited use in time trials and for riders under 130 pounds.
- *Lightweight*, 320 to 380 grams, for smooth roads, criteriums, and track racing.
- *Team weight*, 380 to 460 grams, for general road racing and training.

Selecting tubular rims is fairly straightforward. They almost all use the same box cross section. The main differences are in weight, joint quality, and in the aluminum alloy and its heat treatment. Light, thin-walled rims are harder to make so they're more expensive. They're also significantly weaker. Heat-treated or hard-anodized rims are somewhat stronger and a lot more expensive. The new aerodynamic shapes are the exception. They're heavier than box-shaped rims of the same strength. You gain in wind resistance and lose in weight.

The best-quality tubular rims have spoke sockets that extend through the box cross section to join the box together. Aero rims don't use eyelets; you often have to use washers on the nipples, which is a bother. Advertised rim weights and actual rim weights differ. If you're really on a lightweight kick, you should weigh your rims before you buy them. When you talk to the vendors, they all tell you that their competitors understate their weights.

Rim Makers

The gruppo companies have not been interested in rims, so there's still lots of competition.

Ambrosio Ambrosio is an Italian company that's best known for tubular rims. *Durex* is their buzzword for hard anodizing.

Araya Araya is a member of JBM (Japan Bicycle Manufacturers), the Japanese combine that includes Shimano. They're a major supplier of OEM clincher rims.

Assos Assos is a Swiss company that makes very expensive, light, high-quality, aerodynamic tubular rims.

Campagnolo Campagnolo entered the rim market in 1985 with three lines: Victory, Triomphe, and Record. In 1987, they expanded to five lines and named them Sigma, Delta, Omega, Epsilon, and Lambda. In the process, the advertised weights of the lightest rims became heavier. Campagnolo makes their top-quality Sigma rim from Ergal, a heat-treated aluminum zinc alloy.

Fiamme and Rigida Fiamme and Rigida are two small French rim companies. You'll find their tubular rims in the aftermarket but the clincher rims are largely made for the OEMs.

Matrix and Mistral If you believe in buying American, these are your rims. Trek makes Matrix in Wisconsin and Sun Metal makes Mistral in Indiana. They both make only top-of-the-line, hard-anodized rims from heat-treated 6000 series alloy. I wish they would provide spoke sockets with their box-section rims. I made the wheels for my Trek 2000 with Matrix Titan rims. They held up well to the abuse I gave them when I was testing ultra-light clincher tires.

Mavic Mavic is the premier French rim maker. Mavic's Module E rim and Michelin's 27 × 1 Elan tire were the first narrow clincher package back in 1975. The Mavic G-40 was the best selling high-performance clincher rim until 1986, when it was replaced with the MA-40. Wheel builders often prefer Mavic because their rims are true and have uniform joints. The Mavic cross section has an almost flat floor. This means that there isn't a well for the tire bead when you're mounting a tire. I found it harder to mount Japanese Kevlar-beaded tires on Mavic rims than on rims with a deeper well.

Specialized Specialized introduced the Saturae line of imported rims in 1984. The clinchers came from Japan and the tubulars from Italy. In 1987, Specialized appeared to be de-emphasizing rims.

Weinmann Weinmann makes a full line of steel and alloy rims for the OEM market. You find the Weinmann A-124 and A-129 Concave rims in the aftermarket. These rims have a unique cross section. If you were going to pedal your bike for 20 miles on bare rims, they would be your choice. I've used half a dozen Weinmann A-124 rims. They've held up well, but they lack a hooked edge so I can't use them with foldable tires.

Wolber Wolber was an Italian tire company that bought the Super Champion rim company a few years back. The wide Super Champion Model 58 is my favorite touring rim. In 1987, they introduced the heat-treated, hard-anodized Model 59 that has a welded rather than pinned joint. In like fashion, the 430 is an upgrade of their GTA Gentleman narrow clincher rim.

Spokes

After all of the complication of hubs and rims, it's a pleasure to write about spokes. Spokes are the highest-stressed components on your bicycle and when they were built to normal manufacturing tolerances, spoke failures were quite common. Life has become simpler in the last few years because the design of today's top-quality spokes has become quite refined. There are now only two widely distributed brands of top-quality spokes: DT and Wheelsmith.

Today, stainless steel is the only spoke material for serious cyclists. Also, there are only four diameters to concern you: the straight and butted versions of 14 and 15 gauge. The old bicycle books contain a lot of out-of-date information about problems with stainless steel spokes from old spoke companies like Stella and Robergel. The problems just don't happen with today's top-quality spokes.

Spoke Companies

The pressure for better spokes began when companies like Wheelsmith and Performance Bicycle Shop set up computer-controlled wheel-building machines to make top-quality wheels. They found that without absolutely uniform spoke lengths and threads, the machines required excessive adjustments and the wheels needed more final trueing. The Swiss spoke company Drahtwerke Trefilerie (DT) became known for high uniformity at the same time that

Robergel, the old favorite spoke company, was encountering quality control problems. After building 25,000 wheels with DT spokes, Wheelsmith went to Japan to have their own top-quality spokes made to even more rigorous specifications. Wheelsmith and DT spokes are widely available. Alpina and Berg Union also make top-quality stainless steel spokes, but they sell largely to the OEM market.

Spoke Material

Spokes are made from carbon steel or stainless steel. Carbon steel spokes can be chrome-, nickel-, cadmium-, or zinc-plated (galvanized), but none of them lasts very long. Chrome-plating gives a brilliant luster but poor rust protection, and chrome-plated spokes that are improperly heat-treated become brittle. In short, chrome-plated spokes are best for show bikes. Galvanized spokes look crummy on any bike. They rapidly discolor in coastal climates. If you try to true a wheel after a year's service, you may find that your chrome-plated or galvanized spokes are welded to the nipples with corrosion. Low-cost galvanized or chrome-plated spokes are a hallmark of standard-quality bicycles.

The wire used to make spokes is repeatedly cold drawn to develop a very high tensile strength and fatigue resistance. Typical ultimate strengths are in the 150,000 psi (pounds per square inch) range. The old folklore said that carbon steel spokes were stronger than stainless steel spokes for any given size. The tensile strength data that I've seen doesn't support that conclusion. Rather, it suggests that some of the old spoke companies had difficulty making consistently high-strength stainless steel spokes. Today, if you want stronger spokes, use a larger gauge.

Spoke Diameter

The gauge numbers for wire and spokes read backwards. Small gauge numbers are thicker. I remember this by thinking that 16 gauge is about 1⁄16 inch thick and 8 gauge is about ⅛ inch thick. There are only two spoke gauges in common use: 14 and 15. Fourteen-gauge spokes are 2mm in diameter. Fifteen-gauge spokes are 1.8mm in diameter.

Spokes come in butted or straight gauge. Butted (or double-butted) spokes are thicker at the highly stressed ends, and thinner in the main body. Wheelsmith reduces the diameter of the butted section more than DT. Wheelsmith spokes are 14-16-14 gauge and 15-17-15 gauge. DT spokes are 14-15-14 gauge and 15-16-15 gauge. Butted spokes cost half again as much as straight-gauge spokes. Ten years ago, every top-quality wheel was built with butted spokes. Today, there's a trend to straight-gauge spokes, especially for loaded and sport touring wheels.

I like butted spokes because I think that their fatigue life is improved by the reduction of stress at the threads and at the elbow. (Spokes fail from fatigue rather than from overload.) However, it's certainly easier to build a wheel with straight-gauge spokes because they don't twist as much. Wheel-building machines have problems with the twisting of butted spokes.

The weight difference between 36 straight 14-gauge spokes (the heaviest) and 36 butted 15-17-15 gauge spokes (the lightest) is about 3 ounces or 110 grams. If you want very light wheels, it makes more sense to use fewer spokes rather than thinner spokes. That way you also reduce wind resistance. If you break a 14-gauge spoke, the wheel will remain truer, and you can probably open the brake and ride home. Fifteen-gauge straight or butted spokes are for light riders. For average riders with 36-spoke wheels, I suggest straight 14-gauge spokes for your touring wheels and 14-gauge butted spokes for your light racing wheels.

Nipples

Nipples are usually made of nickle-plated brass. Aluminum nipples are available, sometimes anodized in pretty colors. The 1-ounce saving per wheel isn't worth the hassle of dealing with the softer material. Extra-long nipples are available for certain extra-thick rims.

The ISO standard thread is 56 tpi and most spokes now use that standard. In theory, you can swap nipples of the same gauge. However, if you do, your wheels will shout, "amateur builder!" Use the nipples supplied by the spoke maker. The typical quality spoke has about ⅜ inch of threads or 22 threads. The typical nipple has a counterbored lead-in hole and about 16 threads. Wheelsmith nipples have a shallower hole and a few more threads, which gives a bit more tolerance in selecting spoke length.

Spoke Length

The perfect wheel has all of the spoke threads inside the nipple and no spoke end projecting beyond the nipple. It really isn't all that critical, but it looks prettier. Determining the exact spoke length for each combination of hub diameter, rim diameter, number of crosses, and rear wheel dish is lots of fun. I usually build one wheel that's a bit off and get it exactly right the second time. *Sutherland's Handbook for Bicycle Mechanics* (4th ed.) takes 26 pages to list all of the combinations. Wheelsmith sells a rim caliper and a hand-held computer to precisely calculate spoke length. Spokes come in 1mm steps in the most common lengths.

Flat Spokes

Flat or aerodynamic spokes are for wind resistance fanatics. There are three kinds. One kind has a double bend instead of a head. These can be wiggled head first through the spoke holes in the hub. The second kind has a conventional head and you have to slot the spoke holes in the hubs to allow the flat blade to be inserted. The slotting weakens the highly stressed hub flange (and voids the warranty). The third kind has an aero profile that can be pushed through the hub. Aerodynamic spokes are exotic items, and I have the feeling that the experts specifying wheels and spokes for Olympic record bikes may not need to read this book.

Wheels

Now that you know all about hubs, rims, and spokes, there's not a whole lot more involved in selecting your new wheels. Spend about the same amount on rims as you spend on hubs. Decide your spoking pattern and your source of supply and you're ready. Wheel building is still part art, part science, and part black magic. Two good books—*The Bicycle Wheel* by Jobst Brandt and *The Spoking Word* by Leonard Goldberg—and an article by Dan Price and Arthur Akers in the June 1985 issue of *Bike Tech* have done much to increase the science and decrease the black magic.

Sources of Supply

You have four choices as to how you acquire your new set of wheels.

- Buy all of the parts and build the wheels yourself.
- Buy hand-built wheels from the local wheel builder with the best reputation.
- Buy ready-made wheels such as those sold by Wheelsmith.
- Buy mail-order wheels.

I think that serious cyclists should build their own wheels. It's one of those satisfying human achievements that rarely happens in our complex technological world. If you can build an adequate wheel, you can also true your old wheels. Home wheel building has been made much easier by Eric Hjertberg's series of four articles in the January, February, March, and April 1986 issues of *Bicycling.* Eric wrote essentially the same instructions in *Bicycling Magazine's Complete Guide to Bicycle Maintenance and Repair.* I sat in my workshop with the February and March articles in my lap and laced up my best ever pair of wheels. A year later they're still true. The only hard part was knowing where to stop as I added more tension to the spokes. John Allen, who is also a musician, says to pluck the spokes and stop at G# or A above middle C. If you feel a bit nervous about the spoke tension in you home-built wheels, get an impartial evaluation from a wheel builder.

If you're not really into the arts and crafts thing, then try to buy your wheels from your local pro bicycle store. Every community has its own builders of "Stradivarius" wheels with super-tight spokes and perfect trueness. Ask five bike nuts and you'll get six different names. Most bicycle shops have one mechanic who is the acknowledged shop champion. These people build better (maybe only a bit better) wheels than you or I, because they've built so many. Custom-built wheels are surprisingly inexpensive. You pay a whole lot more to get your VCR fixed and it might not be fixed right. Just remember that it takes about three hours to build a top-notch set of wheels, so be prepared to pay Stradivarius a fair price for his fiddle.

Wheelsmith's ready-made wheels are a small step down from their hand-built super wheels. I visited the factory and I was impressed. Every wheel is checked for trueness and uniform spoke tension by a builder at the end of the line. If it takes more than a minor tweak, he (he was a she the day I was there) goes over and adjusts the machine. Many busy bike stores sell Wheelsmith wheels because their mechanics are too busy to hand build every wheel. The machines take a lot of work to set up so they require a long run of identical wheels. The machines also demand spoke and rim uniformity and as a result Wheelsmith has a tremendous background on spoke and rim quality control. If you order an oddball, extra-light, 24-spoke, radial wheel, the Wheelsmith bike shop will make it by hand.

I feel more nervous about mail-order wheels than I do about mail-order clothes or components. I'm willing to accept that some of the mail-order houses may have very talented builders, but I worry about what the gorillas at UPS or Federal Express do to those big, fragile wheel boxes. Also, if the wheel goes out of true after a few rides, you don't have the convenience of having its builder nearby to retrue it for you.

There's a type of OEM machine-made wheel that you shouldn't touch with a 306cm pole. I'm referring to the low-cost replacement wheel with steel rims and chrome-plated spokes. Buying cheap wheels of this type is definitely not the way to upgrade your bike.

Spoking Patterns

As part of the study reported in *Bike Tech,* Price and Akers built radial, one-, two-, three-, and four-cross wheels and tested them for torsional, lateral, and radial strength.

There really weren't any startling conclusions. We all knew that the more crosses, the stronger the wheel is torsionally. The torsional load from pedaling is only a small part of the spoke tension. The difference in lateral strength was only 15 percent, with one-cross strongest and four-cross weakest. Shorter spokes brace the wheel better from side loads than longer spokes. The surprise was that radial-spoked wheels were weaker laterally than one- or two-cross wheels. Price and Akers think that radial-spoked wheels are weaker because the uncrossed spokes don't brace each other.

There was a similar variation in radial strength. Radial-spoking was strongest and four-cross was weakest. For some unexplained reason, one-cross wheels were out of sequence. They were about the same as four-cross.

From all of this esoterica, I conclude that there is no significant performance difference between three-cross and four-cross and that none of the other patterns make sense. I make my light racing wheels three-cross and my heavy touring wheels four-cross just in case there is any truth to the old saw that four-cross wheels ride softer.

How about all of the magic asymmetrical patterns that we always read about? For example, I used to make rear wheels radial on the right side and four-cross on the left. The rationale was that all of the pedaling torsional load was carried by the underloaded left side spokes. I used to get all kinds of comments. Then one day I was pedaling along and the rear wheel collapsed. The radial spokes tore a four-spoke wide chunk of metal out of my Dura-Ace low-flange hub. Lesson? The main reason not to build oddball patterns is that they're hard to build; since the spoke tensions aren't uniform, they don't take advantage of all of the spoke's strength.

Frank's Favorite Wheels

I use nothing but Shimano Dura-Ace Freehubs because I like the freewheel design so much. I must confess I haven't had very much recent experience with any other hubs.

From his bicycle-repair-shop viewpoint, Paul Brown feels that middle-quality, cup-and-cone hubs are subject to a variety of quality and misadjustment problems. He feels that only the top-of-the line Campagnolo and Shimano Dura-Ace hubs are as good as the sealed-bearing hubs from Phil Wood, SunTour, or Specialized.

I have two favorite wheels, one for loaded touring and one for fast sport touring. Both use Shimano Dura-Ace, wide-spaced 6-speed Freehubs. I use Wolber Super Champion Model 58 rims on my current loaded touring wheels. I'll use Mistral M 20 rims on my next set. I use Matrix Titan rims on my lightweight wheels. Eric likes Mavic MA-40 rims. I use 36 Wheelsmith spokes on both sets of wheels. The touring wheels use straight, 14-gauge spokes laced four-cross. The light wheels use butted 14-16-14 gauge spokes laced three-cross.

CHAPTER 12

All about Tires and Tubes

Tires don't last forever, so each time a tire wears out you can buy a better one, and you've got lots of tires to choose from. There are two basic kinds of clincher bicycle tires: skinwalls and gumwalls. You can improve the performance of your bicycle by upgrading from a gumwall to a skinwall tire that matches your riding style.

To select the optimum skinwall, you have to select the right size and the right construction. This involves a compromise between lively performance on the one hand and durability and mileage on the other. Skinwall tires come in five sizes and four different constructions. The important thing is to pick the right size and the right kind of tire for you.

Terminology time. There are two classes of bicycle tires: *tubulars* and *clinchers.* Tubular or sew-up tires have the inner tube sewn inside the tire. Tubular tires are glued onto tubular rims. That's fairly straightforward. But, when we turn to clinchers, things get trickier. A little historical background is needed to help sort things out.

When Doctor Dunlop invented the pneumatic tire more than a century ago, he invented a tubular and tubulars were just as troublesome in those days as they are today. The inventors immediately set to work to develop a more reliable tire that was easier to repair. By 1896, there were three broad classes: *tubular, wired-on,* and *clincher.* The tubular tires of that time were just as they are today. The wired-on tires had strong wire beads that held them onto the rims, and clincher tires had two flaps that folded under the tube and bulges in the tire sidewall that fitted into grooves in the rim. It's almost the same situation today except that there's a whole lot of history and terminology that tends to confuse things. Today, everyone calls nontubular tires "clinchers," regardless of how they're retained on the rim. (*Bicycling* once launched a campaign to refine the terminology but we lost.)

Today's clincher tires are designed for two basic kinds of rims: *straight-side* and *hooked-edge*. Tires designed for straight-side rims are called "wired-on" tires by the experts. The tire bead mates with the bead seat of the rim to keep the tire from blowing off. Tires designed for straight-side rims have steel beads. Tires designed for hooked-edge rims are called "hook-bead" tires by the experts. Hook-bead tires are a bit like the ancient clincher tires. The hook-bead is forced under the rim's hooked-edge by the air pressure. This retains the tire securely at high inflation pressures. Tires with Kevlar beads must use hooked-edge rims. (See figure 12-1 for a depiction of clincher, wired-on, and hook-bead tires.)

Tires are donuts and they have two diameters. The big outside diameter is what is usually termed the *tire diameter* and the little diameter is the *tire width.*

Tire Sizes and Tire Marking

While we've taken time out for terminology, we'd better talk about the strange numbers that designate tire sizes. There are three basic sets of numbers: ancient English, ancient French, and ISO-ETRTO (International Standards Organization–European Tire and Rim Technical Organization). The first two go back to the turn of the century and were based on the outside diameter of the tire. (Probably because that's how buggies with solid rubber tires were sold.)

Ancient English System

The tire size 27 × 1¼ is an ancient English designation. Eighty years ago, the tire outside diameter was 27 inches, the tire width was 1¼ inches, and the rim outside diameter was 24½ inches. The English system covered both tires

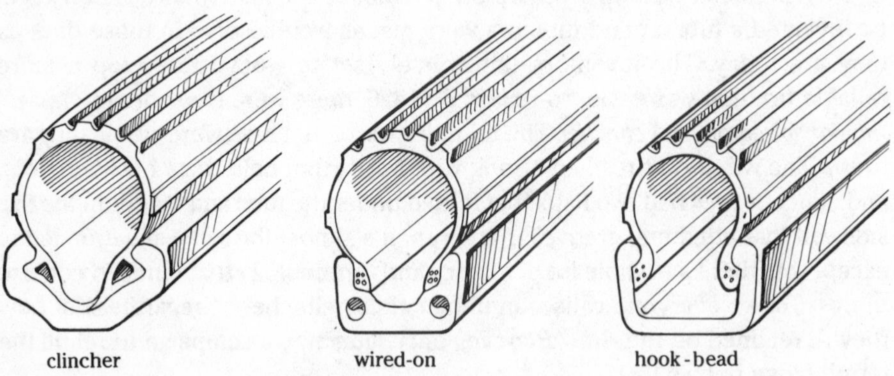

FIGURE 12-1 Three kinds of tires and rims.

and rims. Thus, a 27 × 1½ tire required a smaller-diameter rim (24-inch) to provide the same 27-inch outside tire diameter.

After a while, certain rim sizes became national favorites. When the tire maker produced a 1-inch-wide tire to fit the standard 27 × 1¼ rim, it was labeled 27 × 1¼ × 1. You still see the dual designation occasionally, but today most makers call the tire 27 × 1.

There's another little subtlety. A tire designed for a straight-side rim with a bead seat is supposed to be marked in fractions, say 26 × 1⅜. A tire designed for a hooked-edge rim without a bead seat is supposed to be decimal marked, say 26 × 1.375. But, in the 27-inch and 700C sizes, hooked-edge rims have both hooked edges and bead seats so the tires don't have decimal markings.

Ancient French System

The tire size 700 × 39C is an ancient French designation. Eighty years ago, the tire outside diameter was 700mm, the tire width was 39mm, and the rim diameter was 622mm. The C was a code number that defined the tire width: 700A tires were narrowest (1⅜ inches), 700B tires were wider (1½ inches), and 700C tires were widest (1¾ inches). Today, in France 700A and 700B rims are still used. With an outside diameter system, they have larger bead seat diameters than 700C.

Today, at least in the USA, the C in 700C says in effect, "Stop all of this nonsense! This rim has a 622mm bead seat diameter. Period."

ISO-ETRTO System

The object of tire and rim marking is to ensure that a standard-sized tire fits a standard-sized rim. This means that the inside diameter of the tire has to be just a tiny bit larger than the bead seat diameter of the rim. The ISO-ETRTO size designation is based on bead seat diameters, not outside diameters. This is clearly a better system, which is why the ETRTO designation has become an ISO standard. If everyone provided accurate ISO-ETRTO markings, we would be in clover.

Here's how the system works. The ISO-ETRTO marking for a 27 × 1¼ tire is "32-630." The first number, 32, specifies the section width in millimeters. The second number, 630, is the diameter in millimeters of the bead of the tire or the bead seat of the rim. All widths of 27-inch rims have a bead seat diameter of 630mm. All widths of 700C rims have a bead seat diameter of 622mm. Now you see why narrow rims designed for 27 × 1 tires are labeled 27 × 1¼. The ISO-ETRTO number is often embossed on the tire tread rather than printed on the label.

Section width is ISO-ETRTO's method of measuring tire width regardless of what width rim is used. The section width is the width of the tire measured over the tread, divided by 2.5. To measure section width, you wrap the tire around a dowel and measure the width from bead to bead around the outside (see figure 12-2). The 2.5 converts tire circumference to tire diameter. You don't divide by Pi (3.14) because a clincher tire isn't a complete circle; there's a gap between the beads for the rim. If a tire is mounted on the correct rim, the section width and the measured tire width (figure 12-3) are nearly the same.

In theory, a tire labeled 27 × 1 has a section width and a mounted width of 1 inch (25.4mm), while a tire labeled 700 × 25C tire has a section width and a mounted width of 25mm. In practice, all three systems are very loosely interpreted and there's considerable imaginative labeling. This does you a disservice, because the labeled size doesn't have a standard meaning between brands or even within the same brand.

Clinchers versus Tubulars

If you add the total weight of tire, tube, and rim, you'll always get more strength and performance per pound from tubulars. I suspect that this will continue to be true in spite of any future improvements in clincher tire or clincher rim design. The clincher rim is the real problem. It always weighs more than a tubular rim of equal strength. Bicycle racers put up with the disadvantages of tubulars because pound for pound, tubulars perform better than clinchers.

However, tubulars have a potful of disadvantages. First, they're very expensive, especially the handmade silk tubulars that the old books rave about. Second, the tread isn't very thick so they puncture easily. Third, it's difficult to repair the punctures. Sometimes, you can find a pro bike store that has an old racer who will repair tubulars on his kitchen table for, say, $20 a pop. (That's a

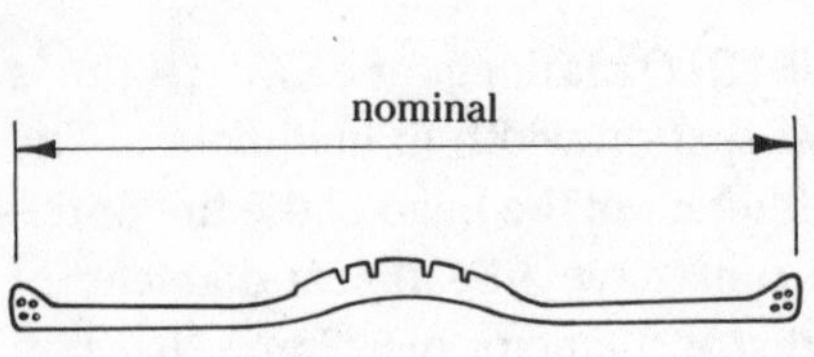

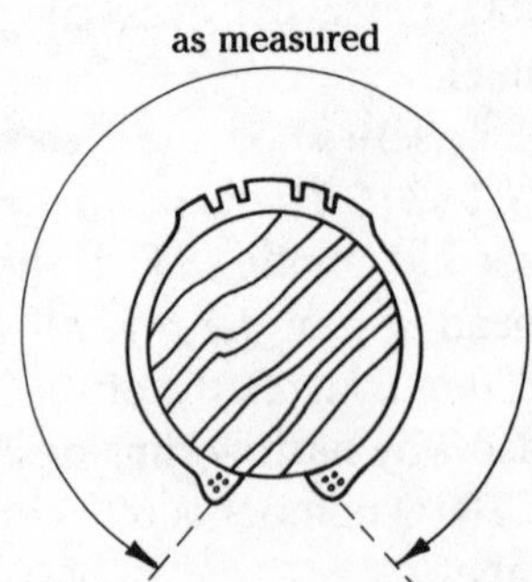

FIGURE 12-2 ISO-ETRTO section width.

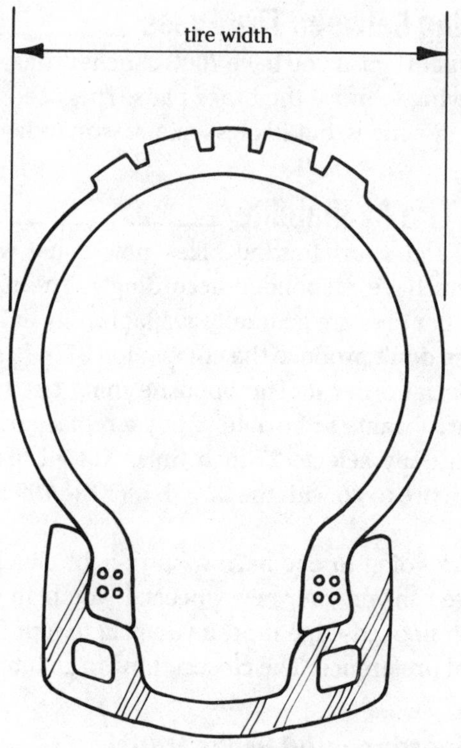

FIGURE 12-3

Measured width of a mounted tire.

pun, son.) The normal choice is to repair them yourself or throw them away. Unfortunately, fixing tubulars is not a satisfying job like building wheels. Finally, you have to glue the stupid things back onto the rims, which is another messy, time-consuming task.

All of the old bicycle books wax ecstatic about tubulars. The key point to remember is that they were comparing old handmade silk tubulars to old clinchers, and clinchers have improved dramatically since those books were written. I haven't rated tubulars since they represent such a small share of the market.

Rim Size Selection

When you buy a new set of wheels, or a new bicycle, you have to choose between two rim sizes: 27-inch (630mm bead seat diameter), or 700C (622mm bead seat diameter). Once you've bought the wheels, you buy tires to match the rims. The 8mm (0.3-inch) difference between the two sizes is so small that they perform exactly the same. It's one more maddening bit of nonstandardization. If you're buying a new set of wheels, think about the following factors.

Switching between Tire Types

All tubulars use 700C tubular rims. If you have 700C clincher rims, then you can switch wheels without having to move the brake pads. This used to be the main reason for picking 700C clinchers, but it's less of a reason today because so few people use tubulars.

Tire Availability

Most high-class racing and sport touring bikes now come with 700C clincher rims. The tire makers have responded accordingly. The narrowest, best-performing, lightest clincher tires are generally available only in 700 × 19C or 700 × 20C sizes. The makers don't produce the companion 27 × ⅞ size, or, if it's available, you have to special order it. The opposite thing has happened with fat touring tires. The tourist wants to be able to buy a replacement tire in Lodgepole, Montana, so he usually selects 27-inch tires. Not all tire makers offer the companion 700 × 32C tire to go with the 27 × 1¼, or the 700 × 35C tire to go with the 27 × 1⅜.

Plan accordingly. If you're going to use narrow, ultra-light clincher tires, buy narrow 700C hooked-edge rims on your new wheels. If you plan to use fat touring tires, buy wide 27-inch hooked-edge rims. If you plan to tour in Europe or Bangladesh, check the local preference. The closest thing to an international tire size is 650A.

Fender Clearance and Brake Reach

When you buy a new set of wheels for your present bicycle, you can sometimes correct the original maker's lack of prescience. For example, few bicycles designed for the U.S. market have adequate fender clearance, especially with fat touring tires. You'd like to have about ⅜ inch between the outside of the tire and the inside of the fender. If you want to ride in the rain but your bicycle doesn't have enough clearance for fenders, switching from 27-inch to 700C wheels will give you an extra ⅛ inch.

If your old bicycle used centerpull brakes and you want to install one of today's fancy short-reach sidepull brakes, you may find that the brake mounting hole is a bit far from the rim. If the bike also used 700C wheels, then switching to 27-inch wheels will move the rim a bit closer to the brakes.

Tire Performance

When selecting a set of clinchers, you have to make two decisions. The easy choice is between cheap, poor-performing gumwalls or expensive, good-performing skinwalls. The sidewall of a gumwall is ⅓ cord and ⅔ rubber. In a skinwall, the proportions are reversed. Flexing all that rubber makes thick gumwall tires harder to pedal.

Your second choice between fat clinchers and skinny clinchers is harder. You have to decide if you want wider, lower-pressure tires and tubes that feel sluggish and are heavier, softer riding, harder pedaling, longer wearing, and more puncture-resistant. Or do you want narrower, higher-pressure tires and tubes that are lively, lighter, harder riding, easier pedaling, shorter wearing, and more puncture-prone? Note that each advantage has a companion disadvantage. In bicycle tires, there's no free ride. (Pun intended.)

There is, however, still a lot of mystique in bicycle tire advertising. Yesterday's snake oil peddlers now sell bicycle tires. They'd have you believe that there's a magic combination of rubber compound, tread, and sidewall design that will roll uphill without pedaling.

Before writing this chapter, I talked to the tire experts at Avocet, CyclePro, Michelin, and Specialized. I took their expert advice and integrated it with my own experience. I tried to pick out the important differences between tires. Then, I obtained a pair of each of the more than 50 widely distributed, top-of-the-line clincher tires, weighed them, and measured their key dimensions. Finally, I prepared table 12-1, which shows the significant differences between tires. You can see the advantages along with the disadvantages and pick the features that are important to you.

Let's look at the major differences in tires, in order of importance.

Tire Size

There are five nominal English sizes, each with a companion nominal French size as shown in table 12-2 on page 240. Neither the English, French, nor ISO-ETRTO markings indicate the actual tire section width or the actual tire width when mounted on a proper rim. In the narrowest size, tires are larger than the labels. In the wider sizes, tires are smaller than the labels. Each maker exaggerates in a different way. It's as if there's a Tire Labeling Politburo with a rule that the label must not tell the truth.

Avocet's labels are closest to the truth. Michelin makes three tires that have a section width of 25mm. Because of the Politburo, they can't be labeled 700 × 25C. So Michelin labeled the Hi-Lite Road and Hi-Lite Comp 700 × 23C and the Select 700 × 28C. Actually, the mislabeling has gone on for so long that now you expect a 1⅛ tire to be about 1-inch-wide and a properly labeled tire would be hard to sell.

I used the French sizes for my measurements. I also show the companion English size in tables 12-1 and 12-2. Each English size tire is exactly the same width as its companion French size tire. They're 1 percent larger in circumference and they weigh 1 percent more. Table 12-1 shows the labeled ISO-ETRTO

(continued on page 238)

TABLE 12-1.

Tires

Make and Model	Cost ($)	Marked Size English 27 × __	Marked Size French 700 × __	Marked Size ETRTO 630 or 622 × __	Maximum Inflation Pressure (psi)	Weight (gr.) Advert.	Weight (gr.) Meas.	Actual Widths (mm) ETRTO Section Width	Actual Widths (mm) Meas. Mounted Width	Tread Type
Avocet										
FasGrip Time Trial 30	19–25	⅞	20	—	125	165	173	22	20	smooth
FasGrip Time Trial 20	13–20	⅞	20	—	125	215	221	22.5	21	smooth
FasGrip Time Trial K20	18–24	⅞	20	—	125	245	249	22	21	smooth
FasGrip Criterium 30	19–25	1	25	—	115	190	198	24	23.5	smooth
FasGrip Criterium 20	13–20	1	25	—	115	225	231	24.5	23.5	smooth
FasGrip Criterium K20	18–24	1	25	—	115	260	260	24	23.5	smooth
FasGrip Road 30	19–25	1⅛	28	—	105	230	251	27.5	26	smooth
FasGrip Road 20	13–20	1⅛	28	—	105	265	285	27	25	smooth
FasGrip Road K20	18–25	1⅛	28	—	105	300	311	27	25	smooth
FasGrip Duro 20	13–20	1¼	32	—	95	300	324	31	29.5	smooth
FasGrip Duro K20	18–24	1¼	32	—	95	335	—	—	—	smooth
CyclePro										
Linear/F	18–24	1	23	23	115	195	195	22.5	20.5	sm. cnt.
Linear	15–20	1	23	—	115	220	237	22.5	20.5	sm. cnt.
Discovery/F	16–21	—	20	—	125	200	190	22	20.5	sm. w/sipes
Discovery/F	16–21	1	25	—	115	220	205	24	23	sm. w/sipes
Discovery/F (KB)	17–23	—	20	—	125	195	200	22.5	21	sm. w/sipes
Discovery/F (KB)	17–23	1	25	—	115	225	223	24.5	23	sm. w/sipes
Discovery	11–15	—	20	—	125	220	238	23	21	sm. w/sipes
Discovery	11–15	1	25	—	115	225	265	24.5	23	sm. w/sipes
Discovery	11–15	1⅛	28	—	105	265	282	27	26	sm. w/sipes
Discovery	11–15	1¼	—	—	100	270	342	30.5	29	sm. w/sipes
Discovery (KB)	13–18	—	20	—	125	220	258	23	21	sm. w/sipes
Discovery (KB)	13–18	1	25	—	115	240	260	24	23	sm. w/sipes
Discovery (KB)	13–18	1⅛	28	—	105	285	292	27	26	sm. w/sipes
Discovery (KB)	13–18	1¼	—	—	100	290	314	29.5	28	sm. w/sipes

Bead Material	Threads Per Inch	Thickness			Rim Required			Special Features	Durability	Mileage	Rolling Resist.
		Tread (mm)	Sidewall (mm)	Under Tread (mm)	Inside Width (mm) *Min.*	*Max.*	Type				
Kvlr	127	1.05	0.55	0.85	11	16	H		P	P	E
Stl	127	1.00	0.60	0.90	11	16	S		P	P	E
Stl	127	1.20	0.65	1.30	11	16	S	Kv1r belt	VG	F	VG
Kvlr	127	1.25	0.60	0.90	12	17	H		F	F	VG
Stl	127	1.25	0.55	0.85	12	17	S		F	F	VG
Stl	127	1.50	0.60	1.20	12	17	S	Kvlr belt	VG	G	G
Kvlr	66	1.90	0.60	0.90	14	20	H		G	E	G
Stl	66	1.60	0.60	0.90	14	20	S		G	VG	G
Stl	66	2.15	0.60	1.20	14	20	S	Kvlr belt	E	E	G
Stl	66	2.00	0.60	0.90	16	22	S		VG	E	G
Stl	60	—	—	—	—	—	S	Kvlr belt	—	—	—
Kvlr	120	1.45	0.55	0.80	11	16	H		F	F	VG
Kvlr	120	1.45	0.50	0.70	11	16	H		F	F	VG
Kvlr	130	1.70	0.55	0.85	11	16	H		F	G	VG
Kvlr	127	2.05	0.50	0.80	12	17	H		G	VG	G
Kvlr	130	1.75	0.55	1.15	11	16	H	Kvlr belt	VG	G	G
Kvlr	127	2.10	0.55	1.10	12	17	H	Kvlr belt	E	VG	G
Stl	130	1.40	0.60	0.90	12	16	S		F	F	VG
Stl	127	1.95	0.65	1.00	12	17	S		G	VG	G
Stl	66	2.10	0.60	0.90	14	20	S		G	E	G
Stl	66	2.70	0.60	0.90	16	22	S		VG	E	F
Stl	127	1.55	0.60	1.20	12	16	S	Kvlr belt	VG	G	G
Stl	127	1.70	0.60	1.20	12	17	S	Kvlr belt	VG	G	G
Stl	66	2.05	0.60	1.15	14	20	S	Kvlr belt	E	E	F
Stl	66	2.10	0.60	1.15	14	20	S	Kvlr belt	E	E	F

(continued)

Tires—*Continued*

Make and Model	Cost ($)	Marked Size			Maximum Inflation Pressure (psi)	Weight (gr.)		Actual Widths (mm)		Tread
		English 27 X __	French 700 X __	ETRTO 630 or 622 X __		Advert.	Meas.	ETRTO Section Width	Meas. Mounted Width	Type
Michelin										
Hi-Lite Pro	17–25	—	19	19	110	210	214	21.5	20.5	smooth
Hi-Lite Comp	17–25	—	20	20	110	220	223	22.5	22	smooth
Hi-Lite Comp	17–25	⅞	23	23	110	235	242	25	23.5	smooth
Hi-Lite Road	15–21	—	20	20	105	220	213	22.5	22	cnt. rib
Hi-Lite Road	15–21	⅞	23	23	105	235	228	25	23.5	cnt. rib
Hi-Lite Road	15–21	1⅛	—	28	100	265	266	29	27.5	cnt. rib
Hi-Lite Tour	15–21	1⅜	35	35	85	320	343	32.5	32	zigzag
Select	12–16	1	25	25	105	270	285	23	21.5	sm. w/sipes
Select	12–16	1⅛	28	28	100	290	299	25	23	sm. w/sipes
Select	12–16	1¼	32	32	95	330	321	30	29	sm. w/sipes
Classic Speed	12–16	1¼	—	32	85	495	555	32.5	30	ribbed
Specialized										
Turbo VR	32–45	—	25	20	115	165	172	23.5	20.5	smooth
Turbo VS	32–45	—	25	20	115	165	188	23.5	20.5	checker
Turbo R	17–23	—	19	18	125	170	177	20.5	19	smooth
Turbo R	17–23	1	25	20	115	180	194	23	21	smooth
Turbo R	17–23	1⅛	28	25	110	240	258	27	24	smooth
Turbo S	17–23	1	25	20	115	180	187	23	21	checker
Turbo S	17–23	1⅛	28	25	110	240	251	26.5	24	checker
Turbo S	17–23	1¼	32	28	105	275	288	28.5	26.5	checker
Touring II	11–15	1	25	—	110	270	266	23	21	sm. cnt./H-bone
Touring II	11–15	1⅛	28	—	105	290	284	27	24	sm. cnt./H-bone
Touring II	11–15	1¼	32	—	100	330	333	29	26.5	sm. cnt./H-bone
Touring II-K4	14–18	1	25	20	110	335	276	23	21	sm. cnt./H-bone
Touring II-K4	14–18	1⅛	28	25	105	355	318	26.5	24	sm. cnt./H-bone
Touring II-K4	14–18	1¼	32	28	100	370	340	28.5	26.5	sm. cnt./H-bone
Touring X	11–15	1¼	—	—	100	400	—	—	—	—
Expedition	12–18	1⅜	35	—	75	475	480	35	31.5	cnt. rib/H-bone

section widths, where the makers show this dimension. It also shows the actual ISO-ETRTO section width based on my measurements.

I mounted all 50 tires, inflated them to the listed pressure, and measured the mounted width at four places. The narrow tires (1⅛ or 28mm and smaller) were mounted on 14mm, narrow rims. The wide tires (1¼ or 32mm and larger) were mounted on 16mm, medium-width rims. Table 12-1 shows the mounted

Bead Material	Threads Per Inch	Thickness: Tread (mm)	Thickness: Sidewall (mm)	Thickness: Under Tread (mm)	Rim Required: Inside Width (mm) Min.	Rim Required: Inside Width (mm) Max.	Rim Required: Type	Special Features	Durability	Mileage	Rolling Resist.
Kvlr	N/A	1.30	1.10	1.10	11	15	H		G	G	E
Kvlr	N/A	1.35	1.10	1.45	11	16	H	nylon belt	VG	G	E
Kvlr	N/A	1.40	1.00	1.30	13	18	H	nylon belt	E	VG	E
Kvlr	N/A	1.60	1.10	1.10	11	16	H		G	G	VG
Kvlr	N/A	1.70	1.10	1.10	13	18	H		VG	VG	VG
Kvlr	N/A	1.55	1.00	1.00	14	20	H/S		G	G	VG
Kvlr	N/A	2.30	0.95	0.95	16	23	H/S		E	E	G
Stl	36	1.10	1.05	1.50	11	16	H/S		G	P	G
Stl	36	1.20	1.05	1.50	13	18	H/S		G	F	G
Stl	36	1.15	1.05	1.50	15	21	H/S		VG	G	G
Stl	—	1.60	2.00	2.00	16	23	S		E	VG	P
Kvlr	110	1.20	0.65	0.65	12	17	H	Kvlr casing	P	F	E
Kvlr	110	1.55	0.65	0.65	12	17	H	Kvlr casing	P	F	VG
Kvlr	106	1.00	0.75	1.15	10	15	H		F	P	VG
Kvlr	106	1.30	0.70	1.10	12	16	H		F	F	VG
Kvlr	66	1.70	0.80	1.15	14	19	H		G	VG	G
Kvlr	106	1.30	0.65	1.00	12	16	H		F	F	VG
Kvlr	66	1.75	0.80	1.15	14	19	H		G	G	G
Kvlr	66	1.85	0.85	1.25	14	20	H		VG	VG	G
Stl	66	1.25	0.90	1.35	12	17	S		G	F	G
Stl	66	1.80	0.65	1.00	14	19	S		G	VG	G
Stl	66	1.95	0.85	1.25	14	20	S		VG	E	G
Stl	66	1.30	0.85	1.70	12	16	S	Kvlr belt	VG	F	G
Stl	66	1.90	0.85	1.80	14	19	S	Kvlr belt	E	VG	F
Stl	66	1.90	0.90	1.90	14	20	S	Kvlr belt	E	VG	F
Stl	66	—	—	—	—	—	S	Kvlr belt	—	—	—
Stl	36	2.60	0.90	1.35	16	24	S		E	E	F

tire widths. Use these actual mounted widths rather than the labeled size when you want to switch to a comparable tire of a different brand.

Inflation Pressure

Inflation pressure is the other significant variable. You can make a major change in the feel and performance of any tire by carrying ten psi more or less

TABLE 12-2.

Five Nominal Tire Sizes

Labeled French Size	Labeled English Size	Typ. Mounted Width (mm)	Typ. Mounted Width (in.)	Typ. Inflation Pressure (psi)
700 × 19C/20C	27 × ⅞	21.0 ± 1.0	0.82 ± 0.06	125
700 × 23C/25C	27 × 1	22.0 ± 1.5	0.87 ± 0.06	115
700 × 28C	27 × 1⅛	25.0 ± 2.0	0.98 ± 0.09	105
700 × 32C	27 × 1¼	28.0 ± 2.0	1.11 ± 0.07	95
700 × 35C	27 × 1⅜	32.0 ± 0.5	1.25 ± 0.01	85

than the recommended inflation pressure. Table 12-1 shows the inflation pressure marked on the sidewall of each tire. When properly installed on the correct rim, tires are supposed to withstand twice their marked inflation pressure without blowing off the rim. And, as a matter of fact, most tires *are* strong enough to withstand such pressure, but keeping the tire on the rim is a different matter. If you install a maximum tolerance tire on a minimum tolerance rim and overinflate it, it may just blow off.

In the process of installing the 50 tires on rims to measure them, 3 tires came off the rims at less than the rated inflation pressure because I didn't make sure that the beads were properly seated. Hooked-edge rims are much better at preventing blow-off than straight-side rims. Straight-side rims are really only suitable for casual riding at pressures less than, say, 85 psi. If you're going to overinflate your tires, read the instructions about seating the beads and be careful. There's a lot of energy stored in that compressed air.

The stress in the casing of a tire goes up directly with tire diameter and with inflation pressure. A 1½-inch-wide tire at 75 psi has the same casing stress as a ¾-inch-wide tire at 150 psi. There's a bit of a Detroit horsepower war going on with inflation pressures. Tire buyers believe higher pressure ratings are better. Some tires now show a recommended pressure and a maximum pressure. This reflects the fact that the blow-off pressure is higher with hooked-edge rims, so the maximum pressure can be higher.

I used to think that the pressure listed on the sidewall was the maker's recommendation for heavy riders. From my conversations with the makers, I've now concluded that they don't have a magic formula that says this inflation pressure gives the best possible performance for some given rider weight. Their pressure ratings are based on casing stress, blow-off pressure, and legal liability considerations.

Experiment a bit with inflation pressure. Heavy riders on narrow tires should try an extra ten psi, especially on the rear tire. Both overinflation and underinflation cause tires to wear out prematurely. It's essential to keep a narrow 27 × 1 or 700 × 20C tire fully inflated or you'll get a "snakebite" puncture when your rim bottoms out going over potholes or bumps. The tube is trapped by the folded tire between the rim and the bump. The tube is folded, which is why there are two holes ¼ inch apart. Snakebite punctures tell you that your tire pressure is too low, your tire diameter is too small, or your waist diameter is too large.

This sounds like all you need is a good high-pressure tire pump and lots of pressure. Unfortunately, overinflated tires aren't much fun either. The ride beats you up like a jackhammer and they "feel" insecure when you corner. If you're a lightweight and your tires feel too harsh, try lowering the pressure ten psi. The ride will be more comfortable and the bicycle will corner better.

You need an accurate pressure gauge to find your optimum inflation pressure. I wrote an article on pressure gauges in the May 1987 issue of *Bicycling.* I concluded that the hand-held Kingsbridge and Meiser pressure gauges were accurate and that the gauges that are installed on pumps take a beating with time and tend to read high.

Tire size ties in with inflation pressure. Narrow tires can withstand higher inflation pressures than wide tires. Over a narrow range, you can match the tire size to the rider weight and the road surface by raising or lowering the inflation pressure. At some point, the heavy rider finds that he has to grossly overinflate

PHOTO 12-1 Tire labeling problems: top, Michelin 700 × 28C Select (actual width, 23mm); bottom, Michelin 700 × 23C Hi-Lite Comp (actual width, 23.5mm).

a narrow tire. He needs a wider tire. Similarly, the light rider doesn't get much comfort from lowering the pressure more than say ten psi. He needs a narrower, lighter tire.

I've tried just about every narrow, high-pressure, high-performance, clincher tire made, starting with the Michelin Elan in 1975. I've had hundreds of flats. Literally, because I'm working on my third box of 100 Rema patches. To me the message is very clear. At 180 pounds, the smallest tire that I should use is 27 × 1⅛ (or 700 × 28C). However, like Charlie Brown trusting Lucy to hold the football, I want to believe the snake oil salesmen. There's no doubt that my 24-pound Trek 2000 with 27 × 1 (or even 700 × 19C) tires at 125 psi is a joy to pedal. I can repair a rear flat and be moving in less than ten minutes and I always carry a spare tire and tube when I'm playing lightweight tire games.

I've learned something from all of this. I get a different kind of fun riding properly-sized or even oversized tires. On my long distance tours, I use 27 × 1⅜ (or 700 × 35C) tires and I've learned to love them. I leave the Michelin Hi-Lite Tours inflated to 80 psi on the Columbine touring bike all year round. They're easy riding, insensitive to road surface, and they almost never get a flat. It's reassuring to know that I can run off the shoulder of the road onto the gravel and nothing happens. On city streets, wide tires shrug off paving grooves and ridges that would dump you on narrow tires.

The wide tires seem to be about 10 percent harder to pedal. It takes me about 15 minutes longer to do the same 33-mile ride on the Columbine than on the Trek. I keep reminding myself that at 15 mph, 70 percent of my power input is spent overcoming wind resistance and that the wind resistance goes up as the cube of the speed. Going down steep hills, the Columbine with a Zipper fairing coasts away from the Trek with no fairing.

Picking the right tire size is a personal matter. Jim Merz, Specialized's tire guru, weighs 190 pounds and rides narrow Turbo VRs. I asked him if he gets lots of flats. He answered, "I don't get flats, I'm careful."

Figure 12-4 is my effort to quantify rider and bicycle weight against inflation pressure and tire size. It's my own idea. I couldn't find anything like this in the manufacturers' literature. It's conservative, but take it as a starting point to pick your tire size and inflation pressure.

Weight

The total weight of the tire, tube, and rim is the most important weight on the bicycle. Most bicycle writers have written that they would rather pedal a Varsity with Paramount wheels than a Paramount with Varsity wheels. I'm not sure I agree, but it makes the point. The rotating weights on the outside of the wheel have the greatest influence on how a bicycle accelerates and how it feels.

PHOTO 12-2 Six tire sizes (widths in parentheses): left to right, 700 × 19C Specialized Turbo R (19mm), 700 × 23C CyclePro Linear F (20.5mm), 700 × 25C CyclePro Discovery (23mm), 700 × 28C Specialized Touring II (24mm), 700 × 32C Avocet FasGrip Duro 20 (29.5mm), and 700 × 35C Michelin Hi-Lite Tour (32mm).

The easiest way to reduce the weight of a tire is to reduce its size. A narrower tire takes less cord and rubber so it automatically weighs less.

A narrower tire has less air pressure force acting on the casing and the rim. The casing can be thinner and lighter and the tire can carry a higher pressure without blowing off the rim. The corollary is that a narrow tire must carry a higher pressure to support a given rider. On the surface, the obvious answer is to buy the lightest and narrowest tire that you can get away with. This is true as long as the light tire is comfortable and reliable. This gets right back to my first priority item: pick the right tire size.

For any given size, lighter tires cost more money. Thinner sidewalls, skinwall construction, finer cord thread, exotic Kevlar beads, and tight quality control all add to the cost. This is a classic "less is more" situation. The tire makers charge a legitimate premium for lighter tires.

Now comes the rub. Tire making isn't a precise micrometer-controlled process. There's a weight tolerance of about plus or minus 10 percent on production line tires. The manufacturer doesn't list the heaviest tire in the batch or even the average one. Usually, he weighs a bunch of tires and advertises the weight of the lightest ones. Table 12-1 shows the advertised weight and the average weight of my two samples. Where you see a significant weight difference, it probably means that the tires that I weighed were different models from the tires that were weighed for the advertising.

There's a sneakier approach to the weight game. You can label a tire as larger than it really is. That's why I show the actual ISO-ETRTO section widths and the actual mounted widths in table 12-1. Tires with the same section width are the same size.

Feel

Feel is often called "liveliness." Either way, it's what keeps the snake oil salesmen in business. Tubular tires feel great. You can hear them hiss over the

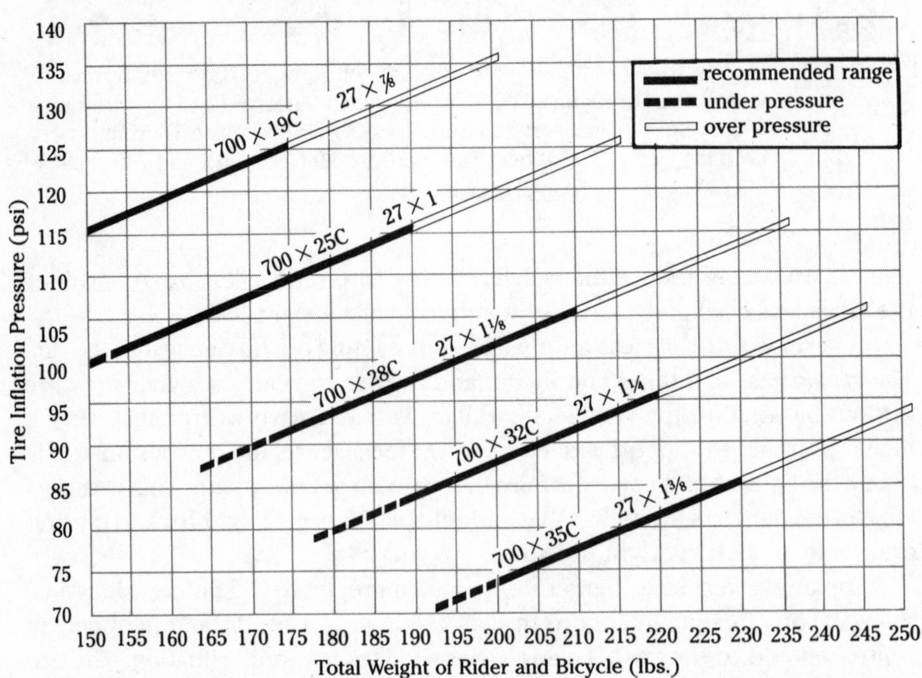

FIGURE 12-4 Tire size and inflation pressure in relation to weight of rider and bicycle.

road. Feel is an undefinable combination of many characteristics. Some of these characteristics can be measured, including parameters like shock absorption, adhesion, and rolling resistance. Feel is also affected by inflation pressure, sidewall flexibility, rubber compound, tread thickness, tread pattern (or the absence of tread), tire size, and type of rim.

Adhesion

There are two kinds of adhesion: *friction* and *mechanical linkage.* The coefficient of friction measures how much force it takes to push a one-pound block of rubber along a given road surface. We old-school mechanical engineers were taught that it always took less than one pound, so the coefficient of friction was always less than one. The old textbooks had to be revised when drag racers began turning 200 mph in the quarter mile, which requires a coefficient of friction of more than one. That's when we learned about mechanical linkage.

We now know that tires are literally geared to the texture of the road. Rubber compounds that provide good friction have poor mechanical linkage and the reverse. Both friction and mechanical linkage drop when you lubricate the surfaces with water. You can see the reason why the tire business attracts snake oil salesmen.

Cornering ability and adhesion are tied together. You can measure cornering ability by coasting around a constant radius corner faster and faster, which requires you to lean the bike farther and farther over. When the bike slides out, you measure the angle or the speed. Then you replace the tire (and probably the tire tester) with a different model and repeat the test. Fortunately, the cornering test can also be simulated in the laboratory on a very expensive testing machine. Unfortunately, the USA has 60,000 under-employed trial lawyers, so the test results are always confidential.

We know that overinflation causes bouncing instead of shock absorption on rough surfaces and this reduces adhesion and cornering ability. The most significant factor in adhesion is sidewall flexibility, which keeps the tire patch on the road. I don't think I can properly predict adhesion from tire measurements so I don't show a rating for it in table 12-1.

Rolling Resistance

This can also be measured, either by coasting the bicycle down a slight ramp and measuring the speed or by measuring the deceleration of a loaded cart. Rolling resistance depends on rider weight, inflation pressure, road surface, and tire construction. When a tire rolls over a road, both the tire and the road deflect. When the tire and the road surfaces return to normal, not all of the energy that went into in the original deflection is recovered. The phenomenom is called "hysteresis." The tire print left in a soft dirt path causes a major loss, which is why it's so hard to pedal on soft roads. According to Frank Rowland Whitt and David Gordon Wilson in their book, *Bicycling Science,* the rolling resistance of the road surface can vary by a factor of five. In most cases however, the road hysteresis loss is minor.

The tire hysteresis loss is the significant part of the total rolling resistance. The more the tire flexes under load, the greater the rolling resistance. That's why a high inflation pressure reduces rolling resistance on smooth roads. A steel wheel on a steel rail has minimum rolling resistance, but it rolls on an extremely smooth surface. On a rougher surface, a steel wheel not only gives an extremely uncomfortable ride, it also has a high rolling resistance. The pneumatic tire averages out the road bumps. When Doctor Dunlop invented the pneumatic tire a century ago, it was much more comfortable than the solid rubber tires previously used. On the rough roads of the period, pneumatic tires were also much easier to pedal.

Minimum-hysteresis bicycle tires with minimum rolling resistance should have thin, flexible sidewalls, a thin, flexible casing under the tread, a thin tread, and a thin tube. The rubber compound probably enters into the equation somewhere, but it's not as important as the first four items. I measured the sidewall thickness, casing thickness, and tread thickness of the 50 pairs of tires. I used the measurements to calculate the rolling resistances shown in table 12-1.

Sidewall Thickness and Flexibility Sidewall thickness is very important and it's also easy to measure. As part of my rough-and-ready tire quality evaluation, I measured the sidewall thickness at five points on each side. This thickness is shown in table 12-1. Equating rolling resistance to sidewall thickness is undoubtedly an oversimplification, so I also asked the makers about sidewall construction.

All of the tires except the Specialized Turbo VR and VS and the Michelin Hi-Lites use the same construction. The casing consists of two plys of nylon cord in the sidewalls and three plys under the tread. The ply starts on the right side of the middle, goes around the left bead, back over the middle, around the right bead, and back over past the middle. (See figure 12-5.)

The Specialized Turbo VR and VS and Michelin's Hi-Lite tires are special and they are described in the Specialized and Michelin sections at the end of this chapter. The sidewall construction of Michelin Hi-Lite tires is completely different from normal skinwall tires so Hi-Lite sidewall thickness isn't comparable to the rest of the tires.

I also asked the makers what "denier" nylon cord they used. *Denier* is similar to wire gauge. Larger numbers are smaller in diameter. Basically, the higher-quality tires use twice the number of cords in their plys, but the cords are only half as thick. The plys are coated with rubber and the excess rubber is squeezed out by rollers. More cord and less rubber provides a more flexible sidewall. This is the fundamental difference between gumwall tires, which have thick sidewalls with extra rubber on either side of the cord body, and skinwall tires, which have thin sidewalls with most of the rubber squeezed out. Of the two, gumwall tires are harder to pedal because there's more rubber to deform. Still, according to *Bicycling*'s rolling resistance tests, the best of today's high-pressure gumwalls don't come off too badly, but you pay a significant weight penalty.

Casing Thickness under the Tread This is a continuation of the concept that flexible tires have lower rolling resistance. To differentiate between casing thickness and tread thickness, I started out by abrading the tread from brand-new tires so that I could measure what was casing and what was tread rubber. This was painful, even with free tires. After a while, I noticed that the casing under the tread on most of the tires was 1½ times as thick as the

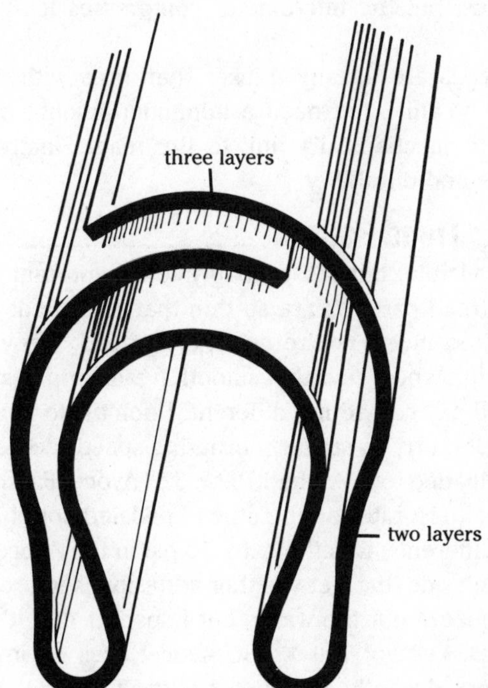

FIGURE 12-5

Ordinary two-three-ply tire casing construction.

sidewall. This is logical because top-quality tires are made with two plys of cord in the sidewall and three plys of cord under the tread. After this brilliant discovery, I subtracted the calculated casing thickness from the total thickness. I still had to abrade the Kevlar-belted tires to find the thickness of the belt.

Tread Design

There are four parts to the tread design equation: tread thickness, tread pattern, rubber compound, and rubber hardness. Tread thickness is the most important and it can be measured. The other three are important but they fall in the snake oil department. After listening to quite different stories from the experts at Avocet, CyclePro, Michelin, and Specialized, I have to say that they're all honorable men, they all believe what they say, but they can't all be right.

Tread Thickness

Tread thickness is very important to rolling resistance. Rubber has significant hysteresis loss; the more rubber, the higher the rolling resistance. It's easy to measure tread thickness. I just measure the total thickness of the tire in the center and subtract the casing thickness. There's usually a little ridge in the center where the mold closes, but the micrometer compresses it so that it doesn't matter.

Tires with patterned treads are usually thicker than tires with smooth treads. There's another side to this. You need a minimum amount of tread thickness to allow the tire to mechanically link to the road. Finally, tread thickness ties in with mileage and durability.

Tread Pattern

Tread pattern is highly visible, but it's probably less important than it looks. First off, some of the tread patterns are so thin that as soon as you've used the tire for a few hundred miles, you're on smooth tread. Wet-weather adhesion is the crucial element. Avocet says that smooth treads grip best in the wet. Michelin and Specialized say something different. I don't ride in the wet that much, and when I do, I don't try to set any cornering speed records.

On my British Columbia loaded tour, we had 700 × 32C Avocet FasGrips on one bike and 700 × 35C Michelin Hi-Lites on the other. I pedaled both bikes on the day it rained. The main difference was the extra 10 psi in the Avocet tires. I'm willing to believe Michelin's ads that wet-weather adhesion is improved by sipes or radial grooves to squeeze out the water, but I suspect that it's more important in automobile tires. I've got 700 × 28C Avocet tires on my sport touring bike. They corner very decently, although I haven't approached the lean angle shown in the Avocet ads.

Rubber Compound and Rubber Hardness

I'm sure that there are significant differences between the rubber compounds used in the different tires. I haven't seen any measurements that indicate that one rubber compound is better than another or that hard rubber is better than soft rubber, but it seems logical that hard rubber should wear better and that soft rubber should adhere better. I suspect that hysteresis has more to do with both wear and adhesion. For the mileage, durability, and rolling resistance ratings in table 12-1, I assumed that all the rubber was the same.

PHOTO 12-3

Tire treads: top to bottom, smooth tread on Avocet FasGrip, minimum tread on Specialized Turbo VS, siped tread on CyclePro Discovery, and deep tread on Michelin Hi-Lite Tour.

Durability and Mileage

Almost all of the tire features that make for good feel and low rolling resistance also make for poor durability and low mileage. I define durability as resistance to punctures and other failures. Mileage is the number of miles before the tread wears through. I throw away far more tires with durability failures (sidewall and tread cuts or ozone cracks) than I do with worn out treads. My son, the racer, trains on light clinchers and he has the opposite experience.

It's a classic compromise situation. You have to decide what's more important to you, lively feel or minimum care. It's nice when you have two (or more) bicycles. Then you can pick the bicycle with the tires that suit your mood for each ride. You can get much of the benefit with two sets of wheels, but it takes a bit of time to switch.

Durability

There are two kinds of durability: *puncture resistance* and *casing integrity.* They're both covered in the durability column in table 12-1. I arrived at the durability rating by adding the thickness of the tread, the thickness of the casing, the thickness of the sidewalls, and my own personal riding experience. For greater durability, you can either use wider tires with thicker treads or you can use special puncture-resistant belted tires.

Puncture Resistance You avoid punctures by using a tire that's wide enough. On the surface, it would appear that a wide tire sweeps a wider stripe of road, therefore it rolls over more glass and gets more flats. Not so! A skinny, high-pressure tire presses much harder on the road and it has a much thinner tread. A fat tire shrugs off tiny pieces of glass that puncture a skinny tire. The fat tire also avoids snakebite flats because there is more air volume to absorb bumps and potholes before the rim bottoms through.

Some riders are much more observant than others. I notice that when I draft my son, he always points out the glass on the road. When I lead, I just roll right through it, which makes him indignant, especially when he's riding tubulars.

Broken glass also affects how far you keep to the right. If you stay out to the left, you'll be on the part of the road that's swept by the cars. You'll also have more cars waxing your left pant leg as they pass too close. The throw-away glass bottle and the throw-away mentality is the bicycle tire's worst enemy. States with bottle bills are more pleasant for bicyclists. (The lobbying organization for the throw-away bottle makers calls itself "Keep America Beautiful."

How's that for chutzpah?) So, match your tire selection to your riding style *and* your road surfaces.

Casing Integrity The sidewalls on the top-quality skinwall tires are so thin that they're translucent. Light passes through them and so does glass. Because the sidewall is so highly stressed, even a tiny cut destroys the tire. You can patch it with a piece of duct tape and pedal home but you'll never be able to hammer it up to maximum pressure.

There are lots of other failure modes. Hooked-edge rims cause the tire to bend around a sharp radius corner. The tire has a special strip of tape to prevent cord chafing at this point, but I've had flexure failures at the base of the sidewall. Then there's ozone and aging cracks. The classic test for ozone is to bend a section of natural rubber, expose it to the smoggy atmosphere, and wait for the cracks to appear. The tire makers use additives to increase ozone resistance. One saving grace is that top-quality tires have very thin treads, so they usually wear out before they smog out. However, when you have lots of bikes or lots of wheels, it takes longer to pile on the mileage.

If you ride on poor roads or you don't consciously avoid glass, you have another option: *belted tires.* The casing construction of Michelin's Hi-Lite tires is inherently puncture resistant. The Avocet FasGrip K20, CyclePro belted Discovery, and Specialized Touring II-K4 are puncture-resistant tires with a Kevlar belt under the tread. You pay a feel and rolling resistance penalty because the Kevlar armor belt isn't as compliant as the nylon plys, so there's more hysteresis loss. Avocet claims that their Kevlar belt is specially designed to reduce this penalty. Thorn-proof tubes and belts that you install between the tire and the tube are much worse. They make your tires feel as though they're inflated with sand.

Mileage

Tire mileage depends on rider weight, inflation pressure, road surface, and slippage. Front tires typically last three times as long as rear tires because all of your power goes through the more heavily loaded rear tire. Braking also wears away the rubber. If your rim has a wide spot, it will cause the brakes to lock at that point and wear out a spot on the tire tread. If you use smooth tires, don't plan to ride them until the cord shows through. You lose adhesion when the tread gets too thin and you'll get more flats in the last quarter of a tire's mileage. I usually throw my wide touring tires away while they've still got tread, because of the aging cracks or because I'm tired of looking at them.

The mileage rating in table 12-1 is based on tread thickness, tire size, and the ratio of rubber to voids in the tread pattern. For a given tread thickness, a smooth tread will wear longer because there's more rubber and less air. An excellent-mileage tire should last at least 4,000 miles on a back wheel. A poor-mileage tire should last about 1,000 miles.

Tire-Rim Compatibility

I've already talked about the two rim and tire diameters, 27-inch and 700C. They have to match or you won't be able to mount the tire. There are two other factors involved in tire-rim compatibility. The rim has to be the right *width* for the tire and it has to have the right kind of *edge construction.*

Rim Width

The only rim dimension that matters is the inside width. There are three inside widths: narrow (13mm to 14mm), medium (15mm to 16mm), and wide (16.5mm to 20mm). (Rim inside widths are listed in table 11-3 in chapter 11.) Narrow rims are for narrow tires and wide rims are for wide tires. Tire size 27 × 1⅛ or 700 × 28C is the transition. It's about the widest tire that you can use with a narrow rim and the narrowest tire that you can use with a medium rim.

Fitting a wide tire on a narrow rim doesn't properly support the beads. The tire may blow off and it will certainly ride in a squirmy fashion. A narrow tire on a wide rim can't take the proper round shape and it will be very prone to snakebite punctures.

The 18mm- to 20mm-wide rim is ideal for 27 × 1⅜ or 700 × 35C loaded touring tires. Unfortunately, wide rims that come with hooked edges are hard to find. You're much better off with a medium-width, hooked-edge rim than you are with a wide, straight-side rim. Table 12-1 shows the minimum and maximum rim inside widths suitable for each tire model. They are based on the ISO-ETRTO recommendations. According to my "bible," *Sutherland's Handbook for Bicycle Mechanics* (4th ed.), tires with section widths between 1.4 and 2.0 times the rim inside width should fit well. If you're trying to find tires to fit uncommon rims, *Sutherland's Handbook* is an indispensable guide.

Bead Material and Rim Edge Type

The main reason to use a Kevlar bead is to save 50 or 60 grams per tire compared to the same tire with a steel bead. The second advantage is that you can fold a Kevlar-beaded tire since the bead is flexible. The Japanese Kevlar-beaded tires are a bit prone to stretching. They are made on the small side, which makes them harder to mount. Michelin's Hi-Lite tires have a different kind of Kevlar bead, which stretches less. They're made slightly larger so they mount easier and Michelin allows use of some sizes of tires on rims that don't have a prominent hooked edge.

If you use foldable tires with Kevlar beads, you must use hooked-edge rims. Otherwise, if the bead stretches a bit, the tire will blow off. If you plan to use high-performance skinwall tires with steel beads at full inflation pressure, you should also use hooked-edge rims. They provide more security against blow-off. When you see a tire with a reinforcing tape over the bead, you know the maker was thinking about hooked-edge rims. If the tire doesn't have the reinforcing tape, it may chafe through where it bends around the sharp-radius hooked edge; this probably won't happen for a few thousand miles.

If your present rims have straight sides or just a vestigial hook, use tires with steel beads and keep your inflation pressure down a bit. Tires can't be made with zero tolerances. A maximum size tire at maximum inflation pressure will probably blow off a straight-side rim.

Road Test Results

When I had completed the first draft of this chapter, I gave it to five different experts for their review and comment. I was particularly interested in their input on figure 12-4 where I make recommendations on tire size and inflation pressure in relation to rider weight. The response was unanimous. All five were succesfully using narrower tires than I recommended. I had a shop full of tires and I had to mount them on rims to measure the mounted width. So, for a three-month period, I rode a different set of tires on every ride. With careful mounting and careful riding I was able to test ride the 700 × 19C, 20C, and 23C tires.

I'd like to tell you that I have a vernier caliper on my backside and the results of the road test confirmed my calculated tire ratings, but that would be a lie. I can readily tell the difference between a tire with an "excellent" rolling resistance and one with a "good" rolling resistance. But, I wouldn't want to wager that I could tell a "good" tire from a "very good" tire in a blind test.

Here's what I learned in the process of riding 50 different tires:

- Good-feeling tires hiss as they roll but a head wind or a tail wind masks a lot of rolling resistance.
- Polyurethane tubes are a significant improvement. They'll raise any tire one rating.
- When you overinflate wide tires, they feel like you're riding on the rims. A 700 × 20C tire at 125 psi is much more pleasant to pedal than a 700 × 28C tire at 125 psi.

- You should use a good rim tape (Velox) and mount and inflate narrow, high-pressure tires very carefully. I always dusted the tube with talcum powder. I was able to mount most of the tires without using tire irons.

I experienced six flats in the three months (and 1,200 miles) of tire testing. Two were punctures. One was a snakebite and three were just strange pinholes that appeared in the tube on the rim side. Most of my previous flats with narrow tires were caused by poor mounting rather than punctures.

Tire Makers and Distributors

Just four companies make top-quality bicycle tires: Inoue Rubber Company (IRC), Michelin Tire Corporation, Mitsuboshi Belting Limited, and National Tire Company. In the USA, the three Japanese companies sell most of their tires under different names. Inoue makes tires for Avocet and West Coast Cycle. Mitsuboshi makes tires for Specialized. National makes tires for West Coast Cycle, Western States Imports, Schwinn, and others. West Coast Cycle calls their tires CyclePro. Western States Imports calls their tires Panaracer.

Avocet and Specialized have done considerable research and development work with their Japanese suppliers so that their tires are unique. Still, most Japanese tires are quite similar. Michelin Hi-Lite tires are quite different. Most bicycle stores contract with one of the major distributors for their complete tire requirements to get the best possible volume price. Michelin distributes their bicycle tires themselves.

I picked the four largest distributors and I've listed all of their top-quality tires in table 12-1. I also show their best-selling economy skinwall or top-quality gumwall for the bargain hunters.

Avocet

Avocet got into tires in 1985. They're convinced that smooth treads are the proper approach for both wet and dry conditions. FasGrip tires use a special rubber compound for smooth tread service. Avocet showed me the results of their rolling resistance and adhesion tests. Some of the tests involved the kind of brute force and awkwardness that appeals to me. They paved several sheets of plywood and arranged them so that they could be tilted at an angle. Then they rode bicycles across them and increased the angle until the tires lost traction. They played the same game with water running down the paving. In 1987, Avocet introduced the FasGrip K20, a Kevlar-belted tire with the belt woven from a special Kevlar mixture to minimize energy loss. Avocet claims that the rolling resistance of their belted tire is only 4 percent higher than the nonbelted model. The usual penalty is about 30 percent.

Avocet calls their steel-beaded tires FasGrip 20. The Kevlar-beaded tire is called FasGrip 30. The Kevlar-belted model with steel beads is called FasGrip K20. Avocet's width and model designation is logical. Each size has a different name. The 700 × 20C Time Trial tires have a very thin tread and they're designed for light riders on smooth roads. The 700 × 25C Criterium has a one-third thicker tread than the Time Trial. I've used them succesfully and they're very lively. The 700 × 28C Road has a one-third thicker tread than the Criterium and the 700 × 32C Duro has a one-third thicker tread than the Road.

I fitted Duros on one bike and Michelin Hi-Lite Tours on the other for my 1986 British Columbia trip. I hoped to be able to give you all kinds of insightful advice, but you don't get a whole lot of liveliness feedback from a loaded touring bike. Both tires felt almost exactly the same. The Duro was a bit firmer riding, but it was narrower and carried ten more psi.

CyclePro

West Coast Cycle distributes CyclePro tires and accessories and Nishiki bicycles nationwide. CyclePro Discovery tires are made by IRC and CyclePro Linear tires are made by National. The Discovery has IRC's unique oval shape. They accomplish this by making the tread about 50 percent thicker and about half as wide as a typical skinwall tire. It's almost like a wide, raised-center tread. CyclePro says that all of the Discovery tires have been tested to wear 3,000 plus miles. The Discovery is available in four models, with or without Kevlar beads and with or without a Kevlar belt. The Linear is the smooth tread model that features National's dual hardness concept, harder rubber in the center of the tread for long wear and softer rubber on the edges for better cornering.

Michelin

Michelin's Hi-Lite bicycle tires are different. *Vive la différence.* Michelin has always been innovative. Fifteen years ago, their Chevron 50 was the first high-performance bicycle tire. The Elan was the first narrow tire and the Elan RS was the first Kevlar-beaded tire. The Elans weren't very nice narrow tires, but they proved the concept of narrow, high-performance clinchers. I get the idea that the Japanese tire engineers look over each other's shoulders. Michelin doesn't look over anyone's shoulder.

The Hi-Lite series of tire is a real breakthrough. Michelin wanted a very flexible carcass but they didn't want to pay the durabilty penalty involved in thin sidewalls. Hi-Lite tires don't fit into the two-three ply pattern. Their unique three-ply carcass construction uses a two-way mesh instead of parallel cords. A fine-mesh, pressure-containing ply, which Michelin calls N-2, is sandwiched between two coarse-mesh plies, which Michelin labels N-1 (see figure 12-6).

Based on my experience, I think that the Hi-Lite package offers the best combination of durability and performance. The 700 × 19C Hi-Lite Pro is the lightest model. In the course of riding it about 300 miles, I only had one puncture and one snakebite flat. The Hi-Lite Pro includes a wedge of rubber to fair the tire to the rim for minimum wind resistance. Hi-Lite Comps come in two sizes, 700 × 20C and 700 × 23C. These have an extra belt of nylon under the tread for better puncture resistance. I've used the 23C for more than 1,000 miles. Both the Pro and the Comp are sweet-handling tires. Hi-Lite Roads have a fine tread, no extra belt of nylon and a thicker tread for longer wear. The 700 × 35C or 27 × 1⅜ Hi-Lite Tour is Michelin's super tire for tandems and loaded tourists. It's my favorite loaded touring tire.

Michelin's Select tires are conventional skinwalls, designed and priced to meet the Japanese competition. They also have "approximate" size designations to match the competition.

I feel that Michelin tires are more subject to ozone cracking than other top-quality brands. But, it may just be that the treads wear for so long that the sidewalls show the ozone cracks. The only other negative feature I see in the Hi-Lite tires is that they look different. I think they're ugly.

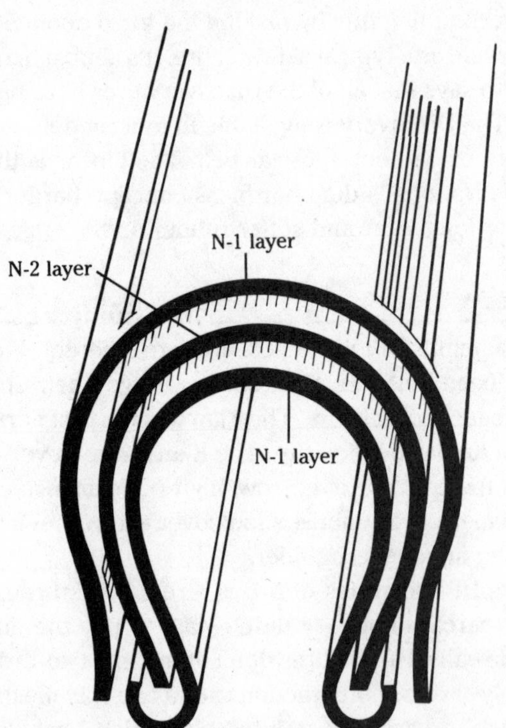

FIGURE 12-6

Michelin Hi-Lite tire casing construction.

Specialized

Specialized got into bicycle tires in 1976. They hit on the idea that buyers would pay a premium for a better-quality, better-performing tire. They picked up the narrow, high-performance clincher idea and ran with it. The Specialized Turbo was their breakthrough tire and I just happened to write a comprehensive article on tires when it was introduced. My tire testers loved it. So did the buyers, and the dealers couldn't keep them in stock for six months. I was very enthusiastic about the raised center ridges of the old Specialized Turbos, though there's now pretty general agreement that a raised center ridge adds more to rolling resistance than it subtracts. The key point was that the Turbo was the first widely available, high-performance clincher tire with a thin, flexible sidewall. I credited the center ridge instead of the tire construction. Today, Specialized sells more tires than anyone and their lineup is the most complete.

The top-of-the-line Specialized tire is the Turbo VS and VR. ("S" means rough tread and "R" means smooth tread for some inexplicable reason.) These tires grew out of a program to develop a breakthrough mass production tubular tire. Specialized abandoned the tubular program because the market was too small. However, the research results indicated that a very high performance clincher could be made at a high price. The VR and VS are the most expensive clincher tires made. They use a proprietary cotton-Kevlar casing and they're two-ply rather than two-three-ply. There's almost no rubber in the sidewalls.

The labeling on these tires is odd. They have a 20.5mm mounted width and a 23.5mm actual section width. The tire label says 700 × 25C and the ISO-ETRTO label on the sidewall says 622 × 20. Take your choice.

The skinniest Specialized tire is the 700 × 20C Turbo R. Specialized also makes the steel-beaded Turbo LR and LS series at a lower price. The Touring II series for general sport touring is their best-selling skinwall clincher. The Touring II-K4 has a Kevlar belt. The Touring X is a lower-priced, heavy-duty skinwall. The market for extra-wide loaded touring tires was so small that Specialized stopped importing my favorite 700 × 35C Expedition tire. I show it in table 12-1 because it's still available. I've now switched over to the Michelin Hi-Lite Tour.

Everybody Else

Everybody else consists of the other people who import IRC and National tires and sell them under different names. National Tire and Panasonic Bicycle Company are both divisions of Matsushita Electric. Western States Imports is the U.S. importer and distributor for Panasonic bikes and National's Panaracer tires. Schwinn's top-quality tires are also made by National. IRC has it's own distributors, and tires labeled IRC are widely sold.

Tube Selection

It's funny, the same person who will endure all sorts of pain and suffering to save 50 grams of tire weight will waste most of the saving by using heavy tubes. Find a tube that matches your tire selection and it will make a surprising difference. The new polyurethane tubes are a real breakthrough. They make any tire feel like it's one size lighter. All tubes of the same type are about the same so I haven't picked a favorite. I'll cover the important tube features in order of their importance (these features are all shown in table 12-3).

Size and Weight

The same tubes are used for both 27-inch and 700C tires. Tubes come in three or four different sizes (widths). Tubes stretch so that you can stuff a fat tube into a skinny tire but it will really degrade the performance. You can also put a skinny tube into a fat tire, but you'll get a few more punctures and snakebite flats. As a general rule, use the same size tube as the tire.

Cheap tubes are heavy. Light tubes cost more money because it takes better quality control. It's less expensive to save weight with tubes than with tires.

Material

The basic choices for tube material used to be *butyl* and *latex*. Butyl rubber is a much more forgiving tube material, although it absorbs more energy than latex. The important thing is to buy the right size. Latex tubes are lighter and they have a better road feel. However, latex tubes are fragile. Sometimes they go flat all by themselves. (My bad vibes on latex tubes may be because I used to use them on my ultra-skinny tire tests.) Sometimes when a latex tube gets punctured, it self-destructs with a big long rip. This can be distressing since they cost ten bucks or so. Finally, latex tubes don't do a very good job of holding air, so you have to pump them up before every ride.

Many people think that since latex tubes work well in tubulars, they'll be fine for clinchers. The tubular tube, safely sewn inside it's sleeping bag leads a much easier life than a clincher tube. The clincher has to adapt to the transition from tire to bead seat to rim tape, and the tube moves around as the tire deflects.

Polyurethane is the hot new tube material. It has even more liveliness than latex. Polyurethane tubes also resist punctures. Still, they have their disadvantages. They don't like to stretch at all, so you have to buy the exact size (both diameter and width) to match your tire. If you do get a puncture, you have

TABLE 12-3.

Tubes

Make and Model	Cost ($)	Weight (gr.)		Marked Size		Material	Valve Available	
		Advert.	Meas.	English 27 × ___	French 700 × ___		Presta	Schrader
Avocet								
Feather Lite	5–7	75	67	⅞, 1	20C, 25C	butyl	X	
Presta/Schrader	3–5	—	101	1	25C	butyl	X	X
Presta/Schrader	3–5	—	133	1⅛	28C	butyl	X	X
CyclePro								
PolyTex	11–15	85	86	—	23C, 25C	Polyur	X	
PolyTex	11–15	90	94	—	28C	Polyur	X	X
PolyTex	11–15	—	—	1	—	Polyur	X	
PolyTex	11–15	—	—	1⅛	—	Polyur		X
PolyTex	11–15	—	—	1¼	—	Polyur		X
Deluxe	4–6	105	106	1	25C	butyl	X	X
Deluxe	4–6	115	115	1⅛	28C	butyl	X	X
Michelin								
Hi-Lite (28-4MTS)	5–7	65	68	—	19C, 20C, 23C	butyl	X	
Airstop (28-4M)	5–7	85	89	—	19C, 20C, 23C	butyl	X	
Airstop (28-5M)	5–7	125	132	1, 1⅛, 1¼	25C, 28C, 32C	butyl	X	X
Airstop (28-6M)	5–7	150	174	1⅜, 1½	—	butyl		X
Specialized								
Latex	8–11	65	67	1, 1⅛, 1¼	25C, 28C, 32C	latex	X	
Turbo UL	4–6	75	67	⅞, 1	19C, 25C	butyl	X	
Standard S-1	3–4	110	100	1, 1⅛	25C, 28C	butyl	X	X
Standard S-2	3–4	135	133	1⅛, 1⅜	28C, 35C	butyl	X	X

to use a special patch repair kit and the patch has to cure for 20 minutes before you can use the tube. As I write this, polyurethane tubes are just coming into general use and their problems are being defined.

Valve Type

There's no contest in the valve department. Use Presta valves, not Schrader valves. The Presta valve is faster to inflate because it doesn't have a spring and it loses less air when you pull off the chuck. It's the only valve you can use with very narrow rims. The smaller hole weakens the rim less, it seals tighter, and it's even five grams or so lighter. Use Presta valve tubes even if your rims have big Schrader valve holes. You can put a washer of rubber around the valve stem or not. (Tourists sometimes order Schrader holes in their rims even though they plan to use Presta tubes, so that in a pinch, they can use a Schrader tube.) Some cheap tubes have bolted rather than vulcanized valves. Don't use these in narrow rims. There isn't room for the valve and the tire beads.

Rim Tape

When you use lightweight tubes, narrow clincher tires, hooked-edge rims, and very high inflation pressures, you get flats for all kinds of interesting reasons. To prevent the spokes or the rim from puncturing the tube, you need a good rim tape. There are four kinds: rubber bands, reinforced plastic bands, strapping tape, and Velox tape. Rubber bands are only suitable for inexpensive single-wall rims. Double-wall (box-section) rims have big spoke recesses in the inner wall. They need a stronger rim tape, especially at high inflation pressures. You want a tape that's wide enough to cover the holes, but not so wide that it covers the bead seat.

CyclePro, Michelin, and Specialized make bands of reinforced plastic. These work well if they're exactly the right width for the bed of the rim. Otherwise, they move around and uncover the spoke holes. CyclePro makes two widths and the narrow width is just right for dropped-center rims.

Fiberglass-backed strapping tape is used to seal cardboard boxes. It's available in ⅜- and ½-inch widths. I had good luck with it until my first trials with 700 × 19C tires and 130 psi pressures. I found that if I used two overlapping layers of tape, it was too thick and it was hard to mount the tires, and one layer wouldn't always keep the tube out of trouble.

Velox rim tape is made in two widths, #56 for rims with a narrow dropped center section and #51 for the double-wall rims without a dropped center section. Velox tape is fussy to use, but it's worked well for me.

Frank's Favorite Tires and Tubes

In most of the other chapters, I tell you exactly what I like and why. Tires aren't so cut and dried. Many of the Japanese tires are similar. For a given size and inflation pressure, it's difficult to feel the difference on the road, especially when you get away from the exotic ultra-light models. I believe in smooth treads. After I completed my tire-a-day tests, I picked five different tires for my five bikes. (Next year, I'll probably be using something different.)

Working our way from the lightest to the most rugged, the Trek 2000 has 700 × 23C Michelin Hi-Lite Comps. If I use any other tire that small for the long pull, I get too many punctures. The Schwinn Paramount has 27 × 1 Avocet Criterium 30s. The Redcay has 27 × 1⅛ Specialized Turbo Rs. The Windsor commute bike has 27 × 1¼ Specialized Touring II-K4s and the Columbine has 700 × 35C Michelin Hi-Lite Tours. I used polyurethane tubes in the lightweight tires.

CHAPTER 13

All about Brakes

Over the past five years, most of the action in bicycle brake design has taken place in the mountain bike arena. Nearly all the bicycle makers have now adopted cantilever brakes, or similar types with the pivots brazed on to the forks or the stays, as the standard for mountain bikes. You can't install cantilever brakes on your 10-speed without brazing on the mounting studs, which is a major expense. However, some of the mountain bike technology has rubbed off onto racing and touring brakes. We've learned that good braking requires rigid calipers, high mechanical advantage, strong cables, stiff casings, large pads made of suitable material, and minimum friction.

I especially like two new features found on many of the new brake models: aerodynamic levers that have the cables coming out the back and lever return springs that produce a lighter lever action. With few exceptions, all of the latest 10-speed brakes are sidepulls. The centerpull brake has become obsolete, so I won't lead you through a long centerpull versus sidepull discussion.

Terminology time. The word *brake* can mean either the whole lever-caliper-cable-casing assembly or it can mean just the calipers. The word *brakeset* means the whole front and rear assembly. Similarly, the word *cable* can mean the combined cable and casing or just the inner cable.

At the risk of losing friends among the brake salesmen, I'll begin by saying that your old brakes are probably adequate. In dry weather, they have enough stopping power to skid your back wheel or to lock your front wheel and rotate you over the handlebars. What more do you need?

Though your present brakes may be adequate, I do see two main improvements in contemporary brake design. First, the best of today's brakes give much better interaction between lever effort and stopping power. Second, they have more stopping power for the extreme situations—stopping in the rain or stopping a heavily loaded touring bicycle. In addition, today's aerodynamic sidepulls are so handsome that you might decide to upgrade simply because you like their looks. If you do decide to stick with your present brakes, you can make a noticeable improvement in their operation by installing new cables and casings and new pads.

Two parts of the bicycle deserve the overworked word "system." One system, the gear train, makes you go, while another system, the brakes, makes you stop. There are six parts to the braking system: levers, cables, casings, calipers, pads, and the brake track surfaces of the rims. Let's first talk about them one at a time, then look at the entire package.

For their January 1987 issue, *Bicycling* ran a very complete series of tests of braking systems that covered wet and dry stopping power and sensitivity. I've reused the results of those tests in this chapter. The tests revealed how much progress has been made with brake design. Many of the brakes tested produced a 0.5-G stop with only a 13-pound lever force. (A 0.5-G deceleration is a commonly accepted standard for the maximum braking pressure an inexpert rider can generate before locking the front wheel of the bike and flipping over the handlebars. It takes a skilled rider to keep the rear wheel of a bike on the ground during a 0.5-G stop.)

Brake Levers

For the discussion that follows, I've assumed that you're upgrading a bicycle with dropped handlebars. If you want flat handlebars, you'll have to use brake levers designed for them and you have a wide variety of touring or mountain bike levers to choose from. But since this chapter is primarily about brakes for bikes with dropped handlebars, I will focus on levers that fit dropped handlebars.

Auxiliary Brake Levers

First, let's dispose of the hallmark of gaspipe bicycles: auxiliary brake levers or "safety" levers. These awkward devices are actually the antithesis of safety because they reduce lever travel, especially if they're misadjusted so that they bottom out on the handlebars. Auxiliary levers force you to place your weight in a poor position for maximum braking. Also, you can't have rubber hoods with auxiliary levers, and rubber hoods are worthwhile. You rest your hands on them in one of the top positions. In fact, my favorite hand position for loaded touring is on top of the brake hoods.

Aero Brake Levers

The label *aero* was first applied to brake levers during Shimano's aerodynamic design era, when they came out with the AX Parapul brakes. The aero type lever is more accurately described as *rear cable exit,* because it has the cable and casing coming out the back of the body instead of the top. This allows you to tape the brake cables to the handlebars. The resulting cable path from the lever to the calipers is shorter, but the curves are sharper. With old cables and casings, these sharp bends would create an undesirable amount of friction. However, with the new lined casings and careful cable routing, the brake response with these levers is the same as with conventional levers.

I'm slowly converting all of my bikes to aero levers. I bury both the brake cables and the bar-end shift lever cables under the handlebar tape. (Look Ma,

TABLE 13-1.

Brakesets

Make and Model	Cost ($)	Weight (gr.)	Type	Mechanical Advantage			Stopping Power		Respon-siveness	Quick-Release	
				Lever	Caliper	Total	Dry	Wet		Location	Type
Campagnolo											
C-Record	400–500	830	*	4.7	1.3	6.1	—	—	—	Lvr	O
Cobalto	250–350	765	SP	4.4	1.1	4.8	E	VG	F	Br	V
Nuovo Record	180–280	730	SP	4.6	1.1	5.0	E	VG	F	Br	V
Nuovo Victory	140–180	770	SP	4.6	1.1	5.0	E	VG	F	Br	O
Nuovo Triomphe	90–120	770	SP	4.6	1.1	5.0	E	VG	F	Br	O
Dia-Compe											
BRS 400	90–120	730	SP	4.7	1.1	5.1	VG	E	E	Br	V
BRS 300	60–80	680	SP	4.7	1.1	5.1	—	—	—	Br	V
BRS 200 (Alpha II)	50–70	660	SP	4.7	1.1	5.1	—	—	—	Br	O
Mathauser Engineering											
Hydraulic Brake	175–200	690	*	N/A	N/A	4.6	—	—	—	Br	V
Modolo											
Super Prestige	180–240	720	SP	4.4	1.1	5.0	G	E	G	Br	V
Speedy	80–120	710	SP	4.4	1.1	5.0	G	E	G	Br	V
Scott											
Superbrake	150–190	—	*	—	—	—	E	E	VG	none	—
Shimano											
Dura-Ace	150–200	790	SP	4.2	1.2	5.0	VG	G	E	Br	V
600 EX	75–110	730	SP	4.5	1.2	5.4	VG	F	VG	Br	V
105	60–90	740	SP	4.9	1.0	5.0	G	G	VG	Br	V
SunTour											
Superbe Pro	160–240	760	SP	4.1	1.2	5.0	VG	E	G	Br	V
Sprint	75–110	760	SP	4.1	1.2	5.0	VG	E	G	Br	V
Cyclone	45–70	780	SP	4.1	1.2	5.0	VG	E	G	Br	V
Weinmann											
590SQ	40–60	—	SP	4.0	1.0	4.0	—	—	—	Br	V
Delta Pro	—	770	*	4.7	1.4	6.6	—	—	—	Br	V

* This is a unique model that does not fit into one of the common categories.

no cables!) It takes me an afternoon to get all of the casings in exactly the right position and cut to exactly the right length. It's almost as much fun as wheel building. Most of the high-quality brakesets now offer aero levers as an option.

Table 13-1 shows the type of levers that are available with each model of brakeset. "Aero" means only aero levers are available; "std" means only standard levers. "Std/A" indicates the availability of either type of lever, and "both" means the lever can be used with either top or rear exit cables.

Lever			Calipers					Cables and Casings		Features
Reach (mm)	Type	Return Spring	Drilled	Reach *Short (mm)*	Reach *Long (mm)*	Thrust Bearing	Adj. Pads	Cable Dia. (mm)	Lined Casing	
59	both	no	no	38–56	—	—	yes	0.18	yes	var. mech. advtg.
55	both	no	yes	43–52	48–56	no	no	0.18	yes	
54	std	no	no	43–52	48–56	no	no	0.18	yes	
54	std	no	no	43–52	48–56	no	no	0.18	yes	
54	std	no	no	43–52	48–56	no	no	0.18	yes	
64	aero	yes	no	39–49	47–57	no	no	0.16	no	
71	aero	yes	no	39–49	47–57	no	no	0.16	no	
63	aero	yes	no	40–55	47–57	no	no	0.16	no	
69	aero	—	no	44–66	—	—	no	—	—	hydraulic
59	both	no	yes	40–52	46–58	no	no	0.17	no	sintered pads
59	both	no	yes	40–52	46–58	no	no	0.19	no	sintered pads
—	aero	no	no	40–54	—	—	—	—	—	
—	std/A	no	no	40–50	—	yes	no	0.16	yes	
62/74	std/A	no	yes	40–50	47–57	yes	no	0.16	yes	
67/74	std/A	yes	no	40–50	47–57	yes	no	0.16	yes	
64/66	std/A	no	no	39–49	47–57	yes	yes	0.18	yes	internal coil spring
64	aero	no	no	40–50	47–57	yes	no	0.18	yes	
64/66	std/A	no	no	40–50	47–57	no	no	0.18	yes	
—	std/A	yes	no	—	47–57	no	no	0.16	yes	
69	aero	no	no	44–57	—	—	no	0.16	no	var. mech advtg.

Lever Return Springs

Lever return springs are another of those neat little improvements that reduce brake lever force and make cycling more pleasant. After you bicycle for a few years, you learn to live with a $\frac{1}{10}$-HP engine, which teaches you that friction is your mortal enemy. When you apply the brakes, you first have to overcome the cable-casing friction, then you have to overcome the caliper return spring force, and finally you pull the pads against the rims. Lever return springs fight cable-casing friction. If the only return spring is the one located in the calipers, then that spring has to be made to overcome worst-case, cable-casing friction. With two light springs, one in the lever and one in the caliper, brake response becomes lighter.

Shimano and Dia-Compe came out with lever return springs at about the same time. Shimano introduced *Shimano Linear Response (SLR)* in the 105 gruppo and is letting it percolate up the line. The logic is that racers are used to Campagnolo brute force brake response and they'll have to gradually become accustomed to light brakes. Dia-Compe calls their lever return spring design *Balanced Response System (BRS),* and they've installed it on all of their aftermarket brakesets. I feel that once you try either of them, you'll want it. (Table 13-1 shows which levers have lever return springs.)

Lever Reach

Lever reach is the distance from the inside of the handlebar to the outside of the brake lever. Brakes with a longer reach can move farther before they bottom on the handlebar, which lets you either use a caliper with a higher mechanical advantage or set your brake pads with more clearance.

The reach of your levers should match the size of your hands. If you have small hands, buy a pair of Dia-Compe, SunTour Superbe Pro, or Weinmann short-reach (junior) levers. Short-reach levers typically have a reach of 55mm compared to 65mm for standard-reach levers. This means a 10mm reduction in lever travel, which means less braking power. Small hands also have less power. Thus, riders with small hands need a highly efficient brakeset.

When you brake from the drops, the span from the crook of your thumb to the crook of your first finger has to be larger than the brake lever reach. When you brake from the tops, with your thumb resting on the brake hoods, your fingers have to reach even further out. I obtained 12 different brakesets and I made a special jig to measure lever reach. (Figure 13-1 shows how I measured lever reach, while table 13-1 records the actual measurements.)

Handlebar Clamp Diameter

Handlebar clamps come in three diameters: 22mm for steel handlebars, 23.8mm for inexpensive alloy handlebars, and 24 or 24.2mm for quality alloy handlebars. Almost everyone supplies the large 24.2mm clamp, which works on 24mm or 23.8mm handlebars with no problem. The better levers use an Allen wrench rather than a screwdriver to tighten the clamp. Campagnolo uses a nut and you need a Campagnolo 8mm T-wrench to install the brake levers.

Lever Mechanical Advantage

Mechanical advantage is the ratio of the travel of the low point of the lever to the travel of the cable. Most brake levers have a mechanical advantage of about 4:1 so you can mix and match brakes and brake levers. (Figure 13-2 shows how I measured mechanical advantage and table 13-1 shows the mechanical advantage of the various brake levers.)

Brake Lever Construction

The best brake levers have forged alloy bodies with a bushed pivot for the lever and a separate attachment for the clamp. (All of the levers in table 13-1 are

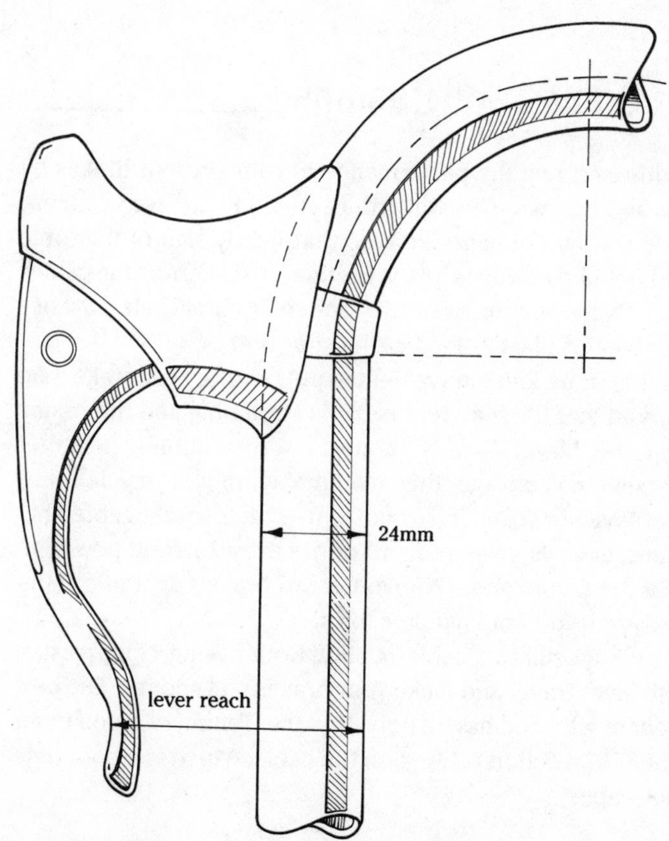

FIGURE 13-1

Brake lever reach.

made this way.) Economy levers have bodies pressed from sheet aluminum and a single shaft serves both the clamp and the lever, which pivots on plastic bushings. This is not a good construction because overtightening the clamp can bind the lever. Levers with cable length adjusters and/or quick-releases are usually a sign of an economy brakeset. Quality brakes usually incorporate these features in the calipers.

In the past, top-quality levers were always drilled because buyers expected it. However, drilled levers aren't always lighter. Campagnolo makes their drilled Super Record levers from a heavier gauge aluminum than their undrilled Nuovo Record levers, which are lighter. (Table 13-1 shows which levers are drilled.)

Brake Hoods

All quality brake levers have rubber hoods, which provide a comfortable hand position. Many of the current levers have anatomically molded hoods with grooves for your thumbs. These are right- and left-handed. Some hoods are made of softer rubber than others. The soft hoods don't last as long in smoggy climates.

Cables and Casings

You can significantly improve the performance of your present brakes by installing better cables and casings. This will reduce friction and give you more powerful braking. Tests run by Shimano indicate that nearly half of the force transmitted through an unlined casing is lost in friction. Just keeping the cables greased isn't adequate. That's why most of the top-quality brakesets now use either plastic-coated cables or plastic-lined casings, or both.

If it takes significantly more lever movement to put on your rear brake than the front, that's telling you that the long rear cable is stretching and the casing is compressing. When the Marin County pioneers were cobbling together mountain bike prototypes ten years ago, they mated Magura motorcycle brake levers with Mafac cantilever brakes. They had to use motorcycle cables because bicycle cables and casings gave away all of the extra braking power. In the same vein, much of the Campagnolo Nuovo Record brake's splendid reputation came from the oversized Campagnolo cables.

Casing quality is as important as cable quality. Both casing compression and cable stretch waste lever travel and make your brakes feel spongy. The best casings are made of square wire and have a polyethylene, Teflon, or nylon inner liner. Some makers put a low-friction coating on the cable, which is a poor idea if it results in a thinner cable.

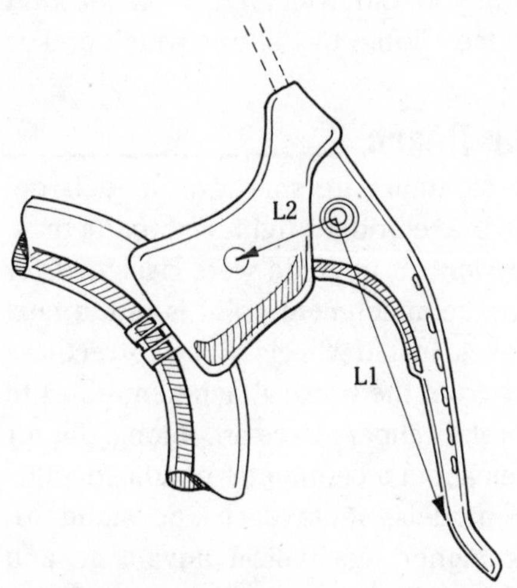

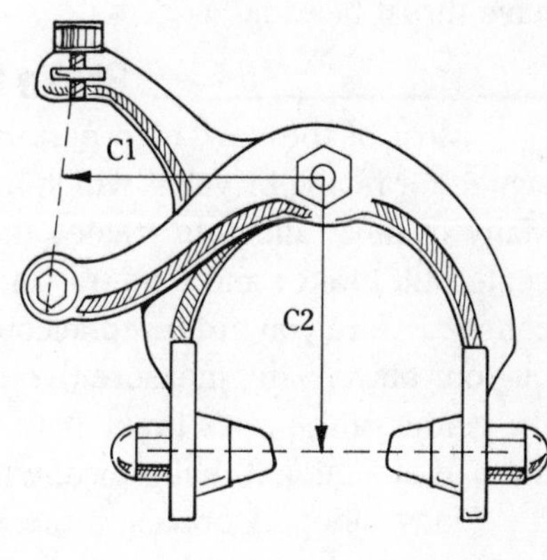

FIGURE 13-2 Mechanical advantage.

Everything else being equal, a low-priced bicycle with open cables and short sections of casing stops better than an expensive model with full-length casings. Everything isn't equal of course, especially when the exposed sections of cable get rusty. When you replace your brake cables, don't buy the $2 specials. Instead, buy an expensive set with lined casings and oversize cables. One of these sets will cost you about $10, but it will double your braking pleasure. (Table 13-1 shows cable diameter and casing construction.)

Brake Calipers

Table 13-1 describes 16 sidepull models and 4 unique brake designs: the Campagnolo C-Record, the Mathauser Hydraulic Brake, the Scott Superbrake, and the Weinmann Delta Pro. It used to be that the main criterion for sidepull brake quality was how faithfully the maker copied the Campagnolo Nuovo Record. No longer. The best of today's sidepulls start where the Nuovo Record leaves off. This includes anti-friction thrust bearings between the calipers, stiffer caliper arms, and lighter springs. A thrust bearing is needed because the calipers are forced together by strong braking. If there's friction between the calipers, they won't respond to small changes in lever force.

Many of the new sidepulls offer either a recessed attachment bolt or the normal exposed bolt. Watch out for this option. Short-arm sidepulls usually come with the recessed bolt, which won't fit your old front fork. Order the kind that matches your fork and rear brake bridge. (Table 13-1 shows which brakes have thrust bearings.)

Brake Caliper Reach

Most of the new, high-performance sidepulls are short-arm models designed for racing bicycles, which have the brake bridges right next to the tires. Many of those nice old frames that you want to upgrade were designed for centerpull brakes and fenders, and the brake attachment point is in the next county. Before you order replacement brakes, install wheels of the correct size on your bicycle and measure the distance from the brake attachment holes to the center of the rim's brake path. The brake calipers have an oblong slot for the pad attachment that typically provides about a centimeter of adjustment.

Many sidepull brakes come in two models, short-reach and standard-reach. The short-reach models have a higher mechanical advantage and they're stiffer, but your bicycle must be designed for short-reach brakes. (Table 13-2 gives typical brake reach dimensions for the various kinds of brakes, while table 13-1 shows the actual figures for both the short-reach and standard-reach brakes. Figure 13-3 shows how brake caliper reach is measured.)

An offset bolt can be used to lower the mounting point for sidepull brakes by 5mm, 8mm, or 10mm. This lets you use short-reach brakes on bicycles designed for standard brakes. I think offset bolts are ugly and they reduce the brakes' rigidity. It makes more sense to buy the right reach brakes for your bicycle. Using 27-inch wheels on a bicycle designed for 700C moves the brake path 4mm closer to the mounting bolt.

TABLE 13-2.

Brake Reach

Brake Type	Min. Reach (mm)	Max. Reach (mm)
Extra-short sidepull	35	42
Short-arm sidepull	40	50
Long-arm sidepull	47	57
Short-reach centerpull	42	55
Long-reach centerpull	60	78
Campagnolo C-Record	38	56
Mathauser Hydraulic	44	66
Scott Superbrake	40	54
Weinmann Delta Pro	44	57

The Centerpull Option

Weinmann and Dia-Compe make short-, medium-, and long-reach centerpull brakes in two or three different price levels. Some mixte frames are designed to use a medium-reach, centerpull brake on the rear. It makes a very neat installation. However, for most normal 10-speed applications, a modern short- or medium-reach sidepull brake will stop more positively and more sensitively than a centerpull. The exception is old bicycle frames that need brakes with a 60mm+ reach. For these, the long-arm centerpull is your best choice.

Caliper Mechanical Advantage

The mechanical advantage of the brakeset is the product of the mechanical advantages of the brake levers and the calipers. For table 13-1, I measured the mechanical advantage of the calipers by measuring the length of the two caliper lever arms. The typical long-reach sidepull caliper has a mechanical advantage of 1.0. The short-reach model has a mechanical advantage of about 1.2. It isn't a precise measurement because it changes when you raise or lower the brake pads in the slots.

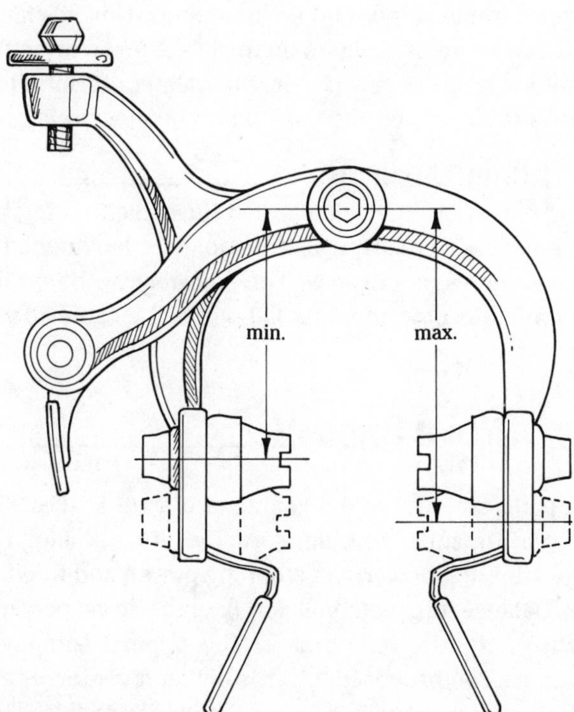

FIGURE 13-3

Brake caliper reach.

Brake designers keep inventing dream brakes that have a low mechanical advantage for the first part of the movement—until the pads contact the rim. Then the mechanical advantage increases for better braking efficiency. The old bicycle books show all kinds of exotic brakes that tried to achieve this dream.

The dreaming process continues today. The Cunningham Powermaster and the similar SunTour Roller Cam brakes for mountain bikes use a contoured cam. Shimano's Parapul brake also used a contoured cam. Campagnolo's C-Record and Weinmann's Delta brakes use a parallelogram to give a variable mechanical advantage. All five of these brakes have to be precisely adjusted. You can't just set the pads the proper distance from the rim with the cable adjuster. Shimano has decided that the adjustment (calibration is probably a better word) is too complicated, so they've dropped the Parapul brake and replaced it with a high-performance sidepull.

Caliper Quick-Releases

A brake quick-release lets you spread the calipers and pull a bicycle wheel down between the brake pads without deflating the tire. The adjustable type of quick-release, which has a range of positions between open and closed, allows you to open your brakes wide enough to still be usable while limping home with a broken spoke. You used to get the second type of quick-release on Campagnolo Nuovo Record sidepulls and not on the imitations. Now it's fairly common. The quick-release can be on the caliper, on the brake lever, or on the cable attachment point. Only the quick-release on the calipers is infinitely adjustable. (Table 13-1 shows the kind and the location of the quick-release.)

Cable Adjusters

As brake pads wear and cables stretch, you shorten the cable to bring the pads back to their proper position. Actually, the cable adjuster lengthens the casing, but this accomplishes the same purpose. The adjuster can be on the brake lever, the caliper, or (with a centerpull brake) at one of the cable attachment points.

Brake Pads

A pair of replacement pads can change the character of your brakes. The makers balance a range of performance characteristics, including braking efficiency, wear resistance, dry stopping power, wet stopping power, and freedom from grabbing. They also balance the potential for lawsuits from powerful brakes against that of lawsuits from anemic brakes. The original equipment pads on lower-priced brakes are compromised towards higher lever forces and nonexpert users. Consumer's Union can take some of the credit for this. They think that front brakes should be so feeble that even the most incompetent cyclist can't go over the handlebars. The pads on top-quality racing sidepulls are also compromised towards higher lever forces because that's what the racers are used to.

The aftermarket pads from Aztec, Kool-Stop, and Scott-Mathauser are designed for high braking efficiencies, both wet and dry. An efficient brake pad gives more stopping power for a given lever pull. Carried too far, this gives grabby brakes. Efficient brake pads require high-quality, low-friction brakes that are responsive to small changes in lever force. If you install efficient brake pads on worn, spongy old brakes, you won't be able to modulate the delicate pressures needed to stop smoothly.

If you use your brakes heavily on a long descent, the pads will get very hot. This is a major problem with tandems. Though I haven't seen any test data on pad melting, Aztec, Kool-Stop, and Mathauser advertise high-temperature performance. The Modolo sintered metal brake pad is also designed for high-temperature service.

There are no advantages to notches or slots on brake pads. They only cause the pads to wear faster, and there's good evidence that wet-weather braking is made worse by slotted pads, which act as water reservoirs. Some pads include hemispherical washers to let you precisely align the pads with the rims. This avoids the awkward task of bending the calipers to toe in the pads at the front and reduce the squeal. Bending calipers is a poor idea anyway, especially with top-quality forged calipers. The brake makers suggest that you sand the back of the pads instead. Most quality sidepulls include a wheel guide between the caliper and the pad so that racers can change wheels faster. The latest pads are molding this guide into the rubber. (Table 13-3 provides a description of the surface found on a variety of different pads and evaluates their stopping power.)

Brake Track Surface

A good set of calipers and pads alone does not guarantee good braking. The wheel rim material and the nature of the brake track surface are also involved. Special pads are made for wet-weather stopping with steel rims, but they're hard to find. The Fibrax Raincheater is one model that I know about. The problem in marketing these special pads is educating the unsophisticated bikers who ride cheap bikes with steel rims.

The brake track on the rim should be smooth, not serrated or dimpled. Dimples don't help dry braking and they make wet braking worse since it takes more wheel revolutions to wipe off the water. Serrations or dimples also greatly increase brake pad wear. I feel that brakes work better when the brake tracks are vertical rather than slanted.

TABLE 13-3.

Brake Pads

Make and Model	Cost ($/pr.)	Stopping Power Dry	Stopping Power Wet	Area (sq. in.)	Surface
Aztec	8	E	E	—	2 vees
Campagnolo black	6	VG	VG	0.45	3 slots
Campagnolo gray	6	E	VG	0.33	3 slots
Dia-Compe RGC	4	G	F	0.38	3 vees
Kool-Stop Supra	6	E	VG	0.67	1 slot
Mathauser Engineering	—	—	—	0.78	1 slot
Modolo sintered	6	G	E	0.56	solid
Scott-Mathauser	15 (2 pr.)	E	E	0.84	solid
Shimano Dura-Ace	12 (2 pr.)	VG	VG	0.60	4 vees
Shimano 105	5	G	G	0.58	3 vees
Shimano 600	5	VG	G	0.58	3 vees
SunTour Superbe	5	VG	E	0.43	3 vees
Weinmann Delta	—	—	—	0.45	2 slots

Brakeset Makers

Although you can mix and match brake levers and calipers, you're more likely to buy a complete brakeset. Table 13-1 shows you the performance and mechanical details of the widely available, top-quality brakesets and several medium-priced models. The weights shown in table 13-1 are for the complete front and rear brakeset, with the short-arm brakes and cables and casings. A set of front and rear cables and casings weighs about 180 grams.

The trend of OEM and aftermarket buyers to include the brakes in a gruppo is affecting the brake marketplace. The small companies are having a hard time getting a profitable share of the market, regardless of their product quality.

Campagnolo

Campagnolo makes brakes at six different price levels. The names are confusing. The top brake is called Record, C-Record, or Delta. Take your choice. With 65 separate parts in just one housing, it's a very sophisticated brake. Only Campagnolo could pull it off. The parallelogram housing moves the pads quickly at first and then the mechanical advantage increases. The original 1984 version was recalled while the prototypes were being tested. They added adjustments and changed the materials. The present C-Record has individual Allen screws at the front and rear of the pads for precise toe-in adjustment.

In 1983, to celebrate their 50th Anniversary, Campagnolo produced the Cobalto sidepull brake, which has a beefier front caliper than the old Record (now called Nuovo Record) and a jewel at the center of the calipers. The Cobalto brakeset was included in the C-Record gruppo while the Delta brake was being revised. C-Record and Cobalto levers allow you to route the cables out the top or out the back of the lever body. Cobalto brakesets are sometimes included in Super Record gruppos. A frugal dealer may include a Super Record brakeset in the Super Record gruppo. The Super Record is a Nuovo Record brakeset with drilled levers and Cobalto calipers without the jewel.

The Nuovo Record brakeset is Campagnolo's original Model 2040 sidepull that was introduced for the 1968 Olympics. Nuovo Victory uses the same calipers as the Super Record except that the quick-release is two-position rather than variable. Nuovo Triomphe uses the same calipers as Nuovo Record with a two-position quick-release. The 1988 Chorus sidepulls continue Campagnolo's unique mixture of art and engineering.

Dia-Compe

Dia-Compe started out 15 years ago cloning Weinmann sidepull and centerpull brakes so precisely that the parts were interchangeable. Dia-Compe has grown a lot since those days. They now have a major assembly plant in Fletcher, North Carolina that supplies a very broad range of brakes to the OEM market. Dia-Compe's model names have been confusing because the OEMs mix and match levers and calipers.

Dia-Compe is making a serious run at the aftermarket with three sidepull models that incorporate their Balanced Response System. All three have aerodynamic levers with lever return springs and light caliper springs. BRS 400 uses Royal Gran Compe calipers. BRS 300 uses Royal Compe II calipers. BRS 200 uses the SunTour Alpha II calipers. Dia-Compe is particularly proud of the stiff new tighter-weave cables and molybdenum-impregnated casing liners that are used in the BRS brakesets.

Mathauser Engineering

Bill Mathauser and Ed Scott were partners in Scott-Mathauser. The partnership dissolved in 1975 with Scott keeping the rights to the Mathauser name. Bill Mathauser now runs his own firm, Mathauser Engineering. He has developed a hydraulic bicycle brake that's a beauty. He avoids the problem of fluid leaks by providing a completely sealed system and using "bellofram" instead of pistons and O-rings. The brakes are elegantly engineered and have a very light feel.

Modolo

Modolo is an Italian brake company that has good availability in the aftermarket. They produce three basic models: Master Professional, Professional, and Speedy. All three models have the same dimensions but they differ in material and finish. The Master Professional is hard anodized and has a titanium mounting bolt. The Super Prestige is the white finished version of the Professional. The Speedy is Modolo's bargain brake. All Modolos use sintered metal brake pads that stop splendidly in the rain and erase the hard anodizing from your rims in jig time.

Scott

Ed Scott makes Scott-Mathauser brake pads. He developed the Scott Superbrake to overcome all of the design deficiencies that he perceives in conventional brakes. It's a design tour de force. It's probably the most rigid brake made, with the largest, stiffest pivot bearings. It's a center-pivot, top-pull

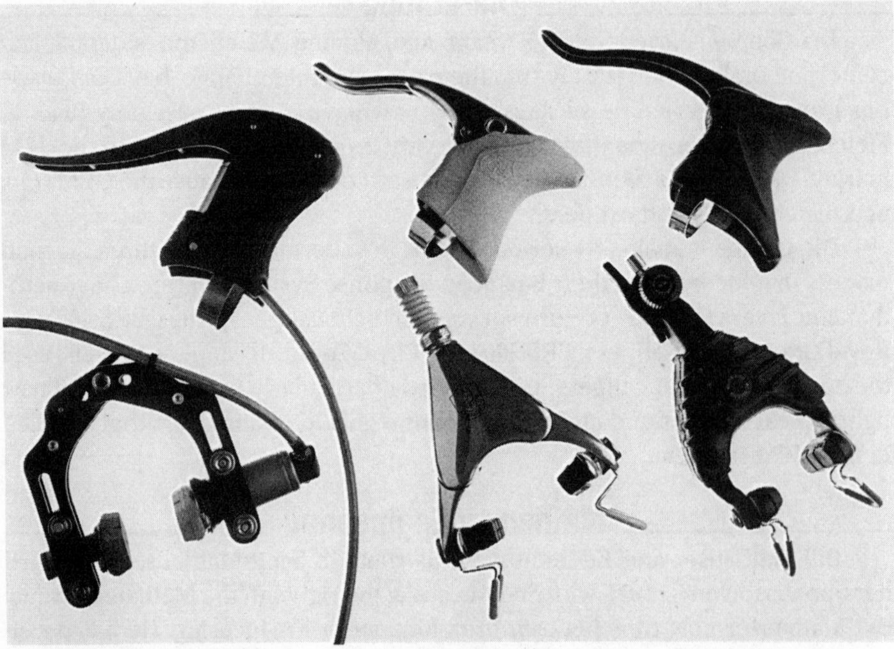

PHOTO 13-1 Unconventional brakesets: left to right, Mathauser Hydraulic, Campagnolo C-Record, and Weinmann Delta Pro.

rather than a sidepull. The calipers are like a pair of scissors and the cable comes in from one side. The cable leaves the bottom of the front lever and runs directly to the front brake. The Superbrake requires very little lever movement.

Shimano

The three lines of Shimano brakes—Dura-Ace, 600 EX, and 105—all reflect Shimano's extensive design and road testing effort in 1985. When the aerodynamic bubble burst, Shimano decided that the users of quality components wanted conservative equipment that looked like Campagnolo. Campagnolo Super Record brakes were their design benchmark; "less friction, less flex" was their battle cry. The key improvement was caliper thrust bearings, but there were dozens of other minor improvements.

I think that Shimano succeeded in meeting their design goals. All three Shimano sidepulls stop with less lever effort and more sensitivity than the Super Record or any other brakeset that I've tried. You can have aero or standard levers with all three series. I particularly like the 105 brakes with the lever return springs.

SunTour

SunTour brakes are made by Dia-Compe. The three lines—Superbe Pro, Sprint, and Cyclone—are very similar, with more bells and whistles on the top line. Superbe Pro and Sprint have a ball thrust bearing between the inner caliper and the bolt and greased washers between the calipers. Superbe Pro has internal coil springs for the calipers and pads that can be adjusted for toe-in. Aero levers are available for all three and a short-reach standard lever is available for Superbe Pro.

Weinmann

Weinmann is a full-line brake company with factories in five countries. They make a complete line of sidepull, centerpull, and cantilever brakes for the OEMs. They're being hurt by the current trend to include brakes in the gruppo. Weinmann makes two exotic brakes. The Delta Pro is a knee-action brake with a variable mechanical advantage. The Turbo is a centerpull that wraps the cable around a threaded drum and screws the pads into the rim. I've only seen Turbos at the bike shows. The 590SQ is Weinmann's low-priced sidepull for the aftermarket.

Everybody Else

CLB, Galli, Mavic, and Zeus make Campagnolo Nuovo Record look-alike sidepulls. Distribution of the brakes made by all these companies is quite limited.

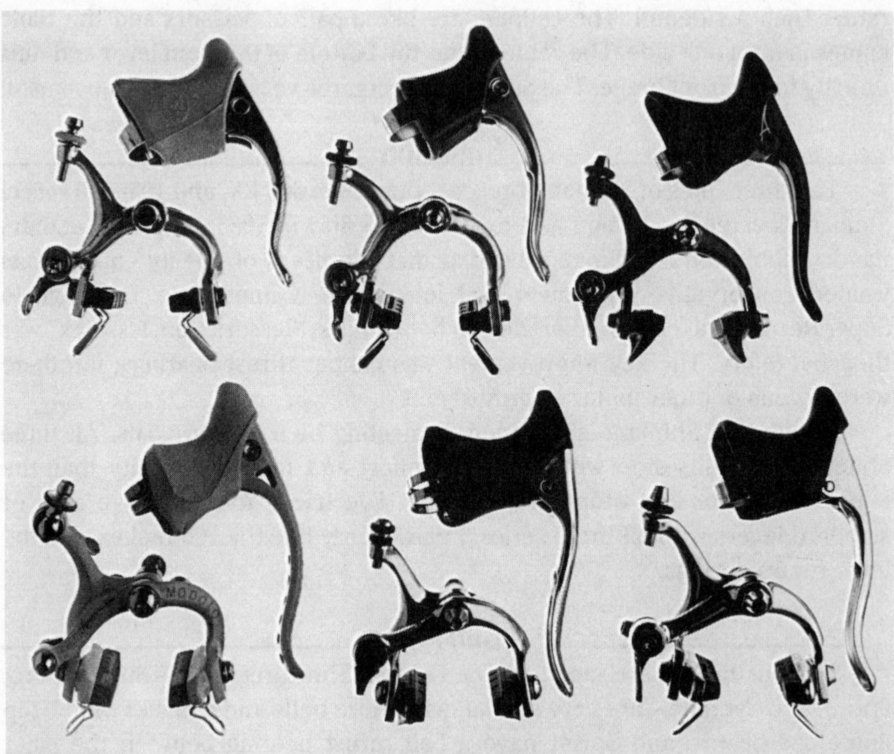

PHOTO 13-2 Sidepull brakesets: top left to right, Campagnolo Cobalto, Campagnolo Nuovo Record, and Dia-Compe BRS 400; bottom left to right, Modolo Professional, Shimano 105, and SunTour Superbe Pro.

Frank's Favorite Brakes

The Shimano Dura-Ace on the Trek and the Shimano 105 on the Paramount are my favorite brakes. I've got an old set of Campagnolo Nuovo Records on the Redcay that I've souped up with Dura-Ace pads. This is my reference standard, and there's no doubt that the Shimano brakes take less lever force and are more responsive than brakes made by their competitors.

I've been playing mountain bike brake games with my loaded touring bike. I started out with Dia-Compe braze-on centerpulls. They were pretty, but they really weren't up to stopping a loaded touring bike in the wet. So I had the Dia-Compe bosses removed and SunTour Roller Cam bosses brazed on, with the rear brake located under the chainstays. This worked well, gave good control, and I was able to lock my wheels under all circumstances. Then, when Shimano came out with the U-Brake, I got a pair, since they fit on SunTour bosses. They're just as powerful and require even less lever force.

CHAPTER 14

All about Saddles and Seatposts

The first 13 chapters of this book have focused attention on the important mechanical components found on your bicycle. This final chapter will describe two major nonmechanical components—saddles and seatposts. These nonmechanical items are often overlooked and neglected. We simply accept what came with our bicycles even though it reduces our riding pleasure and comfort. That is both unfortunate and unnecessary, since these components, which your body contacts as you ride, can be easily upgraded.

Saddles

A bicycle saddle is a very personal item and every rider has to make a judgment about what best suits his or her backside. In the past two or three years, there have been some improvements in this critical area. Today you have more options to choose from, though it's hard to separate the facts from the advertising hype.

As with so many other bicycle components, when you pick a new saddle you have to strike a compromise. In this case the compromise is between a wide, soft saddle that's more comfortable for short rides and a narrow, firm saddle that's more comfortable for long-distance rides. The narrow, firm saddle doesn't chafe your thighs, it's ergonomically more efficient, and it keeps you from sliding around. Narrow saddles don't have to be extra-firm. The latest gel-padded saddles combine good support with medium firmness. The best way to pick a new saddle is to borrow one from a friend and try it on a long ride.

Saddle Differences

My own feelings (that's the right word because the subject doesn't lend itself to engineering evaluation) can be summarized as follows:

- The beginner has different needs than the experienced rider. You start out needing a soft, wide saddle. Later, when your backside becomes inured to the pedaling process, you switch to something narrower and firmer that's easier to pedal.
- If you ride in an upright position, you put more weight on the saddle and you need a wider and (perhaps) softer saddle. Optimum saddle width at the rear varies from 8 inches for a sprung "Roadster" saddle on a bicycle with upright handlebars to 5½ inches for a racing saddle to as little as 4 inches for a track racing saddle. As you lean further forward and put more weight on your hands, your saddle can be narrower and firmer.
- The wide, soft saddle that feels wonderful for a 10-minute ride may be less comfortable for a century. The problem is that wide, soft saddles cause more friction. They waste energy and chafe your legs after a while. If your average ride is 30 to 50 miles, you'll probably prefer a firmer and narrower saddle.
- You need to spread the pressure at the two points where your ischial tuberosities ("sit bones") contact the saddle. There isn't that much "meat" between these bones and the saddle. It doesn't help to put great layers of foam over the whole saddle. That just increases the friction and chafing.
- Women's pelvic structures are different from men's and they need a different saddle. Women's ischial tuberosities are about 4¾ inches apart compared to 4¼ inches for men. Women's saddles are ½ inch wider than the similar men's models. They're also about 1 inch shorter. I used to think that the makers did this so that you knew it was a women's saddle and not a wide touring saddle. It makes sense though—the women's saddle is shaped more like a letter T than a letter V, so you can't sit very far forward without coming off the padding.
- The clothing between the skin and the saddle has almost as much influence on comfort as the saddle itself. If your underwear has seams or your sweaty skin slides around in your underwear, long-distance cycling won't be much fun.

Kinds of Saddles

From firm to soft, saddles fall into three main categories: tensioned leather, plastic foundation, and gel-padded.

Tensioned Leather Saddles The *tensioned leather* saddle is the classic saddle design that's virtually unchanged from the days of the safety bicycle. There used to be dozens of manufacturers and hundreds of models of leather saddles. Now there are just two quality makers, Brooks and Ideale, and they make just a few models. The word tensioned describes the method of construction. A triangular piece of top-quality leather about 3/16 inch thick is formed into shape. Then it's riveted to front and rear frame supports and stretched like a hammock over the saddle rails. A tension bolt at the front allows you to adjust the amount of sag and to take up stretch.

Your first ride on a brand-new leather saddle can be a painful experience. It feels like it was carved from wood—hard wood at that. After a few thousand

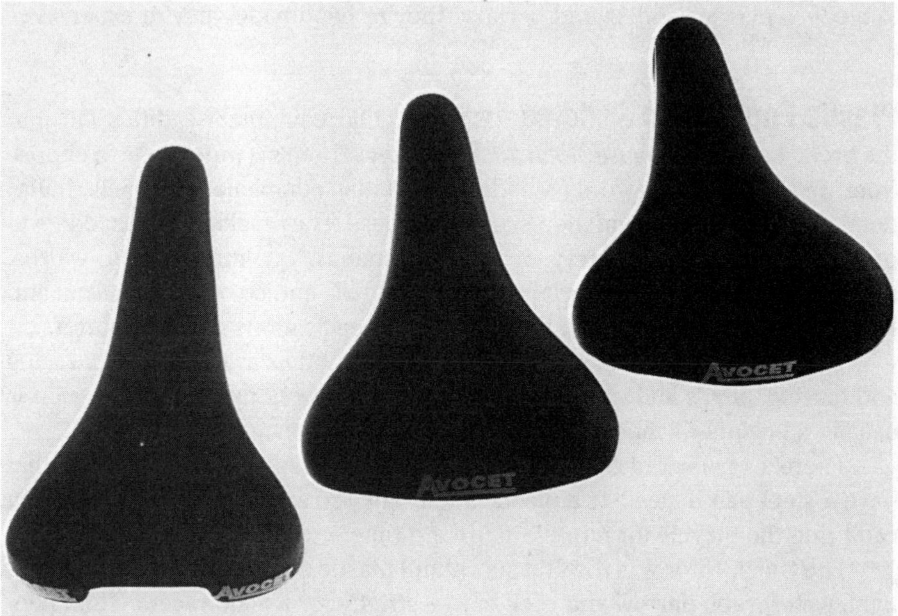

PHOTO 14-1 Three basic saddle shapes: left to right, Avocet Gel-Flex men's racing saddle, Avocet Gel-Flex men's touring saddle, and Avocet Gel-Flex women's saddle.

miles of riding and liberal applications of Brooks Proofide or some other leather preservative, the leather takes a permanent deformation from the pressure of your ischial tuberosities. When this finally happens, you treat the saddle like an old friend and move it from one bicycle to the next.

In our modern, fast-paced world, not everyone is willing to be uncomfortable for six months, so Brooks and Ideale now sell pre-softened versions of their top models. The pre-softening shortens the time for the leather to take a permanent set. Ideale calls its pre-softening the "Rebour process" after Daniel Rebour, who edited *Le Cycliste* for so long and did the beautiful pen and ink drawings that are so valuable to bicycle historians.

Tensioned leather saddles are quite comfortable when they're properly broken in. They give firm support with minimum friction and they "breathe" a bit on hot, sweaty days. At the same time they have liabilities. They're firm, even when well broken in. They can't be left out in the rain or the leather rapidly deteriorates; most users carry a plastic saddle cover for wet weather. The Proofide, even when applied only to the inside, stains your shorts (one reason why traditional shorts are black). Leather saddles are heavy compared to modern plastic saddles and because they're handmade, they're expensive.

Plastic Foundation Saddles Most original equipment saddles fall into the broad category of *plastic foundation* saddles. There's a wide range to choose from. *Selle* is the Italian word for saddle and Italian companies (e.g., Selle Italia) dominate the plastic foundation saddle business. They make plastic saddles to order in a bewildering array of models, shapes, qualities, prices, widths, shapes, firmnesses, rail materials, cover materials, and colors. Specialized and Pearl Izumi saddles are made in Italy to the specifications of the importers.

The pattern for Italian saddles is that most models are available in racing and touring, men's and women's, and firm or soft versions. The soft version is usually a beginner's model and it's less expensive.

There's a subset of American and Taiwanese gaspipe-quality saddles that have a steel pan instead of a plastic shell. They're so uncomfortable that you can't ride the bicycle for more ½ hour at a time.

The Unica-Nitor was the first successful plastic saddle that I noticed. It was light, waterproof, narrow and rock hard—strictly for macho racers. Then people began to work them over with a drill. If you drilled just the right number of holes in the ischial area, it would conform to the shape of your backside and it was almost comfortable. In the mid-1970s, padded models appeared with ⅛ inch or so of foam padding over the nylon base. This was topped with a vinyl cover, or leather in the top models. The next step was to thin out the nylon under the ischial area to spread out the pressure point. Finally, Avocet came out with the "two-bump" anatomic saddle, which had thicker padding over the thinned out area. Avocet has a patent on the combined thin shell–thickened padding design.

Gel-Padded Saddles In 1975, Cool Gear brought out "The Seat," which had a nylon base and three little packets of ski boot liquid gel under a vinyl cover. There were the usual start-up problems. Just about when they had it all sorted out, the factory burned down. By that time, Avocet had pretty much taken over the quality saddle aftermarket. I didn't see anything more of gel-padded saddles until 1983 when the Pearl Izumi Flolite appeared. In 1986, Avocet introduced the Gel-Flex saddle. I used an early Gel-Flex saddle on my British Columbia tour and found it very comfortable. Now the Italian *selle* companies offer an array of gel-padded saddles with words like "visco-elastic polymer" to describe the gel.

Saddle Construction

A saddle has a pair of rails that attach to the seatpost and support either the front and rear frames of a tensioned leather saddle or the shell of a plastic saddle. Ten years ago, saddles had either two or four rails. The rails were round rods or flat bars. They were spaced 43mm or 27mm apart. All of the diversity ended when Sakae made inexpensive, alloy, micro-adjusting seatposts and the OEM and aftermarket buyers began to insist on them. These require two 7mm diameter rails spaced 43mm apart. Virtually all of today's saddles now use this construction and saddles no longer come with clips to attach them to straight seatposts. If you need a clip to attach your new saddle to an old straight seatpost, your bike store probably has a drawer full. The rails on most saddles are made of steel. Sometimes there's a top model available with aluminum rails that weighs about 80 grams less and costs about $10 more. See table 14-1 for a description of the materials used in various saddle models.

Saddle Dimensions

There are three important dimensions on a saddle: the overall length, the width at the rear, and the width at the halfway point. This last dimension is informative because a wider mid-width gives you more support, which is comfortable on short rides and chafes you on long rides. Figure 14-1 illustrates how these dimensions are measured and table 14-1 provides this kind of information for several current models.

Cover and Shell Material

Leather is the best cover material if you keep your bicycle out of the rain. Leather "breathes" and it doesn't get slippery from sweat. Some of the top-

(continued on page 286)

TABLE 14-1.

Saddles

Make and Model	Cost ($)	Weight (gr.)	Width (in.) Rear	Width (in.) Halfway	Length (in.)	Materials Cover	Materials Padding
Avocet							
Anatomic Racing							
Model II	35–45	345	5.7	2.4	10.8	suede	foam
Anatomic Touring							
Model I	25–35	375	6.4	3.0	10.6	leather	foam
Gel-Flex M-20	30–40	450	6.5	2.8	10.6	Lycra	Spenco gel
Gel-Flex R-20	30–40	385	5.7	2.7	11.7	Lycra	Spenco gel
Gel-Flex W-20	30–40	475	6.9	3.2	10.0	Lycra	Spenco gel
Brooks							
B-17	30–40	530	6.7	3.2	11.1	leather	—
Professional	35–50	540	6.4	2.6	10.7	leather	—
Team Professional	35–50	540	6.2	2.5	11.2	leather	—
Professional S	35–50	500	7.0	3.5	9.6	leather	—
Ideale							
Model 90	30–40	554	6.1	2.5	10.3	leather	—
Model 92	35–45	620	6.8	3.1	10.8	leather	—
Pearl Izumi							
Model 100	35–50	425	6.0	2.6	10.6	leather	Flolite
Racing Model 300	45–60	415	5.7	2.6	10.9	leather	Flolite
Selle Italia							
Bio Turbo	50–80	390	5.8	2.4	10.8	leather	gel
Super Turbo	35–50	370	5.8	2.4	10.8	buffalo	—
Turbo	25–35	340	5.8	2.4	10.8	buffalo	dense foam
Selle San Marco							
Concor	25–35	350	—	—	—	buffalo	dense foam
Regal	50–65	380	—	—	—	leather	foam
Rolls	30–40	410	—	—	—	buffalo	foam
Specialized							
Delta S (Racing)	25–40	365	5.9	2.8	10.9	suede	foam
Lambda S (Touring)	25–40	380	6.7	2.8	10.9	leather	foam
Carina S (Women's)	25–40	350	7.3	2.5	9.8	leather	foam
Vetta							
Anatomic Maxi	15–20	430	7.0	3.3	10.8	leather	foam
Ergonomic	15–20	400	6.0	2.6	10.6	leather	foam
Nuvola Maxi	30–40	550	6.7	3.3	10.9	leather	gel
Nuvola Racing	35–45	450	6.0	2.6	10.6	leather	gel
Nuvola Ladies	30–40	450	7.2	2.7	9.9	leather	gel

Materials Shell	Materials Rails	Women's Model Available	Touring Model Available	Firmness	Padding Thickness (in.)	Tension Adjuster	Features
nylon	ChrStl	yes	yes	med.	0.6	no	
nylon	Stl	yes	shown	soft	0.7	no	
Polyeth	Stl	yes	shown	soft	0.8	no	
Polyeth	Stl	yes	yes	soft	0.6	no	
Polyeth	Stl	shown	yes	soft	0.8	no	
—	—	no	yes	X-firm	N/A	yes	
—	—	yes	no	X-firm	N/A	yes	pre-softened mod. avail.
—	CpPlStl	yes	no	X-firm	N/A	yes	pre-softened mod. avail.
—	CpPlStl	shown	no	X-firm	N/A	yes	pre-softened mod. avail.
—	Stl	yes	—	X-firm	N/A	yes	
—	Stl	yes	shown	X-firm	N/A	yes	pre-softened mod. avail.
Polyeth	Stl	no	no	med.	0.8	no	
Polyeth	Stl	no	no	med.	0.8	no	
nylon	Stl	no	no	med.	0.6	no	
nylon	Stl	no	no	firm	0.6	no	textured cover
nylon	Stl	yes	no	firm	0.6	no	
nylon	Stl	no	no	firm	—	no	
nylon	alloy	no	yes	med.	—	yes	
nylon	Stl	no	no	med.	—	no	
nylon	ChrStl	yes	yes	med.	0.45	no	lower-priced Delta avail.
nylon	ChrStl	yes	shown	med.	0.65	no	lower-priced Lambda avail.
nylon	ChrStl	shown	yes	med.	0.70	no	lower-priced Carina avail.
Polyeth	ChrStl	yes	shown	med.	0.80	no	
Polyeth	ChrStl	yes	yes	med.	0.70	no	
nylon	ChrStl	yes	shown	soft	0.85	no	
nylon	ChrStl	yes	yes	soft	0.80	no	
nylon	ChrStl	shown	yes	soft	0.90	no	

quality saddles use buffalo leather. Some saddles have suede leather but these become smooth leather very rapidly. Nylon or Lycra cloth makes a less expensive cover that stretches and resists water. Vinyl is the least expensive and least pleasant cover material. It doesn't "breathe" at all and it gets slippery with sweat.

If you leave your bike out in the rain a lot, you should buy a vinyl-covered saddle. Padded covers are available from Spenco and others to fit over your present saddle. I don't like the idea. If the cover slides around at all, your bike is harder to control. I'd rather buy the right saddle with the padding or gel built in, which is also lighter.

The shells of the less expensive plastic saddles are made from polyethylene, while the more expensive models use nylon. The shell is often thinned out in the ischial area to spread the pressure.

Firmness, Thickness, and Weight

The firmness or softness of a saddle is determined by a combination of factors: the density of the padding, the thickness of the padding, and the flex of the shell. I don't have the instruments to measure firmness, but I wanted to give you a feel for the differences, so I poked my thumb into the padding at the ischial area. This unscientific measurement is the basis for the firmness ratings found in table 14-1. Obviously, my thumb test cannot produce a precise prediction of how each saddle will feel after you've spent several hours riding on it.

The total thickness of the shell, padding, and cover of each test saddle was measured with calipers at the ischial area and recorded as padding thickness in table 14-1. The weights shown in the table are for the models with steel rails. All

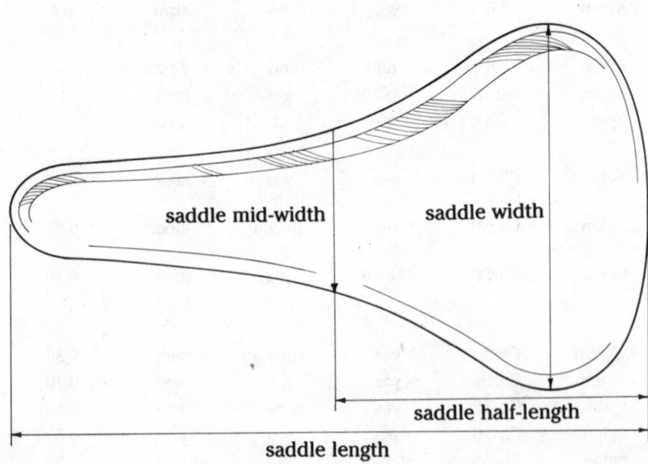

FIGURE 14-1

Saddle dimensions.

tensioned leather saddles include a nut at the front to let you increase the tension as the leather stretches with age. A few plastic foundation saddles also include a tension adjuster. This feature is also noted in the table.

Saddle Makers

Brooks and Ideale make tensioned leather saddles. Avocet, Pearl Izumi, and Specialized have saddles made offshore to their specifications. Selle Italia, Selle San Marco, Selle Royale, and Vetta make millions of saddles for the OEMs and thousands of saddles for the aftermarket. The Taiwanese make large numbers of inexpensive OEM saddles, but they're generally the kind that you ought to be replacing.

Avocet Avocet is a major supplier of aftermarket saddles. They have the most complete selection and a straightforward naming system. There are three models, and each model includes a racing, a touring, and a women's version. Model I saddles have a softer cushion and a more flexible shell; they are intended basically for beginners or short-distance cyclists. Model II saddles have denser foam padding and a firmer nylon shell. Gel-Flex saddles have a horseshoe-shaped band of Spenco gel.

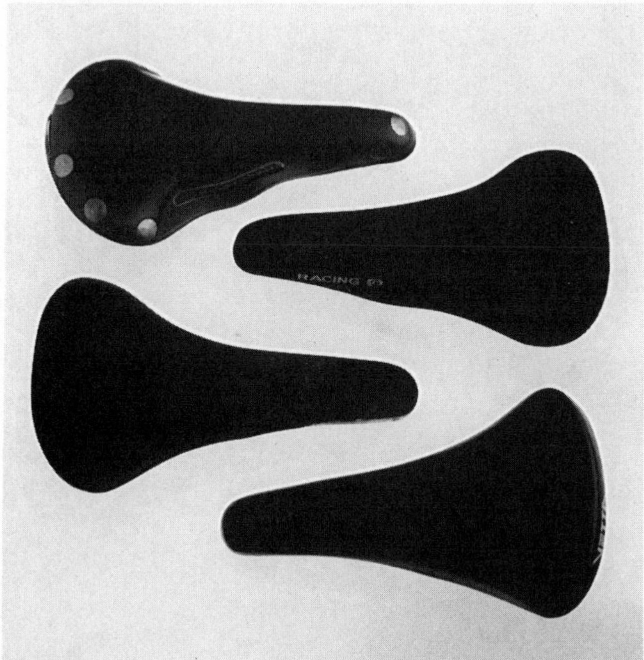

PHOTO 14-2

Racing saddles: top to bottom, Brooks Team Professional, Pearl Izumi Flolite Model 300, Selle Italia Super Turbo, and Vetta Racing.

Avocet has a long-standing dream of producing "Made in America" bicycle components. They built a large, efficient saddle factory in California and mass-produced Avocet-USA saddles there for two years. The low-priced competition became too fierce in 1986 and Avocet moved the factory offshore.

Brooks Brooks has been making bicycle saddles since 1866. The Brooks catalog still shows wide, sprung "roadster" saddles. There are five racing and sport touring models in the aftermarket. The lightweight Team Professional has distinctive ⅝-inch-diameter copper rivets. The Professional has 7/16-inch-diameter copper rivets. The B-17 is available in wide touring and narrow racing versions, but it only has mingy little ¼-inch-diameter rivets. Women should know that there's a new Professional S model designed just for them. If your shop doesn't stock it, nag the owner.

In bygone days, people used to take their leather saddles apart to torture and beat them to hasten the breaking-in process. The large-diameter rivets allowed the saddles to be reassembled. Today, Brooks doesn't need large-diameter rivets any more than Levis need riveted pockets or Marines need Sam Brown belts. Brooks got tired of seeing Ideale get all of the sales of pre-softened

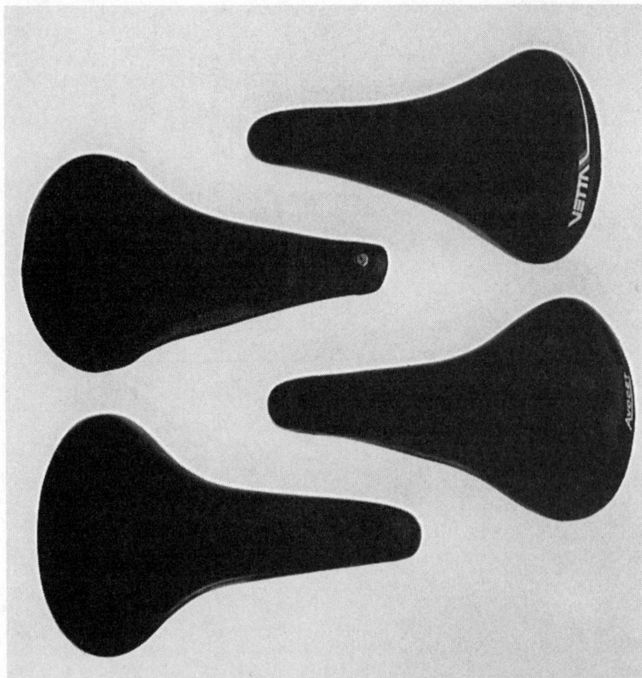

PHOTO 14-3

Touring saddles: top to bottom, Vetta Nuvola, Ideale Model 92 with Rebour treatment, Avocet Touring Model I with bumps, and Specialized Lambda S.

saddles. They now offer pre-softened versions of the Team Professional and the Professional S for about $10 additional.

Ideale Ideale is the French equivalent of Brooks. They fell on hard times a few years ago and there were bankruptcy "sales." The company has barely survived and it's now part of Zefal. They sell two saddle models: the narrower 90 and the wider 92. Both are available with Rebour pre-softening.

Pearl Izumi Despite the Japanese name, Pearl Izumi saddles are made in Italy by Selle Royale. There are three models. Model 100 is the softest touring saddle. Model 200 is the firmer touring saddle and Model 300 is the firmest racing model. All three models use a ⅜-inch-thick layer of Flolite ski boot liquid, which actally flows under pressure. The Pearl Izumi Flolite got raves for comfort in *Bicycling*'s saddle test in 1984.

Selle Italia Selle Italia makes dozens of models and the importers often specify slightly different versions. The Turbo is the racing model. The Super Turbo has a perforated (sometimes textured) cover. The Bio Turbo is the racing model with gel padding. The Tri-A is a slightly wider Turbo. Selle Italia's Turbo racing saddles are a bit less firm than Selle San Marco's Concors. They also have a different shape. Most riders pick one style or the other and stick with it. Most Selle Italia saddles are available in women's models and in higher-priced, lightweight versions with aluminum rails.

Selle San Marco The name Concor is applied to a whole range of racing saddles made by Selle San Marco. They also make the classy Rolls racing saddle with brass-plated rails, a buffalo cover, and a gold nameplate. The Regal is a plastic saddle disguised with large copper rivets to look like a Brooks Team Pro. It's available with a perforated cover.

Specialized Specialized got into the saddle business in 1985. Avocet got into the tire business in 1986. You can draw your own conclusions. It has certainly provided more competition. Specialized saddles are imported from Italy. There are three models: Lambda for touring, Delta for racing, and Carina for women. Each model comes in a standard and an S version. The S version has firmer shell material and a leather cover. All Specialized saddles have thicker padding in the ischial area, but it's set into depressions in the shell, giving a smooth top cover.

Vetta There are three series of Vetta saddles in the aftermarket: Racing, Anatomic, and Nuvola. Each series is available in men's, women's, or Maxi

PHOTO 14-4

Ladies saddles: top to bottom, Avocet Gel-Flex, Brooks Team Professional S, Specialized Carina S, and Vetta Ladies.

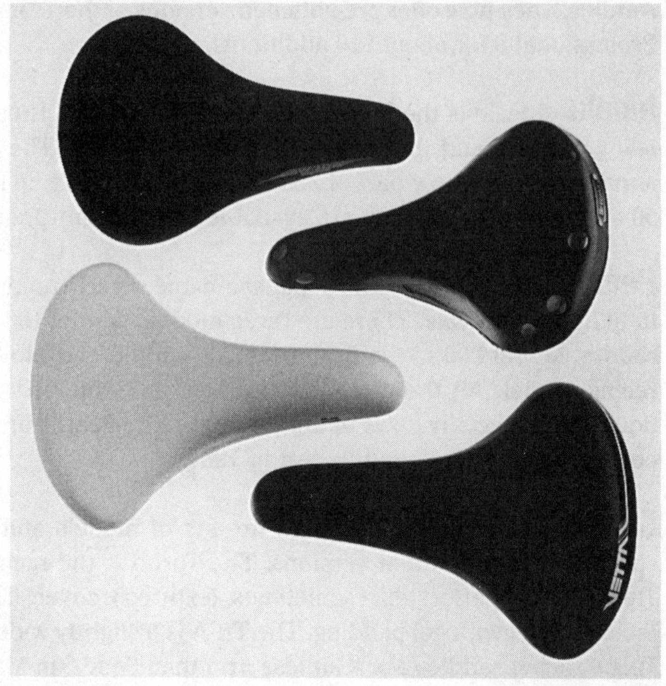

models. The Maxi is wider and has softer padding. Vettas are also available with vinyl covers at a lower price. The Vetta Nuvola (*nuvola* is the Italian word for "cloud") has the gel material enclosed in a foam cavity and covered with latex. It's available in racing, touring, and women's models.

Frank's Favorite Saddles

I rate saddles with considerable misgiving because there's no good reason why a saddle that suits me should suit you. Before writing this chapter, I was using Avocet Gel-Flex touring saddles on my two touring bicycles. I've done several centuries and a long tour on Gel-Flex saddles. I had a well broken in Brooks Professional on one racing bicycle and a Specialized Delta S on the other. I had an Avocet Touring II with a sheepskin cover on my commute bicycle. The idea was to keep my suit pants from getting shiny.

For this chapter, I tried three of the new saddles to get a "feel" for their performance. The Pearl Izumi Model 100 was the best of the three. It feels very firm at first and then it molds to shape. I pedaled the Model 100 on a 75-mile ride and found it comparable to the Avocet Gel-Flex. The Selle Italia Bio Turbo was close, but a bit less comfortable than the Gel-Flex. The Vetta Nuvola Maxi is an extra-wide touring saddle and I found it uncomfortable after 15 miles. My son

Ben commented that I should pick one saddle and install it on all of my bicycles. Your leg muscles get used to the support of a particular saddle. Switching saddles is hard on you. If your present saddle feels good to you, stick with it.

Seatposts

Seatposts are also called "seat pins" or "seat pillars." There's almost no performance difference between expensive seatposts and the lower-priced versions. Buy the one that looks best to your eyes and your pocketbook. The big improvement in the past five years is the availability of inexpensive micro-adjusting alloy seatposts.

Before these became available, seatposts were a straight tube of steel or aluminum with a reduced top section. A seat clamp fit on top of the seatpost and locked onto the saddle rails. There were about 50 serrations in the seat clamp, which meant that the minimum change in saddle tilt was 7 degrees. The odds were that this would be 3 degrees too high or 4 degrees too low. Many cyclists can notice a change of just a few degrees. Ideale, Brooks, and Simplex make clamps with infinite adjustments but they aren't widely used.

The old Campagnolo Record micro-adjusting seatpost, introduced in the 1950s, solved the adjustment problem. By the mid-1970s, you could buy Campy-copies from Sakae, Zeus, and others. The old Campagnolo Record (now called Nuovo Record) isn't that nice a seatpost because it's hard to adjust. You have to grope under the saddle with a wrench to tighten the two bolts. Campagnolo makes a special bent wrench just for the purpose.

The Sakae Foursir (Laprade) seatpost, introduced in 1980, could be adjusted from below and it was available in a range of prices. Now you can get Laprade-style seatposts from American Classic, Shimano, Sugino, SunTour, and even Campagnolo.

Many seatposts have a fluted strut that slides in a bit easier. In 1981, Shimano introduced an aerodynamic AX seatpost with a narrow pillar. It didn't improve wind resistance very much, but it looked pretty and Shimano still makes it. Campagnolo's new C-Record, Victory, and Triomphe seatposts also have a narrow pillar.

Seatpost Diameter

There are about a dozen standard seatpost diameters, starting at 25mm and then going in 2mm steps from 25.4mm to 27.4mm. There's not a whole lot of scope for standardization because seatposts have to fit into seat tubes. Seat tube inside diameters vary with the wall thickness and the tube butting. Just

TABLE 14-2.

Seatposts

Make and Model	Cost ($)	Weight (gr.)	Style	Lengths (mm)		Available Diameters											Features
				Min.	Max.	25.0	25.4	25.8	26.0	26.2	26.4	26.6	26.8	27.0	27.2	27.4	
American Classic	30–40	160	Lapr	200	280	X	X		X		X	X	X		X		
Campagnolo																	
C-Record	75–100	220	Lapr	130	180	X		X	X	X	X	X	X	X	X		aero tube
Super Record (4051/1)	65–90	220	Lapr	—	180	X		X	X	X	X	X	X	X	X	X	fluted tube
Nuovo Record (1044)	45–60	300	2-bolt	130	180	X		X	X	X	X		X	X	X		
Victory/Triomphe	30–40	240	Lapr	130	180	X				X	X		X	X	X		aero tube
Sakae																	
Custom (CT-P5)	13–20	335	Lapr	190	250		X	X	X	X	X	X	X	X	X		fluted tube
MTE-300	13-20	335	Lapr	250	330							X	X	X	X		
Shimano																	
Dura-Ace AX (SP-7410)	45–65	260	Lapr	200	200	X								X	X		aero tube
Dura-Ace (SP-7400)	40–60	245	Lapr	200	200						X	X	X	X	X	X	fluted tube
Sugino																	
SP-KC	15–25	290	Lapr	230	230				X	X	X	X	X	X	X		fluted tube
SP-C	10–20	245	2-bolt	200	200					X	X	X	X	X	X		
SunTour																	
SP-XC	40–60	285	Lapr	300	300						X	X	X	X	X		
Superbe Pro	40–60	240	Lapr	200	250	X					X	X	X	X	X		

make sure you measure first and buy the right size. "Close" isn't good enough. Table 14-2 shows which models are available in which diameters.

Seatpost Length and Weight

You need about 2 inches of seatpost buried in the seat tube. Most seatposts have a minumum insertion mark. More insertion than that is just extra weight. If you have more than about 4 inches of exposed seatpost, it usually means that your frame is too small. Many racers like small frames because small frames are stiffer and the rider can lean lower. I think that small-framed 10-speeds with extra-long seatposts and stems look ridiculous. Lots of serious riders disagree with me. Mountain bikers use smaller frames than 10-speeds for a number of good reasons.

Campagnolo makes short (130mm) and standard (180mm) seatposts. Sakae makes three lengths: 190mm, 220mm, and 250mm. You can now buy 330mm (13-inch) high-quality mountain bike seatposts from Sakae, SunTour, and others. Some seatposts come with insertion graduations, but I simply put a scratch on my seatposts to mark my insertion level. The range of lengths available for various seatpost models is shown in table 14-2.

Seatpost weights aren't too exact. To make the different outside diameters, the makers machine more aluminum from the outside. The hole remains the same diameter. Table 14-2 shows the weight of the 27.2mm-diameter short model.

Seatpost Makers

The large gruppo makers are now supplying seatposts and stems. However, they are both low-technology items, so an efficient small maker can survive.

American Classic This American-made seatpost with a Laprade clamp is the lightest available.

Campagnolo There are five Campagnolo seatposts available. All but the Nuovo Record now have Laprade-type clamps. If you can find one, the Triomphe is the bargain. It has the same svelte styling as the C-Record at half the price.

Sakae Sakae dominates the seatpost business. They make seven different micro-adjusting seatposts for the OEM market. The model that Sakae calls the Foursir and everyone else calls the Laprade is the one you'll find in the aftermarket. For the mountain bikers, Sakae makes a seatpost with a quick-release that lets you adjust the tilt and the fore and aft positioning on the move.

Shimano Shimano still doesn't include seatposts in their gruppos. There are two Dura-Ace models available: the old AX from the aerodynamic era, and the Dura-Ace EX with a round fluted pillar.

SunTour SunTour's seatposts are made by Sugino. The Superbe Pro model uses a Laprade-type clamp. The extra-long mountain bike model is widely available.

Frank's Favorite Seatpost

Picking my favorite seatpost is no big deal. Most of my bicycles have Shimano Dura-Ace AX seatposts because I like their looks.

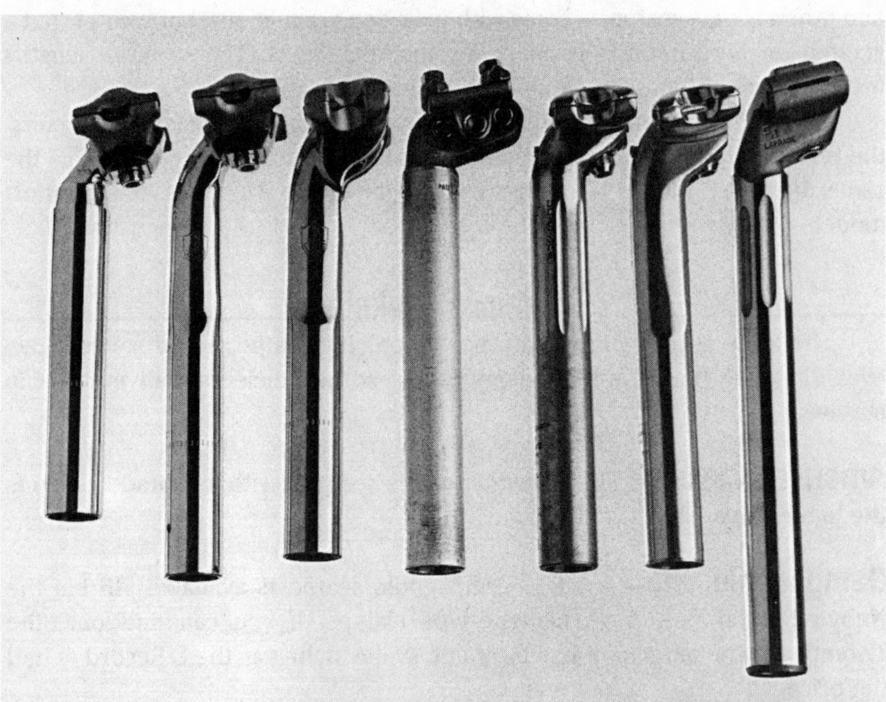

PHOTO 14-5 Seatposts: left to right, Campagnolo C-Record (130mm), Campagnolo C-Record (180mm), Campagnolo Triomphe (170mm), Campagnolo Nuovo Record (170mm micro-adjusting), Shimano Dura-Ace B-Type (170mm), Shimano Dura-Ace A-Type (170mm), and Sakae CT Extra Long (250mm).

APPENDIX

Guide to Abbreviations Used in Figures and Tables

Category	Abbreviation	Meaning
Bicycle parts	B.B.	bottom bracket
	Br	brake
	CW	chainwheel
	FW	freewheel
	Lvr	lever
	Pl	plate (chain)
	QR	quick-release
	SP	sidepull brake
Chain plate shapes	Bul	bulged
	Chmf	chamfered
	Flr	flared
Finishes	An	anodized
	C	colored
	HAn	hard anodized
	P	polished

Category	Abbreviation	Meaning
Locations	Bot	bottom
	Cnt	center
	Fr	front
	Frw	forward
	Hdn	hidden
	Rr	rear
Materials	Al	aluminum
	ChrStl	chromed steel
	CpPlStl	copper-plated steel
	Cr-Mo/CrMo	chromium-molybdenum
	Fbrgl	fiberglass
	Kvlr	Kevlar
	Plst	plastic
	Polyeth	polyethylene
	Polyur	polyurethane
	Stl	steel
	Ttnm	titanium
Material processing	Ca	cast
	Fg	forged
	MFg	melt-forged
Ratings	E	excellent
	F	fair
	G	good
	P	poor
	VG	very good
Strapless shoe-pedal systems	Cl + Ad	cleats plus adapters
	P + Cl	pedals plus cleats
	P + Sh	pedals plus shoes
Types of bicycles and cycling	ATB	all-terrain bicycle
	City	city riding
	I	intermediate between racing and touring

Category	Abbreviation	Meaning
	LT	loaded touring
	MB	mountain bike
	R	racing
	ST	sport touring
	TT	time trials
Types of bearings	CB	cartridge bearing
	C&C	cup and cone bearing
	SCB	sealed cartridge ball bearing
	SCN	sealed cartridge needle bearing
Types of brake quick-release	O	on/off
	V	variable
Types (or spacing) of chains and freewheels	I	intermediate between narrow and wide
	N	narrow
	W	wide
Types of handlebars	Cri	criterium
	Rnd	randonneur
	Rd	road
	Str	straight
Types of pedals	R. plat.	racing platform
	T. plat.	touring platform
Types of rims, levers, hubs, and seatposts	A	aero
	Cncv	concave
	H	hooked-edge
	HF	high flange
	Lapr	Laprade
	MF	medium flange
	S	straight-side
	SF	small flange
Types of threads	Eng	English
	Itl	Italian

Category	Abbreviation	Meaning
Types of tire treads	cnt. rib	center rib
	H-bone	herringbone
	sm. cnt.	smooth center
	sm. w/sipes	smooth with sipes
Units of measure	deg.	degrees
	dia.	diameter
	$	dollars
	$/pr.	dollars per pair
	gr.	grams
	gr./pr.	grams per pair
	in.	inches
	in.-lb.	inch-pounds
	mm	millimeters
	%	percent
	lb.	pounds
	psi	pounds per square inch
	sq. in.	square inch
Other	adj.	adjustable
	adjust.	adjustment
	advert.	advertised
	advtg.	advantage
	attach.	attachment
	avail.	available
	avg.	average
	℄	centerline
	const.	construction
	deflec.	deflection
	flx	flexible
	ht.	height
	int	intermediate
	laby	labyrinth
	max.	maximum
	meas.	measured

Category	Abbreviation	Meaning
	mech.	mechanical
	med.	medium
	min.	minimum
	mod.	model
	N/A	not applicable
	no.	number
	part.	partial
	plst. bush	plastic bushing
	pos.	position
	pr.	pair
	resist.	resistance
	std	standard
	stf	stiff
	typ.	typical
	var.	variable
	X-firm	extra-firm

Note: In the tables, spaces marked with a "—" represent information the author was unable to obtain by press time.

Index

Note: Page numbers for tables appear in **boldface** type; page numbers for figures and photos appear in *italic* type.